THE DIVORCE FROM HELL

THE DIVORCE FROM HELL

*How the Justice System
Failed a Family*

Wendy Dennis

Macfarlane Walter & Ross
Toronto

Macfarlane Walter & Ross
37A Hazelton Avenue
Toronto, Canada M5R 2E3

Canadian Cataloguing in Publication Data

Dennis, Wendy
    The divorce from hell: how the justice system failed a family

Includes index
ISBN 1-55199-000-8

1. Gordon, Ben. 2. Divorce – Law and legislation – Canada.
3. Divorce – Canada – Case studies. I. Title

KE569.D46 1998   346.7101'66'092   C98-932361-7
KF535.D46 1998

Macfarlane Walter & Ross gratefully acknowledges financial support for its
publishing program from the Canada Council for the Arts, the Ontario Arts
Council, and the Government of Canada through the Book Publishing
Industry Development Program.

Printed and bound in Canada

For Deja and Zoe and Ben

CONTENTS

Acknowledgments   xi

1   Marriage   1

2   Mediation   21

3   The Lawyers   34

4   The Assessment   43

5   The Game of Law   72

6   The Trial   121

7   Assessment Again   144

8   The Trial Resumes   177

9   The Settlement   205

10   Catastrophe   253

11   Loss   293

Epilogue   322

Postscript   350

Selected Sources   354

Index   358

ACKNOWLEDGMENTS

This story would never have been published had it not been for John Macfarlane, the editor of *Toronto Life* magazine. From the start, he and Anne Collins understood what I was trying to accomplish by telling this story and published it when they had many good reasons not to. A writer is lucky to meet one editor with real courage during her career. I had the good fortune to meet two.

Sheilagh McEvenue, a member of the original *Toronto Life* team, reprised her efforts on this book. Sheilagh undertook the hellish task of fact-checking and always did so with good cheer as long as she was kept well-fed, which I considered a small price to pay for her insightful suggestions and unflagging generosity and support.

Thanks, too, to Veronica Cusack, whose research assistance was inordinately helpful. I owe a debt of gratitude as well to Tim Lipson and Robert Schipper, who put up with my endless calls and patiently walked me through some legal thickets.

I would also like to thank Senator Anne Cools and her assistant Candice Clark for the tremendous help they provided, as well as journalists Margaret Wente, Frank Jones, Donna Laframboise, and Christie Blatchford for lending a measure of intelligence and balance to the controversy surrounding "The Divorce from Hell" when it was first published.

I would also like to thank the many people who called or wrote to Ben and me after the *Toronto Life* story was published. Their touching stories and words of support not only sustained me through a difficult time but reminded me why I'd written the story and encouraged me to write this book.

Thanks also to the remarkable team at Macfarlane Walter & Ross: to John, Jan, and Gary for believing in this book; to Paul Woods for his good nature and production support; and to Rosemary Shipton for reading the manuscript and suggesting improvements. My deepest thanks also to editor Barbara Czarnecki, who not only brought her dauntingly keen eye to my manuscript but cared about this book as much as I cared.

I owe deep thanks to my editor Jan Walter. Not only did she bring her formidable intelligence, honesty, curiosity, open-mindedness, and skill to bear on the editing of this manuscript, she held my hand and talked me through its countless drafts. I have been remarkably blessed to have acquired in her not only a great editor but a great friend.

I want to say thanks as well to the loved friends and family who supported us through this ordeal. They know who they are. My thanks especially to Ellen Vanstone and Debby Bernstein, who knew the truth because they watched it unfold and who never shirked from setting the record straight when someone questioned it.

To my daughter, Sara, I owe a great deal, not only for putting up with a mother who disappeared into the writing of a book for a couple of years, but for having the maturity and wisdom to understand its larger purpose.

And finally, there is Ben, who for the past two years endured my tough questions and lived surrounded by many reminders of a deeply painful time. For Ben, it would have been so much easier to turn the page on a hideous chapter in his life, but he chose instead to have his story told, not only so that his own children would have an answer, but to spare others the suffering that he, Deja, and Zoe have endured.

I hope I have done justice to their story.

CHAPTER ONE

MARRIAGE

Spring 1980–Spring 1989

ON a Saturday night in January 1983, my husband, David, and I attended a dinner party at the home of close friends. Four couples sat around the dining table that evening sharing banter and Beaujolais. Everyone was in high spirits. Within a few weeks, three of the couples announced they were breaking up.

The hosts, the only couple to survive the wreckage, vowed facetiously never to arrange another dinner party. The rest of us made arch jokes about the wine being spiked. It was as if six healthy people had suddenly been struck by a mysterious virus. Three couples who seemed perfect matches were kaput, splitsville, on their way to dividing the china.

After going public we lived through the interminable death throes, trying everything people try when their marriages turn sour: counselling, shrinks, a trial separation, one last trip to a resort. About the only good thing I remember from that period was losing ten pounds without even trying. In the end we crashed anyway.

In retrospect, I realized I must have been watching several Academy Award performances that night. Putting on a cheery face in the terminal stages of a marriage, when there are no illusions left to control the pain, requires Stanislavskian skill. I don't know what tawdry domestic melodramas were unfolding at our friends' houses, but I can tell you what was playing at ours.

At the end, after a particularly nasty scene, I walked quietly out of the house and drove downtown to the Holiday Inn, where I sat in my car reflecting on the inescapable fact that I was thirty-four years old, the mother

1

of a four-year-old daughter, and parked outside a hotel at midnight with a toothbrush in my purse. Sitting in that car, I finally acknowledged that my marriage was over. I knew I'd hit rock bottom because I preferred to spend the night in a Holiday Inn rather than with my husband.

Of course, I didn't always feel that way. At first I thought we were made for each other. He was Jewish; I was Jewish. Our families had grown up together. He was the practical, feet-on-the-ground one; I was the whimsical, impetuous other. It was Tracy and Hepburn, Gable and Lombard. So we moved in together and sent each other funny cards and had three-star dinners and trips to the south of France and bought a house and got married and had a kid – and nine years later he claimed I had a narcissistic personality disorder that could be treated only in the States, and I thought he was a cheap, controlling prick.

Nora Ephron says that marriages are just the perfect meshing of two neuroses, that every time you turn around you get involved with the one person on earth you shouldn't. You fall in love with someone's differences, then you get married and the differences start to drive you crazy. This was certainly true in my case. In our early, hormone-rush phase, I'd given him a scrapbook alluding to what I viewed as his many adorable idiosyncrasies – the exact same traits for which, later, I wished to impale him on one of his golf clubs.

Whose fault was it? I had a list on him and he had a list on me. But in my more clear-headed moments I have to admit it was nobody's fault – we were just stunningly incompatible. I won't go into the gory details but there was much slamming of doors and Stop-the-car-I'm-getting-out. We kept up appearances, though. By the end I was ready to implode from the energy it took to have a lousy marriage and pretend I didn't.

Eventually I mustered the courage to check in at that Holiday Inn and make it past the levitating eyebrow of the desk clerk. I found my room, ran a bath, got undressed, and climbed into the tub. Then I began to think seriously about my future. My to-do list was daunting. First, get a divorce. Then, get a life. But what kind of divorce was I to have? There were good divorces and bad divorces. I wanted a good divorce. But how to achieve it? Nobody talked about such things. How were you supposed to manage a civilized break-up with the same person you couldn't get through a peaceful bowl of cornflakes with, by the end?

First I thought about money. I was terrified about money, mainly because I didn't have any. I'd left teaching to go to journalism school five years before, so what I had was a nascent career as a writer, no idea when my next cheque would arrive, and a fear of becoming one of those poor single mothers who lived on Kraft Dinner. I told myself I'd been arguing for years that women should be independent. Now I was going to become one of those truly independent women. But what if I wound up on the street? You didn't get much more independent than that. Then I got panicky and started wishing a man would take care of me.

Next I thought about moving. One of us would have to go, and I didn't want it to be me. The thought of scanning want ads, looking for a place, packing, hiring a van gave me palpitations. But I assumed David wouldn't want to move either. Moving is way up there on those lists of life's major stress points, and who needs more stress when your life is coming unglued? I thought about other couples who'd split up. Almost always the woman stayed in the house with the kids and the guy moved out. I didn't know why this was so, because it struck me as an exceptionally bad deal for the guy. Yet it seemed to be step one in the divorce manual.

I tried to find a reason why I should stay in the house. It was definitely in my best interests to come up with a brilliant argument. But I kept slamming up against fifteen years of feminist ideology. The house belonged to both of us because women had lobbied to change the family laws. How could I argue that men and women were equals, then claim occupancy of the house because I have the Fallopian tubes? That was the problem with having principles. Sooner or later they came up and bit you on the ass. I shelved the house problem for the moment.

Then there was our daughter, Sara. In most of the divorces I knew of, the kids lived with Mom and visited Dad. I didn't know why this was so either. I'd read about couples whose children went back and forth between their households every other week, but in 1984, the year I was sitting in that tub, I didn't personally know any couples with that arrangement.

I thought about Sara, and how, four years earlier, she'd opened her eyes in the delivery room to the adoring gaze of her mom and dad. The experts said kids needed one home base to feel secure. I was no expert. But I thought kids needed devoted parents who showered them with love every day to feel secure, and if Sara was lucky enough to have two who did, it made most sense for us to continue that arrangement. I simply couldn't comprehend how adjusting to a life under two roofs was harder on a child than having one of her beloved parents suddenly evicted from her life and labelled a visitor. Anyway, who'd be the evictee? I knew that nobody would expect it to be me, including David. Dads moved out. Moms stayed with the kids. If push came to shove, I'd win, not only in court but in the court of public opinion.

If you added it up, I did more of the household and parenting tasks, just like those surveys always say women do. (That was true even when we had a nanny, which we did until Sara started school full days that fall.) David wouldn't win any awards as a Sensitive New Age Guy. He worked a litigation lawyer's usual hours and golfed both days of most weekends half the year. Throughout our marriage I'd pushed David to golf less and share more of the parenting responsibilities. What was I supposed to say now? Sorry, honey. Equal parenting applies only in marriage. Now that we're divorced, new rules: send money and get lost.

I'd always hoped that Sara would grow up with a dad who did "mom" things some of the time and vice versa. Of course, I'd wanted this arrangement under one roof, but that was clearly not in the cards. Then I realized divorce would force us both to truly become equals, a goal we'd never managed to achieve in our marriage. David would have to start making some compromises in his schedule and doing more of the mom stuff. And I'd have to develop my career and become self-supporting again.

It did not escape me that my life would be easier if I could make decisions without the aggravation of having to deal with David. I didn't want that aggravation, and it's safe to assume he felt likewise about me. As tempting as the option was of not having to negotiate with David, I didn't think that was best for Sara. We had this child together, and we had to find a way to make joint custody work. I knew I was signing on for headaches, but I figured we'd manage because we agreed on the big decisions and the lifestyle we wanted for our daughter.

I had another reason for wanting David to share the parenting load: I didn't want to turn into a bitter, exhausted crone who resented her life and took it out on her child. I loved being a mother, but I knew single parenting would be tough, and I'd need some time off. Of course, wanting time away from the kids is not the sort of thing a woman ordinarily confesses publicly. Even today a woman is supposed to long to be with her children every waking and working moment; anything less is considered aberrant or selfish. A mother always feels that expectation, whether it's spoken or not. But if David and I divided the day-to-day responsibilities, we'd each get a break. And with two demanding careers, we'd both need a break. Furthermore, one day we might actually want a social life again. I knew I'd miss Sara dreadfully when she was with her dad. When you've just split up, your self-esteem is in the toilet, and having a little person underfoot is about the only thing that fills the silences and makes you feel worthwhile. Also, I found it sad and strange to think of missing out on half my daughter's life. But I couldn't imagine David feeling any different.

Next to Sara, my biggest worry was how David and I were going to settle the financial issues. During our marriage money was the deadliest subject. Of course, money was just the metaphor; what we were really fighting about was control. He was for. I was against. But don't get me started. Suffice it to say I knew money would be the deal-breaker, and for Sara's sake, I was determined not to fight about it.

I pulled the plug, climbed out of the tub, and wondered why no one ever tells you how hard you have to work at a divorce.

■ ■ ■

Some time in November 1984 we sat down in our living room and drafted a separation agreement. I was proud of us. It was the first civilized collaboration we'd achieved in a long, long time. I told David my thinking. I had to sell him a little. Not because he didn't want to be with Sara as much as possible, because he did, but because in 1984 I was proposing a radical concept and David Wilson is not a radical-concept kind of guy. His greatest concern was the same as every working mother's: how he'd manage to balance the demands of his work with the responsibilities of caring for a child.

I told him I knew the arrangement went against the current, but my instincts told me it was best for Sara and that if he couldn't manage, he at least could afford to hire household help, and we should give it a try. With some trepidation, he agreed. This was the deal: Sara would live with each of us half the time. On Mondays and Tuesdays she'd be with me, on

Wednesdays and Thursdays with David; on weekends she'd alternate between us. I'd discovered this schedule in a book about divorced parenting. It seemed appropriate for us because it allowed Sara at least two days a week with each parent, plus an uninterrupted five-day stretch every two weeks with either David or me. For instance, I'd see her Monday and Tuesday and then Friday through the following Tuesday, while David would see her Wednesday and Thursday the first week, then Wednesday through Sunday the next. An alternating weekly arrangement would have been less complicated for us, but even though our daughter was mature beyond her years, she was still only four, and I reasoned that seven days away from her mom or dad might be too hard for her, especially at first.

David and I would consult on all the major decisions and remain intimately involved in the day-to-dayness of our daughter's life. We wouldn't sell the house right away. Fortunately, neither of us needed our equity immediately, and with no pressing debt we decided it would be best to avoid that disturbance for the time being. In the interim, I'd stay in the house for practical reasons: I worked on a flexible schedule at home and could be more readily available to Sara. Moving would have meant disrupting my office as well as my home at a time when I needed to focus on earning more income. Once David had moved out, I'd carry the house (unless the roof caved in or the furnace conked out) and assume responsibility for all my own expenses; he'd cover his living expenses, and when either one of us wanted to sell the house, we'd put it on the market, split the proceeds, and divide the rest of our belongings.

Next on the list was child support. First we drew up a budget of Sara's monthly expenses. We tallied household costs, such as food, shelter and entertainment (the cost of an amusement park outing or *Star Wars* video). Then we factored in non-household expenses, such as her clothing and haircuts. We didn't include "extras" like camp, orthodontics, and private school fees in the monthly tally since they were one-time-only or once-a-year costs; those we agreed to pay proportionately (and directly) on a two-thirds (him), one-third (me) basis, reflecting the difference in our incomes.

Once we knew the monthly total, we had to do an arithmetic calculation taking three factors into consideration. Since Sara would be dividing her time equally between us, we figured our household costs for her would be the same. David devised a formula allowing him to deduct his household costs from the total. That enabled him to receive full credit for those costs. Even though I felt his formula wasn't equitable – his ability to pay those costs far exceeded mine – I agreed in order to settle matters. Then we settled the logistics: David would pay me a monthly cheque representing his share, then I'd kick in mine and administer her bills.

However, David said he wanted to be able to buy Sara things when she was with him, but since he was already paying support for his share of those items, he didn't want to have to lay out any more money. So he insisted, and I agreed – once again, to settle matters – that we both keep records of Sara's expenses and reimburse each other as necessary. If, for instance, he took Sara to the skate exchange or bought her an outfit, or school supplies one year, then he'd send me those bills and I'd pay him back. The success of that arrangement depended, of course, on David exercising judgment about the bills he sent me, and me keeping my word about paying him back. Finally, since at the time David could deduct his support payments while I had to pay tax on them, he calculated an adjustment to compensate for that differential.

For several reasons our arrangement was unusual, ahead of its day – and by any account a great deal for David. (My break was getting to stay in the house for a while.) First, his daughter would be living with him half the time. Second, most fathers did not receive any credit for child care costs incurred in their household – although, to be fair, most fathers did not have as much time with their children as David did. (Had Sara lived primarily with me in a conventional custody arrangement, David would have had to pay a great deal more support. In that case I'd have incurred almost all of Sara's household costs, and he'd have had to pay more to offset that imbalance.) Third, the credit formula he had worked out for household costs was greatly to his advantage because he earned twice what I did. Fourth, most women who received child support did not reimburse their ex-husbands for money the dads spent on their kids when they were with them.

In the end we settled on $650 a month. All in all I figured I was probably getting screwed on child support, and David probably thought he was paying too much. But I didn't press the issue. I was determined to begin our divorce in the right spirit.

7

We hung on until Christmas, the traditional time for Jewish couples to split up. That's when many of their parents leave for Florida condos, and the divorcing grown-up children can move temporarily into rent-free apartments. Which David did, until he found a townhouse to rent not far from Sara's school.

Once arrangements were in place, we took a deep breath and walked into our daughter's cheery yellow room where she was drawing at her desk to explain that her world was about to collapse. In that dreadfully forced-but-chipper way adults have of breaking terrible news to kids, we told her that Mommy and Daddy weren't going to live together any more. We assured her that we still loved her tons, only now we'd love her in two houses. Just before David moved, we tried valiantly to make a game of having her select the toys and books she wanted at each house. None of us will forget the pain of those moments.

When we told family and friends our plans, you'd have thought we'd announced the earth was flat. Many people – divorced or not – had an opinion on what was best for Sara. And what was best, they insisted, was for a child to live in one home with the mom and visit the dad one night a week and every other weekend.

I'm not saying everything went perfectly. Sara was listless and melancholy for a while and we all had our share of problems and adjustments. But I can report that all the Cassandras were wrong: there is no blanket solution for every situation. Sara flourished. When she was eight or nine, she asked me why other kids whose parents were divorced lived only with their mothers. She thought that a curious and inadequate arrangement. Didn't they miss their fathers too much?

Our arrangement greatly eased the burdens of single parenting for both of us. The truth is, when the children are little, enjoying respite from the relentless grind of parenthood is one of the best-kept secrets about joint custody. Soon my married friends with kids began to joke that maybe they should split up, too, since it seemed the only way to steal some guilt-free time for themselves.

In almost every other way, however, joint custody was nothing but aggravation for David and me. In retrospect, I suppose it wasn't all that surprising that our high-conflict marriage became our high-conflict divorce.

Our problems were the same as they'd always been. We had endless arguments – about money, about Sara's activities, holidays, schedule. Ever the optimist, I'd begin each exchange hoping to find a solution through a meeting of minds, but wind up babbling insanely at my ex's lawyerly propensity to wear me down by turning every issue into a right-or-wrong, winner-take-all, let's-play-hardball fight to the finish. Or to engage in another legalistic ploy that drove me nuts: interpreting the rules to serve whatever his interests might be that particular day. When the issue was one worth fighting for, I could hold my own as his worthy opponent in our private divorce court, but I didn't want to fight and such exchanges bored me stupid.

Eventually we couldn't stand to talk to each other any more. So we started faxing. Still, despite the ongoing, teeth-clenching frustration the joint custody arrangement caused us both, for many years it continued to work wonderfully for Sara. Somehow, David and I managed to keep her out of the fray. We dutifully showed up together for teacher interviews and camp visitors' days, and Sara continued to thrive in two households.

Two years after we'd split, we decided to sell our house and work out a formal agreement. By the summer of 1986, David had bought a new house of his own. All we had to do was refine the deal already in place: review Sara's expenses, update the figure for child support, and, in accordance with Ontario's family laws, split the house proceeds, figure out an equalization payment, and divide the rest of our possessions. It should have been routine. After two more years of mediation, cash-flow charts, arcane tax calculations, affidavits, financial statements, cross-examinations, a file of correspondence, and around $20,000 in legal fees, we finally settled. (The $20,000 was what I had to pay a lawyer out of my share of the house proceeds; I don't know what David spent.) That was my first encounter with the process our finest legal minds have devised to help couples through a divorce.

What happened? If you asked David, he'd say he was a paragon of flexibility and I was totally demanding and unreasonable. If you asked me, I'd say David had a teensy problem with independent women and that to David, being unreasonable meant refusing to capitulate to his petty demands.

Maybe he was right and maybe I was. But let's say, for argument's sake, that David was right, that I was the intransigent one, the neurotic, the crazy. Or the bitch, out to take my ex-husband to the cleaners. If that's true, then for Sara's sake, why didn't anyone make me stop my nonsense? And why wasn't there a less costly and destructive way to help us dissolve our marriage?

■ ■ ■

I bought a smart little semi in the city, fixed it up, and began to focus on the second item on my agenda: getting a life. David found someone new almost immediately. Her name was Jan. First they lived together, then they married and adopted a baby. I would like to say that none of this bothered me, but I'd be lying. I didn't want David back. I was just annoyed that he had a new person in his life and I didn't. Then I had to adjust to the idea of another woman mothering my daughter. I struggled with that one. In my most vulnerable moments, it felt threatening to think of Sara turning to another woman for motherly comfort and advice, especially one who didn't necessarily hold the world view I wished for my daughter. But Jan was kind and affectionate to Sara and it was obvious that Sara loved her, so I had to eat that one too.

By the fall of 1990 I'd been holed up in the house for a year writing a book about sex, but not getting any. My research was telling me you had to be proactive in these matters. So I lobbied my friends. First I called Judy. "Who do you know?" I asked. "I need some fun." Judy and her ex had fixed me up with David. "Leave it with me," she said. "I owe you one."

The first time I met Ben Gordon he was standing shirtless in his living room amidst a hodgepodge of furniture that appeared to have been donated by the Salvation Army. He was just over six feet tall, with broad shoulders, fair, freckled skin, and hair, the little that was left of it, the colour of sand. Judy and I had knocked on his apartment door and opened it to find him standing in a state of semi-undress. He crossed his arms across a woolly chest and popped his eyes wide in mock embarrassment at being caught half-naked.

The second time I met Ben he turned up, at Judy's invitation, to have a Christmas drink with a group of our friends. Judy had discovered that we had several acquaintances in common, two of whom, unknown to me, had already pressed my number on him. (Later, he referred to this evening as his "go-see.") He arrived late, perspiring heavily from the flu, went directly to the john, and threw up. When it was time to leave he helped me on with my coat and made a funny crack about the hat I was wearing. I liked his attitude, his courtly manners, the dignity of his posture, and the way his broad shoulders looked in a cashmere overcoat.

Ah, but I'm getting ahead of myself. Ben lived downstairs from Judy in a fourplex on Relmar Road, around the corner from Forest Hill Village, a prosperous neighbourhood in midtown Toronto with a large Jewish population. He was recently separated and since October had been living in one of the lower flats. Judy had graciously furnished his CV: late thirties, Jewish, shoe business, show business, two kids, in the throes of a nasty divorce. She'd chatted with him in the hall, seen him playing with his two young daughters in the park across the street. He'd brought her several pairs of Keds wholesale. As Judy saw it, how bad could a guy be who brought you shoes wholesale? I, on the other hand, told her to do more digging and report back.

Meanwhile, I did some digging of my own. Reports in the television industry were favourable. My friend Debby, an executive at the CBC, told me to move quickly. If I didn't, somebody else would. Debby was right. I soon discovered that Barb, a mutual friend of Ben's and mine, had already set him up with another of her girlfriends. Barb confirmed the general tenor of the reports I was hearing: Ben Gordon was a smart, funny, decent guy. "But he's going through a bad divorce," she added. "Whaddya need it for?"

"Going through a bad divorce" was girl code for Trouble. A man so marked would be bitter, gun-shy, unable to commit. He'd be needy. He'd have kids you might loathe but would have to mother. Any woman dumb enough to get involved with a guy going through a bad divorce would become his Transitional Relationship. She'd sustain him through his darkest days, then he'd recover and dump her for a twenty-year-old with great tits.

I knew Barb's advice was well intentioned, but I had to consider the source. She'd been married for eighteen years to the world's sweetest man. What did she know about divorce or the difficulties, in our age, of meeting someone even marginally appropriate? It seemed draconian to disqualify a man on whom reports were favourable just because he was going through a bad divorce. Half the people I knew were divorced, and so far as I could tell, at any given moment, the other half were scrambling to keep the lawyers at bay. Furthermore, in spite of my most determined efforts to ensure that my divorce would be amicable, it was no picnic. No, I wasn't about to draw conclusions about Ben Gordon on the basis of uninformed speculation by a second-hand source who'd been happily married since 1972.

He called on New Year's Day to ask me out. Later that week he called again to talk arrangements. "Do you still like me?" he asked. He sounded tentative.

I laughed. "So far, but give me time. We haven't gone out yet … Why do you ask?"

"Because you might not like me after you hear what I'm going to suggest."

He had tickets for the hockey game – the Los Angeles Kings were in town. He did not, as a rule, go to the games, but this particular one he wanted to see.

"Ahh … Gretzky."

I was no hockey fan but I'd never seen Gretzky on skates, and turning down a chance to see the Great One would be like turning down tickets for Pavarotti, so I said sure, why not?

En route to the car after picking me up that Saturday night he said he had a funny story to tell me. A few minutes earlier, on his way out the door, he'd bumped into Larry, Judy's boyfriend. "I told him, 'Larry, I've got a hot date tonight. This girl wants it, I can tell. I can feel the heat over the telephone wires. But I'm running late and I can't get to the drugstore. Have you got any protection?' So Larry says, 'Aw Ben, whaddya taking out girls like that for? Why don't you take out a nice girl? Judy has a friend Wendy. Wendy Dennis. You should take her out.' Meanwhile, Judy's standing at the top of the stairs listening to this conversation. 'So, who are you taking out?' she asks. And I say, 'Wendy. Wendy Dennis.'"

And so began my first date with Ben Gordon. By the time we'd arrived at Maple Leaf Gardens I was having so much fun I forgot I was on a first date. "Do you know what your best line has been so far?" I asked as an aside during the second period, while we were both engrossed in the action on the ice. Amused, he turned to stare at me for a moment. "I don't usually get reviewed this early in the evening," he replied.

Back at my place later, I asked him to tell me about his divorce. He outlined its history in the broadest brush strokes. He said only that he and his wife were in court and many things were at issue between them. He didn't speak bitterly of his wife or portray himself as a victim, but it was clear he was living through an ordeal. I think I clucked that matters would improve now that he was out of the house. It was only later, when I saw for myself what he was actually experiencing, that I realized the remarkable restraint he'd shown and how hideously platitudinous my comment must have sounded.

He asked about my divorce. I delivered my set piece. You need a set piece about your divorce for first dates. You want to sound mature, even-handed, like someone who has weathered a storm but grown and moved on. You save for later the stories about how the cheap sonofabitch was sending you invoices for birthday party streamers. As he listened, I noticed a flicker of cynicism in his eyes. "Everything you just said about David," he said when I'd finished, "Terry would say about me." Over the next while, we exchanged stories, as people do. Here is the story that Ben Gordon told me about his life.

■ ■ ■

He grew up as Bruce Gordon in suburban Toronto in the fifties, the only child of middle-class Jewish parents. He remembers his childhood as a lonely time. Though his parents were loving and liberal, their marriage was unhappy and they divorced when he was in his twenties. His dad, a sales agent in the shoe business, travelled a lot selling shoe lines, and with his father away he was left to look after his mother in his father's absences. Raised by fifties television, he longed for a family like the one he saw on *Father Knows Best*.

After Grade 8 the family moved to a highrise apartment in Forest Hill. Though he didn't live in a grand home like many of his schoolmates, moving to an affluent Jewish neighbourhood was like arriving in society. In high school he was the class clown and classic academic underachiever. He had buddies but no close friends, and he didn't date. His father, the salesman, had taught him to do jokes to put others at their ease. He had a talent for making people laugh.

After Grade 12 he studied theatre at Boston University's School of Fine

Arts, graduating in 1973. The following year, at twenty-three, he married a Toronto girl. Within a year, because another actor had his name, he had changed his to Ben and moved to Los Angeles to become a comedy writer for a series of NBC specials. He hated Hollywood – the phoney, dog-eat-dog atmosphere, writing schlock comedy. After a season he came home, but by then the marriage was over and he realized he'd been in love less with the girl than with the idea of family. The next year they split.

He got a call from the director of Second City. Would he join their new cast? He replaced Dan Aykroyd and joined Dave Thomas, Andrea Martin, Catherine O'Hara, and John Monteith doing improv onstage. He landed roles in Canadian movies, working with Alan Arkin, Burgess Meredith, and later Armand Assante and Rod Steiger, among others. By 1979 he was twenty-eight years old, writing and performing in a network comedy series, acting as a brand spokesperson for a string of award-winning radio and TV commercials, working regularly in movies, earning around $80,000 a year – and deeply unhappy.

He wasn't driven to be a star. He'd gone into show business because he had a talent for performing, and it was an easy way to become successful and meet his father's expectations. Once he'd taken care of that obligation, it was time to take care of the next: become a model family man.

Terry Nusyna called his office in the spring of 1980, looking for her old friend Danny Mann. Mann was staying at Ben's place while he was visiting from Los Angeles. The night before, Mann had taken Terry to a party. She'd met a good-looking guy there and was calling to see if he'd set her up. Ben took the call. "Yes, I know the guy ... Great guy ... Very good-looking. And charming? Absolutely. Let's see ... did I say dull? Me, on the other hand? Not good-looking, not much hair. But fascinating."

On their first date they went out for Chinese food and to the show at Second City. Just before the curtain Ben excused himself to go to the washroom. When the show began, Terry discovered that her date was part of the cast, performing sketch comedy while the audience choked with laughter.

She moved in with him a few months later. She too had grown up in a middle-class Jewish family. After York Mills Collegiate, she'd studied film and television production at York University. She met the rock singer David Clayton Thomas while on vacation and married him the year she graduated.

She was twenty-three years old. Her girlfriends were just starting out in life, but the marriage to Thomas catapulted Terry into the limousine life of a rock star's consort, travelling with her husband to concerts across North America. By the time Ben met her, five years later, she was separated from Thomas, working freelance as a production assistant for a company that made television commercials, and living in a highrise building on Jarvis Street in the city's red-light district. The story she told him about her first marriage was that she'd fled a relationship she claimed was abusive with nothing but her white Camaro Z28 and the shirt on her back.

He didn't know much about her past and he didn't care. She was five feet ten, slender and attractive with a small waist, beautiful skin, and large breasts. She laughed at his jokes. They had a circle of acquaintants in common and shared a certain familiar comfort from having grown up in Toronto's Jewish community. He longed to be part of a close family, and Terry's relatives adored him: a nice Jewish boy with a sense of humour who loved Friday-night dinners and was good to Grandma.

Around this time the country's top casting agent and agent/manager, Stuart Aiken and Deborah Peck, were courting him to go back to Hollywood. They opened doors for him there, set up meetings with Hollywood's most influential casting directors, and packaged him as their premier comedic actor. This is it, they told Ben, now's your chance to be a star. But Ben lacked the desire or ambition to be a star. He wasn't driven or competitive. He was insecure. He didn't think he was particularly funny.

Terry wanted him to have a career in Hollywood. According to Ben, she saw him as her return ticket to the show business life. She believed she was destined to be the wife of a celebrity; she also thought she was a starmaker. Terry told him his agent was incompetent, that she should be managing his career. She said that David Clayton Thomas owed his success to her and that his career had stalled only when he'd stopped taking her advice. What Ben needed, she told him, was for her to show him the way.

He didn't believe she had any real connections in the entertainment business, and he knew that her job as a production assistant was to be a gofer, to organize the catering and visit bars to scout for extras. He thought that what she'd learned travelling in limos and hanging around backstage was not how to manage a star but how to demand star treatment. Still, a part of him felt empathy for her. Underneath Terry's braggadocio there was a deep and transparent insecurity that he identified with and that made him want to take care of her.

He went to Los Angeles but was ambivalent about being there. He'd go into casting sessions with Lynn Stalmaster and other top casting agents in town but act as if he was there only as a favour to his agent. He didn't have the juice. He cut the trip short, closed the door on Hollywood, and came back to Toronto and Terry.

The first time he proposed, she told him he wasn't good enough. He'd have to prove himself to be a reliable husband and provider. Having blown his chances in Hollywood and failed at one marriage, he had too low an opinion of himself to disagree. The message he'd learned from his parents was that if he took care of others then they would take care of him. He made it his mission to take care of Terry. He was considerate of her needs, provided her a certain lifestyle, introduced her to his show business friends. Shortly after moving into his apartment in the summer of 1980, she quit freelancing as a production assistant, worked for a liquidation company for a few months, and, after being fired from that job, helped produce a low-budget television commercial for the local retailer Alan Cherry.

In December 1981 Ben and Terry bought a spacious but run-down home, badly in need of a facelift, a few doors from Bathurst Street in lower Forest Hill. Buying a home held tremendous symbolic significance for him, not only because his family had always rented apartments, not even because it meant he'd achieved a certain level of financial success. What thrilled him most was that at last he'd begun to build the foundation for the family life he so desperately wanted.

They married in the spring of 1982, but almost immediately there were problems. Ben described them as cohabiting, but without any sense of passion, harmony, mutual affection, or respect. Having seen no other model, he thought all marriages were supposed to be that way. He thought his role was that of the affably resigned husband in the classic wife joke: say "Yes, dear" and survive. If he bought the right house, if he attended the Friday-night dinners at the Nusynas, if he surrounded himself with all the trappings of a good husband and family man, then he would be one.

Married only a few months, they went to Los Angeles to attend a personal development seminar to improve their relationship. Looking back later, he thought their marriage would probably have ended at this point: he was beginning to understand that there was more to life than the kind of marriage he had and that without any centre, theirs was doomed. But Terry became pregnant. Now fatherhood beckoned. This was the moment he'd been waiting for all his life. He'd pour his energies into becoming a superdad.

He spent that fall in Edmonton producing two comedy specials for cable television. He was happy on his own and didn't miss Terry. He had a fling while he was away, but he saw the affair not as a reason to leave his marriage but as a way to meet the needs it failed to provide so that he could stay in it.

Deja Victoria was born on May 4, 1983. The Jamaican nurse who helped out when Terry came home from the hospital told them delightedly that their squirmy daughter was a clever, independent soul with mischief in her eyes. Between auditions and gigs, Ben spent much of Deja's first year at home with Terry and the au pair. At first he had to learn the mysteries of caring for an infant, but he wanted to learn it all and he adapted quickly. He was good at the details, like checking to make sure the diaper bag was stocked. He loved to strap Deja in her stroller and walk her up to Eglinton Avenue to buy groceries.

Even though he was performing in commercials, making movies, and earning a good income, he felt Terry's dissatisfaction. Disappointed by his lack of ambition to become a star, she criticized him at every turn. If he revealed his vulnerabilities, she'd use them against him later. For a long time, he blamed himself for their problems, but then they went into group therapy and he began to see matters differently. He recognized that he'd been deeply insecure his whole life, looking for affirmation and a sense of identity in others' expectations and approval. He began to view Terry as a woman with a grandiose sense of self who expected a man's devotion but did little to earn it. In Ben's account, Terry had come to different conclusions: there was nothing wrong with her and everything wrong with Ben.

Misery and recrimination lost its appeal for him and when she berated him for his shortcomings, he was less and less willing to listen. He did a movie in the Bahamas and, while working on the picture, had a couple of one-night stands to which he later confessed. Still, he didn't leave the marriage. For Deja's sake and theirs, he hoped some semblance of family might still be salvaged.

In the spring of 1985, Zoe Nicole came along. A cuddly, affectionate infant, Zoe was Deja's personality opposite. The marriage continued its downward spiral, but making a living and the joys of fatherhood distracted him. While Terry was busy with the baby, he spent hours with Deja at her co-op nursery, helped organize her birthday parties, and took her to toddler music classes.

They hired an architect and contractor and began renovations on the house. These too were welcome distractions. He was working full-time for CTV in Toronto, writing and producing a situation comedy series starring Don Adams, and so wasn't around the house as much as he had been during Deja's infancy. But Terry was a stay-at-home mom and by then they had live-in help.

After Zoe was born, Ben craved more time with the kids, yet the animosity between himself and Terry intruded on his efforts to be a father. If he was diapering Zoe, Terry would mock him for doing it all wrong; if he'd forgotten some toy or piece of child's clothing on a visit with friends or family, she'd draw attention to his lapses and bemoan the general stupidity of men. He grew more distant, sullen, and cruelly sarcastic. Their fights always began the same way. She would belittle him in front of the kids or the housekeeper. He would ignore her or demand that she stop. She'd pump up the volume. He'd lose his temper and yell at her in fury. Then she'd play the victim.

In 1986 Ben's father, Jules, was beginning to think about retiring from his shoe sales agency and wondered if Ben was interested in coming into the business. The opportunity appealed to Ben: his father had been on the road a great deal during his boyhood, and here was a chance for the two of them to spend time together. Moreover, he was unhappy in show business and, with a family to support, needed a more stable and regular income than it could provide. He would help out his father and still keep a hand in the entertainment world. Terry was appalled by his decision. According to Ben, she made it clear that she had no desire to be the wife of a shoe salesman.

Nonetheless, Ben started making sales calls with his father. He continued to take roles where he was called upon to be funny, but by 1987 his marriage was a battleground and he was finding it harder to play the clown. It continued to crumble. By 1989 the recession hit. Ben was offered only the odd job in show business. On top of a disintegrating relationship was a serious financial crisis: they were living beyond their means.

Their marriage finally drew its last breath in the early spring of 1989, in the office of Larry Nisan, Terry's therapist. Ben remembered the scene vividly: for the first time, someone forced Terry to face the reality that whoever was to blame for the demise of their marriage, it was over, and there was no way or good reason for it to continue. "Do you love her?" Nisan asked him. Ben said no. Nisan turned to Terry: "Do you want to live with a man who doesn't love you?" he asked. Terry was caught off guard by her therapist's question. Haltingly, she answered no. "Then shit or get off the pot," said Nisan. Advising them to stay away from lawyers, he wrote down the name of a mediator to see for separation mediation.

That meeting in Nisan's office had taken place almost two years before our first date. Since then, Ben said, he'd tried everything possible to work out a joint custody agreement with Terry, but to no avail. Meanwhile, his children, now seven and five years old, were suffering from the continuing conflict and no one was doing anything to help.

■ ■ ■

I listened to this story with a certain scepticism. On the one hand, Ben struck me as a man not without problems, certainly, but sincere, thoughtful, and self-aware. I appreciated the fact that he didn't try to portray himself as blameless, justify his actions, or pass them off as inconsequential. Furthermore, having married a man who was breathtakingly wrong for me, I could identify with some of the bad judgments he'd made. I was well aware, too, that it didn't always take two to have a messy divorce. Sometimes one spouse could wreak all kinds of damage.

On the other hand, I was aware that I was hearing only one side of the story. Having spent six years trying to make joint custody work with an ex-husband whose version of who was causing the problems clashed wildly with my own, I knew that the truth at the centre of any divorce was not as simple as it appeared to the wounded parties. I imagined the hurt Terry must have felt at Ben's infidelities and rejection, and her terror at the prospect of having to support herself without any man or career to fall back on.

I knew nothing about Terry Nusyna other than what Ben had told me, but on some elemental female level my heart went out to her. Because of my divorce and the stories I'd heard from girlfriends or had read in the media, I tended to think of women as the victims in divorce and ex-husbands as generally troublesome creatures. Those who were particularly nasty I lumped into two categories: the so-called deadbeats who walked away from their kids and support obligations, and the pathological control freaks with deep pockets and unresolved rage who used the courts to jerk around, bully, and punish their ex-wives. In those first few weeks of my coming to know him, Ben Gordon did not strike me as either sort of man. However, until I'd seen more, I wasn't prepared to rule out the possibility that he belonged in column A or column B. Although I did not speak of my feelings to Ben, the truth was that if there was a benefit of the doubt to be given at that point – and there was – I was more than willing to give it to Terry.

Still, I liked this man, who seemed to worship his kids and to want little more than to carry on being a good father. Ben's desire to remain a deeply involved parent struck me as a worthy and reasonable ambition. So I decided to reserve judgment, keep my eyes open, listen carefully, and draw my own conclusions. What, I wondered, was taking him so long to get divorced? What were he and Terry fighting about? To what extent was Ben the architect of his own misfortune? What did Terry want?

CHAPTER TWO

MEDIATION

May–July 1989

After the meeting in Larry Nisan's office in March 1989, Ben was eager to start mediation with Terry. As he saw it, disentangling their lives didn't have to be complicated. They had two kids, a house, some RRSPs, furniture, and belongings. All they had to do was devise a parenting schedule, sell the house and do some equalization calculations, split the proceeds, divvy up their possessions, and work out child support. As divorces went, it was routine.

However, money was a serious concern. Ben's income had dropped precipitously from the height of his entertainment career in the early eighties, but their expenses were still around $7,500 a month. On a $60,000 income he was paying for all their household expenses, which included a gardener and live-in nanny/housekeeper, their dental and medical bills, and the kids' expenses such as clothing, jazz and piano lessons, spring break program, camp, and religious nursery school. Now he had their mediation fees as well. (Terry had agreed to participate in mediation only if Ben paid.)

Ben had a shortfall of approximately $2,400 a month and was trying to make ends meet by writing off whatever expenses he could through the business and borrowing from his dad. But Terry was looking for work. Once she'd found a job, her earnings would buy them some time. He preferred not to sell the house right away if they could hang on. The real estate market had recently taken the first downward turn in years, and it was probably best not to disrupt the kids immediately anyway. Still, he knew it was inevitable they'd have to sell the house in the near future.

All their equity was tied up in the house. They'd bought it in 1981 largely with the savings he'd accumulated before meeting Terry. He'd put in approximately $90,000, Terry had contributed about $10,000 from her own savings, and he'd committed any extra money he'd earned since then to the mortgage and renovations. It had been a point of pride with him to pay down the mortgage. In eight years, he'd managed to reduce it from $155,000 to $57,000. The house was their only significant asset, but it had turned out to be a smart investment. Bought for $255,000, it was now worth over a million dollars in the overheated Toronto real estate market. He did some mental calculations. They would have roughly $800,000 to split when they sold it. Ben knew this was hardly a penurious situation for them to be in and counted his blessings.

When he and Terry broke the news of the divorce, the girls made only one request: to stay at John Fisher Public School. Terry had heard about the school on the moms' grapevine and sold Ben on it, and he was glad she had. The girls had been in French immersion there since junior kindergarten, and both had close friends among their classmates. Ben had no intention of depriving the kids of a crucial source of stability in their lives. The principal, Terry Mokriy, was a gentle, easygoing man who truly liked children. He set a wonderful tone for the staff and students, and Ben felt confident sending his kids off every day to such a child-friendly environment. He'd enrolled them at the school, consulted with their instructors regularly to find out how they were doing, and met with them every spring to arrange the kids' best class placements for the following year. Often he accompanied the moms and other dads like him on apple-picking excursions or outings to Harbourfront. Every year he ran a booth with the kids at the June Fair. If he happened to be driving by the school at recess or lunch, he'd often drop in to see what was doing, look for the girls, and goof around with them and their pals in the schoolyard.

After the house was sold, Ben expected, he and Terry would each find a place to live near the school so the kids could travel between them. They'd both been deeply involved with the girls from infancy, although with Terry at home in those early years she'd spent more time caring for them. Nevertheless Ben's freelance schedule allowed him more flexibility than many fathers, and he always did many of the things that mothers might normally do. By the school years particularly Ben and Terry were sharing the myriad responsibilities of child care, so he figured alternating weeks with each parent would be the natural extension of the roles they'd always played.

They'd have to cut back, no question. The nanny/housekeeper would have to go, and they'd no longer be living in a four-bedroom, three-bathroom home in lower Forest Hill Village with a finished basement and all the amenities. But there were charming, albeit more modest neighbourhoods closer to the school. Fortunately, they had enough equity in their house to allow them both to move into smaller homes.

Once relocated, they could ease the kids into the new arrangements. He felt Deja and Zoe would be fine if he and Terry treated the idea of moving in an upbeat way. He'd already been reassuring them, talking up their new life, getting them excited about how great it was going to be, how they'd have two homes, a bedroom in each place with all their stuff, maybe a cat or a dog, too. Best of all, Mommy and Daddy wouldn't be fighting any more. The adjustment would take time, but he saw no reason why the kids couldn't adapt. He'd miss them terribly when he wasn't with them. He'd just have to cope.

Once Terry had a job, they could crunch some numbers to figure out child support. They'd have the same household expenses for the kids, but her income would likely be lower so she'd need some support to make up for that disparity. But that was just a matter of reviewing the numbers and doing an arithmetic calculation. Dividing their property should be straightforward as well, Ben thought. Terry had owned a few pieces of mismatched furniture and some posters when they'd met, most of which she'd dispensed with when she moved into his apartment. The bulk of their furniture, such as it was, dated from his college days and first marriage, and there were odds and ends he'd picked up from his grandmother's apartment when she died. They'd never really decorated.

In Ben's mind, mediation was the only sensible way to end their marriage. Until they separated, the kids would be living in a corrosive atmosphere, and he wanted matters resolved as quickly and painlessly as possible. He imagined the mediator sitting the two of them down, butting heads if necessary, and assisting them in working out a joint custody agreement and all the financial mechanics. He had every expectation that, with the mediator's help, they could dissolve their marriage expeditiously and, with a minimum of rancour, get on with their lives.

■ ■ ■

In 1989 hiring a mediator instead of lawyers to negotiate a separation agreement was an increasingly popular alternative for divorcing couples. (Sensing a shift in the wind, law firms were themselves offering mediation and alternative dispute resolution services.) Mario Bartoletti, whom Larry Nisan had advised Ben and Terry to consult, was a respected marital and family consultant who'd published and given media interviews about the burgeoning discipline. Throughout the spring and early summer of 1989, still living under the same roof, Ben and Terry attended eight separation mediation sessions with Bartoletti.

According to the summaries he gave Ben and Terry after each session, the mediator devoted the introductory session on May 2 to background. "Ben," he noted, "has turned the corner and looks forward to a mediated separation"; Terry had "unhealed wounds inside which still hurt." He recommended weekly double sessions of two and a half hours to "negotiate a mediated resolution of their concerns," and he noted at the end of session two that "*kids* and *family finances* [emphasis his] emerge as two very important factors which are going to require careful attention." However, Bartoletti devoted almost all of the first three sessions to recapitulating issues in the couple's marriage. His summaries reveal two people hopelessly divided. Still, on one crucial matter, they seemed to agree: *Session Summary,* May 9: "Underlying these exchanges between them is some anxiety about custody – which is clarified, i.e. *neither wishes to initiate legal action to wrest custody of and responsibility for the kids from the other* [emphasis his]."

By the end of the third session, Ben was growing impatient. Terry spent the entire session each week telling Bartoletti what a lousy husband Ben had been, and Bartoletti let her go on and on. (According to the mediator's summaries, Terry castigated herself only for having been "stupid" for loving too long and "because I didn't stand up to Ben.") After years of therapy and marriage counselling, Ben had no desire to rehash their marital differences with a mediator acting as referee. He thought Bartoletti was allowing Terry to vent her anger about the past so she'd be ready to deal with the future, but in the meantime, the sessions were costing a hundred and eighty bucks each while their unpaid bills were continuing to mount, they weren't resolving any of the issues they'd come to mediate, and the situation at home was growing more poisonous by the day.

Ben had entered mediation under the impression that a mediator helped couples work out finances, divide their assets, and devise a co-parenting plan. The mediator would troubleshoot differences and arbitrate issues they couldn't resolve themselves. He thought that he and Terry had implicitly agreed to accept Bartoletti's judgment because the mediator had come so highly recommended by Terry's therapist and, presumably, they both trusted his credentials. Instead, Bartoletti acted as a father confessor and marriage counsellor, devoting far too much time, in Ben's view, to the regurgitation of marital issues and not nearly enough to mediated resolutions, which, according to his first session summary, was their purpose for being there.

Ben walked into their fourth session on June 6 with a concrete proposal to separate right away. His idea, which he'd heard of other couples trying, was that the kids would stay put, while he and Terry would each find a place to stay and then they'd rotate weekly in and out of the house. Ben saw this rotation plan as the ideal short-term solution until they sold the house. Since they couldn't afford to carry the house and rent an apartment, they'd have to impose on friends or family for a while and put up with a little inconvenience themselves. But he believed his proposal was doubly advantageous for Deja and Zoe: he and Terry could separate right away without disrupting the girls, and the move would immediately spare them the pain of further exposure to their parents' animosity.

Terry said she wasn't comfortable with the idea. She found it too "unstable." Her suggestion was that she remain in the house while Ben found an apartment big enough for the kids to make overnight visits. She wished to encourage "significant quality time between Ben with the children," maintaining flexibility for considerable "access." However, if she was away for business or other reasons, she said she had no objections to Ben looking after the kids in the home. Ben wasn't interested in having "access" to his children. The word itself and everything it represented were profoundly offensive to him. He'd always been their parent and he intended to continue in that role. Furthermore, he resented Terry's assumption that he should be the one to move out of their house while she took control and dictated how much time he would be allowed with his daughters. With Bartoletti's encouragement, Terry eventually agreed to try the rotation plan.

Ben made arrangements to stay with a friend for six months, but the first week he had to return to the house to pack for a business trip. Bartoletti noted that in those circumstances "both were dealing with the other daily without any clear control of the situation." Terry had no such arrangement; indeed, Bartoletti recorded, "she was not expecting to find a place outside the home. She was going to return home, after the children were in bed, and spend the nights in the home." She complained that during one of her absences Ben had thrown out some of her medicine cabinet items. She criticized his parenting skills and accused him of upsetting the kids. After half-heartedly attempting the experiment for a week, Terry, according to Bartoletti, "had no investment in a rotating residency plan."

Ben agreed the kids were upset and routines had broken down that week but denied that the problem was his parenting skills. He said Terry had been "against the plan from the beginning," was threatened by his ability to handle a job, the house, and the children, and had sabotaged the arrangement to inflate her importance as a mother and create the impression that looking after the kids was beyond Ben's capacities.

At Bartoletti's urging, Terry agreed to try the arrangement for a second week. At the following session the mediator noted that Ben viewed the experiment as a "qualified success," but "Terry is definitely not interested in a rotation plan. She finds it too stressful and wants a place she feels is her own." Once Terry refused to carry on with the experiment, it died.

After the first week of rotation, Ben had told Bartoletti that he could see only two other options. Option A was for him to become primary caretaker and for Terry to move out, find an apartment where the kids could make overnight visits, and devote her energies to launching her career while Ben provided her considerable "access" and encouraged "significant quality time" between her and the children. He was mocking Terry, trying to hold up a mirror to make her understand that being told to move out of the family home and settle for "occasional access visits" with one's children was as ludicrous a notion to him as it was to her.

Option B was for them to sell the house, split the proceeds, and both relocate. The reality was that they could no longer afford to live the lifestyle they'd been living, and even if their marriage hadn't dissolved they would have had to drastically cut back their expenses. That they were divorcing added even more stress. Two households couldn't live as cheaply as one. They needed money, and the only money they had was tied up in their house. As far as Ben was concerned, the solution to their problem was obvious.

Furthermore, even if they'd had the luxury of keeping the house, Ben believed that if Terry stayed in the family home with the girls while he moved into an apartment where they came for occasional "visits," it would send them the message that divorce had suddenly altered their parents' roles. Selling the house wasn't just their only practical financial alternative, it was a vital symbolic step if they were to launch their joint custody arrangement in the right spirit.

Terry rejected the first option. *Session Summary*, June 13: "Terry feels that Ben does have the sensitivity and ability to raise the children, but isn't sure he could handle it on a full-time basis on his own … Being girls, they would need a woman they trust to turn to about 'female issues'." Then she vetoed selling the house. Terry saw only one scenario: "She wants to remain in the family home with the children, while Ben sets-up in an apartment large enough for the children to spend overnights." Ben was disturbed by Terry's idea of joint custody. It emerged that her notion of the concept involved him moving out and having the kids for occasional overnight visits. This she saw as an inconvenience to herself, requiring considerable compromise on her part, since she would still have to deal with him about the children from time to time. Ben was beginning to doubt the sincerity of Terry's commitment to negotiating a cooperative parenting plan, Bartoletti noted. "Feeling very depressed now, Ben expresses great concerns that he is going to become a part-time parent."

By late June the discussions had moved to the strained family finances. In their session on May 30, Ben had told Bartoletti he didn't think Terry was facing the facts that he wasn't earning the same kind of money he once did and that they were in serious debt. He didn't want any more "crisis calls," with Terry saying, "I need another thousand by next week!" In the June 22 session Terry said she was "not feeling comfortable" that the bills weren't being paid. She'd "told Ben she needed a cheque for about $1,700.00," but Ben hadn't given her any money. The mediator noted that Ben reminded her that he didn't have the money.

To begin separating their finances and "anticipate financial needs once separated," Bartoletti had given them each budget forms to complete at the end of their third session on May 30 and proposed that they draft personal budgets to review at their next session. However, three sessions passed and Terry still hadn't completed hers. *Session Summary*, June 22: "Terry has those items ... differentiated, but grouping into the three categories is the next stage." Bartoletti never referred to the budgets in his reports again.

It was the end of June. They'd had several double sessions but were no closer to any resolution. Typically, the dynamic in their sessions followed a pattern. Ben would make various practical proposals that would require some sacrifice or inconvenience but would allow them to separate right away, spare the kids more conflict, and continue to co-parent them. Then Terry would shoot them down because none of them suited her. The only proposal she would seriously entertain was for him to move out.

Through all this, according to Ben, Bartoletti remained scrupulously neutral. He would nod and confirm Terry's feelings and he would nod and confirm Ben's. If Ben pushed him, he would dutifully lay out the various options Ben proposed for separating, but he refused to put himself at odds with the will of one of the participants or express an opinion on the proposals he considered most constructive for the children. He stepped in to offer a point of view only as a last resort. And so, with a voluntary, open-ended process whose success depended entirely on the willingness of both parents to cooperate and a mediator whose function was largely that of a feel-good therapist lacking any authority to determine the best joint custody arrangement for the children, the process seemed to Ben to be a complete waste of time and money.

If a mediator focused more on the logistics of separation, Ben could see the process being useful for couples who were willing to put their kids first. However, because one uncooperative party could simply refuse to follow through on mediated resolutions and sabotage the process without being held accountable – the session summaries made it clear that Terry had never seriously looked for a place to live, given the rotation plan an honest try, or completed her budget – non-mandatory mediation without binding arbitration was useless for the very families who needed it the most.

Meanwhile the stalemate in mediation aggravated the situation at home. He and Terry weren't communicating. Confusion reigned. The kids were being used to relay messages. They had to resolve the housing and budget issues before school began in the fall. At the sixth session, on June 22, the mediator noted that Ben suggested they address the "major issues impacting on them." Although Ben had raised their strapped finances and the possibility of selling the house in previous sessions, they'd never reached any conclusions about how to resolve their financial problems. Now, for the first time, Ben was emphatic about their options: Terry had to "find a job." They had to face "a drop in socio-economic status." They had to recognize the "possible loss of living in the family home." It is the first unequivocal reference in the reports to the inevitable lifestyle changes closing in on them.

The following week, Ben was leafing through some bills on the kitchen desk, deciding which ones he could pay that month, when he found a bankbook he'd never seen before. He discovered that Terry had $3,703.86 in a personal account. When he confronted Terry, she told him the money was hers. According to Ben, she said she'd wound up with nothing from her first marriage because she couldn't afford a lawyer and she'd vowed that was never going to happen to her again.

Ben was furious. He asked her why she needed money for a lawyer when he already owed Bartoletti close to a thousand dollars to mediate their separation agreement. Terry said she felt insecure in their financial discussions and needed to know her rights. Ben reminded her of the deal they'd made when they began mediation: they'd each have their lawyers review their agreement before they signed anything, but it was Bartoletti's job to get them to that point without a fight. Consulting a lawyer now was premature. Terry remained unmoved.

Unable to pay all their bills, Ben asked Terry to cover her personal Visa expenses – her car insurance, incidentals like cosmetics and pantyhose – from the money she'd put aside while he was struggling to support their family. In Ben's recollection, Terry's attitude was that she'd never had to pay for things like pantyhose before, so why should she have to start now? It was his job to look after her.

The next session, on July 5, was heated. Bartoletti noted that the "pressure between them is building rapidly." Terry was upset that Ben wasn't paying the bills and the kids were being used as messengers. Ben was upset that Terry wasn't following through on mediated resolutions and their struggle was hurting the children.

Bartoletti noted that Ben was "no longer co-operating with Terry's interpretation of what the marriage should be" and wanted to "get apart" as soon as possible. *Session Summary*, July 5, under the heading "Ben's Issues": "Mediation sessions which are used just for arguing are useless and a waste. Unless resolutions are directly to her best interests, she doesn't cooperate ... She only wanted the status quo [of her lifestyle] to be maintained. The children are not the priority yet for Terry; they come further down the line."

After two months of unproductive mediation sessions, Ben had had enough. He demanded that Bartoletti put the major issues on the table and turn his attention to their separation. At Ben's insistence, Bartoletti laid out an agenda and they finally began to deal with realities. Terry had secured a real estate appraisal of their home: it was worth $1.1 million. They discussed the state of the real estate market, the improbability of finding two affordable homes in lower Forest Hill, the logistics of selling and relocating in other nearby but less tony neighbourhoods. They agreed to approach agents about renting or buying their own separate homes. "A conservative estimate of disposable net proceeds from the sale of the family home," Bartoletti recorded, "is $800,000.00 ($400,000.00 to each parent)."

For the first time Terry seemed ready to mediate a truly equitable joint custody agreement. Under the heading "Priorities," Bartoletti noted that Terry's were: "Sell the family home, even if there is a financial loss [against a possible market upturn], as soon as possible. Each to locate and become settled in a home of their own. (Close, if possible, and in same neighborhood as school.) Each parent be responsible for 50% of the children's needs, i.e. develop a Parenting Plan." He also wrote that Ben "concurs with the three priorities as stated by Terry. He wishes to maintain all negotiation within mediation for the present."

Ben told Bartoletti about discovering Terry's bank account and explained that until they sold the house and freed up some equity, he wanted her to start sharing the load and covering her personal expenses from her savings. Ben had stopped paying for her notional items and car insurance but continued carrying their other household expenses and supporting her and the children in all respects. Eventually, he said, he resumed paying her car insurance because he feared the financial ramifications if Terry was involved in an accident without any coverage, and she'd flatly refused to pay the bill.

Bartoletti noted: "Ben will make *paid receipts* [emphasis his] available to Terry, so she knows what bills have been paid," and "Ben proposes that Terry's personal expenses are to be paid from her personal savings ... until those savings are exhausted." Ben recalls Bartoletti himself suggesting to Terry that she should cover her own expenses; however, his summaries do not indicate any mediated resolution of that issue.

Session Summary, July 5: "At the next session, the information and facts obtained by each parent will be shared and discussed." Beside the list of options they'd agreed to investigate for the next session, scheduled for July 19, Bartoletti noted, "Both ... ready to separate." Ben was relieved but his elation was short-lived.

The following week, Ben received a letter dated July 12 from Carl Orbach, a lawyer acting for Terry. "Our client is in absolutely dire financial circumstances as you have declined to give her any money whatsoever in the past several weeks," the letter read. "Accordingly she has been unable to purchase any food, or other necessities. Unless you are prepared to make immediate arrangements to advance to our client the sum of $350 a week for food and other necessities, we would have no recourse but to commence an action."

Ben had two weeks to pay up. Otherwise, Terry would take him to court. Terry was prepared to settle out of court if Ben met the terms set forth in her lawyer's letter: she'd agree to "joint custody, provided the wife has daily care and custody." Ben would move out. She'd give him "liberal access to the children in and out of the matrimonial premises." She'd live in the house with the kids for a year, and they'd list the house for sale in August 1990. When the house sold, she'd be entitled to 60 percent of the house proceeds. They'd determine net worths and calculate equalization payouts. She'd divide their furniture "equitably" but "taking into consideration" that the children lived with her. Meanwhile, Ben was to pay "all expenses in connection with the matrimonial home" until it was sold, $2,000 a month in child support, $2,000 a month in spousal support (increased annually according to a cost-of-living index, reduced "in part" if she took a part-time or full-time job), cover Terry's and the kids' dental and medical expenses, give her an insurance policy, and secure part of the house sale proceeds to ensure his support payments.

At the next session, Ben showed Bartoletti Orbach's letter. According to Ben, Bartoletti took a stand for the first time and implored Terry to reconsider, telling her that not many women who came into his office walked away from a marriage with close to half a million dollars. When lawyers finished with them, he told her, there'd be nothing left. But Terry was upset about other matters. She'd given Ben her Visa bills but he hadn't paid them. He'd denied her adequate grocery money, providing only "about $200.00 for the past three to four weeks. (Though Ben continues to eat at home.)" He was "taking no responsibilities for the children other than for a few hours at a time." Bartoletti noted she'd accepted "a job in advertising" and was due to start the following week.

Ben went over the facts again: Terry had $3,700 in the bank. He was borrowing to pay their bills, including $14,000 to Revenue Canada in May to pay their taxes. He thought it reasonable under the circumstances to ask Terry to cover her incidental expenses. As for Terry's claim about the grocery money, he had cancelled cheques "well in excess of $200.00 over the past four weeks, which prove that he has given Terry adequate funds for groceries."

What was really going on, Ben believed, was a contest over whether Terry's lifestyle was going to change, and over who was going to run the household. During their marriage, whenever Terry needed money he'd write her a cheque, but he liked to shop regularly, too. It gave him a sense of pride to stock the larder. Although Terry was at home, he wasn't some Bay Street suit with a traditional marriage who went off to work and came home expecting his wife to have dinner on the table.

After Terry had refused to spend any of her money on her expenses, he was so strapped for cash that he thought it reasonable to give Terry less household money than usual, continue to shop himself, and ask her to fill in during the week, if necessary, with the money she had in the bank. But Terry didn't want to spend her own money on the family. At the same time she didn't want a situation developing where Daddy was buying all the groceries, because that would mean Daddy had control of the household. When Terry claimed she didn't have grocery money, what she really meant, Ben believed, was that she was unwilling to dip into her savings for household expenses and that her husband wasn't giving her exactly the same amount of money he'd always given for *her* to buy groceries, too.

Bartoletti's summary indicates that Ben then asked Terry a question: "If he pays the Visa and auto insurance bills; if he gives Terry $1,000.00/month for groceries and household supplies; if he pays for a live-in child care person, would she continue with mediation as opposed to litigating their separation?"

Terry said she would.

In fact, Ben couldn't afford to make that offer. He had asked the question only so Bartoletti could see Terry's priorities and lack of commitment to mediation. Ben believed that for Terry none of what had gone on in mediation was about the children. It was all about money. The moment he'd asked Terry to spend a few hundred dollars of her own money, she'd walked away from mediation, hired a lawyer, and threatened to sue. The moment her lifestyle seemed imperilled she reacted like a cornered animal and attacked.

When Ben protested against the involvement of lawyers, he heard the refrain that would run through all of Terry's subsequent actions: "I have no choice," she told him. "My back is against the wall."

Session Summary, July 19: "The [lawyer's] letter makes no mention of mediation. Obviously Terry feels: (1) her back is against the wall, and (2) Ben is not negotiating in good faith. Terry acknowledges that she has given to her lawyer the last money in her account ... being saved in case of an emergency. That has been a retainer, and he has acted, i.e. the letter ... Until the house is sold, they will be going into debt at the rate of $3,000.00 to $4,000.00 per month."

Carl Orbach's letter ended mediation.

CHAPTER THREE

THE LAWYERS

July 1989–January 1990

Terry had a lawyer so now Ben needed one, too. He met with Ken Cole on July 24, 1989, five days after their final mediation session. Cole was a partner at the firm of Epstein, Cole, one of the city's top family law specialists. He'd been recommended as a smart, level-headed negotiator with a reputation for settling his cases. Anxious not to inflame the situation any more, Ben wanted a lawyer with a low-key but firm approach to work out a joint custody agreement.

He showed Cole Orbach's letter and explained how shocked he'd been to receive it after almost three months in mediation. He assured Cole that Terry's allegations were absurd. He was still the sole supporter of the family and, except for Terry's Visa statements, was paying all the bills. They were eating. He was paying the mortgage. The water, heating, and hydro hadn't been cut off. And he'd stopped paying Terry's Visa bills and starting providing less household money than usual only when he'd discovered that she had more money in the bank than he did. Her lawyer's letter said she was in "absolutely dire financial circumstances" with no money for food and necessities. How could she have no money for food but enough money to retain a lawyer?

And what did it mean that Terry would agree to "joint custody" as long as she had "daily care and custody"? That just sounded like bullshit lawyerly semantics to Ben. He'd never been a weekend father and wasn't interested in starting now. Furthermore, considering his income was approximately $60,000 a year, her financial demands were outrageous. And they'd increased exponentially the moment she'd hired a lawyer. He told Cole that

Terry had just started working in the office of a one-man advertising agency, presumably as an assistant or trainee, but he didn't know what she was doing or earning. What could Cole do to help him?

Even before hearing the specifics, Cole wasn't encouraging about Ben's chances for joint custody. The reality was that the court didn't like to order joint custody when parents battled over their kids. The court took the view that it had to pick one parent over the other in such cases, and overwhelmingly it picked mothers. All things being equal, if there was a fight, Mom was going to win custody. But he told Ben not to worry. He'd contact Orbach and begin negotiations immediately. Both of them had to make full financial disclosure. Once he and Terry had exchanged financial statements, Cole would present Orbach with a settlement proposal. Then the four of them would meet to hammer out an agreement. He asked for a $1,000 retainer to cover his fees and gave Ben a financial statement form to complete.

Until they had an agreement, Cole advised him not to leave the house. If he did, he'd jeopardize his chances for joint custody. Lawyers knew from experience that if custody was at issue, both spouses should stay in the home unless they were going at each other with knives. It was the court's practice not to upset the status quo; if one spouse left the home without an agreement in place, it was easier for the other to argue that a new status quo had been established, claim exclusive possession of the home, and block its sale. Most important, the spouse who stayed could argue that the other parent no longer cared for the children on a regular basis, which would damage that parent's chances in a custody dispute. Ben learned his first lesson on how the family court looked out for the "best interests of the children." The moral course of action was legal suicide.

Ben left that meeting sick at heart. Cole had remarked offhandedly that negotiations should take only a couple of months at most. But for a family in turmoil, two months were an eternity. The kids needed their parents to separate right away. How were Deja and Zoe to live through another two months of discord? How was he? And how was he supposed to pay their bills? House prices were falling. Their equity was beginning to evaporate. Now there was real urgency to sell. He tried to get a grip. Cole seemed like a sensible straight-shooter. The good news was that Terry was working and could begin sharing their expenses. He'd just have to hang on a little while longer.

That day Cole called Orbach to notify him that he'd been retained by Ben. Three days later he wrote to request details of Terry's income and propose that their clients exchange financial statements to "commence productive negotiations." "We assume that the status quo will continue with both parties living separate and apart in the same dwelling and sharing parental responsibilities," he wrote. "Both parties should be contributing to the needs of the children and the household to the extent of their respective financial abilities." A month passed. Then another month. But Cole did not hear back. Ben called his lawyer periodically to find out if there was any news, but Cole had nothing to report. He advised him to be patient and sit tight.

The atmosphere in the house grew more unbearable. According to Ben, he kept trying to reassure the kids about how great it would be when they had two homes, but Terry was portraying him to the girls as a cruel home-wrecker. He said her solution for how to end the rancour was for him to leave. She'd say that if he wanted a divorce he should get one, but what did his divorce have to do with her? She'd tell him bitterly in front of the children that they didn't want him there, that they had a nice life and he was ruining it, that if he didn't want the marriage, he should just find an apartment on Bathurst Street somewhere and get out. The animosity between them was so pronounced that shoving matches would sometimes erupt.

Ben pleaded with Terry to have her lawyer contact Cole. Still Cole heard nothing. He told Ben that the only way to make Terry respond and bring her to the table was to begin a legal action. But Ben still hoped to negotiate a settlement; a confrontational court battle was the last thing he wanted. Although Terry had been working full-time at the ad agency since August, Ben was paying virtually all of the family's expenses. Ben had no idea what she was earning. Wasn't there something his lawyer could do?

In mid-October Cole wrote another letter. He alluded to the trouble at home, said Ben couldn't continue carrying the house without a "substantial deficit on a monthly basis," and asked again if they could exchange financial statements: "We assume," he wrote, "that we will have details of her remuneration in the very near future."

Then he outlined Ben's settlement proposal: the house would be sold but not immediately, given market conditions. In the meantime, Ben would find a place nearby to take the kids half the time. Although Ben saw no reason why he should be obliged to vacate their home any more than Terry, he would offer this concession in the interests of sparing the kids ongoing conflict and of hastening a settlement. The girls (and their nanny) would alternate between their households. They'd each support the kids in their own households, and they'd split costs such as the nanny's salary, religious school tuition, clothing, and camp and extracurricular activity fees. To pay their respective housing costs, they'd take out a line of credit against a collateral second mortgage on the house, share the bank debt, and divide the balance according to their equalization payouts when they sold the house. They'd each cover their personal expenses, and the house would be listed in the spring.

On October 24, three months after Cole had first requested Terry's financial statement, Orbach finally responded. He didn't yet have it. Terry was "reviewing" it and would deal with the matter "shortly." "Without going into your proposals in detail," Orbach wrote, "it would appear to be, on the face of it, inappropriate as you intend that both parties equally share all the expenses. Obviously, Mr. Gordon has a substantially larger income than Mrs. Gordon, and he, of course, would be liable for a substantially larger share of the maintenance of the property, and the children than Mrs. Gordon would. In any event, we will wait until we hear from Mrs. Gordon and advise you thereafter."

Another week passed. Cole wrote a third letter. Could they please exchange financial statements? Would Orbach please review Ben's settlement proposal with his client? He'd suggested sharing expenses because they'd both share equally in any increasing value of the home until it sold. Ben preferred to sell right away, but "that might prove too disruptive for the family." There shouldn't be any need for support since the children would be spending approximately equal time with each parent, but he was "certainly prepared to discuss with Mr. Gordon his additional contribution to certain predictable expenses related to the children." However, until they knew Terry's income, Cole pointed out, it was premature for the lawyers to have any discussion about expenses.

"I would like to proceed with this matter in an expeditious fashion," he concluded, "but I would like to also keep matters as calm and co-operative as we can."

Two days later, on November 2, Cole learned that Orbach had left town for three weeks. That day Cole wrote him again, presumably so that Orbach would deal with the matter immediately upon his return. Cole said the file was "becoming more difficult," and it was "becoming urgent" to take "some steps … to resolve the frictions … in the home." He reminded Orbach of the "very realistic" settlement proposal in his earlier letter. Ben had seen some places for rent close to the home, which would allow them to work out a co-operative parenting arrangement. "The proposal that I have made to you is very fair, requiring the parties to share the cost of both accommodations and use the equity in the home for that purpose." Cole implied that it would be disadvantageous for Terry to reject Ben's proposal and veto the sale of the home. In that case, Ben "would not be obliged to pay spousal support, as your client is now working full time. Your client then would be responsible for all of the expenses of the matrimonial home. Child support would be relatively modest in light of the fact that the children would be spending approximately one half of their time with Mr. Gordon." Cole noted that Ben was already attending to most of the children's needs and most of the household responsibilities, and he signed off by urging him "to consider this matter with Mrs. Gordon." Then he learned that Orbach was no longer representing Terry.

Ben was slowly going out of his mind. It wasn't so much what Cole had told him about what to expect; it was more what the lawyer hadn't told him. Cole had been upbeat about the possibility of settling promptly for a predictable fee. Ben was discovering it worked that way only if you had two settlement-minded clients and two settlement-minded lawyers. What Cole hadn't explained was that if Terry or her lawyer simply refused to cooperate, Cole had no way of controlling the costs and Ben was powerless to do anything about it, unless he wanted to litigate and escalate the problem. That was Ben's second lesson on how the family court looked out for the best interests of his children.

Almost four months had passed since Ben had retained Cole. During that time he'd waited patiently while his level-headed lawyer wrote conciliatory letters to Terry's lawyer in a futile effort to settle. Orbach no longer had Terry's file, but Terry wouldn't say who she'd retained, and it was unclear whether Orbach or Terry's file was still with his firm. More time was lost while Cole did some detective work to find out who was representing her. According to Ben, Cole got a lead and said he wasn't certain but thought Terry's lawyer might be Ronald Zaldin. Zaldin was a litigation lawyer about forty years old who practised at the downtown firm of Lyons, Goodman, Iacono, Smith & Berkow. Cole didn't characterize Zaldin to Ben one way or another.

Meanwhile, as Ben described it, he was living under siege in the house. Terry regularly demonized him to the kids and their nanny, Cheryl – whom she instructed not to do his laundry. She called him a "bastard" in front of Cheryl and the girls, rhetorically asked Deja, "How come Daddy can't buy you any clothes?" and told Cheryl that Ben had "tons of money" and "wasn't supporting her and the girls."

At the end of November, Cole wrote to Zaldin: the home situation was "increasingly intolerable." He urgently wanted Terry's financial statement and a response to their settlement proposal. He'd already waited several weeks. Ben had been pressing Cole to do something to move matters forward; now, in an effort to bring the other side to the negotiating table, Cole took a more aggressive stance in his correspondence: "Mr. Gordon will have no alternative, in the absence of a response from you, but to institute proceedings for exclusive possession or sale of the matrimonial home." The threat elicited no response from Ronald Zaldin.

Early in December, the pressure cooker in which the family was living finally exploded. Ben's version put him in the kitchen around 8:30 in the morning, helping Cheryl get the kids their breakfast and taking lamb chops out of the freezer for dinner that night. Terry came downstairs and in front of Cheryl and the girls began berating him for his choice, insisting that the kids didn't like lamb chops, then coaching them to agree with her by saying, "You don't like lamb chops, do you, kids?"

He walked out of the kitchen and into the den nearby to avoid engaging her, but she followed him and began threatening that she had a lawyer who was going "to take care of him." "Fine!" Ben told her angrily. "Just tell me your lawyer's name, just get him to answer my lawyer, so we can get on with negotiations!" (Although Cole had written to Zaldin, Zaldin had not yet responded, so Ben didn't yet know for certain if he was representing Terry.) According to Ben, Terry kept goading him and refusing to reveal her lawyer's name. Finally, in complete exasperation, he stormed out of the room, angrily sweeping a pile of magazines off the coffee table and upending it in her direction as he left.

Terry called 911 to report a domestic assault. The investigating officers arrived, interviewed them separately, and found no basis to lay charges. The police advised them to have their lawyers talk. Terry consulted Ronald Zaldin. Zaldin advised his client to press assault charges through a justice of the peace.

In Ontario, a justice of the peace is empowered to lay charges without investigating the complaint. All a complainant need do is provide a sworn statement. Terry's account of the incident that morning was that "around 8:30 a.m. we were sitting in our living room ... at 24 Dewbourne Avenue. At that time, I was concerned about continuing our marriage and the subject of divorce came up. As the discussion of separation and divorce continued, my husband became very angry. He stood up and grabbed the side of the coffee table and propelled it towards me ... flipping it over and landing in front of the chesterfield where I was seated. I was terrified and feared that he would continue his behaviour and harm me, so I reached for the telephone and called '911' for the police while he continued his angry tirade. After the police left, I consulted with my lawyer and then attended this courthouse and laid this charge." The matter would hang over Ben's head for months.

Ben called Cole. They couldn't go on like this. Didn't anyone give a damn about the kids? The lawyer wrote another letter. This time he suggested hiring an assessor to review the "present dynamics of the family." "Mrs. Gordon has hinted that she is involved in detailed tactical considerations with you. I would urge you to engage in a dialogue with me prior to the commencement of [divorce] proceedings."

Ben scribbled a note to himself and threw it in his file: "Press Cole. Apparently Terry's lawyer has finally responded. Suggestion he's never actually met Terry. They [Terry and lawyer] apparently have meeting today." On December 18 he received a letter from Cole: he'd been in touch with Zaldin, "who was ill for a couple of weeks." Zaldin had recently met with Terry, he expected details shortly. He was trying to stay on top of the matter.

The next day, five months after Cole had responded to Orbach's letter threatening to take Ben to court and two months after he had forwarded a settlement proposal, Cole finally heard back: "[Terry] may very well consent to your proposal, without prejudice." "Without prejudice" meant that Zaldin was speaking within the context of settlement negotiations, and his client was therefore not bound by any offers he proposed. First, though, Zaldin wanted to see Ben's tax returns going back four years, details of his current income, and corroboration of the loans and debts he was claiming. "Upon receipt of this information," he wrote, "I shall get Mrs. Gordon's sworn Financial Statement to you." He thanked Cole for his indulgence due to his "recent illness (bronchitis)" and proposed a four-way meeting for early January.

Cole had told Ben that both parties were obliged to provide full disclosure. Ben had furnished a financial statement, but Terry hadn't even disclosed her income. Why did he have to hand over more information when Terry hadn't revealed even that? When did she have to start playing ball? Ben said Cole told him his only options were to commence a legal action, or continue to be patient and cooperate. In Cole's opinion it was best to take the high road and keep the situation as unadversarial as possible. Ben was incredulous at how the process penalized the cooperative party and rendered him (or her, he imagined) powerless to do anything except wait until the other side decided to play fair.

Nonetheless, he began to pull together the documents Zaldin was demanding. Cole wrote Zaldin promising to present a sworn version of Ben's financial statement, with any changes, on the day of their meeting. He asked again for Terry's financial statement, adding that while he would wait until the date of the meeting for a sworn copy, he needed a draft copy as soon as possible so that he might review it and, if necessary, request any additional documentation before they met. Because of the delay, he advised Zaldin, Ben had lost several potential apartments, but he was still looking for accommodations, assuming Terry was amenable to their settlement proposal.

The four finally met in Ken Cole's office on January 31, 1990, almost a year after Ben and Terry had decided to divorce and more than six months after Terry had walked away from mediation and retained a lawyer. When Zaldin and Terry arrived, Ben got his first look at the lawyer Terry had chosen to represent her in their negotiations. According to Ben, Zaldin was a stubby-framed man in a wrinkled suit who lumbered into the room listing to one side under the weight of a heavy briefcase. He made no attempt at pleasantries. The thought crossed Ben's mind that if he'd been producing an episode of *Night Court*, he would not have cast Ronald Zaldin as the dignified and stately barrister.

Just that morning, Zaldin had at last supplied Terry's financial statement, and it was not the sworn copy Cole had specified. There had been little time to review it, let alone request supporting documentation. At least, after six months of polite requests, Ben and Cole had it in hand.

For the first hour and a half, Zaldin grilled Ben about his finances. Ben was puzzled. They were there to negotiate a settlement, but he felt as if he were being cross-examined. In exasperation, Cole finally demanded they get down to the business at hand. He asked Zaldin to state his client's terms. Zaldin said Terry wanted $2,000 a month in child support, possession of the home for five years, and sole custody of Deja and Zoe.

Ben's stomach turned over. Terry had never before mentioned sole custody. Throughout their mediation sessions, it was money she had always talked about. And, to Ben's knowledge, Zaldin had never raised that possibility with Cole.

"Are you telling me we have a custody fight on our hands?" Cole asked Zaldin sharply. Zaldin nodded. Ben tried to focus on what was happening, but he was in shock. All he knew for certain was that the sole custody of his children had never been an issue until Ronald Zaldin took over the file.

CHAPTER**FOUR**

THE ASSESSMENT

February–December 1990

After the meeting with Terry and Zaldın, Ben started looking for a new lawyer. He'd found Cole to be a gentleman, and he was grateful that Cole was prepared to release his file even though he hadn't fully settled his account. He believed the lawyer had done the best possible job under the circumstances. But Cole hadn't been as available as Ben would have liked, and he'd been all business. That was fine when all he needed was a lawyer to negotiate a separation agreement. But his needs had changed. Now he was in a crapshoot to remain more than a weekend dad in a system with lousy odds for men with such aspirations. He was desperately worried and wanted a lawyer who'd be willing to hold his hand a little, too. Susan Himel, a family lawyer of his acquaintance who worked in the Official Guardian's Office (now the Office of the Children's Lawyer), had given him two names when he'd called for a referral six months earlier. He would try the second: Judith Beaman.

In late February, Ben parted amicably with Cole and hired Beaman. Beaman, like Ken Cole, came highly recommended as a solid negotiator who liked to settle her cases. Unlike Cole, who practised in a downtown space for downtown fees, Beaman worked in a cosier midtown brownstone and charged lower rates. Furthermore, Beaman's high-profile all-female firm, Dunbar Sachs Appell, had a reputation for championing women's issues. Besides offering him comfort and reassurance, Ben also hoped a female lawyer would be less intimidating for Terry and might have more luck in persuading her to settle.

When he told her about himself and the role he'd played in the girls' lives, Beaman made no promises, but she was more encouraging than Cole about his chances. She'd represented fathers who'd been much involved in their children's upbringing and, judging by his account of his history, felt he had a decent shot at joint custody. However, when he asked her to suggest another father willing to have a drink and answer his questions about what to expect, Beaman couldn't come up with any names. That concerned him. There had to be other men going through this. Maybe Beaman didn't act for any fathers who were as emotional about their kids as he was, or as willing to do whatever it took to remain their parent. He felt utterly alone.

Nor was she able to assuage his most pressing worry, which was that the kids would continue to suffer as long as he and Terry were forced to live under one roof. Until they had an agreement on custody, nothing was going to change. And now they were to have an assessment. At the four-way meeting, the lawyers had recommended that Ben and Terry arrange for an assessment before the court ordered one. They'd shortcut the process and, depending on the outcome, maybe even settle.

When custody was at issue, the court often ordered an assessment of the family by a psychiatrist, psychologist, or social worker, who then made recommendations. Although the quality of assessments varies widely – some comprise only a couple of interviews – ideally the process lasts a few months, involving about thirty hours of psychological testing, observation, and interviews with the parents, children, and significant others.

Lawyers recommend an assessor to their clients; then the two sides tangle over the choice and the method of payment. The clients pay the assessor's fees; in 1990, assessments cost anywhere from $3,500 to $8,000. At the time, assessors wielded tremendous power in family court, since judges tended to accept their word. (Judges today are more inclined to view the assessment as just one important piece of the evidence, though a respected assessor's recommendations still carry a great deal of clout.)

Both Cole and Beaman recommended Irwin Butkowsky as their first choice. Because of the money to be made conducting assessments, many of those getting into the business weren't particularly well qualified. But Butkowsky had a PhD in clinical psychology and, although he wasn't a favourite of all lawyers, was certainly considered one of the top names in the field. He was much in demand and he had a great deal of influence with the court.

Cole pointed out that because Butkowsky was a middle-class Jewish father like Ben, he'd be likelier to understand their family dynamics and Ben would be judged by a peer. In addition, Cole had used him in the past and, as assessors went, thought Butkowsky more inclined than most to be pro-father (in lawyers' parlance), meaning that he believed the assessor to understand and be sympathetic to the importance of a father's role.

Ben knew an assessment would cost more money and mean more long months living in the house with Terry. He also expected it would be upsetting to have a stranger poking and prodding in their lives. But if they had to travel this road, surely a psychologist well known to the family court, highly recommended by two respected lawyers, would look closely at their family, see it couldn't be pigeonholed into some conventional slot, and decide that joint custody was the only appropriate recommendation in their case. If it took an assessment to ensure that he remained an involved father to Deja and Zoe, then he would endure an assessment. He would do whatever it took.

Despite his apprehensions about both the process and the outcome of the assessment, Ben was eager to begin right away if it would hasten the end of the excruciating tension at home. He was sick about its effect on the kids. He was conscious of his growing debt load and the fact that they were losing equity in the house every day. And on top of these worries was the humiliating prospect of his criminal court appearance to answer Terry's assault charges.

Ben later said that since Terry had begun working in July, he and Cheryl were managing most of the workload for the household and children. His daybook that year was crammed with reminders: "Kids to circus ... Deja to Kortright Centre – class trip ... buy bread Food City ... dinner at Sticky Fingers," and so on. Sundays he'd drive Deja to piano classes in the morning, do errands with Zoe, give the kids lunch, drive Deja to religious school at 1:30, take Zoe grocery shopping, then collect Deja at 3:30.

He'd sandwich his family responsibilities around meetings with shoe buyers, auditions, studio tapings, and commercial shoots, but he was so unglued he was finding it impossible to perform. In studio one day doing a voiceover for a carpet commercial with the comic Robert Cait, Ben kept stumbling over words, botching his timing and delivery. Cait knew something was terribly wrong. Later he likened the experience to "getting a chance to be on the ice with Jean Béliveau, but discovering, to my horror, that Béliveau couldn't skate."

It took two more months for the lawyers to settle on Butkowsky. Then they haggled over how he'd be paid. Butkowsky estimated his assessment would take thirty hours over six months and cost approximately $6,000. Before starting, he required the lawyers to personally guarantee their clients' share of his fees, and he insisted on some money up front. According to Ben's financial statement, his gross income was $48,000 and he'd accumulated more than $50,000 in debt. Nevertheless, he continued to support the family. Terry, who'd been working full-time for eight months, and whose financial statement disclosed her gross income at approximately $28,000 a year, was still contributing only nominally towards the children's expenses or the household; for instance, Ben said, she would pay if she took the kids to McDonald's or picked up a few things at the drugstore. Nor had she produced a pay slip to confirm her earnings.

Beaman wrote to Zaldin that Ben had an "enormous shortfall" each month "carrying *all* [emphasis hers] the expenses related to the house and children," while Terry "seems to be keeping her entire salary for her own use" and was in a much better position to afford the assessment. If she couldn't raise the cash through her salary, Beaman suggested they remortgage the house and pay Butkowsky off the top.

Terry would pay only one-third of the assessment fees. Ben agreed to pay the rest. "He doesn't think things should be held up arguing about money," a colleague handling Ben's file in Beaman's absence wrote in an internal office memo. "The assessor should be booked and financial matters dealt with separately later. It is [the] children's welfare he is worried about."

Butkowsky was too busy to begin until later that spring. Meanwhile, the lawyers wrote him letters of instruction. "Ben Gordon is an actor and you might have seen him on TV," wrote Zaldin. "It is the wife's feeling that her 'actor' husband will attempt to 'act' his way through the assessment and convince you that he is more interested in the children than he ever was prior to their in-house separation. The husband's position ... is that he is as dedicated and caring as the mother and there should be joint custody … The husband feels that the wife doesn't pay enough attention to the children and he can do a better job of it. The wife … feels that the husband's interest is only to 'punish' her out of bitterness and to save him lots of money by reducing the child support he wouldn't [sic] otherwise pay in a normal custody/access situation." Zaldin assured the assessor he'd guarantee Terry's portion of his fees, since "the matrimonial home is probably worth over $700,000, even in this depressed market."

The formal assessment process began at last in May. First the lawyers met with Butkowsky; then, at mid-month, Ben visited his office for an introductory session. According to Ben, it was similar to most modern doctors' offices, except for an adjacent viewing room replete with books and toys where the psychologist could observe children at play.

Ben's first impression of Butkowsky was of a man around his age, perhaps slightly younger, with salt-and-pepper hair, a medium build, a large head on a thin frame, and a delicacy of manner. As Ben recalled, Butkowsky sat down in a swivel chair at a desk situated in front of a wall lined with framed degrees and certificates from McGill and Duke University and began their meeting by saying that he intended to lay down the ground rules. Then, by way of introducing himself, he pointed to his degrees on the wall, making much of his credentials, his accreditation and accomplishments, attempting, as Ben saw it, to impress upon him how influential his decision would be with the court.

For the next forty-five minutes, Ben said, Butkowsky lectured him in this vein, making it clear that Ben was not to mess with him or think he could fool or trick him, that he was in a position to decide his future and the future of his children. He'd interview Terry and Ben separately a half-dozen times, bring the girls in for some visits, and if necessary take some personality and IQ tests.

Ben left the meeting queasy with fear. He'd imagined that a reputable assessor with the power to make custody recommendations would be an astute, compassionate professional with wisdom and life experience. Instead, Butkowsky had struck him as an arrogant and self-aggrandizing bureaucrat.

■ ■ ■

For the next three months, while Butkowsky conducted his investigations to arrive at a recommendation on custody, Beaman tried to wrap up the house and money matters, which didn't fall within the assessor's jurisdiction. "Your client," wrote Beaman to Zaldin on April 24, "is enjoying the benefit of living separate from my client under the same roof, without any of the responsibility ... The only realistic solution for all concerned is to sell the matrimonial home and split the proceeds." But Terry didn't want to hear about selling the house or moving. According to Ben, she believed she was entitled to custody and the house, and was going to get both, so why should she negotiate? She expected Ben to move out.

Terry also refused to acknowledge that Ben had money problems. As Ben told it, she insisted to him, Zaldin, Butkowsky, and anyone who was willing to listen that he had deliberately destroyed his acting career and intentionally depleted his income to deny her child support. "For some reason your client does not believe that Mr. Gordon's financial picture is exactly as it is portrayed in the financial statement," Beaman wrote. To allay Terry's suspicions, Ben offered to answer any questions about his income and assets under oath and to have his accountant do so as well. Beaman asked Zaldin to reply soon. She wanted to know how much money Terry would contribute to their household; they had to discuss the logistics for listing the home. But Zaldin did not respond.

Ever since Terry had abandoned mediation the previous summer, she and Ben had been operating as a separated couple leading separate lives under the same roof. (The court requires couples to pick an official separation date to facilitate post-separation division of property and assets; they'd selected March 1989, after the meeting in Larry Nisan's office.) For almost a year they'd been coming and going without communicating where they'd been or what they'd done. Desperate to escape to some female warmth and companionship, Ben had gone out on a few dates. For all he knew, Terry had done likewise. The court had put them in the position of waging a struggle over who'd retain primacy in the home and who'd be evicted and thus reduced to second-class parenting status. The battle played out symbolically on other fronts, too. According to Ben, Terry insisted the master bedroom was "hers," just as she insisted their house and children were hers. Unwilling to become the discarded parent that Terry was trying to convince the children he should be, Ben found himself in the ludicrous position of seeing who'd claim the bedroom first in the evenings. Against this backdrop, an assessor figuratively peered over their shoulders to evaluate the family dynamic and make recommendations on custody.

Ben told Beaman that Terry was constantly belittling him in front of the kids, their housekeeper, the kids' teachers, and his family. He continued to document the situation in the house by scribbling notes on backs of envelopes, shopping lists, and scratch pads, and in his appointment diary. Ben was driving carpool, racing home by 4:00 to greet the camp bus, making dinners, meeting with another divorced father to borrow a book about divorce for the kids, teaching their new housekeeper how to make French toast, buying birthday party invitations, promising Deja's music teacher to work with her on theory, buying the kids skates, retrieving Zoe's scarf and gloves from the lost and found, readying the girls for school in the morning, bathing them, reading them stories, and cuddling them at night. While he managed their family life and paid for it, Terry was calling him "immature," accusing him of refusing to support her, and vilifying him to the kids and the housekeeper. She told Ben's mother her son was a sick person who needed help. Zoe told Ben, in hysterics, "Mommy says you won't buy us milk."

When they were at home together, Ben said, he tried to respect Terry's parenting time, and if they managed to communicate about her plans to take the kids on a certain day at a certain time, he wouldn't stand in her way. In the past, whenever he'd taken the girls out, he was just Daddy taking the girls out. Now that Terry wanted sole custody, and an assessor had them under a microscope, Ben said Terry set herself up as the commander-in-chief of all parenting decisions and treated him like a lackey obliged to report for instructions. She would give him the third degree beforehand and grill the kids on their return, trying to create the impression that she was in control, constantly asking, "What are you going to feed them? What are you going to make them wear? Who's going to be there?" – all of which were questions he wanted to ask her but, given the situation they were living in, didn't.

Events that would have been viewed as natural in the course of a family's life were suddenly magnified with meaning and fraught with fearful subtext. Now everything was Evidence. Early in July he took the kids to his former brother-in-law Brian Evans's cottage for the weekend. (Evans, who had his daughter, Alyssa, that weekend, had recently split from Terry's sister, Lynne. Before they'd split, Ben said, he and Brian would jokingly make private bets at the Nusynas' Friday-night dinners about who'd be the first to leave his wife.) At the cottage, they waded out to a wooden raft and Evans began horsing around, playfully tipping the raft this way and that. The raft overturned and everyone fell off. Ben dove underneath, grabbed the kids, and lifted them above the water; everyone was fine, but they'd been scared. Ben had been angry at Brian, but because he would not censor the girls he'd spent the balance of the weekend terrified about what would happen when they told Terry. He imagined her blowing the incident out of all proportion, then running to Butkowsky to say "her" children had almost drowned.

In Ben's account, Terry repeatedly told Deja and Zoe how pathetic men were. She portrayed the girls as Ben's victims and positioned herself as their protector, claiming "your father is trying to take our home away from us … things will get worse if he has his way … but I'm not going to let him hurt us." On April 7, Ben made a note of a remark from Zoe: "I smiled at Mommy and said [I] love you, but I really don't. I just did it so she won't know I love you."

In these ugly circumstances, Ben was a tinderbox, and exchanges between himself and Terry escalated easily into shouting and insults. Still, he kept hoping Terry would come to her senses. He couldn't believe a mother would continue upsetting her own children the way Terry was hurting Deja and Zoe. He asked an old friend to speak to her, but she said Terry wouldn't listen. In desperation, he asked Butkowsky for ideas. The psychologist suggested he write Terry a letter requesting her cooperation. On June 15, he faxed Beaman: "Butkowsky recommends I write Terry a letter regarding care of the children," read the cover sheet. "Here's a draft. What do you think?"

June 6, 1990

Dear Terry,
Once into the assessment process I had hoped that your antagonistic behavior towards me (and its residual effects on Deja and Zoe)

50

would cease. Unfortunately not. You have said to me and I've heard you say to others that I'm "... an animal, inhuman...", ... and that my lawyer is "... a fool". If you are so confident of the "outcome" of our conflict then why do you persist in trying to antagonize me? Why must you continue to insult, belittle and accuse me?

It is clearly in the best interest of our children that you stop making such remarks to me in the presence of Deja and Zoe. Aside from being provocative and disturbing to me, these unnecessary and uncalled for remarks are torturing our children and have no doubt already caused serious and lasting psychological damage to them both.

Ben had a number of specific suggestions for reducing conflict over the bedtime routines of the girls as well as those of their parents, such as alternating in the master bedroom, making use of the sleeping quarters in the basement, or setting up a bedroom in the study. As for the morning routine, he asked Terry to "refrain from throwing insults and put-downs from the sidelines" while he was getting the kids up and out the door, a parental duty he greatly enjoyed. Similarly, Ben noted Terry's "contempt and low regard" for their new housekeeper and asked Terry to stop her verbal abuse of Mavis, especially in front of the children. (Mavis had begun working for them in April after Cheryl could no longer bear the situation in the house and quit.)

<u>With regard to my/your financial status, the maintenance of our home and our living expenses:</u> ... You have admitted to making approximately $500 a week at a job you've been at since about July of last year. Currently your only expenses are your personal ones. In spite of this you continue to plead poverty, make no significant monetary contribution to our home or the family. Instead you accuse *me* of not providing for you and the children (often in their presence). You won't even buy yourself a box of "Q-Tips" or a jar of the coffee you prefer (when the de-caff I bought wasn't acceptable).

With Ben's debts now amounting to close to $60,000 and growing by $1,000 a week, he was particularly outraged at Terry's remark to Deja's teacher at their parent-teacher interview in March: "He hasn't brought five cents into the house."

> This and numerous other such comments to others does nothing to promote a positive resolution of our domestic situation or enhance the relationship we must continue as parents. Please stop it.
>
> Considering your behaviour as I've outlined above (and much that I haven't) it's not surprising that I find it difficult being open, trusting and friendly with you. I hope that you will soon begin coming to terms with the fact that our marriage is over. I suggest that it's time that you begin taking responsibility for your behavior, your children and your own financial needs. Most importantly I think that it is essential that you become specific about what child-care responsibilities you wish to assume and at what times. I have no problem communicating with anyone with regard to the care and well being of my children. However I do have difficulty co-operating with someone who is vindictive and untrustworthy and acts not in the best interests of my children.

He ended with a plea for "an early reply." On Beaman's advice, at the bottom of a later draft, Ben added:

> P.S. I very much want to work *with* you to resolve our differences. I accept that our marriage is at an end. As we enter a new phase of our relationship (namely as a divorced couple and forever co-parents of Deja & Zoe) we are *compelled* to overcome our negative feelings for one another and concentrate on providing our children the most loving, supportive and peaceful environment possible. (If nothing else, we can exemplify for their benefit how two people can agree to disagree and live co-operatively in spite of their differences.)
>
> Ben

According to Ben, Terry did not respond to the letter and it accomplished nothing. He pleaded with anyone who might have Terry's ear to talk to her. He begged Terry's parents to intervene. They said they had to support their daughter, right or wrong. Morris Nusyna accused him of provoking Terry and "putting on an act," then threatened to "get you out of that house so fucking fast," to get his lawyer after him and call the police.

One day in early July, Ben said, he was in the front vestibule around 8:30 in the morning preparing to leave for the office: putting on his coat, throwing back a glass of orange juice, grabbing his keys, watching for his father, who was picking him up, through the open front door. Deja and Zoe were outside on the front steps waiting for the camp bus when something set Terry off and she started in on him in front of the children and neighbours, hurling accusations. "You're no good. You're wrecking this family. You're pathetic. You're not supporting us. You're ruining everybody's life. We have a good life here. Why don't you just get out?"

He knew better than to try to talk to her when she went into a rant and he kept walking away from her, but then he came back and tried to get her to stop, saying in a low, clipped voice, "Terry, stop, Terry, shut up. Terry, not in front of the kids." But whatever he said only provoked her more. She was standing with her arms crossed, barring the front door, taunting him to try to get past her, saying, "Why don't you just walk out?" The kids were only a few feet away on the steps with their heads bowed, pretending not to listen but hearing it all. She went on and on and there was no stopping her or getting away from her, and he wanted to slap her to make her stop, but all he could think of to make her shut up was to stomp on her toe. That's what he did. Then she began to wail as if she'd been bludgeoned, rushing out to the kids, crying, "Oh my God! Oh my God! Deja, look! Look what he did! Look at my foot! Look what he did!" The kids started withdrawing, hanging their heads, darting their eyes here and there, and once she'd involved them she charged into the house, shoved him against the wall on her way into the kitchen, dialled 911, and reported a domestic assault. Ben phoned his friend Mark Anshan to get the kids out of the house before the cops arrived.

Once again the police arrived, interviewed them separately, and found no basis to lay charges. Once again Terry pressed assault charges through a justice of the peace.

Ben called the Jewish Family and Child Service. He said his children were being emotionally abused. He begged for their help. He was told the agency couldn't intervene unless the kids were in immediate physical danger. According to his diary notation that day, he was advised not to react to Terry's outbursts and to keep a record of them.

He called Beaman. This was insane. His kids were being harmed and his life was being destroyed. They had to get apart. Was there *nothing* she could do?

Beaman wrote a letter to Zaldin. "It will not come as news to you that the already strained relationship between our clients has deteriorated even further ... [They] simply cannot continue to live together under the same roof. My client has long been concerned about the impact of the present arrangement on the children. Dr. Butkowsky's observations confirm that the damage to the children is serious and ongoing. Something must be altered immediately if any members of this family are to be salvaged."

At his wits' end, but lacking another alternative allowing them to separate, Ben resurrected the rotation plan idea that Terry had vetoed in mediation.

> Mr. Gordon has instructed me to advise you that he will be taking the initiative in moving out of the matrimonial home as soon as he can make alternate arrangements. He expects that your client take this opportunity to find herself another place to live as well. The children will not be moved at this time. The house should immediately be listed for sale. Until such time as the property can be sold, the parties can alternate living at the matrimonial home with the children – either on an alternating weekly or half-weekly basis. This arrangement would be on a strictly without prejudice basis. I telephoned Dr. Butkowsky to determine how much longer the assessment would take, and he indicated he would need until approximately the middle of August before he would be holding his disclosure meetings. During this conversation, I raised Mr. Gordon's plan and he wholeheartedly endorsed the physical separation of the parties at this time.

Once again Beaman said Ben couldn't keep accumulating debt and carrying the family's financial burden alone. Once again she said Terry was employed and "should be contributing a fixed sum each week toward the household expenses." Once again she said it was inevitable they'd have to sell the home at some point and explore new accommodations for the children in time for school in the fall, that they had to choose a real estate agent and decide on a listing price. Once again she asked for a response within one week. And once again she heard nothing from Zaldin.

■ ■ ■

Ben soon had grave misgivings about Irwin Butkowsky. He'd expected the assessor to come to their house, get a feeling for how they lived. But Butkowsky said it wasn't necessary. Ben urged him to interview their house-keeper, Mavis. Since April, she'd witnessed what was going on at home and could testify to what she had observed. According to Ben, Butkowsky said no way. Butkowsky's methodology, we later learned, was standard practice.

The psychologist did talk to the grandparents on both sides and to Ben's friends Mark Anshan and Brenda Spiegler. Anshan was a lawyer and Spiegler a neuropsychologist at Toronto Western Hospital. Ben had argued that although they were his friends, Mark was Zoe's godfather, the couple had spent a lot of time in their home, and they were wholly credible wit-nesses. Anshan later told Ben that they gave Butkowsky their "spin" on the situation: they were seeing "real negative conduct" from Terry, who was trying to control and dominate and making it difficult for everyone involved to have a healthy relationship. They saw Ben as trying to encourage strong bonds between the girls and both parents and doing nothing to undermine their relationship with their mother, despite the terrible marriage break-down. But Spiegler got the feeling the assessor was interviewing them only to "placate Ben." She described Butkowsky's technique as "fairly passive" and "pretty low-level stuff." To her, "it felt like we were tattling."

Ben and Terry were paying a top assessor handsomely for an in-depth assessment. Ben wondered how Butkowsky would form an accurate picture of their family without more in-depth investigation or corroboration of what each parent was telling him. Butkowsky had told him that children needed one home base to feel secure. Ben didn't think this was necessarily true, certainly not for all children, and he firmly believed he knew his own well enough to feel confident that they could readily adapt to living in two homes if the arrangement was presented to them in a positive light. (According to Ben's notes, after Deja's music class one Sunday in early

February, he'd dropped in with her to check out a house for rent at Redpath and Eglinton Avenue, near the school: "Deja is enthusiastic," he'd noted. "She picks out a potential bedroom for herself and Zoe.")

Besides, he thought an assessor needed wisdom more than book learning, but Butkowsky didn't inspire confidence in that realm. And while Ben did have the impression that Butkowsky understood the ferocity of the conflict at home, he didn't think the assessor had the faintest idea of his financial pressures or the responsibilities he was carrying on his own, for the kids. How then could he possibly do a fair evaluation? Furthermore, Ken Cole had wanted him to be judged by a peer, but Ben would never have described Butkowsky as his peer; he found it difficult to establish a therapeutic rapport with a professional whose sensibilities were so far from his own and who seemed to lack empathy for his situation. He had the uneasy feeling he'd been handed over to the nerdy kid in the class, the browner with the big briefcase whom nobody picked for baseball but who'd suddenly been given the chance to act out all his power fantasies.

And while Butkowsky was Jewish, Ben thought they had radically different ideas of what it meant to be Jewish. For starters, Ben didn't think Butkowsky had any sense of humour or understood his own brand of humour or irony, which was troubling because it caused Ben to question the psychologist's intuition and self-awareness in a broader sense. He had the worrisome feeling, which grew over time, that the assessor was never going to "get" him. The more he acted like himself in the assessment process, the greater distance he travelled from the assessor and his values. To communicate with Butkowsky, he had to be more like Butkowsky. But then he would be acting.

Butkowsky was a man he'd avoid in an airplane or bar, but now he practically had to tell him the colour of his pubic hair. And he couldn't walk out the door, as he could have if he'd found a therapist's approach questionable or manner objectionable. He had the feeling he was just another file to Butkowsky and found it excruciating to describe his hopes and fears for his children to someone who appeared interested only in evaluating and categorizing him, just as he was doing to the assessor in his own mind. But there was one significant difference: Ben didn't have the power to take the other man's children away from him.

What worried him most, however, was that his future as a dad lay in the hands of a man who seemed unable to conceive of a father who should have more than weekend access and a backseat role. Butkowsky had told him that he had a traditional marriage and family, that he worked and his wife stayed home. What underlay everything Butkowsky said was the assumption that since Ben's children were daughters, they should be with their mother. But Ben wasn't a bad guy, so he'd give him a little more time than the usual. The possibility that the kids might also make their home with their father did not even seem to be up for discussion. Moreover, Butkowsky seemed to view a father who did less than he did as not good enough, and a father who did more as threatening.

Ben said to him one day, "I'm making the kids' lunches, taking them to the dentist, going on their school trips. I'm getting them ready for the school bus." Then Butkowsky responded with a remark that made him realize these details just weren't registering, a sort of admonition to the effect that, "Well, you should do that. I waited for the camp bus and that's one of the most important things a father can do for his kids."

It was a pivotal moment in the assessment. From the first Ben had sensed Butkowsky's biases all over the process, but at that instant he knew he was in trouble. What had this man been hearing all these months? Did Butkowsky not have a glimmer that he was patting himself on the back for having done on occasion what Ben was doing day in and day out? That he was putting them on the bus every morning, then turning himself inside out to leave work early and racing uptown and downtown and all over town to greet their bus at an earlier drop-off point so they didn't have to sit another twenty minutes in the heat, that he'd diapered them and nurtured them and talked to them and educated them and loved them, that he'd always done it and was doing it still? And now this vain, condescending man was telling him, "You know, you really should meet your kids at the camp bus. It's a good feeling."

■ ■ ■

By late July, Butkowsky was preparing to release his recommendations. Ben doubted that joint custody could work without Terry's cooperation, and he had good reason to believe she wouldn't cooperate, but he assumed she would suffer consequences if she didn't. If she persisted in drawing the children into battle and alienating them from him, Ben thought she would ultimately lose any form of custody. Ben knew from the lawyers he'd consulted that the law said the children were entitled to a relationship with both parents, and the court was supposed to rule in their best interests. Terry's attempt to alienate the children from him was so obviously a form of emotional abuse that he could not imagine the court allowing it to continue.

He now believed it was crucial for him to have joint custody. If this was how Terry behaved with a court authority involved in their lives, what would she do if she had the dictatorial power of sole custody, unbridled and unsupervised? Without joint custody, how would he protect Deja and Zoe from her behaviour and attitudes or retain any voice in shaping their future? Despite his reservations about Butkowsky, Ben was still hoping for joint custody, and trying to impress upon the assessor how vital joint custody was for his children. However, he was growing increasingly alarmed by what he was hearing from the psychologist.

As Ben recalls, Butkowsky told him he believed joint custody was in the children's best interests, but he wished to refrain from classifying it as such in his report because he didn't want to convey to Terry the idea that she'd "lost" on that issue. If Terry felt she didn't have complete custody of the children, Butkowsky explained, then she would be socially embarrassed and psychologically upset. That upset would have such a dramatic effect on her that she wouldn't be able to cope and, as a result, would be unable to properly parent the kids. Consequently, the children would lose the benefit of her mothering. And that would not be in their best interests. Terry had to have peace of mind so that she'd be better equipped to be a good parent and get on with her life.

Ben reviewed this logic. Joint custody was best for the kids. But joint custody wasn't best for Terry. Terry had to believe she was the most important parent. A recommendation of joint custody would be threatening to her self-image. Ben told the psychologist that if he thought joint custody was best for the kids then he should say so. His job was to make a custody recommendation to ensure the kids' security, not Terry's. Anything less was just coddling an insecure mother and catering to her hysterical personality. If he lent credence to the notion that Terry was the more important parent, he'd only give her more ammunition to sabotage his parenting and denigrate him to Deja and Zoe. They'd hired him to help resolve a conflict. They needed clarity, not ambiguity. But Butkowsky told him he knew best in these matters.

Deeply worried, Ben wrote the psychologist a letter.

August 3, 1990

Dear Doctor Butkowsky,

...With regard to the proposal sent in a letter to Mr. Zaldin and copied to you last July 17th, 1990 ... regrettably we have not received any response from either Terry or Mr. Zaldin. Terry has not altered her position since first stating it last May of 1989. She expects sole possession of the matrimonial home, sole custody and will allow me every other week-end and one night a week with the kids. I on the other hand have changed my thinking. Where I once felt joint custody the best solution, I see now that without any co-operation between the two parents, joint decision making is impossible.

By then, Ben had realized that joint custody could never work unless Terry cooperated. His "changed thinking" led him to suggest an indirect path to the joint custody arrangement Butkowsky had said was best for the kids. Because the system did not begin with a presumption of joint custody and provided no incentive for a mother to cooperate with a co-parenting arrangement – just the opposite, in fact – the only way he saw to ensure joint custody in practice was for him to have custody in theory. He didn't think he should have total control of the children any more than Terry; if he got custody, he would ensure that she remained just as involved with the girls as he was. But he doubted she'd do the same for him.

Ben went over their financial predicament and Terry's refusal to even acknowledge it, let alone help out. He, by contrast, was moving forward: he had rented "the ground floor of a fourplex in the same neighbourhood as our house ... Now that I have alternative living accommodations for me and the kids, Terry and our housekeeper can continue to live in the matrimonial home until it can be sold. Arrangements can be made for the house-keeper to work at both residences and care for the kids on a schedule relative to your recommendation."

Acknowledging that the whole situation was "not a pretty picture," Ben nevertheless expressed his confidence that Butkowsky's recommendations would help them all. Because he believed that "the sooner that this conflict can be resolved the better it will be for everyone," Ben vowed that it was his "intention to accept and support the advice and recommendations of your report and make the best of it." He added that he hoped Butkowsky would stay on to provide the "considerable guidance and mediation" they would need "in order to re-organize and conduct our lives."

To a certain extent, Ben was trying to score points with the assessor, to make him feel needed and important, particularly because, as the father, Ben was so far behind the eight ball in the process. But he truly hoped for the best, too. Despite his feelings about Butkowsky, Ben still hoped he'd make a decision, stick by it, and help them put a co-parenting plan into practice.

Returning to the custody issue, Ben explained that initially he never gave custody much thought because he never felt that he and Terry "differed much" on major decisions like schooling, religious training, and so forth, and he "naively thought that was all there was to it. 'Getting custody,' as it were, wasn't important to me. Now, however, I see it as being extremely important, a situation that will have a significant impact on all our lives for years to come."

Ben also put in writing the doubts that had been plaguing him about what the assessor had told him. What harm would be done, he wondered, to spare Terry "social embarrassment" and "psychological upset"? Might there not be more damage done if she had custody? Would she be "more or less likely to get psychological help," to "co-operate with regard to me and the children," to "cope with the pressure of home, office and personal life?" And what of the "social embarrassment" she had caused Ben? "Perhaps some 'social embarrassment' of her own might prompt her to begin taking responsibility for her own behavior and stop attributing all her actions to the deeds of others?" Ben added that he didn't make such comments "in a vicious way," and recognized how important it was for them all that Terry felt secure, but he simply wished to point out it was also important for them that Terry begin to "confront some personal issues and be a mature role model for our daughters."

> Personally I do feel much embarrassment. I'm ashamed for having my innocent children suffer because of my inability to resolve this marital situation. There are things I would have done differently and things I regret doing. To a certain extent I believe Terry and I through our actions have lost the "sole right" of parenting Deja and Zoe. Now we leave to others the discerning of our children's best interests ... hardly the epitome of responsible parenting.
>
> I want the custodial responsibility for my children because I believe that if so granted Deja and Zoe will be better off. I see custody as a privilege, not a right. I know that I will be co-operative and make every effort to have our lives (Terry's included) organized (but still flexible) enough to allow for the most loving and support-ive environment possible. I would expect this privilege to be moni-tored by a family mediator on a regular basis to ensure that the terms and spirit of our separation and parenting arrangements are met.
>
> And finally, I hope that [the] time will come when there is enough trust and co-operation between Terry and I so that, as I had originally hoped, a true joint custody can be achieved...
>
> Sincerely yours,
Ben Gordon

Butkowsky never responded to Ben's letter. Later that month, he released his recommendations and parenting plan (setting out a parenting schedule, transportation arrangements, and all the rules for holidays). The report con-firmed Ben's worst fears. The psychologist recommended a conventional weekend father schedule. The kids were to go to Ben's one night a week, on alternate weekends, and for some extra time at holidays. Terry's place would be the kids' "primary" residence; Ben's residence would be their "secondary" one. Ben was deeply offended by those terms. He had hoped for alternating weeks, and he worried he'd now become Uncle Dad. But his gravest reser-vations lay in what the report had failed to recommend.

Butkowsky had written that both parents were "mutually obligated to solicit each other's input and opinions in relation to major decisions affecting the lives of the children." To "facilitate communication and joint decision-making" Ben and Terry were also to meet monthly for a year with a mediator/arbitrator. Mutual consultation and joint decision-making concerning major decisions about and for a child are the hallmarks of a joint custody arrangement. But nowhere did Butkowsky actually use that term. Ben was convinced that the omission of those two crucial words would pave the way for more conflict.

Ben met with Butkowsky. He recalls them talking about his letter briefly and Butkowsky telling him he understood what Ben was saying but this was what he thought was best.

As Ben remembers it, the psychologist admitted he'd been cagey about the recommendations and, as he'd intimated he would, had purposely left Terry with the impression that she hadn't "lost" custody. Ben reminded him that a joint custody recommendation didn't mean Terry would be losing custody. It meant she'd be obliged to share custody with the other parent. He said Butkowsky could view a joint custody recommendation as a loss for Terry only if he operated on the same assumptions as Terry did: that the kids belonged to her, that mothers should have custody and fathers should become visitors in their children's lives.

Ben was especially disturbed that Butkowsky had recommended that the kids live primarily with Terry when he seemed to consider Ben the more stable parent. Ben recalled Butkowsky explaining that if Terry thought she'd lost custody, she'd have a mental breakdown, and what good would she be to the kids then? Ben remarked that this must be the first time in history that a father couldn't get equal time with his kids because their mother might be "socially embarrassed" or "psychologically upset" by the fact that their father was just as capable and important a parent. But Butkowsky told him it wasn't unusual to make recommendations based on the kind of logic he'd used.

For Ben, this was another defining moment of the process. The assessment, it seemed, wasn't about finding the truth. It wasn't about investigating what was going on in the family to determine the best alternative for the children. It was about making an expedient decision to serve the system and to reinforce its biases.

Now Ben understood how it worked. If you showed that you were a good father, that you were capable of handling the kids, the assessor didn't have to worry about you. You'd always put your kids first and you'd always suffer in silence. The thrust of the process was, "How do we get the mother to mother the children? What does she require to do that? What are her needs financially, emotionally, and psychologically?" If she is a troublesome, emotionally unstable mother, then we have to do whatever it takes to make her feel secure. A weak or problematic father shouldn't be around. But if we have a strong father who wants to be involved, that's great, because then it'll be easier for her. We can use him to help her. We'll toss him a crumb. We'll give him every other weekend and one night a week. And a good father will take it, make the sacrifices, go to the moon and back to have a visit with his kids.

Ben warned the psychologist that his recommendations were a terrible mistake that would have devastating consequences. Butkowsky asked Ben to trust his judgment and try the plan for a year, then he'd review the recommendations. If Ben gave the arrangement an all-out effort for a year, and it still wasn't working, then Butkowsky would know that either Terry wasn't cooperating or he'd made a bad decision. That was the only way he could be proved wrong.

Ben agonized. He believed the schedule would be disruptive for the kids and ached at the prospect of suddenly becoming a shadowy presence in his children's lives. He wondered how he would ever manage to counter Terry's influence if he saw his daughters only eight days a month. In almost every way, Ben's instincts told him Irwin Butkowsky's recommendations would do his children far more harm than good. And he bristled at being the parent expected to make all the sacrifices.

If he and Terry supported the assessment, they'd avert a full-scale custody battle. And Ben had no doubts that a custody battle would be devastating for the kids. Even though Butkowsky had recommended that the kids live primarily with Terry, he and Terry were obliged to consult about the kids and make all major parenting decisions together. Butkowsky had assured him that, in every sense except the amount of time he'd have with the children, theirs was a joint custody arrangement.

Whatever their fate, it had to be better than prolonged hostilities. On that factor alone his decision turned. He'd try his best for a year, if Butkowsky supervised their arrangement. Despite his feelings about the assessor, he was already familiar with their case, and Ben reasoned that it made more sense to stick with him than to start all over with someone new. He consented to the recommendations, on condition that Butkowsky would act as the mediator/arbitrator he had recommended to resolve disputes at monthly meetings. The psychologist agreed.

Beaman then wrote to Zaldin. The first part of her letter dealt with discussions she'd had with Zaldin about dividing household possessions and listing the house; in particular, what agent should list the property. "The sooner we have the house listed, the sooner our clients are going to be able to get on with their lives." Then she took up the custodial arrangements. "My client wants to be very clear about the fact that he is prepared to honour the spirit of the recommendations of Dr. Butkowsky ... More than anything else, he wants the children's lives to be normalized, so that they can begin to enjoy the time spent with both of their parents."

The assessment process had gone well for Terry. Butkowsky's parenting plan was a cookie-cutter weekend father arrangement. And, decades after feminists demanded that fathers play an equal role, she wouldn't have to cope with the "social embarrassment" a reputable family court assessor believed a mother would suffer if a father did in fact assume that equal role. She'd be entitled to more child support because she'd have the kids more often. If she agreed to Butkowsky's report, the only concessions Terry would have to make were to let the kids see Ben occasionally and to consult with him about major decisions. All that was needed was Terry's agreement to support the recommendations and sell the house. Then Ben would move out.

On September 6, Zaldin wrote to Beaman. His letter made no mention of Butkowsky's report. As for the house, Terry dismissed Ben's suggested listing agent and named one she preferred. His letter also confirmed Beaman's promise of the previous day that Ben would not remove any items from the house until they had an agreement or court order, "on the understanding," she'd written, "that when the time comes for discussion about the division of these items, your client will act in good faith."

Zaldin also wrote: "Without prejudice, my client is willing to list the property at this time, in principle, but is naturally anxious as to how the property will be maintained and family (she and the children) are supported in the interim." Zaldin wanted a recent pay stub from Ben and his proposal for interim support until they sold the house.

Zaldin was playing equivocation games again. His letter conveyed the impression that Terry intended to put the house on the market – after Ben made one more concession. Zaldin's letter, which was couched in qualifying phrases like "without prejudice" and "in principle," in no way obliged Terry to list the property – even if Ben complied with her latest demands. She might list the house, and then again she might not, but first Ben had to confirm what he'd pay to continue carrying a property he couldn't afford and supporting her and the children in it until it sold – whenever that might be.

Ben refused to hand over one more piece of paper or make one more concession until Zaldin and Terry started negotiating in good faith. How much documentation did Zaldin need? At the four-way meeting in January, Zaldin had requested – and shortly afterwards Ken Cole had supplied – Ben's 1988 corporate tax returns for Ben Gordon Enterprises Inc., his personal income tax returns for the past three years, and the financial statements of Ben Gordon Agencies Ltd. for three previous years. He'd also requested – and Ben said he'd provided – information about whether he was a shareholder of Jules Gordon Agencies Ltd., a copy of his most recent résumé used for auditions, details of the RRSP and credits to the ACTRA Benevolent Fund, documentary evidence corroborating the present value of his RRSP, copies of his bank statements from each active bank account over the last year and any passbooks that might cover the same period, and copies of his credit card statements for the same period. At the same time, Cole had requested Terry's recent RRSP statements, details of her Canada Savings Bonds and other security holdings and corroboratory information, statements or passbooks from Terry's bank accounts for the past two years, credit card statements for the past two years, a letter from her employer confirming her salary and other employment benefits, and a copy of her personal chequebook record over the past year. Terry had produced none of it. Zaldin had not even provided her sworn financial statement yet, nor confirmation of what she was earning.

Ben recognized Zaldin's tricks by now. He was stalling, trying to secure his client more support while keeping her in the house. Zaldin would play this game as long as there was money in it. Terry had found herself the perfect lawyer in Ronald Zaldin, Ben fumed. They grabbed whatever they could and then said, Okay, that's ours, now what else have you got? For over a year Ben had taken the high road to avoid a fight. He'd sought lawyers known for their ability to negotiate and settle. Both Cole and Beaman had stellar reputations, both had behaved like ethical professionals, both had struck him as decent human beings. And neither one had been able to do a thing for him in the face of a lawyer like Ronald Zaldin.

Ben called Peter Israel, a litigation lawyer who knew the family, for yet another referral. He clearly required a different kind of lawyer, one with enough experience, toughness, and credibility to end this nonsense once and for all. Israel recommended Moishe Reiter, a Queen's Counsel who had thirty years' experience practising family law and was certified as a civil litigation specialist by the Law Society of Upper Canada. Ben recalls Israel explaining that Zaldin was known in legal circles as a "gutter fighter," and he characterized Reiter as a tough, scrappy lawyer whom Zaldin would not be able to push around.

In September 1990, Ben met with Reiter. According to Ben, the lawyer expressed shock that Ben had already racked up $6,000 in legal fees for so little result. He explained that the issues in his case were all simple, clear-cut family law matters, and that he was familiar with Zaldin's modus operandi. He advised staying with Beaman for the time being, however, and using him only if a problem arose. If necessary, a stern letter from him would demonstrate to Zaldin that Ben wasn't fooling around.

Ben had an instant and visceral reaction of distaste towards Reiter. He struck him as pompous and belligerent. He took phone calls from other clients throughout their meeting. But Ben felt as if he'd fallen down a rabbit hole into a looking-glass world where nothing was as it seemed, a nether world ruled by predatory creatures. Liking Reiter personally wasn't important. Under the circumstances, maybe disliking the man was a good sign. Given the world in which he was travelling, Reiter seemed exactly the sort he needed to protect himself from Ronald Zaldin.

For it was Zaldin Ben was after, not Terry. Ben reasoned that either Ken Cole and Judith Beaman had been naive in their dealings with Zaldin, which seemed unlikely given their reputations, or they hadn't wanted to dirty their hands dealing with him. So they'd written him courteous letters and the months had passed. Ben needed a lawyer to put an end to Zaldin's tactics and bring him and Terry to the table. Not on bended knee – just to the table. To talk, deal fairly with the issues, and settle. According to Peter Israel – and the Law Society of Upper Canada – Moishe Reiter had all the right credentials.

■ ■ ■

Three weeks had passed since Beaman had written to Zaldin confirming Ben's agreement to Butkowsky's recommendations. Still no word from Terry. Ben wouldn't move out of the house until she agreed. "Mr. Gordon needs the reassurance of knowing that his wife will join him in honouring the spirit and substance of Dr. Butkowsky's plan for the children," Beaman wrote Zaldin. "The sooner the girls can get involved in their new routine, the better it is for all concerned."

On September 27, Beaman finally received the letter Ben had been waiting for: "I have just spoken with Terry Gordon," wrote Zaldin, "and she has requested me to advise you that she accepts the recommendations of Dr. Butkowsky concerning the children provided that Mr. Gordon leave the home promptly, ie within 5 days." Beaman advised Ben that she'd spoken with Zaldin and they had a deal to sell the home. Only the logistics remained to be worked out. They could deal with those details after he moved.

As thrilled as he was to finally have Terry's agreement on custody, Ben resented the threat of Zaldin's arbitrary deadline, especially after all he'd endured. Was he saying Terry's agreement to support the recommendations hinged on his moving in five days – otherwise all bets were off? That his children would continue to live in jeopardy unless he heeded this eviction notice? Ben knew Zaldin was just throwing his weight around, showing who was boss. How offended he was by this small man, and how disinclined to be bullied yet again. But on October 9 – his thirty-ninth birthday – believing that custody was finally settled and that Terry had agreed to sell their home, Ben finally felt secure enough to move into the apartment on Relmar Road.

Two friends, one with a company truck, helped him transport some furniture, mostly odds and ends Terry didn't want, like his pine blanket box from college days. (According to Ben, Terry had told him he wasn't to remove anything else from the house; of the kids' belongings, she had allowed him only some underwear and like items for which she had no use.) He left most of his wardrobe and personal belongings behind, figuring he'd collect them later. On his way out the door, he grabbed two prized baseballs he'd caught at Blue Jays games.

The apartment was small but ideal. Not only was it on a quiet dead-end street adjacent to a park and ravine, with lots of shops around the corner, but it was three blocks from Deja's piano teacher and Zoe's ballet school, four blocks from Zoe's morning school, and well within the boundaries for the school bus. There were plenty of kids on the street, and both the girls had old friends within walking distance. It was also close to both Ben's parents' apartments. Now that he was officially a single parent without any backup, he knew he'd need his parents' help, particularly when he had to go out of town on business for a few days, three or four times a year. On those occasions the kids could visit Pops, Bubby Nettie, and Bubba Zel.

With two bedrooms, a galley kitchen, and a tiny bathroom, the apartment was a far cry from the spacious residence with all the amenities he'd left behind, but he couldn't have cared less. He was relieved to finally have a home for the kids away from Terry, and anyway it was a temporary arrangement. The house would soon go on the market. Life was beginning anew.

A few days later, having made arrangements with Terry beforehand, he returned to the house around 5:00 to collect the girls for the weekend. When he called from the car, Mathewrina, the new housekeeper (whom Terry had hired to replace Mavis), told him the kids weren't packed yet. According to Ben, he went inside only because Terry's car wasn't in the driveway and the kids weren't ready. Deja and Zoe waited by the car while he went upstairs to pack a suitcase with a few of his belongings and items the girls would need for the weekend. On his way downstairs, in the front hall, he encountered Terry, who had apparently arrived home while he was upstairs. Ben said she confronted him about the contents of the suitcase and pulled at his raincoat pocket to see what was in it as he went out the door. After he was gone, Terry changed the locks.

Terry later told police that she and the girls were waiting for Ben to collect the kids for a weekend "visit" when he started walking through the house, putting things in suitcases. When she asked him what he was taking, he'd refused to say. They became involved in a "verbal dispute" which she'd "tried to keep...low keyed in front of the children," but when she insisted that he tell her, he struck her with the suitcases. But at the time Ben had no inkling that Terry had viewed their momentary exchange that day as any more significant than any other. Then he received a summons advising him that, for the third time, Terry had charged him with assault.

■ ■ ■

Two and a half weeks after Ben moved, there still hadn't been any progress on listing the house. He'd expected it would go on the market immediately. Then Beaman heard from Zaldin. Terry was still "considering" agents. Terry was "wondering" about child support. "Before she can make her final decision on listing the house," she needed Ben's proposal for child support, another sheaf of documentation, and an exchange of "freshly sworn updated Financial Statements, reflecting the new status quo for each."

For Ben, this was the last straw. Zaldin was trying the same stalling tactics again, and they were getting nowhere. On October 27, Ben hired Moishe Reiter. Reiter asked for a $1,000 retainer and said it would probably take a couple of weeks to close the file. Then, to Ben's surprise, Reiter advised Ben to give Zaldin what he wanted. Here we go again, thought Ben. Every time another lawyer took over his case, he was advised to be a good boy, to fill out more forms, to cooperate. Ultimately, he was just another file to these people, an opportunity to docket billable hours and engage in another round of bracing competition. But he was sick and tired of their game. Ben told Reiter he wouldn't play this time. First Zaldin and Terry had to demonstrate some cooperation and good faith by listing the house.

■ ■ ■

Shortly before Christmas, Ben sat in his car in the driveway of the home he'd recently vacated, waiting to pick up the kids. Deja and Zoe came bounding down the front steps, chattering and trailing their paraphernalia. "There's something for you from Mommy in my knapsack," announced Zoe. Ben glanced towards the house. Terry was standing on the porch, her arms folded. The kids grew silent. "Consider yourself served," Terry shouted.

The document Ben recovered from Zoe's knapsack was a notice of application dated December 18, 1990, and filed in the Ontario Court of

Justice (General Division) by the Applicant, Terry Risa Nusyna Gordon. It was sent by her solicitor, Ronald V. Zaldin, who'd left the firm he'd been with to establish his own firm, Zaldin & Zaldin, in partnership with his brother. The front page of the document bore a large seal in the upper left-hand corner.

Court File No. CL1589/90

BETWEEN:

TERRY RISA NUSYNA GORDON

Applicant (Wife)

-and-

BENJAMIN GORDON

Respondent (Husband)

APPLICATION UNDER: The Children's Law Reform Act, R.S.O. 1980, Chapter 68, as amended and The Family Law Act, S.O., 1986, Chapter 4, as amended.

<u>NOTICE OF APPLICATION</u>
TO THE RESPONDENT: BENJAMIN GORDON

A LEGAL PROCEEDING HAS BEEN COMMENCED by the Applicant...
IF YOU FAIL TO APPEAR AT THE HEARING, JUDGMENT MAY BE GIVEN IN YOUR ABSENCE AND WITHOUT NOTICE TO YOU ...

The document, which was not a divorce petition but an application to the court for specific "relief," was accompanied by an eight-page affidavit. The application contained twenty claims in total. In the main, Terry was seeking sole custody of the children with "access" for Ben, $2,000 a month in child support ($1,000 per child on both an interim and permanent basis), and the right to possess the matrimonial home and its contents exclusively until trial, and "post-trial for five (5) years in the best interest of the children." Under the heading "The Grounds for the Application," Zaldin had set forth seven that conveyed the overall impression that his client – the wife –

was desperate for funds and that her husband was an abusive mate and deadbeat dad with lots of money who, since abandoning his family, was refusing to cooperate with the court process and divulge the truth about his finances.

The parties, the document read, had separated around March 31, 1989, but the respondent had left the home "on or about October 8, 1990, after a lengthy and detailed Assessment by Dr. Irwin Butkowsky." The children had "resided with the Applicant since the . . . separation." She was "in need of child support and the Respondent can well afford to contribute to the children's expenses but [since leaving] has refused to render any financial assistance for children's expenses or the home": he had "stopped paying for everything, including the taxes, utilities, Mortgage and other carrying charges of the home and other expenses." Moreover, he had defaulted on his "promise through his third solicitors to forward a fresh Financial Statement reflecting his financial state of affairs."

The document also stated that the wife wanted "exclusive possession of the matrimonial home and contents" because the husband had returned and removed items "contrary to his undertaking and agreement through counsel not to do so." This was presumably a reference to the incident shortly after he'd moved out when he had taken some of his belongings and an overnight bag for the children and Terry had charged him with assault. Although all of Terry's criminal charges against Ben were still only allegations, Zaldin told the court his client wanted exclusive possession in order "to prevent a further assault by the husband of the wife, three so far."

CHAPTERFIVE

THE GAME OF LAW

December 1990–October 1991

Ben spent that December of 1990 careering between rage, fear, and despair. Being with the kids for the holiday week was all that distracted him from worry. Zaldin had advised Beaman that Terry supported Butkowsky's recommendations, and Beaman had assured Ben that the home would be sold. But as soon as Ben was out of the house, Terry had sued for sole custody, and Zaldin now disputed that Terry had ever agreed to sell. He vehemently maintained that their discussions of agents had always been within the context of "without prejudice" settlement negotiations, and Terry's willingness to sell had always depended on how much child support she'd get. Either Beaman had misunderstood Zaldin, or he'd tricked her. Either way, it hardly mattered.

Ben had no doubt that it had all been a set-up to evict him from the house, Zaldin's calculated strategy to give Terry the advantage in her battle for sole control of the children and exclusive possession of the home. The tipoffs were the phrase "new status quo for each" in Zaldin's last letter, the distortions in Terry's court application, and the slanderous accusations masquerading as fact in her accompanying affidavit.

Because of the court's practice of not upsetting the arrangements that were already in place for children, Ben was convinced Zaldin was trying to imply that he'd left the matrimonial home, that Terry was now the custodial parent caring for the girls, and that therefore a "new status quo" existed. He recalled Zaldin having tried this tactic in the spring, when he'd taken the kids to spend the night at his dad's after Terry had started in on him in front of them. Then, Beaman had had to write to Zaldin that "one sleep-over does not a new status quo make."

Having tricked him into leaving the home, Ben believed, Zaldin was now trying to strengthen his client's claims by insinuating to the court that Terry was a battered woman. He imagined Zaldin having advised Terry to agree to Butkowsky's recommendations for now; once Ben was out of the house they could always go after custody from another angle. Ben felt like a fool for having trusted either of them, even for a moment.

He bristled at Butkowsky's role in the fiasco, too. The assessor had left a hole in his report a lawyer could drive a tractor-trailer through. Because Terry had agreed on the record to support Butkowsky's recommendations, she had to be seen by the court to be honouring that agreement. By refusing to be clear on custody, however, Butkowsky had left the issue open for interpretation. Without the words "joint custody" on paper, Zaldin could use the primary residence/secondary residence designations in the report to claim that Terry read the recommendations to mean she already had sole custody – and Ben had only access rights. And that's exactly what he did. In her affidavit, Terry said she accepted the psychologist's recommendations "in principle" and was "therefore requesting interim custody of the children [meaning until the matter was finally resolved at trial], subject to the access as set out by Dr. Butkowsky."

■ ■ ■

Ben faced another impossible choice. Now that Terry had sued him for sole custody, he could walk away from the fight or ask the court to let him continue parenting his children. If he walked away, he also walked away from fathering them, at least in any sense in which he understood that concept, and that he couldn't do. Nor could he comprehend why anyone expected him to.

If Terry had sole custody, she'd have no legal obligation to involve him in decisions about the children's daily lives, and although she would be obliged to provide him "access" and let him know about decisions regarding their health, education, and welfare, he'd have to rely on her good will to see the girls and get information about them. He had no reason to trust her good will, and many reasons not to. Most terrifying was the prospect of losing any influence over the people his children would become. Only a court order with the words "joint custody" in it, he believed, would protect his right to parent Deja and Zoe, and their right to be parented by him. He had to hope that a judge would impress upon Terry that the kids were entitled to a relationship with both of them. A judge would see that all he wanted was to remain a parent.

Even if he could prove he'd been an exemplary parent who defied stereotypical notions about fatherhood, Ben knew he would be facing an uphill struggle to remain more than a casual visitor in his children's lives. Had he been seeking sole custody, as Terry was, he'd have had almost no chance. He'd have had to convince the court that he'd been the primary parent during the marriage, or that awarding him custody was in the children's best interests – the latter a virtually impossible task given the court's extreme reluctance to take custody from a mother, and many assessors' reluctance to risk making an unconventional recommendation.

His remaining options were limited. According to Reiter, his best chance was to seek a court order that incorporated Butkowsky's report and spelled out its joint-custodial intent. Only then would Terry be legally bound to follow recommendations she'd already agreed to support. The irony of this predicament was not lost on Ben. He'd now have to beg the court to let him keep a custodial arrangement he'd always considered to be harmful to his children.

■ ■ ■

The first year of my courtship with Ben played out against the backdrop of Ben's divorce litigation and the consequent upheaval in our lives. There were many reasons for me to flee this relationship rather than try to invest in its future. But I saw goodness in Ben, and gentleness, and something that was decent and honourable and brave, and despite the nightmare of his circumstances, I decided to fall in love with him.

I'd heard some motherly advice after my marriage broke up that I always remembered: "Marry the kindest man you meet." Ben was certainly that. He was a man of many talents, but in some ways his greatest was the ability to nurture others. Some men are driven by career ambition, but he went brilliantly about the business of taking care of others by anticipating their needs, then quietly attending to them. Subtly, without fanfare, he'd freshen a drink here, orchestrate the best restaurant table there, drop off a humidifier filter he'd noticed I needed, turn up with groceries or a magazine he thought I'd like to read.

There was a gallantry about him, too, that I appreciated. Not just with women, although he knew how to treat women and adored flirting with them. I had discerned early on that this was a man who truly liked the opposite sex. He was a natural-born kibitzer, friendly, courteous, and charming to everyone he met, one of those people who had a magic way with kids, dogs, and grandmothers.

And he was funny, of course. By far the funniest person I'd ever met. Not in that in-your-face showbiz way, but rather in a cerebral, take-no-prisoners way that razored through pretence and cut straight to the truth. Leaving a room he'd mutter some barely audible throwaway line and reduce me to convulsive fits of laughter. Or he'd do an impersonation of someone we knew that was so true to the original, he'd make me swear never to ask him to do it in front of the person. He was possessed, too, of a bratty irreverence for authority to which I immediately warmed.

He had a dark side, as all comics do, and sometimes his depressions frightened me. He also had a temper. I saw it flare only when provoked by someone who'd abused his good nature and taken him terribly for granted, or when the helpless frustration of his situation became too much for him to bear. Still, he was an extraordinarily patient man, and it took a great deal to burst the dam of his self-control. He was also remarkably forgiving and never stayed mad long. When I first met him, he was also predisposed to fits of moroseness, which I hated. I could deal with his vulnerability, and I could deal with his rage, but much as I empathized, I could not stand to see him behave like a victim.

I met the girls for the first time at his apartment about a month after we'd begun going out, in January 1991. I dropped over one evening as he was helping them get bathed and ready for bed. Hesitant to barge in on the intimacy of a family ritual, I called a tentative hello from the living room. Suddenly a slim, pretty girl in an oversized T-shirt came flying down the hall towards me, skidding to a halt at my feet. "Hi," I said, "you must be Deja." She stared at me unabashedly for a few moments, gave me a head-to-toe once-over, then turned on her heel and, without speaking a word, raced back in the other direction to whisper news of my arrival to her younger sister. This I took to be an auspicious beginning.

I'd had fears about how Deja and Zoe would react to this stranger who'd come so soon into their father's life. For the first several months, whenever I turned up at Ben's, I half expected them to slam the door in my face. But, almost miraculously, it seemed to me, the girls welcomed me with generosity and affection. Ben wasn't surprised by their open-hearted reception. He said they'd always lived in the eye of a storm, they'd never seen their father happy with a woman, and they, like him, craved to be embraced by a loving family.

And so they did. Sometimes, when Ella and Louis were playing on the stereo, Ben would come out of the kitchen and take my hand and dance with me in the living room, and Deja would dash for the camera, and Zoe would yell "Kiss! Kiss!" and Ben and I would put our lips together and stage a lingering kiss for the lens and the girls would beam with delight and suddenly the flash would pop, illuminating our happiness.

Then seven and five, they were bright, gregarious children, both tall, slender, and lovely. Deja was the athlete, Zoe the actress. They'd crawl into Ben's bed to cuddle early in the morning and late at night. He'd go on their field trips, take them to appointments, host noisy sleepovers on his living room floor.

Weekends, after piano and ballet, he made their favourite lunches, then strolled the village with a daughter on each arm. Often I'd open his apartment door to find Ben and his long-limbed little girls sprawled in a tangled heap on the ratty old couch. Or I'd find their drawings lying around: childish renditions of grinning faces signed, "I love you, Daddy-O."

Sometimes on the mornings I'd stayed over, Deja would tiptoe into Ben's bedroom, flash a wicked smile, and ask whether there'd been any "sexing" the night before. Soon both kids began to ask when we were getting married – a curiosity, I realized, fuelled mainly by their fantasy of attending in fancy flower-girl dresses at their father's wedding.

Sara too, now ten and a half, swiftly won a place in their affections. For Deja, Sara offered welcome respite from the tyranny of playing with a little sister who was temperamentally her opposite. For Zoe, Sara was a partner for cards or Monopoly or dress-up. But Sara was an only child, happy to play on her own, and for her, the sudden arrival of two noisy step-siblings was fraught with tangled feelings. The first time Ben met her, he arrived with a tiny bouquet. "I brought your mother flowers so I thought you should have some, too," he said, bending to proffer them at the kitchen table where she sat, eyeing him suspiciously. But Sara was not as easily seduced as I. She took her time falling in love. Later, after she too had fallen, she told us how she'd loathed this interloping stranger with whom she'd suddenly had to share her mom. But she wisely admitted that she probably would have resented anyone.

Throughout the winter and spring of 1991, with Butkowsky's schedule in place, Ben tried to adjust to the role of Uncle Dad. The schedule proved to be chaotic. Besides alternate weekends, Ben had the kids on Thursday nights one week and Mondays the next. Because the day changed from week to week, the girls were forever getting confused about what night they were supposed to be with him.

The school bus stopped at Terry's door, and she had Mathewrina to receive them when she wasn't home. To minimize conflicts at exchange time, Butkowsky had recommended that Ben pick up the kids at school. On those afternoons he left work at 3:00 to collect them. On teachers' professional development days that fell on "his" time, he took them to work or stayed home.

That first year the girls seemed to miss him dreadfully. They called him constantly – in his car, at the office, at his apartment. Sometimes they called because they wanted him to sponsor their readathon, or drop off a notebook or pair of skates they'd forgotten at the apartment. But often they called just to connect. On the days they expected him to come for them, they usually called from the school office complaining of stomachaches and begging to be collected early. Most nights one child or the other awoke and crawled into bed beside him.

To further complicate matters, they often arrived at Ben's agitated and ill-mannered, and it took a couple of days to calm them down. With only a night here and there to be with them, there was little opportunity to establish any comforting routine in the household before it was time for them to leave. Ben spent what few hours he had with Deja and Zoe simply trying to settle them. Parenting was almost impossible.

But Ben had promised he'd do his best to make the new arrangements work, and his first priority had been setting up the kids' room. His apartment was furnished in a donated odds-and-ends style I've come to think of as Early Ex-Husband: his mother's patio set doubling as a dining table, his friend Michael's old TV, a bed and coffee table Judy had brought up from her basement locker. But the kids' room was another matter: he bought bunk beds with white cotton eyelet duvets and a matching melamine desk and dresser, stocked their closet with fleece sweatshirts, leggings, nylon jackets, and rubber boots, and hung bright posters on the walls. And unlike some divorced dads I'd seen at McDonald's on their "access" nights, Ben cooked meals at home, often inviting guests for Friday-night dinners or Sunday brunch. Weekends, he encouraged the girls to have their friends play and stay over.

Orchestrating a family life was a challenge. Because Sara followed a different schedule, planning a simple outing when the five of us were *en famille* required strategic manoeuvres worthy of General Patton. One weekend when the whole crew was together I suggested the girls put on a fashion show at my place. After much trying on of garments, Deja strutted down the staircase in a sporty ensemble, her bra stuffed to create a huge bust. (Deja could never resist a joke, especially a sight gag. In that respect she was her father's daughter.) Zoe emerged a vision in bracelets and taffeta, a mini Ivana Trump. Sara, meanwhile, did a vamp schtick.

On the way over with the camera, Ben slipped on some ice, slid headlong into a tree, and arrived with a nasty purple bruise on his forehead. "Hey, you look just like that Russian guy," joked Deja, by which she meant Gorbachev, and we all laughed at the aptness of her observation. I remember catching Ben's eye over the merriment and exchanging a smile, and thinking that maybe one day we'd actually manage to balance the delicate ecosystem called a blended family.

Still, I saw many problems with the kids. Although outgoing and fun, they were also needy, demanding children, possessed of a sense of entitlement I found troubling. They struck me as children to whom much had been offered but of whom little had been asked. I'd grown up in a family where children were respected and adored but not allowed to become the obsessive focus of adult attention every moment. My parents solicited their children's opinions, and when my sisters or I disagreed with their decisions, there was always room for dialogue or debate. But it was freedom within limits, and there was never any question about who was in charge.

And so I found it exasperating to watch Ben offer Deja and Zoe endless choices on every subject, from what meal each preferred for dinner tonight to what drink and sandwich each wanted in her lunchbox tomorrow. Watching these exchanges from the sidelines, I had to suppress the urge to holler "Stop!" particularly when, in spite of the awful stress he was under, he'd drop whatever he was doing to cater to their every whim. Worse, they tended to demand rather than ask, expect rather than appreciate. If denied, Deja could become obstinate and mouthy, while Zoe was prone to hysterical tantrums. They seemed never to have been taught to say please and thank you. They bobbed along the surface of life, taking what they could from anyone who would give it to them, without any sense that they might have to give of themselves in return.

As for Ben, he seemed constitutionally incapable of demanding anything from them, or telling them no. The first time I saw them kick open the door, dump their stuff in the living room, plunk themselves down on the couch, switch on the TV, and yell, "What's for dinner?" – while Ben struggled with the parcels, unloaded the groceries, set the table, and made the meal – my mouth fell open. Not at them, for I believe children are the product of their environment and Deja and Zoe were obviously clever children who'd long ago learned how to manipulate Ben's soft centre and abuse his good nature. That they behaved as most kids would have under the circumstances didn't surprise me. What did was Ben's willingness to allow it.

I recognized in Ben's laissez-faire parenting style the legacy of his upbringing, and a misguided reluctance I'd seen in many boomer parents to set boundaries for their children, lest they stifled independence of mind. I also recognized a parent tortured with guilt about his children's suffering and trying somehow to make it up to them. But most of all I recognized the fear of a father suddenly and inexplicably cast adrift from his children's lives and terrified of losing them altogether. If he said no to them, if he denied them a Freezee or punished them for misbehaving, then they might not like him. And if they did not like him they might tell Terry. And then Terry would denounce him to them and he'd read all about his crimes in an affidavit.

I empathized with Ben's fears, for I was by then beginning to recognize how well founded they were. Still, I disagreed with his response to them. He thought he was Superdad. I thought he was Superdoormat. Where he saw two needy kids begging for indulgence, I saw two needy kids screaming for boundaries, and I thought he was doing Deja and Zoe a disservice by failing to provide them. My motives, however, were equally selfish. Ben came as a package deal. I had no desire to spend my time in the company of two spoiled, poorly behaved kids. Nor was I willing to drag Sara along for that ride.

I was uncertain about the role I should play. I saw two children who seemed desperately in need of parenting, but I wasn't their parent. How would they react if I set limits and made demands that neither of their parents had apparently ever imposed? How would Ben respond if I disciplined his children? What would happen when word of my involvement got back to Terry? And how would Sara cope with the turbulence inevitably in store until we established new ground rules?

I realized that a great deal depended on Ben. Unless we worked as a team and he allowed me the authority to parent along with him, nothing would change. If he was willing to share that authority, I was willing to help him give it a shot. I was hopeful that with a little luck we might have a chance to turn the kids around. What we needed most, though, was a swift resolution in court. Otherwise, how would we ever have the chance of establishing normalcy or calm?

Little by little, Ben began to demand more of Deja and Zoe than he ever had before. He insisted they tidy their room and pitch in around the apartment. (The housekeeper had always picked up after them, he said, and at Terry's she probably still did.) He tried to get them to bed at a decent hour, although they always asked him, and he always obliged, to lie on the bunk with one or the other until they fell asleep. They seemed to crave nearness to his still centre; he longed to make them safe and he savoured every minute in their company. Now and then he'd lapse into his former ways, and, with that sixth sense children have, Deja and Zoe would play him like pros. But he tried to change, and it was seeing him make an honest effort, and the kids gradually responding, that made me willing to hang in.

At first, Deja and Zoe mocked my relentless nagging about their manners, and sometimes I became infuriated when Ben sent me up as a finger-wagging schoolmarm in their presence. (When Ben behaved like Bart Simpson the brat child he was either endearing or maddening, depending on my mood and his timing.) But soon remembering to say please and thank you became a game. The kids knew they'd please me if they remembered, and it was clear they wished to earn my approval. It was a small victory, but it gave me hope.

■ ■ ■

It did not take long before I began to have some serious questions about Terry. Notwithstanding Ben's reluctance to say no to his kids, he was, by anyone's measure, an extraordinary father. Actually, he was a better mother than most I knew. Certainly he had far more interest than did I in the myriad chores of parenthood, and far more time and patience for childish pursuits like games of Sorry! and Fish. He was the flesh-and-blood New Man women like me had gone to the barricades for in the sixties, that often heralded man's man with a "strong feminine side," a hands-on dad who didn't just show up for the fun stuff. Most of the unattached women I knew would have killed for a guy like him.

Nevertheless Terry seemed to be doing almost everything in her power to frustrate his attempts to parent, make him out to be a bad guy, and alienate him from his children. Whatever Ben did to accommodate Terry – and that first year under Butkowsky's regime I watched him turn himself inside out to accommodate her – she found fault with his every effort. If the kids brought home a notice about a school Open House or some such event, she'd cut him out of the loop. If he asked to rearrange their schedule because he had a business trip or studio taping he couldn't switch, she'd tell the girls that their father didn't want to be with them even in the little time he had. (She'd say the same when he took the kids for a sleepover at his parents' places; Butkowsky's schedule, limiting as it was, had severely curtailed the children's opportunity to see their paternal grandparents as well.)

Although Ben had told me about such incidents and said they happened regularly, I will never forget the first time I witnessed a typical exchange via the speakerphone. To my horror, Deja and Zoe were on the other end begging him to pay for some program or other, wailing, "Daddy, please pay! Please pay!" while Terry shouted in the background, "There won't be any camp this summer if your father doesn't pay" and "Your father doesn't give a damn about you," which made them even more hysterical. I heard Ben's voice grow quieter until it was frighteningly muted. He told them they didn't have to worry about such things, that who paid for their activities was an adult concern, that he and Mommy would work it out. Then he put down the phone and the stench of Terry's assault hung between us in the air for the rest of that evening.

I knew of mothers who ached for their children's fathers to be more involved. I knew of mothers who covered for fathers who disappointed their kids, to spare them more hurt. I knew of mothers who detested their ex-husbands but bit their tongues in front of their children. I did not, however, have any experience with a woman like Terry. What kind of mother, I wondered, would want her children to think their father did not love them?

Ben just wanted to be a father, and I saw in him one that any devoted, loving mother would wish for her children. Terry, however, seemed to regard him as a villain trying to seize her house and her children, and herself as a mother bear defending her cubs from a predator. Ben had told me that Terry had often accused him of making her waste money on lawyers when he ought to just take an apartment, leave her and the kids in the house, hand over custody, and send a cheque each month. That's what Brian had done for her sister, Lynne, and that's what divorced fathers were supposed to do. Why did he have to make so much trouble? If he'd only behave like a gentleman, she'd let the kids visit him now and then.

Despite the many times I asked Ben to explain to me what Terry wanted, assuming that she had legitimate concerns I simply wasn't comprehending, it wasn't until I read the affidavit accompanying her court application that I realized what Ben had been trying to explain: Terry saw him as the aggressor in their conflict because he wished to continue to share in the parenting of their children. She'd sworn in that affidavit that after they engaged lawyers, Ben decided to "fight me for custody of our two little girls," and that during Butkowsky's investigations, he "waged a campaign of terror to undermine my will to fight him for custody ... and to force me to sell the house or move out and leave him there alone with the kids." In Terry's eyes, I now understood, Ben was the obstructive one because he wouldn't accept "a normal custody/access situation," as Zaldin had put it in his letter of instruction to Butkowsky. It was also clear from her affidavit that Terry saw

Ben's desire to parent his children and realize an equal share of the equity in their home as a vicious attempt by him to punish her, reduce his child support payments, tap her out financially, and steal what was rightfully hers.

■ ■ ■

In early 1991 Ben was juggling three jobs to make ends meet. He'd been approached to become the director of development for Sunrise Films Ltd. and in November had taken the position on a six-month contract basis. Gordon Agencies (his dad's shoe business and, since 1989, the main source of Ben's income), the film company's office, and Stride Rite Canada Ltd. headquarters (where he picked up shoe samples) were at far-flung points on the map; most of the studios where he acted in commercials were downtown. He spent many days trapped in traffic and in his own head, driving from job to job along the 401, the Gardiner Expressway, and the Don Valley Parkway. I quickly learned to discern his anxiety level by the number of times a day he called from his carphone for no specific reason. In between, he managed his household, picked up the kids at school (that fall they were in two places: he'd enrolled Zoe in the morning enrichment program at Forest Hill Public School), went to monthly mediation/arbitration meetings at Butkowsky's office, and frequently drove downtown to his lawyer's office and the courthouse.

On January 17, Ben had taken Reiter's advice and decided to petition formally for divorce and to seek an order endorsing Butkowsky's recommendations and forcing the sale of the home. (According to Toronto Real Estate Board data, the point at which Ben and Terry had officially separated – March 1989 – had been the peak of the market. Since then, despite the occasional blip, house prices had been steadily declining and by January 1991 had fallen off by about 20 percent.) With Terry refusing to sell, the court order was Ben's only recourse. Her motion for interim child support was scheduled for February. His motion to sell the home was to be heard in April.

With each passing day, Ben was falling deeper into debt. Once he'd moved out of the house, he'd finally been freed of the burden of carrying a property he couldn't afford and had stopped paying the household bills at Dewbourne Avenue. If Terry refused to give up that lifestyle then she would have to bankroll it herself. But he was still supporting the children by paying approximately $10,000 a year for things like orthodontics, religious school, lessons, camp, and Zoe's enrichment program. He had the kids' food and entertainment costs when they stayed with him, plus his personal expenses and living costs at Relmar Road. He also had a $7,000 MasterCard balance collecting interest every month – the expense of setting up the kids' room and outfitting his apartment with housewares and the like – and he had his mounting legal bills. Although Ben's cancelled cheques proved the substantial amount he was paying towards the girls' support, Terry had accused him in her affidavit of "unilateral termination of any contribution towards the financial cost of the children."

As a rule, affidavits are prepared by lawyers for their clients. Clients then come to their offices to review them, swear that they are true, and sign the documents before they're filed with the court. Because lawyers are officers of the court, they must not furnish the court with evidence they know is false. In theory, an affidavit is supposed to be a cogent recitation of the facts for the judge to review. Terry's affidavit, however, read like a scenario from *The Perils of Pauline*. It reminded me of the letter Ben had received from Carl Orbach, accusing him of cutting off Terry's grocery money.

In her affidavit, Terry had declared that she didn't know why Ben (who now resided in what she and her lawyer characterized as "an expensive luxury apartment") would unilaterally "cut off all mortgage and utility bills and other assistance to me and the children," other than her "suspicion" that he wanted to drive "the children and me out of home by forcing its sale due to an economic crisis," which he was attempting to create.

Terry's affidavit conveyed the impression that she and the children were being driven from their home by a swinish lout with lots of money, a man who'd left them huddling without heat and stranded without funds to pay the mortgage. The truth was that this man was in serious debt because for twenty months, although officially separated from the woman, he'd supported her and the children in a lifestyle well beyond his means, while for seventeen months the woman had worked full-time, kept her earnings for herself, and steadfastly refused to sell a home from whose sale she could initially have realized close to half a million dollars.

By February Terry was unwilling to contribute to the cost of the monthly mediation/arbitration sessions with Butkowsky. Terry had agreed to pay one-third of Butkowsky's assessment fees, and the assessor had recommended that the couple share the cost of the ongoing monthly sessions. But because Ben was supporting the children by paying their extra expenses himself and not giving Terry the money, she claimed that she couldn't afford Butkowsky's fees. "If you were paying me a proper amount of child support, I would re-consider contributing," she wrote Ben. (I was growing more dubious of Terry's claims of poverty every day. In August she'd begun a new job with a company that did credit reporting, her financial statement declared that her income was about $27,000 a year, and she wasn't showing any recent debt. Yet she was somehow managing to pay a live-in housekeeper and a litigation lawyer.) Terrified that their fledgling cooperative parenting arrangement would collapse without a mediator/arbitrator to resolve disputes, Ben agreed to pay for it all. To Ben, money was just money. When his life settled down, he would find a way to earn more and pay off his debts. But how could he ever get back his kids?

■ ■ ■

Ben had hired Reiter to control Zaldin and wind up the case. But it was when Reiter took over the file that the fireworks really began. As Peter Israel and Moishe Reiter had intimated, Zaldin was known in Toronto legal circles as a difficult opponent, not because of any particular aptitude for the law but because in the blood sport of family law litigation, Zaldin would get offal on his hands. It was Zaldin's practice to do whatever was necessary to win: litigate at the drop of a hat, attack often, inundate his opponents' offices with notices of motion at the last minute and send them scurrying to react. Like many lawyers, he was also known to be an actor in court.

Ben had done an amusing impersonation of Zaldin for me before I'd actually seen him. Later I discovered that, as usual, Ben's observations had been dead on. Zaldin was a stocky, overweight man who moved in a laboured manner and whose barrister's robes always seemed to be trailing loose threads or a fallen hem. He had a thick unmanicured moustache that gave him a dirty, unshaven appearance. There was a sneering quality about him, particularly when he squinted and adjusted the glasses on his nose. In court, he sat with one buttock splayed on the edge of the counsel's table and addressed the court in an injured voice, whining of the injustices inflicted on him or his client until he got his way. He was like the kid who always had an excuse for not doing his homework, who'd fink on others but run to the teacher if someone played a trick on him.

In court, Reiter was Zaldin's theatrical opposite. He strutted about the courtroom brandishing words like swords, delighting in showdowns with worthy opponents, fancying himself in dazzling command of the language and the law. Outside the courtroom, he corrected those who failed to introduce him with the letters "QC" after his name. Charmed by the sound of his own voice, he liked to light his pipe with elaborate ritual and tell long-winded stories about his boyhood while the clock ticked away at $350 an hour.

The two lawyers were constantly at each other's throats. At the pre-trial cross-examinations, where no judge presides, all hell broke loose. At Ben's, in February, Reiter speechified incessantly, Zaldin told him to "put a lid on it" seven times, and both lawyers threatened to walk out.

Reiter deemed Zaldin beneath him, but as the case wore on, and Zaldin kept gaining the advantage, Reiter became obsessed with finishing off his opponent. Winning that fight, and not Ben's case, became his raison d'être. Ben just had to pay.

Throughout that winter and spring of 1991 the lawyers played the game of law. Desperate for closure, Ben repeatedly pressed Terry to sell their home, divide their possessions, and provide documentation about her income so they could settle the money issues. Terry resisted on every front. Every time Zaldin or Reiter filed another motion, Ben went to court to watch the proceedings. Every time he drove downtown and waited around the courthouse for his case to be heard, he expected the judge to make a decision. And almost every time, he came home to report either another adjournment or nothing finally resolved. That year alone the court adjourned matters a dozen times. Ben and I soon discovered that the family court was a playground for lawyers who didn't like to settle and judges who didn't like to decide. We also saw that a lawyer could play the system to prolong rather than resolve a conflict, if delay was in the client's best interests and prolonging a conflict in his own.

Resolving child support was a classic case. A parent applying to the court for child support was required to submit an itemized budget of all child care expenses. (In May 1997, the federal government introduced new child support guidelines that judges must follow, although the legislation still allows a certain amount of judicial latitude.) Judges and masters (judicial officers who deal with certain interim matters) determined child support in each case by assessing the children's costs and the parents' ability to pay them.

Every case is different – the support level depends on a family's financial circumstances, and parents often disagree on the desired or affordable lifestyle for their kids – but theoretically the court takes the view that children are entitled to be supported at a level commensurate with both parents' ability to pay. (The new child support guidelines look only at the payer's income, payers being overwhelmingly men. Consequently, a budget for a child like Sara, whose father's income is beyond the highest income level on the chart, $150,000, will be substantially higher – per child – than a budget submitted for Deja and Zoe, or for a much lower-income family.)

In February Zaldin went to court seeking $2,000 a month ($1,000 per child) in short-term child support for Terry. Reiter argued Ben was already paying most of the children's extra expenses directly (lessons, camp, orthodontics, etc.) and couldn't take any more stress to his already overburdened financial situation. Master Stewart McBride ordered Ben to pay Terry $958 a month. "Notwithstanding the father's position he pays the expenses of [the] children," he wrote, "the mother inevitably has expense." Based on Terry's budget he estimated her total child care expenses to be approximately $1,500 a month, and he ordered Ben to pay 63 percent of those costs.

Ben was livid. First, Terry had inaccurately claimed that "Mr. Gordon has not contributed [to her itemized expenses] since he physically left the house," when he was in fact paying $10,000 a year for the kids' extras. Second, she claimed she was spending $6,000 for those extra items when she wasn't paying a cent. He also speculated that she'd inflated many of her expenses (she listed nearly $800 a year, for instance, for the children's grooming and dry cleaning). But he had no way of knowing the truth until Terry furnished documentation. (To substantiate his claims, Ben had attached copies of cancelled cheques to his motion materials, but Terry did not produce any documentation to support hers.) Master McBride had no way of knowing the truth either, but he ordered Ben to pay her $958 a month anyway. Ben was stunned that the court would rule on the basis of uncorroborated evidence.

Terry's largest claimed child care expense was $800 a month for a full-time, live-in housekeeper's salary, which she represented to the court as "a nanny for the children," permitting her to "go out to work and be self-supporting." Ben considered it ludicrous for the court to condone this outlay: Terry worked flexible hours, the kids were in school or camp all day, she was pleading poverty on her financial statement, and his showed him choking with debt. If they were still married and carrying this level of debt, they'd have had to cut back, and the housekeeper (no longer a nanny now that the kids were gone all day) would have been the first expense to go. He knew why Terry and Zaldin were pursuing this claim, but what, he wondered, could possibly be the court's rationale in endorsing such a regressive notion?

Ben had been under the impression that family laws had been reformed to reflect notions of sexual equality and fairness, and he had assumed when they'd separated that they'd sell the house and split the proceeds. He also figured Terry would need his help until she found a job and that, once she had, they'd support the kids according to their respective abilities. That struck him as reasonable, fair, and equitable. He was upset by the injustice of the court's failure to look at the big picture and take into account the nineteen months of their in-house separation, when he'd supported Terry and the children and she'd kept her income exclusively for her private use. Where was the justice in ordering him to pay even more money to a woman who'd stubbornly refused to behave responsibly?

The court's underlying assumption seemed to be that as the mother, Terry had need, that need was to provide for the children, and until it determined at trial exactly how much need, it would freeze the status quo and refuse to disturb their standard of living. No other possible motive or context for her claim was relevant. As for him, the underlying assumption seemed to be that he was lying. He was the father and he had money, and until the court determined at trial exactly how much money – so it knew how much more to make him pay – too bad for him. Ben wondered why he kept reading stories in the media about how women were the victims of divorce.

He wanted to appeal, but Reiter told him the judgment would cost him more to fight than he was likely to recover. He was angry, but to get one thing out of the way, he did not appeal. Terry did. She considered the award too low. When Justice Karen Weiler heard Terry's appeal in April, she refused Terry any increase but backdated the award by two months.

Believing that once the truth came out and all the evidence was before the court, the outrageousness of Terry's claims and behaviour would be revealed and penalized, he pressed Reiter to cross-examine her in the pre-trial proceedings. Ben said Reiter kept putting him off, saying he didn't want to cross-examine Terry before trial because he didn't want to give her a chance to prepare her answers. He preferred to take her by surprise on the stand. Then, every time Ben asked about a trial date, Reiter led him to believe it was just around the corner.

The story repeated itself in April when Ben's motion to sell the home came before Justice George Walsh. The session began with another battle over support. Ben had stopped sending Terry cheques after she had appealed McBride's February order. Ben said Reiter had advised him that he didn't have to pay support while that order was under appeal. However, Zaldin brought a motion to dismiss or stay Ben's motion on the grounds that Ben had failed to pay. When the lawyers went into chambers before the judge, Walsh refused to hear Ben's motion unless he paid up. According to Ben, Reiter came out of the judge's chambers and told him to write Terry a cheque on the spot. Ben wrote the cheque, and Reiter went back inside and gave it to Zaldin. (It was not until years later that Ben discovered Reiter had given him erroneous advice – advice that had not only put him in contempt of a court order but, because of the court's highly punitive view of fathers who don't pay support, had unwittingly given Zaldin the ammunition he needed to portray Ben as the stereotypical deadbeat dad. Reiter later denied giving Ben this advice.)

Justice Walsh then heard the motion. Reiter argued that selling the house made the most financial sense. Their financial statements showed both parties in debt, and Ben's debt was growing at the rate of several thousand dollars a month. Terry's only reported debt, besides her share of the mortgage, was $17,500 that she claimed her family had loaned the couple towards their home. If they sold the home and split the equity, they'd solve their money problems and Terry would have more than enough cash to buy another place.

Terry fought the sale as "contrary to the children's best interests." In December she'd told the court the children were "doing well in my care" and had "begun to settle down and exhibit less anxiety now that their warring parents are no longer residing together." In February she'd claimed "the home is the only real home the children know; and it is in their best interests that the home not be sold prior to trial nor for some period of time post trial because the children are suffering emotionally and psychologically due to the warring of the Husband vis à vis the wife … and due to the separation in general (which has greatly upset both children)." Now Zaldin told the court that although "the situation has improved somewhat" since Ben had left the home, because of "parental conflict and family breakdown" as cited in Butkowsky's recommendations, "they are not doing well emotionally and psychologically at the present time … and an order for the pre-trial sale of the property would be contrary to the children's best interests, and, premature."

Terry also denied there was any financial urgency to sell since Ben had a place of his own; she claimed the real estate market was "currently improving" so they'd profit by waiting; and she said the court lacked evidence that she and the children could "be provided with suitable alternative accommodation." Terry again claimed that Ben had stopped paying the mortgage as a "calculated" strategy to force her out of the house.

Terry lost. On April 10, 1991, Justice Walsh ruled that the home be sold "forthwith." Ben was relieved to have finally made some headway on resolving that one issue. On May 7, Terry appealed.

Reiter told Ben that they could not move to strike out or expedite the appeal for at least six months. Ben couldn't believe what he was hearing. After two years engaged in fruitless negotiations with Terry to avoid litigation, he finally had an order to sell the house. The waiting list to be heard by the Court of Appeal was more than two years long. What was the point of a court order if Terry could stay in the house indefinitely simply by filing an appeal?

Even worse than the impact of another delay on his financial problems, however, was the threat Ben believed it posed to their precarious joint custody arrangement. Ben was convinced he'd never have a chance to make joint custody work as long as Terry remained in that house. The imbalance in their living situations was too pronounced, especially with Terry preaching to the kids day in and day out that she was their parent and that was their home.

Had theirs been a situation where the parents confirmed each other's roles, the psychological symbolism attached to that house would probably not have been as important a factor as Ben viewed it to be. Sara lived a much more affluent lifestyle with David than with me, yet was disinclined to make any parenting class distinctions. My impression is that children of divorce whose two parents reinforce each other's roles care less about the nature of the physical space they inhabit with each parent than about the way they feel within it.

But Ben was in a rather different position than David. And Ben had no way of countering Terry's propaganda unless he wanted to tug the kids in the opposite direction. As much as he wanted to set the record straight for Deja and Zoe, he knew it would upset and confuse them more if he spoke ill of their mother. They wouldn't know who to trust or where to turn, and would feel even more caught in the middle. That house symbolized the past. Only when it was sold would Terry break with the past. Only then would the kids be able to think of themselves as having a new life with both parents parenting them, instead of a life where Mommy was in charge, and Daddy had been banished to an apartment and alternate weekend "visitations."

Whenever Ben went off to court in the morning and returned later to report that Zaldin had pulled another fast one, or the court had ruled without evidence, or the matter had been "put over" for another month or two to accommodate lawyers' schedules, I would always ask, in disbelief, "But how can that be?" Convinced there had to be more to the story, I'd fire questions at him. But what about such-and-such? Didn't the judge consider this or that? What about the kids? Every time he'd shake his head wearily and say no. I soon realized there wasn't more to the story.

As the months dragged on, I too began to feel a simmering resentment, but I had to suppress my feelings, for there was nothing to be done about them. I had met a wonderful man living through a horrendous ordeal. I loved him, and, for better or worse, I was committed to helping him and his children make it through to the other side. I wasn't prepared to go on like this indefinitely, but, like Ben, I continued to believe that all we had to do was stick it out a little longer. How long could the court allow this insanity to continue?

91

Certainly, the ongoing brutality of the process was taking a daily toll on us all. Many evenings, tired of waiting in Ben's living room for him to return from putting the kids to bed, I'd tiptoe down the hall to their bedroom and find him asleep on the bunk, a daughter curled in one arm. Or I watched him struggle valiantly to fulfill his promise to Butkowsky, trying to be the Good Parent and position matters to the girls in the most cooperative terms, saying things like, "Mommy and I want this for you" and "Mommy and I think that . . ." He was in an impossible bind: how could he explain to an eight-year-old and a six-year-old that selling their house was about liquidating assets, realizing equity, and letting go of the past?

All he could do was repeat, over and over, that Mommy and Daddy both wanted the best for them. But with what was going on in court, and Terry telling him defiantly, as she so often did, "No one can make me support joint custody," and constantly sabotaging his efforts to co-parent, it was becoming harder and harder for him to stay "up" in front of the girls, or speak well to them of "Mommy." The word was beginning to stick in his throat.

There were the days he'd have to leave work early and rush across town to pick up the kids, and maybe that would also have been a day when Zaldin had given the judge an entirely misleading impression about him, her, or their situation or the lawyers had been constantly bickering and Reiter had ranted and raved and accomplished nothing except to mortify Ben. Or maybe it would have been one of the days Zaldin was cross-examining him, and he'd had to listen to the lawyers get into another one of their pissing contests. Or maybe he'd have waited around the courthouse for hours with Reiter billing an obscene fee but nothing being resolved, or maybe he'd have had another exasperating meeting with Butkowsky, and then arrived home with groceries to unpack and dinner to make and one of the kids would start up. Under such pressured circumstances, it was only a matter of time before he blew up and scorched the kids with angry words about their mother.

Maybe it would be Zoe he'd deny some childish want, and she'd tell him angrily, "Mommy's right. You are stupid." Or maybe Deja, always more low key, would roll her eyes and say, "Men are so pathetic." Or maybe one of them would say, "Mommy says you're not giving us money for food." At such times he'd take a deep breath and say, "Well, Mommy and I have a dif-

ference of opinion, but we both love you and we both want to parent you."
But they'd answer, "But Mommy says you're trying to take our home away
from us and we won't have anywhere to go and if you really loved us you
wouldn't do this to us," and then he'd explode in frustration and yell, "Well,
Mommy's a liar! And it's because of Mommy that I have to go to court
tomorrow and throw away another thousand dollars on another adjournment because she won't sell the goddamn house so we can get on with our
lives!" And then he would storm down the hall and fall onto his bed,
weeping. Afterwards, ashamed for having lashed out at them, he'd crawl
into a gloomy cave of depression. Once the storm had passed and he'd gathered his strength again, he'd tell them he was sorry for what he'd said in
anger about Mommy. Then the cycle would start all over again.

■ ■ ■

In mid-April Ben went to criminal court to stand trial for assault. He'd
hired Tim Lipson, a highly regarded criminal lawyer to whom he'd been
referred by a mutual friend. (As a favour, Lipson had kindly offered to represent him for a reduced fee.) The first charge had been stayed in March
because of the Askov ruling, which allowed judges discretionary power to
throw out cases not heard within a prescribed time. The two others were still
outstanding.

Judge Lauren Marshall, the widely respected presiding judge, heard the
charge involving the incident that had occurred a few days after Ben had
moved out of the house and had returned to pick up the kids for a weekend
stay. Unable to go to court with Ben that day, I later read the trial transcript.

Terry testified first. The Crown attorney, Paul Tait, asked her to begin by
recounting the events of October 12, but Terry took off in another direction.

"First of all, I'd like to premise it ... There have been three charges of
assault against Mr. Gordon, but they've all been ... through this Askov
situation – stayed, and this is the only one that seems to be coming to trial.
[There have] probably [been] many occasions I should have pressed charges
previous to that."

Lipson cut her off, pointing out that only the first charge had been
Askoved and that Terry's reference to other "occasions" was inadmissible.
Judge Marshall explained the rules and gently asked Terry to start where she
was comfortable concerning the day in question.

Terry said that late in the afternoon on October 12, she was preparing the children for a "visit" with Ben. She and the children were standing together at the door waiting for him to arrive, when he "barged into the house, went and got our luggage, and started pilfering through the house and filling the bag with, I don't even know what." When she asked Ben what he had in the bags, he "refused to answer me, and then started slugging me with the suitcases repeatedly." She testified that he hit her "numerous times" with two "full suitcases" of the "family's luggage," bruising her "all over" – in the arm, chest, stomach, and hip – then took the kids, who were crying, and left.

When Lipson began his cross-examination, he focused first on the context: "an all and all war on the matrimonial front." Noting the police evidence showing that Terry had taken four days to see a justice of the peace, Lipson put this fact to her.

"I don't recall," said Terry. "I did have a job to keep."

Lipson read aloud Terry's sworn statement to the JP: "After consulting with my lawyer, I attended this courthouse a few days later and laid this charge."

Even when presented with her own statement, Terry said she couldn't recall consulting her divorce lawyer either. She'd consulted Zaldin before "the very first charge" but "didn't need to" do so again. "I'm on a regular contact with my lawyer and ... I've been briefed on how to start handling these situations years before."

"You were more than familiar with the Courts," Lipson went on. "You would consult with your lawyer [and] lay charges like you were changing your clothes ... This is just another step in your crusade against your husband to get some leverage in that, isn't that true?"

Terry was offended at Lipson's implication. She was merely trying to "get some protection" from situations that had been occurring "for years and years in front of my children." She simply wanted Ben to know that he "can't just abuse me whenever he chooses."

"All you're doing is using these trumped up charges to hurt him in this fight for money, house and children," Lipson countered. He suggested that a rather different scenario had unfolded at the house that day: when she saw Ben leaving with one suitcase, not two, she became outraged over a "silly audio cassette tape" he had in his pocket and began grabbing at it, screaming hysterically, "You have no right to take anything from the house." Because he was "taking things out of the house which you thought were your things," Lipson said, Terry started clutching at the suitcase as Ben was trying to leave the house.

Terry stuck to her story. She conceded that Ben had arranged a pick-up time but denied Lipson's suggestion that Ben had deliberately arranged to come by when she wouldn't be home in order to avoid problems. All she'd done that day was come home "like usual, prepared my children." Then she'd waited quietly by the door, never raising her voice too much "because my kids were standing beside me," and asked Ben nicely what was in the suitcase. This request prompted Ben, who had his back to her, to fly into a sudden, uncontrollable rage and start swinging the suitcases at her in a backwards motion.

Lipson asked whether the housekeeper had been present, as Terry's statement to the police had indicated.

"I think so."

"You think so?"

"Yeah."

"Or you know so?"

"Well, I know me and the kids were standing at the front door. I don't remember exactly where she was at the time."

"Is she still under your employ?"

"I'm not sure if it's the same girl. We went through a few at that time because he was threatening them – the girls as well."

"You don't even know who your housekeeper was at the home?"

"No, I'm not sure 'cause … at that time when he was still living in the house we went through quite a few."

"There's no housekeeper here today to testify as to what you're telling us, is there?"

"No."

"No. And I suggest to you it's the same housekeeper who [is] working for you now that was there at the time on October the 12th, do you agree or not?"

"I can't agree, or not agree when I'm not sure."

"Didn't this take place in the vestibule of your house?"

"Yes."

"And that's about, what, four feet in width?"

"Well – "

"It's a small little room?"

"Yeah."

"And you're telling the Judge that you want her to believe that my client [was] swinging these two suitcases and hitting you all around?"

"No, not over his head. He swung them directly like this into my body."

"You were clutching at those suitcases and he was simply trying to get out of the house, isn't that true?"

"I was not clutching at these suitcases. This man is much larger than me, and could certainly pull that out of my hand in a minute. He had them in his hands."

"Don't [you] think if he really wanted to hit you with the suitcases, he could really have damaged you – "

"He did."

"I'm sorry. Is there a doctor here to testify on your behalf? Are there picture[s] here? Is there anything at all to support your story of what you're telling the Court? Is there anything?"

"Just me standing here and telling you what happened."

"You're a sophisticated woman, you have a lawyer, you're employed, you would have known that if any of these allegations were true, [you] could have got your housekeeper, you [could] have had pictures taken, you could have had something here to support what you're telling us, but you have nothing, do you?"

"I didn't think I had to go take pictures of my body to plead for help in a situation like this."

"Well, I guess this divorce battle is going to rage on ad infinitum and you and Ben are going to go to Court and spend all your money [on] lawyers."

"Well, that seems to be what he would like to do. I think he's hoping that he'll tap me out so that I can't fight."

"He'll tap you out?"

"I went out and got a job. I've never asked for money or alimony in his whole life. You know, I stayed home and raised my kids, and trying to protect them the best I can."

Judge Marshall had a question. "Did you at any time just step away out of the reach of his arm and the suitcase?"

"There was like – he was just going like this, you know, real fast at me and then it stopped when I moved back. But there's like a chest beside us, so I'm sort of in a corner there."

The judge asked whether any "access" arrangements existed to avoid confrontations. Terry replied that the assessor had said Ben was supposed to pick up the kids from school, "although he often can't live up to [those arrangements] exactly."

"The thing is, madam," said the judge, "that means that your children have to be like little refugees and take suitcases to school." Had she considered any other options? Perhaps she could take the kids to a friend's place, or a neighbour, family member, grandparent, aunt or uncle?

"I haven't got the resources to do that."

"Do you have family?"

"They work and so do I."

"So after work Friday you couldn't take them to a relative's, he could pick them up there?"

Terry repeated: Ben was supposed to pick the kids up at school. The assessor had said so.

"Forget the assessor. Forget the assessor, madam. What about a relative? There's a housekeeper at your house when the kids come home, is that right?"

"Well, that's what we were trying to do that day. I thought there would be no problem with that until he decided to come in."

The judge explored with Terry how things had gone since the October 12 incident. Terry allowed that "it seems to be all right" as long as Ben stayed out of the house.

Lipson said that after speaking with Ben and his matrimonial lawyer, he believed Terry's charge to be a "complete nuisance."

"Isn't it true, madam," he said to Terry, "that the Court has ordered the sale of your house and that you've tried everything you can to prevent the sale of your house?"

97

"That's right. I have, at this time, in this market, yes, I have."

"And the assessor, in fact, recommended joint custody, and that's what's been awarded, but you want sole custody of the children, isn't that true as well?"

Terry denied any understanding of the custody question, saying, "I don't know what those technicalities and words mean."

"Oh come on. You've been with lawyers for hours on this thing – "

"I'm telling the truth."

"What are you telling the judge," Lipson protested, "that you don't know what's going on?"

"I'm telling you what the arrangement is" – primary residence for her and weekend visits for him – "and this is what it's intended to be." She referred to herself as "prime custodial parent."

When Ben took the stand, Lipson asked him to describe his version of events. He testified he'd been unable to leave work early that day to pick up the kids from school and had gone to collect them at the house around 5:00. As was his custom, instead of going up to the house and knocking on the door, he phoned from the car. He testified that the housekeeper – the same woman currently working for Terry – answered and told him the girls weren't ready. So while the kids went out to the car, he went upstairs to their room to pack them a bag of sleepover blankets and overnight clothing. He recalled taking only one suitcase although "my hands may have been full with other things, dolls, and things for the children." Not until he came back downstairs did he have "any understanding of Mrs. Gordon being present in the house. She confronted me at the bottom of the stairs . . .

"The front door was still open. The children were outside waiting. The housekeeper was . . . helping me gather my things as I was coming downstairs. As I walked by, Mrs. Gordon was shouting insults and accusations. She pulled at my raincoat jacket pocket, pulled me backwards and wanted to know what the audio cassette was that was sticking out of my pocket. And I said, 'It was my audio cassette.' I pulled away. I still tried to leave the house. She began grabbing at the suitcase in my left hand." Ben explained that the stairs went right down to the front door and the confrontation had occurred in the small vestibule, where there was a chest and about a four-foot clearance between the stairway and front door.

"So you're heading towards the door, where's your wife standing?" Lipson asked.

"She's standing ... at the foot of the stairs just before the chest ... As I walked by between the chest and the side of the house she grabbed my pocket and threw me around. I pulled myself but she began grabbing at the suitcase, and that's when I pulled the suitcase free and walked out the front door, and got in the car and took the kids and drove away."

"Do you know if the suitcase came into contact with her?"

"I don't believe so. It was behind my back."

"Well, assuming it had, did you ever intend to assault her with the suitcase, sir?"

"Never, sir ... I had no feeling of a significant incident."

Lipson asked if Ronald Zaldin had ever brought up any of the assault charges in the divorce and custody proceedings.

"Her lawyer did try to raise the issues."

The Crown attorney began his cross-examination.

"Technically you weren't supposed to be in the house because of various court orders, is that right?"

"No, there's no court order barring me from entering the home."

"There was no rush or emergency or anything to getting the children out of there?"

"Not specifically."

"So what was the problem with just letting Mrs. Gordon look in the suitcase or have a look at what you had?"

"Mrs. Gordon was hostile ... she was screaming insults at me in front of the children. This was obviously a situation that I was trying to escape."

"Is this a struggle for the suitcase?"

"There wasn't much of a fight over it. She started to pull it away. I pulled it away and walked out the door."

"Is it possible that the suitcase went back and forth a few times then?"

"I don't think so."

After the Crown had completed his cross-examination, Judge Marshall spoke.

"This is a criminal court," she began, and its standards are "proof beyond a reasonable doubt, not suspicion or could have been, but proof beyond a reasonable doubt." Noting that her "reputation in domestic assaults" was "a pretty nasty one around here," but that this was not a typical assault case, she said, "We have a couple [who] at one time loved one another enough to marry and ... produce two children whom they both obviously love very much ... The really horrible factor here is, these children are well old enough to know what's going on here ... They should still be free to love each of you, but when they see or are involved in these terrible conflicts ... you may as well stick a knife in their heart ...

"Now unfortunately my experience has been, both in practice where I did a lot of family law, and since I've been sitting on the bench, that what was once a loving and supportive relationship turns to bitterness ... Unfortunately all the ugly emotions come out, anger, bitterness, hurt, revenge."

The judge described the "tremendous change in your lifestyles" that comes with divorce. "Of course," she said, "the family home [is] likely going to have to be sold ... It's a major financial problem, and two cannot live as cheaply as one, two families that is ...

"I don't believe either of you are deliberately lying to me in terms of this Court today. However, you are relating to me what's happened from your perspectives," the judge continued. "It would appear that there was a scramble over the suitcase, but in terms of whether you [*to Ben*] deliberately struck her with it, I have a problem in terms of law" of meeting the reasonable-doubt standard.

Judge Marshall wanted to emphasize to both Ben and Terry that "there's only so much money here. If you folks don't get this resolved, you're both going to end up in the poor house. Further, you're both going to end up spending what money is left on psychologists for your kids ... because they're going to be a couple of basketcases. Plus if you people spend your energy fighting instead of getting on with your life ... bitterness is like a cancer, it eats you away ... I'm sure you're both basically decent people."

The judge had some thoughts on the custody question. "I guess I'm really amazed to hear that some psychologist for you two recommended joint custody. Joint custody is supposed to be where there's some semblance or ability to work together. Maybe it can happen, but you two are going to have to deal with one another over the next ten or so years while your kids are growing up. And quite bluntly," she said, it was time to try mediation counselling, "getting rid of the crap" and finding some new means of communication. "This is a criminal court. And all that coming back here is going to do is drive that wedge deeper and deeper."

Next – saying, "Forgive me, gentlemen" – Judge Marshall delivered a few choice words about the matrimonial lawyers.

"Lawyers can be there, not just to fight and create problems, they can be there to help the parties resolve them and the really best lawyers, the first [thing they] say to you is, 'Folks, the money should be [in] your pocket, not mine.' Any lawyer who doesn't mention that to you in passing may want to consider their motivation because the way the lawyers really clean up on these things is [to] go to Court on the motions, and the appeals and the fight …

"All right. Enough of my lecture … This is some legal advice [and] you don't have to pay for it. There's a better way to work it out. The other thing I'd remind you is when you do get into physical confrontation, people can be hurt really easily. And [to Terry] that suitcase struck you, but what are you doing fighting over a suitcase? For Heaven's sake, the kids were there. Should it matter if he carried out the piano, you know? Financial things and property you can solve later, anyway."

Judge Marshall said she had a couple of options. One was to have them both enter into a peace bond to stay away from one another, but she preferred not to do that. "For the reasons given, the charge is dismissed and I hope I never see both of you back here again."

"Well, there's still the stepping on the toe charge, Your Honour," Lipson reminded the judge.

To get rid of that charge ("as long as all this hangs around, it's going to fan the flames") and give them both "peace of mind," Judge Marshall proposed the mutual peace bond after all. It wasn't a "criminal thing," but it gave "moral reassurance." She asked Terry how she felt about a peace bond instead of having the court hear her toe-stepping charge.

"I want to keep my own sanity," Terry said. "It's a frightening situation to come in and barge in like that on us."

Then the judge asked the lawyers to take a recess to work out the details. After the break Lipson said Ben would "certainly" sign a peace bond if Terry did, too.

101

Ben agreed with the judge's suggestion that he did not need to enter the house. To Terry she said the kids "should be ready, and ready with all the things they need" when Ben came to pick them up. "If there's a problem, you've got to sort that out through the civil lawyers."

Judge Marshall then directed Terry and Ben "to enter into a bond to keep the peace and be of good behaviour ... Mr. Gordon, in addition to keeping the peace and being of good behaviour in regards to Terry Nusyna Gordon, you will not enter into 24 Dewbourne Avenue except pursuant to a Court order or a written agreement."

"Can I have protection in regards to my residence?" asked Ben.

"Let's be practicable, sir, she's never been there. Look folks ... there's got to be a starting point here."

The judge withdrew the toe-stepping charge and added her hope that "your next visit to the Court downtown will be to settle." Then, after reminding them they really should give mediation a try ("I know from my practice ... there's some very skilled and successful [mediators] around town") she sent them on their way. Her parting words were: "If you want a shock to your hearts, ask your lawyer what it's going to cost if you keep this up much longer for both of you. The old joke is who should own the house here, you two or the lawyers."

■ ■ ■

Based on what I knew of Ben, I didn't think him capable of hitting a woman. Based on what I was learning about Terry, I didn't think she was an innocent victim. I could easily imagine their fights, how they began, how they escalated. And I could see their pathology: Ben getting to Terry by steadily ignoring her, Terry demanding to be noticed and getting to Ben by goading him until he blew. I could imagine the shoving matches and why they'd happened. The transcript gave me a different insight into an incident Terry had considered serious enough to warrant criminal charges.

With Terry having already pressed two assault charges against him, Ben was alert to the possibility of trouble and had arranged to collect the kids around 5:00, as he'd said, when Terry would be unlikely to be home from work yet. I theorized that she'd come home when she knew he'd be there to stand guard at the door and make sure he didn't remove so much as a bar of soap from the house, that when she saw him with the suitcase she perceived him to be violating her home and taking her things and became enraged. That when she began interrogating him about what he was taking, he ignored her; that his ignoring her had enraged her even more and she began clutching at his raincoat and the suitcase; that he'd yanked free from her grasp with angry force and left the house; and that, as was her custom when ignored, thwarted, or denied, she'd attacked. By the time I'd finished reading the transcript and considered Terry's other assault allegations in the context of what I'd read, the only question I had was why she had not been held accountable for a nuisance charge and charged with public mischief.

Despite what I had deduced about Terry from reading her affidavits, witnessing her behaviour, and seeing it play out in the kids, it wasn't until I read that criminal court transcript that I truly understood the magnitude of what Ben and the children were up against: the improbability of her story; the arrogant and decidedly un-victim-like demeanour on the stand; the unsubstantiated claims of being bruised all over but waiting four days to press the charge; the purported inability of a mother, not to mention one seeking sole custody, to recall the name of the person living in her home and caring for her children; the righteous indignation at being asked to "go take pictures of my body to plead for help in a situation like this," indeed, at being asked for any evidence at all beyond "me standing here and telling you what happened." What struck me most, however, were Terry's perceptions of self, for I believed she truly saw herself as the Abused Woman and Good Mother. What was so disturbing was how stunningly at odds with reality Terry's perceptions were, and how easy it had been for her to manipulate the state into believing her and charging an innocent man.

Some time later Tim Lipson told me that when he'd first set eyes on Terry in the courtroom that day, she appeared to be a presentable, well-spoken woman. Because of her manner and appearance, he said, she'd have had no difficulty convincing a justice of the peace to lay a charge. It wasn't until she'd taken the stand, he'd cross-examined her for five minutes, and her story "completely fell apart" that he saw what kind of woman he was dealing with. Lipson told me, too, that Judge Marshall had a reputation for bending over backwards to be fair to women, and that he believed another judge would have reprimanded Terry for wasting the court's time.

In spite of her kid-glove treatment of Terry, Judge Marshall had struck me as a good judge. She'd tried to get a feel for the situation. She'd been decent, humane, and even-handed. She'd dismissed a nuisance charge, ensured the court's time wasn't wasted hearing another, and made sure an innocent man was not convicted. Still, I could not help thinking how little that decent, humane, even-handed judge with her background in family law sitting high on her bench, appealing to the intelligence of both parties and judiciously averaging blame, could know about the story of the man and woman standing before her. The truth was that because of her vantage point and the nature of the forum, she could make only crude assumptions and apply them in the coarsest way.

Ben had told me afterwards that he was just "glad to get out of there," and that the worst thing about being in court was having to endure the judge's lecture. Now I understood. As I read Judge Marshall's words, all I felt was the sting of their ignorance and how galling it must have been for Ben to listen to a judge scold him about how she was "really amazed to hear that some psychologist for you two recommended joint custody" and how she was sure they were "both basically decent people," but if they didn't stop fighting the lawyers would get all the money and the kids would be basket cases and they really should try mediation. Had it been me standing there, I don't know if I would have had the restraint to stop myself from telling her how far off the mark her assumptions were, and how little she actually knew about the truth.

■ ■ ■

Meanwhile Butkowsky's mediation/arbitration sessions were volatile. After Terry sued over the assessor's recommendations, Ben asked him to read her affidavits and see for himself what she was telling the court: that his recommendations meant she had sole custody. Ben believed that if Butkowsky would tell Terry plainly what he'd told him – that he'd never intended for her to have sole custody – and that if he'd impress upon her that he'd testify in court to that effect, then she'd have no choice but to stop litigating. He begged Butkowsky to tell Terry what his recommendations meant. But Butkowsky refused to become involved. According to Ben, he didn't want to hear about court matters and asked if Ben would pay him extra to read court documents. (In June Ben wrote him another letter, enclosing copies of the "pertinent legal documents" Terry had filed over the previous several months.)

104

But Butkowsky wanted only to hear about their scheduling problems and to mediate their daily disagreements over parenting issues, isolated from any larger context. He behaved as if the fact that Terry was now refusing to accept his recommendations and was suing for sole custody – that Ben had been forced to countersue just to have the recommendations endorsed by the court, that he was now at risk of being cut out of his children's lives forever and having them parented exclusively by a woman who'd tried to have him jailed – was irrelevant to the matters he was dealing with in his office. Butkowsky didn't seem to realize or care that these events might have some effect on Ben's state of mind or on how their co-parenting arrangement was working.

According to Ben, the two of them would be in Butkowsky's office and Ben would be simmering with frustration, arguing that Terry was making a mockery of the recommendations, that he was hearing all kinds of terrible stuff from the kids, that Zoe had said to him, "Mommy says you're a jerk and you're making us move and trying to take our home away from us," and Butkowsky would just censure him for becoming so worked up. Then Terry would complain that he'd enrolled Deja in camp without consulting her. And Ben would explain that Deja was dying to go and deserved a break from all the conflict, but if he'd waited for Terry's approval he'd have missed the application deadline. And Butkowsky would give him a "slap on the wrist" for not consulting Terry.

At one point, sitting in his car outside a hockey arena, Ben called Butkowsky on his cellphone and asked him what it was that Terry wanted. Butkowsky said that Terry had told him Ben was an actor merely putting on an act to get joint custody, all so that he wouldn't have to pay her child support. "You mean she's worried about how much money she's going to get?" Ben asked. Butkowsky said yes. "Fine," Ben said. "Then ask her how much money I have to pay to buy my kids."

■ ■ ■

By the spring, Terry also had someone in her life. Ben had seen her new boyfriend, Randolph Steepe, standing in his bathrobe at the front door of the house once or twice when he'd arrived to collect the kids, and Terry had shown up with Steepe at the birthday party Ben had arranged for Zoe at the Bathurst Bowlerama in May. She'd also brought him to the synagogue for

Deja's consecration ceremony. (I had deliberately refrained from attending both events because I thought my presence might upset Terry, and I didn't want to cause more tension for the girls on a celebratory day. Ben reported that he'd saved seats for Terry and the girls so they could sit together as a family, but she arrived late, refused to sit with him, and led the children to another row. A dad seated in that row witnessed the incident, shook his head at Terry's behaviour, and moved over so that Ben could sit beside his daughters.)

The kids said Steepe was living at the house and mentioned him going on outings with them but, beyond that, seemed reluctant to say much. Ben had a bad feeling about the guy. Steepe's look was a little too "disco hustler" for Ben's liking. It worried him, too, that the kids hesitated to talk about Steepe, since Ben knew from the sessions with Butkowsky that Deja and Zoe were talking animatedly to Terry about me. (The kids' reticence didn't surprise me since it was my impression that Terry censored the girls and instructed them to be secretive about her life and their life with her – or any other information she did not want Ben or others to have.)

Ben's former brother-in-law, Brian, told him that Terry had met Steepe at Centro (a tony restaurant with a wine bar popular among upscale middle-aged singles) and that he'd taken one look at the guy and warned Terry off him. Then, through the grapevine, Ben heard a rumour that Steepe was also living in a waterfront condo owned by another woman. Ben consulted Reiter, who advised him that if Terry was asking for sole custody, the court had the right to know something of the character of a man who was living with the kids. He suggested Ben hire a private investigator to check up on Steepe.

In effect, a family lawyer was now advising Ben that if he wanted to improve his chances of remaining a parent to his children, he'd be smart to surreptitiously marshal incriminating evidence to indict their mother. Mudslinging. In the best interests of the children. We considered the idea of hiring an investigator to snoop around in Terry's love life sordid, not to mention an expense that Ben could ill afford. But Reiter was advising it, and Reiter was the lawyer. Furthermore, Ben was no longer a babe in the woods. By then he knew that Deja and Zoe's future turned more on tactics than on truth, and he could feel himself pumping up for the fight. But he was still distanced enough to detest the person he was being forced to become.

We found an investigator willing to make a few calls at no charge. He discovered that Steepe had no fixed address or credit rating – a discovery, he told us, that itself raised a red flag. For a fee, he offered to do more digging. But Ben had neither the funds nor the inclination to pursue that avenue. In any event, by that point Randolph Steepe took a back seat to more pressing problems.

In April, when Justice Walsh had ordered the house sold, he had also set deadlines for both parties' pre-trial cross-examinations to be completed. Terry's was to be wrapped up by May 9. Unable to pin Zaldin to a date, Reiter served Zaldin with a notice to examine Terry on May 3. Zaldin said Reiter couldn't make him attend that day and suggested that Reiter cross-examine Terry on May 6. On May 6, Zaldin said Terry was "too weak" to attend, because of the flu. He forwarded a note, dated May 5 and signed by a doctor whose name Ben did not recognize and whose office was in the west end of Toronto. (The family physician, who had a neighbourhood office, was Dr. Harvey Kaplovitch, or "Dr. Harvey," as the kids called him.) The doctor's note read: "I saw Ms. Gordon today and [she] is too ill and unable to be cross-examined tomorrow. She should be better within 1 week."

The evening of May 6, Ben called the house, and Mathewrina informed him that everybody was out. She also told him that Terry had gone to work that day. Later the kids told Ben their mother had taken them to a children's play that night featuring the music of her uncle, the composer Louis Applebaum. The following day Ben called Terry's office and was advised that Terry was at work. Justice Walsh's May 9 deadline for the completion of Terry's cross-examination passed. Reiter served Zaldin with another notice to examine Terry, this time on May 10. Zaldin said he was unable to attend that day.

Another month passed. On June 10, at the pre-trial conference, Justice Walsh made his second order setting a date for Terry's cross-examination: June 13. (Despite Zaldin's vehement attempts to delay the trial until much later, the judge also set a trial date for October 21.) On June 13, Zaldin tried to have Ben's case thrown out of court because he was behind on his child support payments. Justice Walsh stayed all motions and ordered

Zaldin to present Terry for cross-examination at 2:00 that day.

That afternoon Ben, the lawyers, and a court reporter showed up at the examiner's office, which was near the courts. When Terry arrived and saw Ben, she announced she feared for her safety with him there and refused to be cross-examined unless he left. Ben pointed out that there were two lawyers and a court reporter in the room, many other witnesses were nearby, and they were attending monthly sessions with Butkowsky and transferring the children weekly without incident. Terry still refused.

The official examiner was called into the room and confirmed Ben's legal right to stay. Zaldin threatened to leave unless Ben left the room. Then Zaldin and Reiter got into a sparring match. They decided to head for the courthouse to see if they could get in to see Justice Walsh. The judge ordered the cross-examination to proceed with Ben present. To allay Terry's concerns, the judge instructed Ben to hire a police officer.

Reiter arranged for the officer; a dispute then arose between the lawyers over who would pay the policeman. Ben said he'd pay. He just wanted to get the proceedings under way. As soon as that issue was settled, Zaldin announced he had an appointment with a client being deported the next day and that it was his access night with his children. He said that he could not wait for the officer to arrive. He and Terry left.

On June 19, six weeks past the date when Justice Walsh first ordered Terry's examination to have been completed, and after two court orders requiring that it take place, Terry's cross-examination began. A police officer was present at Ben's expense.

According to the transcript, Reiter spent the first part of the examination questioning Terry about her work history prior to marriage. Then he turned to custody.

"Do you consider that you do have custody of those children?" Reiter asked Terry.

"Yes, I do."

"Did you ever ask Dr. Butkowsky whether you have custody of those children?"

"I think it's an understanding that we've had, yes, that I've been the custodial parent of those children, yes."

"Then why is it that according to Dr. Butkowsky's recommendation, each of you has the right, when the children are with you, each of you, to make the decisions affecting them?"

Zaldin interrupted. "Don't answer that. That's a question for Dr. Butkowsky."

"Where did you get that understanding, if not from Dr. Butkowsky? From your own head?"

Terry said she got the idea from the way they lived, from her time with Butkowsky and their discussions about the children.

Reiter began to read from Butkowsky's report. "Well … it says, in number three, that it is recommended that Mr. and Mrs. Gordon be mutually obligated to share any and all information related to the significant events of the children's daily lives … Number four, it says it is recommended that daily decisions affecting the children be the responsibility of that parent in whose care the children are at that time."

Zaldin interrupted again. Terry's understanding arose from discussions and meetings with Butkowsky after he'd released his report, so the report was only part of the story.

Reiter asked Terry what Butkowsky had said since releasing his report to give her the perception that she had custody of the kids.

"He said that it is improper that Mr. Gordon does not share information with me and consult with me on decisions he decides to make about the children."

"Such as?"

"Such as where they go to camp." Later in the cross-examination Terry recalled Butkowsky saying, "You get a slap on the wrist for that, Ben."

"Is that all? I'm sure there must be more."

"He mentioned in one of our meetings that Mr. Gordon had not made me aware of the fact that he had a girlfriend and because I would have to deal with the children on that issue I should have been made aware of that."

Reiter asked whether there were any other reasons to account for why she believed she had custody.

"I said it was an understanding we had … we discussed these issues [and] it was assumed that I am the custodial parent and therefore this information should all be filtered through me, and all issues."

"That's your understanding of Dr. Butkowsky's position on custody?"

Terry said it was.

"Have you ever asked Dr. Butkowsky specifically, 'Do I have custody of these children?'"

"It never seemed like a necessary question," Terry answered.

After extensive questioning over two days of cross-examination, Terry could not point to anything specific in Butkowsky's report that had led her to believe she had sole custody. Nor could she relate any specifics Butkowsky had said to give her that impression.

The recommendations were clear on one point anyway: both parents were obliged to consult about major decisions. If one looked at Terry's complaint in a vacuum – as Butkowsky had – one could argue that she had good reason to be annoyed at Ben for not consulting her before enrolling Deja in camp. However, if one considered Terry's behaviour pattern – as Butkowsky should have – one could argue Ben had an even better reason to put his daughter's needs ahead of the rules. Most significant, however, was that for Terry to make the quantum leap from Ben's failure to tell her he'd enrolled Deja in camp to the conviction that she had sole custody was ludicrous.

As problematic as Butkowsky's report was – and it was hugely problematic – it was all they had to go on. During cross-examination, Terry testified that Butkowsky had been hired to assess the situation with the children and "decide who should be primary caregiver." But Butkowsky's job had not been to decide a "primary" anything. He'd been hired to assess the family and make whatever recommendations on custody were appropriate. Furthermore, although Butkowsky had recommended that the children live with Terry the majority of the time, nowhere did his report suggest that the parent whose residence was the children's primary one would also be the parent empowered to make all the parenting decisions.

On the other hand, to a certain degree it was understandable that Terry was convinced that she was the "custodial parent." After all, Ben said Butkowsky had told him he'd deliberately led Terry to believe she hadn't "lost" on custody so as not to cause her a mental breakdown or "social embarrassment." It was also understandable for Ben to assume they had joint custody. Not only did the report clearly recommend joint decision-making, but the impression Butkowsky had given him was that although the kids lived primarily with Terry, theirs was a joint custody arrangement, one he'd prevailed upon Ben to try his best for a year to make work.

One couldn't entirely blame either Terry or Ben for the confusion. But one could certainly blame Butkowsky. By making an ambiguous recommendation that indulged a mother's needs but in no way served the children's, Butkowsky had thrown into chaos the one issue he'd been paid $6,000 to resolve.

The simplest and quickest way to resolve the ambiguity was to ask Butkowsky whether he'd meant for Terry to have custody. Reiter asked Terry if she'd ask Butkowsky to spell out his views on custody at their next mediation meeting, then report back. Zaldin said that was a question for the psychologist to answer himself.

"Are you prepared to put your money where your mouth is and have Dr. Butkowsky say what the reality is?" Reiter asked. In effect, would Terry authorize Butkowsky to provide a statement indicating his position on custody?

"Absolutely," said Zaldin. But in fact Zaldin did not seem to be interested in asking Butkowsky to clarify his recommendations. Zaldin seemed to want the answer to a different question: How capable were Ben and Terry of cooperating, and what impact would that have upon their ability to parent in the future?

This was an important strategic distinction. Asking Butkowsky to state his position on custody would have cleared the smoke then and there. Clearing the smoke would unquestionably be best for the girls. However, it would not be in Terry's best interests.

As Zaldin would most certainly have known, Terry's beliefs about Butkowsky's recommendations did not square with their wording. Terry had said she should make all the decisions; Butkowsky had called for "joint decision-making," the bedrock of any joint custody arrangement, and consultation on major decisions. Terry had said all information should be "filtered" through her, suggesting that Ben was obliged to report to her; but Butkowsky's recommendation clearly stated that the parent in whose care the children were at the time was to make the "daily decisions." Indeed, the previous August, after Butkowsky had met with the lawyers to release his report, Judith Beaman had reported to Ben that when Zaldin had learned of the recommendations he'd slammed his fist down on the table —

hardly the reaction of a lawyer who thought his client would be pleased with the result.

Zaldin would also have known that the court would be loath to order joint custody if Ben and Terry couldn't communicate well enough to make parenting decisions. (In February he'd filed an affidavit saying, "The Respondent pleads that she should have sole custody of the children as primary caretaker as per Dr. Irwin Butkowsky's recommendations of August 14, 1990, as the parties do not talk or communicate well.") If Zaldin delayed and Terry frustrated Ben's attempts to parent, if the conflict between them grew steadily worse, and if, after a year, Zaldin put the assessor on the stand and asked him to tell the court about the parties' ability to make joint custody work over the long term, then Butkowsky was likelier to give him the answer he wanted.

Reiter told Zaldin they should arrange for Butkowsky to come to court and "get rid of this nonsense once and for all ... The only one who knows what his recommendation is, is Butkowsky."

Zaldin said he'd agree to Butkowsky "updating" his recommendations in writing.

"I'm saying bring him in," said Reiter.

Zaldin said he'd take the matter "under advisement."

(When Terry's cross-examination resumed two weeks later, Reiter asked her if, in the interim, she'd asked Butkowsky to clarify his views. "There wasn't much chance to ask him too much about that," Terry said, "because Ben was ranting and raving throughout most of the session." And, while her memory was foggy on whether the psychologist had actually said she was to be the custodial parent, what stuck out very clearly in Terry's mind was that "Butkowsky would never agree to joint custody, because of the fact that we do not communicate well.")

Reiter turned next to money matters.

"You have suggested that your husband has depleted his income purposely. Is that not so? That he is deliberately dissipating his income?"

"It seems pretty obvious."

"Why is that?"

"He has never earned as little in his life. He has turned down a lot of work in the past that I was seeing when he was still living with me." Terry couldn't recall specifics, but did recall Ben's agent asking her why he didn't want to further his career.

Reiter asked her Ben's agent's name. Terry gave the name, then added, "He's probably got rid of her by now too."

"Now when did he get rid of her?"

"I don't know. I'm just assuming ... It just sort of fits the pattern that he would get rid of her."

"What did she tell you she wanted to do for his career?"

"Oh, she wanted to promote him more in U.S. films."

"Specifics?"

"No specifics, generally, and that he was saying he wanted to get away from the business."

"What kind of parts did he have?"

"Character roles ... he's a great character actor ... Ben has a very powerful reputation and has had in this country and in California."

"How many films has he made in Canada in the past two years?"

"The past two years? That's when he has been trying to destroy his career, in the past two years."

"You're saying that he deliberately wants to destroy his future?"

"Yes. He had a talk with me once about how he wanted to get away from the business and sell shoes and he wanted my support in that."

"Did you know that Sunrise [Films] scaled back operations because of the fact that the economy is such that they closed down more than two-thirds of their operations?"

"No, I didn't know that."

"Did you know what the general situation is in the film industry at the present time? ... I'm not talking about two years ago. I am asking if you have any idea what the situation is in the film business now in Canada and the U.S."

"Nope."

"Now at that time that you say ... that he was artificially depressing his career, he had worked in the shoe business as a mainstay and he had the entertainment or acting business, commercials and television ... as a secondary business."

"The entertainment business was his primary business."

"Right, but the entertainment business is cyclical, isn't it?... You're not working all the time."

"People like Ben could be."

"Maybe and maybe not, isn't that right?"

"There's always an element of maybe but his past record shows that he could. We bought our home based on the fact that we could rely on his career."

"Tell me about that. The home that you say you made the greater contribution to, you bought it relying on him and his career? Please tell me about that." Actually, Terry had made no formal claim of a greater contribution to the house purchase. But that did not stop either Reiter or Terry from engaging in a testy exchange on the topic.

"Oh, I stopped working to just take care of the children to allow him the opportunity to further his career," Terry replied, "which meant that I was giving up my career."

"What was your income in 1981?"

"I don't know."

"1980, 1979, 1978, tell me about your income that you gave up to let him build his career? Tell me about it."

"I don't think my career is based on income alone."

"Are you seriously sitting there and saying ... that you made the greater contribution to the acquisition of the home, of the property [and] that you had a real career, a solid career in 1981?"

"I had a growing career."

"From what, from production coordinator to ... production ... to producer, I should say? A producer who was getting coffee and who was doing everything on a small commercial for Alan Cherry? Is that what you're talking about?"

"They were all steps that needed to be taken."

Ben's debts had climbed by now to more than $123,000. In June he had filed an affidavit saying he was "hopelessly in debt" – to, among others, his family, two of his lawyers, and MasterCard. Meanwhile, Zaldin continued to demand more financial documents. Although by then he'd accumulated a mountain of paper, and for two days of cross-examination in February and March had grilled Ben exhaustively, Zaldin had been unable to find any undeclared income or hidden assets.

At Terry's cross-examination, however, Reiter got his first chance to look at Terry's documentation and discovered that she was hiding money. She'd earlier failed to disclose three bank accounts (including the account into which she deposited her weekly salary) and had somehow overlooked reporting $17,000 in savings. Asked how she could have forgotten to report so much money, particularly when her lawyer was telling the court that she and her children were going to be out on the street if she didn't get some relief quickly, Terry said she'd made "a mistake."

At the cross-examination, Reiter also got his first look at one of Terry's pay stubs and made a second discovery. Terry had reported net figures on her financial statement instead of gross figures. He determined that her income was not $27,000, as she'd reported, but actually between $42,000 and 44,000. Furthermore, two days after swearing a financial statement in which she'd neglected to report yet a *fourth* bank account, containing $8,144.01, and two days after filing an affidavit in which she'd accused Ben of deliberately depleting his income, Terry had closed and emptied that particular account.

When Reiter asked why, two days after beginning a court action in which she was pleading poverty and going after Ben for more money, she'd cleaned out a bank account containing more than $8,000, Terry said she owed her father $10,000. He hadn't pressed her for the money; she'd just wanted to pay him back. Terry had borrowed the money from her father in the early summer of 1989, when she and Ben were in mediation and Ben was struggling to pay their bills. Reiter now determined that during that period, Terry had had several thousand dollars in the bank.

Reiter asked her why she'd needed to borrow from her father when she had all that money. Terry said she needed a wardrobe to start working, the "legal situation" was "compounding," she had "expenses," and "Ben was not giving us any money." But the only expense Terry could recall having to pay for herself was a wardrobe.

"Is there any other explanation for leaving out all of those things that we found in your tax return?"

"It was irrelevant."

"I see. So assets that produced about $2,000.00 or more a year in interest

115

income weren't sufficiently relevant to be disclosed in your financial statement, is that what you're saying?"

It was unclear from Terry's flippantly dismissive testimony whether she was too ignorant to realize or too arrogant to care that the evidence revealed her to be lying about her assets. Under the circumstances, the best Zaldin could do was cover for his client and try to exercise damage control. He interrupted again.

"She missed that one," he explained, "because she said, and wrongly so, that she didn't consider it relevant ... She made an error."

Zaldin eventually produced a document verifying that about a week after Terry had cleaned out her bank account, her father had purchased a term deposit for the $10,000 amount Terry claimed to owe him.

She had to pay back her father then "so that he could invest it in a term deposit?" Reiter asked incredulously.

"It's not my business what he chooses to do with his money," Terry replied.

Then there was Terry's household and personal financial recordkeeping. At cross-examination, witnesses are obliged to produce documentation supporting the figures they've sworn to on their financial statements. Terry claimed she had "tremendous expenses" but brought virtually no evidence to support this claim. She threw out most of her pay stubs and credit card statements. She didn't have cancelled cheques, copies of bills, or a list itemizing her expenses. She couldn't explain her investments or the movement of money within her bank accounts. She kept only "dribs and drabs" of receipts. In almost every case, Zaldin refused to provide documentation unless Ben paid the financial institutions' search fees.

Her recordkeeping had not always been so lax. Ben had completed his first financial statement for the case while still living in the house by reviewing Terry's chequebook, bank statements, and household records. And Reiter discovered that the tax return Terry had filed in April – only a few months earlier – contained an itemized schedule listing her deductible car expenses tallied to the penny.

In February the court had made an "interim" child support order of $958 a month on the unsubstantiated assumption that a mother's need was pressing. Four months later, it turned out that Terry had not been telling the truth. She'd had at least $32,000 more than she'd disclosed, and she admitted that Ben had paid the bills she'd accused him of not paying. One could argue that she'd projected blame onto Ben for crimes she'd committed: putting on an act out of self-interest, trying to create a financial emergency where none existed, purposely downplaying her assets out of greed. One could also argue that a mother claiming need for her children was evidence enough and the court didn't care about the truth.

■ ■ ■

As the trial approached in the fall of 1991, Ben had wanted to fire Reiter for some time. His lawyering was scattershot and reactive. He never completed Terry's cross-examination. He never provided Ben a standard reporting letter. His conduct in court embarrassed Ben. When Ben complained that his problems seemed only to be worsening, Reiter's advice was to keep fighting: everything would come together at the trial.

Early in October, with the trial date looming, Ben hoped to meet with Reiter to hear his trial strategy and discuss concerns about the interminable delays. Ben was such an emotional mess by that point that he feared he'd lack the strength to press for a straight answer and asked me to come along. During the meeting, which was my first direct encounter with Moishe Reiter, he constantly took calls, evaded my direct questions, boasted how he was going to "get Zaldin and Terry" at the trial, and spent the better part of an hour and a half (a meeting for which he later billed $525) telling insufferably boring stories about himself. I was so appalled by his conduct that right after that meeting we called my cousin Joyce Harris, a lawyer, to ask about dismissing Reiter.

Firing him was no longer a simple matter. The trial was just a month away. Joyce said it was unlikely another lawyer could prepare the case on short notice, and it could be months before another trial date became available. Also, Reiter was Ben's third lawyer. Judges, she explained, frowned on clients who bounced from lawyer to lawyer. Retaining yet another might prejudice Ben's case. Even if he had legitimate reasons for having switched lawyers, from the bench he'd simply be branded a crazy client. (Zaldin had already tried to use this factor against Ben. In one affidavit Terry had referred to his having "switched lawyers again" to his third lawyer.) Anyway, Ben couldn't have come up with another retainer. The deciding factor, however, was that we all believed the trial would be the end of the road. And so, unhappy as he was, Ben decided to stay with Reiter until the trial was over and the case closed.

What with private investigators and hustler boyfriends, Ben and I felt as if we were living a cheesy movie of the week. Our only salvation was black humour and each other. We now referred to Ben's place as the Expensive Luxury Apartment. "Where should we stay tonight?" I'd ask. "My place or the Expensive Luxury Apartment?" Or, punch drunk from stress, Ben would do a hilariously unflattering impersonation of one of the lawyers or judges, and I'd double over in laughter.

Whenever someone asked him how things were going, he had a stock response: "Couldn't be better," he'd say facetiously. But when people sensed the dark irony in his tone, he'd always try to put them at their ease with a quip. "Just don't press me for details!" he'd add, touching their arm and smiling.

Then there were those who knew that Ben and Terry were in court but had no idea what being in court actually meant and wanted to make *him* feel better. They offered platitudes. They were the ones who reminded me of myself in the beginning. "Don't worry," they'd say. "It will be over soon ... everything will work out."

"Sure," Ben would answer drily. "That's what they told Helmut Buxbaum." And they would always laugh at his black joke, but it made them uncomfortable, too, just as I'd drawn back uneasily when he'd first told it to me. It struck me how little I knew then. I'd assumed he was just another disgruntled husband making a snide ex-wife crack.

On the days we were without our kids, we'd pick up Chinese and a video and repair to my place or the Expensive Luxury Apartment, unplug the phone, crawl into bed, eat from cartons with chopsticks, and disappear into the oblivion of *When Harry Met Sally* or the Woody Allen canon. Or sometimes Judy would come downstairs in bathrobe and slippers and she'd say, "Hey, this is just like *Kate and Allie*," and Ben would serve us tea at his mother's patio table with the hideous plastic tablecloth, and Judy and I would yack away and Ben would sit between us like a smiling Buddha, going through his mail. Every now and then he'd read aloud some item from the Holy Blossom Temple bulletin, and I'd look at Judy and say, "How the hell did I end up with a guy who eats from a plastic tablecloth and reads aloud from the temple bulletin?" We'd giggle and, for five minutes, we'd forget.

It was Ben's fortieth birthday that October, which was something else he was trying to forget. But I refused to allow the occasion to pass without marking it in a celebratory way, even though I knew the only way he'd ever get through it was with humour. And so, one weekend that summer, we lay on a raft at our friends' cottage in Georgian Bay and dreamt up the invitation:

Dear Friend,

As you know Ben Gordon is going through a filthy divorce. He is being slaughtered and becoming an endangered species. He is also balding, overweight and now he's turning 40. Needless to say, he's in pretty rough shape. At such a difficult time, he needs friends around him. He needs you – your love, your support, your encouragement. But most of all he needs ...

CASH!

If you love this planet ... please, SAVE BEN GORDON.

Later we designed the invitations to look as if guests were being invited to a fundraiser, but on the front was a funny photograph of Ben looking like an oversized camper, in a T-shirt, flowered shorts, and sneakers, with a rolled towel under one arm and staring at the camera with his classic droll look. Inside, another photo – below the word "CASH!" – showed him smiling broadly with a mischievous glint in his eye.

As a joke, guests were invited to make a pledge to the Save Ben Gordon Fund. All they had to do was tick off the appropriate contribution: Fairweather Friend of Ben Gordon ($10), True Friend ($500), Asslicker Friend ($1,000) and The Full Corporate Sponsorship. That option involved a $5,000 donation but came with "full partnership in the law firm of Stickem & Bleedem." Our friends reported that they'd cried with laughter when they'd received the invitation, which was precisely the point of the exercise, and this cheered us both immeasurably.

We held the bash at the Squeeze Club, a Queen Street restaurant-cum-pool-hall. Ben pulled his baseball cap low on his forehead and played his harmonica on the street out front. Thinking he was just another street busker, a few guests tossed loose change into his hat on the way inside. A video of his less illustrious performances from B-movie tax-shelter days ran on an endless loop, speeches were made, and his former writing partner flew in from Los Angeles to do the roast. I'd known him for years, too, and I remember him wisecracking, "I thought Wendy was pretty hip until someone asked her, 'How'd you like to go out with a balding, overweight Jewish shoe salesman going through a bad divorce?' and she said, 'Yeah, sounds great!'" Everyone laughed and I looked over at Ben and saw his face all lit up, and I cherished that moment in the middle of a nightmare.

He had blinding stress headaches. He'd gobble 222s and fall asleep on the couch in mid-sentence. Or his mind would go blank, as if rebelling at the burdens it was being asked to carry. Nights I stayed, I'd turn over sleepily beside him at 3:00 in the morning and he'd be lying there, eyes wide open. Or he wouldn't be there at all, but padding anxiously around the apartment.

By that fall, the litigation had turned into a voracious beast that had moved into our lives and demanded to be fed every day. Doubtful of Reiter's ability to present Ben's case in a cogent manner, we spent hours poring over documents and preparing notes Ben wanted him to review for trial. Between his various jobs, he continued to drive back and forth to the courthouse and meet with his accountant in an effort to respond to Zaldin's seemingly boundless demands for documentation.

We also struggled to cope with problems that were cropping up, with increasing frequency, with the kids. One night I listened outside their bedroom door as Ben put the girls to bed. Gingerly, he broached the subject of why he thought they needed to be cared for by a mom and a dad who loved them. Zoe interrupted him: "Mommy says it's not so bad if we only see you sometimes, Daddy, because some kids never get to see their daddies, but Mommy thinks we should see you, so she's letting us."

I could feel Ben struggling to contain anger, searching for the words to answer Zoe. But before he was ready, she lashed out: "Why are you taking our money, Daddy? Mommy told us you stole it all from us and gave it to the lawyers."

Outside in the hall, it was now my turn to repress the urge to scream incoherently at a six-year-old child who I knew, in some distant recess of my rational mind, was only the messenger.

CHAPTER SIX

THE TRIAL

October–November 1991

The divorce trial was now scheduled to begin on October 29. The judge had to rule on every issue except the house. Ben later learned that Reiter had misinformed him when he'd said they could not do anything about Terry's appeal on the house for six months; in fact, Ben might have been able to speed up the process. In any event, it took four months to put the weighty judicial matter of whether one couple's matrimonial home should be sold before Chief Justice Charles Dubin and a panel of two other judges at the Ontario Court of Appeal, and the judges had agreed to expedite the matter. A hearing date was set for November.

In advance of the divorce trial, Ben and Terry exchanged Rule 49 offers to settle. Rule 49 (of the Rules of Civil Procedure, the lawyer's bible of courtroom practices) established the parameters judges had to follow when awarding costs. Judges weren't permitted to see settlement offers until after they'd ruled. If a party had made a pre-trial offer that matched or bettered the court's award, that party could argue later for solicitor/client costs. In theory, Rule 49 was meant to deter litigants who proceeded with an unreasonable claim. If they'd refused a fair offer and forced an unnecessary court action, not only could they lose but they could also be hit with the full amount of their opponent's legal bill. However, because awards normally covered only a portion of the costs and judges rarely made costs awards in matrimonial disputes, a spouse who refused to negotiate fairly and forced the other to incur staggering legal bills was rarely held accountable.

Terry offered to accept Butkowsky's recommendations with "no mention of who has custody and who has access," and no mediator/arbitrator. Ben proposed joint custody, fifty-fifty residency, and a court-appointed mediator/ arbitrator if they couldn't agree on a professional. A year after agreeing to support Butkowsky's recommendations, then suing over their interpretation, Terry was offering to accept them again. However, Zaldin's wording made it clear that one parent would have custody and the other access. Ben said no thanks.

By then Ben believed that Zaldin's strategy was to keep custody as ambiguous as possible, so he'd have plenty of leeway to interpret the recommendations as Terry wished. But how was more ambiguity around custody supposed to help his children? Likewise turfing the mediator/arbitrator. As long as custody remained ill-defined and nobody was monitoring them, Terry could do whatever she pleased. Although Ben was disgusted at how an assessor on whose recommendations the court regularly relied had handled their case (in addition to his litany of complaints about the assessment, Ben said Butkowsky had never arbitrated their disputes or kept his promise to review the recommendations), Ben was still convinced they needed a strong authority to govern their arrangement. (Unlike the mediator Mario Bartoletti, who Ben had mistakenly assumed would also arbitrate, Butkowsky had been hired to both mediate and arbitrate, according to his own recommendation.)

On the money side, Terry was offering to settle for $1,500 a month in child support, plus the money Ben owed her in back support payments. Her offer didn't address how they'd pay for the kids' extras. Ben offered to split those expenses and pay Terry $500 a month. If the kids divided their time equally between them they'd have equal expenses. Ben intended the $500 to compensate Terry for the disparity in their incomes.

Terry offered to list the house for sale immediately, but she had two conditions: first, that they'd pay $35,000 off the top to her family before splitting the proceeds. Terry was claiming her parents and grandmother had loaned them $20,000 and $15,000 respectively towards the purchase and renovation of their house. Her grandmother having recently died, she wanted $15,000 paid to her estate. The second condition was that Ben pay the $7,100 in realty taxes she'd let mount since he'd left the house.

Ben offered to divide the house proceeds equally, each of them paying off debts to family members, "if such [debt] exists." According to Ben,

Terry's parents and grandmother had given them some money towards their reno, and Morris Nusyna had insisted that they sign a promissory note. But Ben's dad had been considerably more generous to them over the years, on one occasion buying Terry a fur coat she wanted and on another helping pay a substantial bill for her taxes. His dad hadn't asked for promissory notes. Nor did Ben think for a second that Terry's grandma had intended the gift as a loan or that she or the Nusynas would ask Terry to repay the money. Terry's refusal to sell their house and the court's indifference to her behaviour had cost him thousands in lost equity and legal fees. And having supported Terry while she hoarded her income to hire a lawyer, he was in no mood to assume any more of her "debts." Given the process, the only defence he could see was for him to claim the money his father had given them – towards their home, Terry's taxes, and other expenses – as debts as well.

Once the house sold, the court would calculate an equalization payment from one spouse to the other, reflecting an equitable division of the increase in net value of the assets the couple accumulated while married. If the house sold immediately, assuming equal division of the proceeds, they'd each net approximately $283,000. Of Ben's share Terry wanted $90,000 as an equalization payment. Ben considered her demands ridiculous and offered to roll over $48,000 from his RRSP or to pay the cash equivalent.

Couples had to split belongings they'd accumulated during their marriage but were allowed by law to keep whatever they'd brought into the marriage or had received as gifts or inheritances during that period. Terry owned a diamond ring from her first marriage and a fur coat from her second. Most of their furniture belonged to Ben before he met Terry. He proposed divvying their possessions in accordance with the law; Terry wanted to keep hers and split Ben's.

In two years, Terry's attitude hadn't changed. But after two years of fighting a war of attrition in an adversarial system, Ben had changed. Two years in the trenches had turned him from a conciliator who'd done everything possible to avoid a fight into a hardened antagonist wary of being played for the fool and taken again. The "loan" claims were a perfect example of how the process not only encouraged a tit-for-tat mentality but demanded it since, if one side made a claim that remained uncontraverted, the other party would almost certainly wind up in a lose-lose position.

Because the court tended to grease the squeaky wheel, as opposed to examining claims on their merits and dismissing the outrageous ones, lawyers generally took the view that clients should make claims. That meant the other spouse had to counterclaim in self-defence, just to stay even. A spouse who didn't try to even the score could suffer serious losses.

Hundreds of thousands of dollars later, however, his reason for refusing to walk away from the fight remained unchanged. A year ago Ben had supported Butkowsky's parenting plan because he believed that supporting recommendations already in place was better for the kids than fighting in court to change them. Now he believed that only a trial would finally settle the issue and only a court order would protect him and the kids from Terry's behaviour in the future. He wouldn't settle until he had the words "joint custody" on paper. He wanted his day in court.

Five judges, two masters, and one assessor had handled his case so far, but no single authority had been told the whole story. Finally, a trial judge would hear it all. Ben would have to endure a few days of gut-wrenching embarrassment, but then the judge would rule and they would all have to live with his decisions. The detestable legal manoeuvring would be over, and they would finally have closure.

Ben didn't picture a television-style criminal trial with a prosecutor and defence lawyers jumping up and down arguing technicalities. In his fantasy, the trial unfolded in an orderly manner, with a wise judge listening carefully to both sides of the story, asking pertinent questions, and uncovering the truth. He imagined a character like Judge Hardy in the old Andy Hardy movies, a kindly, decent gentleman who'd hear the evidence, call everyone into his chambers, talk some sense into the parties, then return to court and give his considered judgment. No doubt some of his decisions they'd like and some they wouldn't, but they'd be obliged to abide by his ruling. Ignoring a court order would carry consequences.

Reiter had been uncharacteristically neutral on the subject of Justice Joseph Potts, the trial judge they'd drawn. Beyond divulging a few personal details, Reiter would say only that Ben could have done worse. The remark was unsettling, but Justice Potts had experience in family court and was the father of a large family himself. Ben assumed he'd have encountered other fathers like him, and that any judge charged with the Solomon-like responsibility of making a ruling on child custody would want to hear as much evidence as possible to determine the character of both parents before making any decision. The evidence was the one thing he felt confident about.

If I didn't picture Judge Hardy, I did imagine an astute judge reviewing the evidence and making the most sensible decision for the children. I knew, however, that all the evidence in the world was useless if a lawyer was ineffective at presenting it, and on that score I had many worries. I knew Reiter could easily try the patience of any judge forced to listen to his bluster. And I feared that his monumental ego and need to engage in a game of oneupmanship with Zaldin would get in the way of his arguing Ben's case clearly and forcefully. Still, I kept my misgivings to myself. We'd sought advice and made a judgment call, and, for better or worse, Ben had decided to stay with him through trial. I didn't think it productive to start second-guessing that decision now.

When I'd met Ben I'd been sceptical of his story and inclined to give Terry the benefit of my doubt. But I was sceptical no longer. In my view, Terry had no credibility. She'd lied, shown utter contempt for the court process, done everything in her power to destroy Ben's relationship with his daughters, and used them to trade for dollars. I was aware of the odds Ben faced as a father in that system. I was also aware how well Zaldin's cunning strategy had worked for Terry. Still, it was incomprehensible to me that any judge who knew the facts could possibly decide it was in their best interests to award sole custody to a mother who'd behaved as she had – especially with a father like Ben on the scene. Nor could I imagine him ruling based on biased, decades-out-of-date assumptions about parenting roles and the inviolate mother-child bond, particularly in a case where the evidence demonstrated beyond a shadow of a doubt that those assumptions were ridiculous.

I also believed the judge would see through Zaldin's tactical ploys, which I regarded as immoral. Instead of helping to illuminate the truth and resolve a conflict, Zaldin had used the courtroom rules and procedures to do exactly the opposite. Law was supposed to be a civilized gentleman's game, but Zaldin was an instigator, a bully. His correspondence was inflammatory. He made every issue a do-or-die confrontation. He delayed, equivocated, stonewalled, ambushed, withheld Terry's documentation but made boundless demands for Ben's. He looked for ways to incite skirmishes and exacerbate the situation rather than resolve it. If there was an ember of disagreement, he threw gasoline on it. His strategy was to wear Ben down emotionally and financially so that he would be forced to capitulate. That strategy had been highly effective for Terry. But how Zaldin's tactics could possibly be viewed as acceptable conduct for a family lawyer or helpful to a family in turmoil, I did not know, and I couldn't imagine a judge charged with the task of protecting those children rewarding such unscrupulous behaviour.

I had come to detest this barbaric process that made combatants of divorcing parents. In the end – if it ever came – someone was going to "win" two children, and someone was going to "lose" them, and it sickened me that there had to be a contest at all, let alone that the contest was rigged and the winner took everything. I was affronted by the injustice of a father being forced to fight for the right to parent while a mother's was assumed by virtue of her ovaries. I was outraged by the scandalous reality that a decent parent who desperately wanted to protect his children could be forced to the brink of bankruptcy just to dissolve his marriage and remain a presence in his children's lives. But what most disgusted me was that whoever "won" depended, in large measure, on who had the deepest pockets, the cagiest lawyer, and the will to fight dirty.

This was not a productive or civilized way of helping a traumatized family through divorce, or a remedy in the best interests of the children. This was a corrupt, sadistic process that destroyed lives. This was war and, in self-defence, it had turned a forgiving, conciliatory man into a warrior. I detested the plotting, the strategizing, the fake civility of the courtroom, the hollow pretence of phrases like "worthy opponent" and "learned friend," the hypocritical obfuscations I heard spill from lawyers' mouths. What did any of it have to do, I wondered, with two shell-shocked little girls who called from school with stomachaches? But I couldn't allow myself to go down that road. Instead, like Ben, I told myself we just had to hang on a little while longer.

Ben was worried he wouldn't be able to tell his story and wished Reiter had prepared him. He'd have felt calmer if he'd known what to anticipate. Typically, lawyers spend many hours readying clients to testify, but whenever he'd asked, Reiter had brushed him off with a "Don't worry" and told him just to tell the truth and be himself and answer the questions without giving Zaldin any more information than he asked for. It was the sort of general last-minute advice a lawyer might give his client en route to the courtroom after thorough preparation beforehand.

When Ben was emotional, he tended to lose focus and ramble. Where should he begin? What should he emphasize? What should he leave out? He was nervous, too, about the prospect of having to talk about himself so publicly. Like many actors, he was comfortable playing a role for the camera but shy and uncomfortable in his own skin, inclined to tell a joke to deflect attention from himself. He'd always been introspective, but because of the upheaval in his life, the therapy he'd had, the assessment process, and the counsel of friends, he'd undergone a period of rigorous self-examination. He'd thought intensely about his childhood, about how he'd been parented, about the kind of parent he was. He was emotionally raw, and now he faced a troubling dilemma. Should he open himself up on the stand, be brutally honest and forthcoming, reveal himself, warts and all? Should he say, "This is who I am. I've told you the best and worst of me. I did my best. I love my kids. Please provide for them in a fair and honest way." It was his nature to be open and real, but he was so vulnerable he knew he'd probably break down on the stand.

Or was that too dangerous? Should he just keep his wits about him and play the game, anticipate where Zaldin was going and head him off, making sure to avoid any self-critical admissions for the lawyer to twist and use against him? If he calculated every word, built himself up, said "I'm the greatest, I deserve everything," he feared he'd come across exactly the way Zaldin and Terry were trying to portray him: as a self-serving aggressor who wanted joint custody only to reduce his child support payments, to punish and control his ex-wife.

He was clever enough to be calculating. But it wasn't in his nature to be calculating about matters of the heart, certainly not about his love for his children and his longing to continue parenting them, and it angered him to be in a forum that forced him to be. That's why the Judge Hardy fantasy was so compelling. In the movies, the judge and Andy would have a conversation over tea, and Andy would reveal all his insecurities, and the judge would say, "Now, now Andy ..." Then he'd give him some sage advice, and the two of them would have an honest, human exchange, and everything would turn out fine. He knew his fantasy was hopelessly naive. Still, on some primal level, it was the scenario he wished for.

■ ■ ■

Reiter had lined up several witnesses: Ben's father, on the subject of the money he'd given the couple towards their house renovation; Judith Beaman, about the deal she claimed that she and Zaldin had struck to sell the house; John Stransman, who'd witnessed the incident with Terry and the kids at the consecration ceremony. Reiter also intended to call Brenda Spiegler, the family friend and neuropsychologist; she'd testify about Ben's parenting and relationship with the girls. Zaldin intended to call Terry's parents "to prove the debt owing to them." He also planned to call Butkowsky.

This was a terrible worry. Butkowsky had a tremendous amount of power to influence the outcome on custody, but suddenly Ben had no idea what he would say on the stand. If Zaldin was calling him as a witness, though, and Terry was paying him to testify, Ben didn't like his chances. The week before the trial, Reiter wrote Zaldin: the assessor had assured him he intended to stand by his recommendations, so he'd simply file his report as evidence. "I had not thought that Dr. Butkowsky wished to add anything, but if you feel that he would, please feel free to call him."

Ben believed by then that the process made it most expedient for assessors to tell the court what the court liked to hear. Assessors whose recommendations were predictably conventional, didn't rock the boat or fly in the face of deeply entrenched judicial assumptions about the best custodial arrangements for children were likelier to be assessors the court would want to hear from again. And what the court liked to hear was that mothers should have custody and fathers should have access.

A predictable opinion also ensured that lawyers would recommend an assessor again. Even though the client paid the bill, and his right to parent his children hung on what the assessor recommended, the client had no status in the equation. He was just a file, and files came and went. If the assessor wanted repeat business, he had to develop a relationship with the middlemen. (Later, one of Butkowsky's former clients told me the assessor had bragged to him that whenever business got slow, he just called up a few lawyers and took them to lunch.) Since lawyers recommended assessors to the court, viewed strictly from a business perspective the assessor's first allegiance was to them. In other words, a professional who wished to develop a practice doing assessments was wise not to bite the hand that fed him. And it fed him well: an assessor completing only two thirty-hour assessments a month at Butkowsky's $6,000 rate could earn $144,000 a year.

Just as an assessor who made what the court viewed as controversial recommendations wouldn't stay in business long, neither would one who admitted he made mistakes. Since judges were skittish about ruling on custody and preferred to rely on expert opinions, they had to feel confident about the experts on whom they relied. An assessor who admitted he'd made an error would lose the court's confidence. An admission of fallibility was not going to advance his career.

A day or two before the trial, sitting in Reiter's office, Ben pressed his lawyer to call Butkowsky and ask him what he intended to say in court. After putting down the phone, Reiter reported that the assessor was suddenly being evasive. Reiter feared he was no longer committed to his own recommendations and, as Ben recalls Reiter's words, had "gone over to the other side." Butkowsky had promised to review the recommendations and had led Ben to believe that if they weren't working after a year, he'd address Ben's concerns. Now it looked as if the assessor was going to echo the theme that ran through Terry's affidavits and do exactly what he believed Zaldin and Terry had been plotting all along: testify that the parties couldn't communicate well, and therefore one parent had to have custody. Only a couple of days to the trial and Butkowsky had turned into a loose cannon. But his report was the only ground Ben had to stand on for joint custody. After all he'd endured, he suddenly found himself in danger of losing the only thing he'd ever truly cared about.

Reiter said they had to rethink their strategy. They had to attempt to "knock out" Butkowsky as the expert witness. If Reiter could convince the judge to dump Butkowsky, Ben figured that the judge would hear testimony from him and Terry and other witnesses, then the lawyers would make their arguments, and the judge would decide based on all the evidence.

It was the eleventh hour but, tactically, they had a reason to discredit the assessor's report: it was out of date. The court liked to have the most up-to-date information on which to base its rulings. Butkowsky had conducted his investigations while the family was living in a stage of siege. Since then a year had passed, Ben had established a secure home base for the kids and a stable relationship with a woman they liked, she had a daughter, and they were creating a blended family. In other words, while Zaldin had been busily delaying to create a new status quo to favour Terry, the tables had turned and the actual new status quo put Ben in a more advantageous position to argue for joint custody.

■ ■ ■

Tuesday, October 29, 1991: Ben and I waited in Courtroom 38. The trial was to have begun at 10 o'clock, but as usual, proceedings were late starting. I sat on a bench, waiting. Unable to sit still, Ben tried to take his mind off matters by shooting the breeze with the court reporter and the clerks. He'd been in court so often that the clerks knew him well. They were mostly war vets and retirees, regular Joes. They seemed to empathize with his situation and tried to put him at ease. They appeared a little bored with their jobs, maybe, but Ben related to them more easily than to the lawyers who strode the halls officiously with their expensive briefcases, well-cut suits, and airs of self-importance.

We knew many of the lawyers we saw in the halls but had little in common with them and no desire to chit-chat. For the most part, they seemed oblivious to the fear and worry etched on their clients' faces. They broke stride now and then to gossip and joke with their colleagues, but didn't seem to notice or care how offensive clients found their collegial jocularity in that setting. As for the judges, they seemed powerful, alien, and remote. You didn't chat with them.

It was almost 11:00. Zaldin was leafing through some papers at the counsel's table. Terry sat behind him. No one had come to hold her hand, not her mother or sister, not a girlfriend, not Randolph Steepe. Ben noticed the coat of arms with a unicorn, lion, and various shields hanging on the wall above the judge's bench. He knew the pageantry was supposed to inspire a sense of reverence for tradition, but he found the archaic figures silly. He'd had the same feeling watching Reiter dress for court. He was supposed to find the sight of a lawyer in his robes majestic, but as he'd watched that squat little man primping for officialdom in the basement robing room, all he felt was detachment and a sense of how little the pomp and ceremony had to do with him or his reason for being there. Despite everything, though, he still retained a heightened sense of expectation for the process about to unfold, an archetypal longing for justice.

At 11:27 a.m. the registrar called "All rise!" and Justice Joseph Potts entered the courtroom. The trial could not get under way immediately. The first order of business was a motion from Zaldin. Zaldin said Ben was behind on his child support payments. He asked the judge to throw Ben's case out of court.

The judge dismissed his motion. It would be a "travesty of justice" to delay the trial any longer, he said. If Mr. Gordon was indeed the "scoundrel" Zaldin was portraying him to be, then it would come out in the evidence.

Court resumed at 3:08 after a two-and-a-half-hour lunch recess. That was when Zaldin announced that Terry was abandoning her appeal on the sale of the home.

Ben and I snapped to attention. Zaldin was a professional dissembler paid to argue the most expedient position for his client. What was he up to now?

"It is her position ... My Lord," he said, "that she was not content that the house be sold ... so soon after the separation for a number of reasons, the two major ones being these: a) the children were unsettled at the time, but they're doing much better now, and she sees no reason why the house should not be sold, and, b) the husband never agreed ... on what he might properly pay for child support; she could never know, at the time ... whether or not the children were going to be supported, and you will see ... evidence that those two issues were intertwined in settlement discussions between myself and previous counsel." But now Zaldin said the situation had changed.

In December Zaldin had argued the children were doing well. In February he'd argued they were suffering. In April he'd argued that making them move would be contrary to their best interests. (At her cross-examination in July Terry had told Reiter that the children were "progressively getting a little better all the time" but had to remain in that house for "stability" and she didn't feel it was "a good time to uproot the children." She admitted that no professional had ever expressed that view: she'd based it on her family's opinion and her own "inner voice.") Now Zaldin was telling the court the children were doing much better and his client saw no reason the home shouldn't be sold.

I was suspicious of this latest bafflegab. I did not believe Zaldin's move had anything remotely to do with the children. I believed he'd advised his client to abandon her appeal because he'd played that card as far as he could. I had no doubt he'd find other ways to manipulate the truth, but on that issue, it was time to fold.

Following Zaldin's announcement, the lawyers argued at length about procedural matters. Zaldin's motion and the legal wrangling consumed a great deal of the day. Ben didn't take the stand until 4 o'clock and he testified for twenty-five minutes.

Before Ben began, Zaldin asked anyone who might be a witness to leave the courtroom. The judge said the same, so I left. What little I'd seen in court that day was disturbing. I'd hoped for a judge who'd be fiercely attentive to the evidence. But as the lawyers bickered and Justice Potts sputtered in exasperation, his flushed cheeks turning crimson as he lost his place and his temper, I feared that what this judge wanted most was to flee that courtroom, escape these two insufferable lawyers and their two crazy clients, and scratch this dog case from his list as quickly as possible.

The registrar's record for Wednesday, October 30, shows that court opened at 11:34 a.m. Ben testified. Zaldin frequently interrupted on a number of matters. Court recessed for two hours. The lawyers argued. After approximately three hours in session, court adjourned at 4:30 p.m.

On Thursday, Zaldin wrote to Reiter asking for documentation corroborating Ben's RRSPs, ACTRA pension, and tax shelter. The next day Reiter forwarded most of the documents, promising that Sheldon Derrick, Ben's accountant, would fax the rest, and advising that he might have to call Derrick as a witness to explain Ben's tax shelter to the court.

The lawyers were still sniping at each other. In another letter on the 31st, Zaldin wrote: "The box of documents which Mrs. Nusyna Gordon brought with her to discovery (and which you didn't inspect at that time) is, of course *still* available to you for inspection at our office at your convenience upon reasonable notice."

"As to the 'box brought along by [Mrs. Gordon] to discovery'," Reiter parried the next day, "a transcript of proceedings at discovery will clarify that, I think, sufficiently for His Lordship."

Reiter asked for Terry's grandmother's bankbook and cable television bills. Terry was claiming that Ben's payments of Fanny Applebaum's cable television bills were made in lieu of interest payments on the $15,000 "loan" her late grandmother had made to them. Ben said that was absurd: Terry's grandmother had given them the money as a gift, and she would never have charged interest. He'd paid her bills because he felt it was the least he could do by way of expressing gratitude for her gift and so that she wouldn't have to worry about paying them or having her service disconnected when she went to Florida every winter.

At the trial Zaldin produced a note to support Terry's claim. It read:

To the Court:
Re $15,000 loan

This letter will confirm that I loaned Ben & Terry Gordon $15,000 on or about January 31, 1984 towards their house purchase or renovation.

This was payable upon request.

The note was dated June 20, 1991, written in Terry's mother's hand, and signed by her grandmother in a childlike scrawl. Later that summer, Terry's grandmother had died.

Ben had told me often of the warm relationship he'd had with Terry's grandma. He admired her character and was deeply proud of the fact that she'd told him many times she loved him "like blood." He didn't believe that, on her deathbed, Fanny Applebaum had said, "I want my $15,000 back." The thought of Terry or her mother going to a dying woman to extract her signature for such an avaricious purpose turned his stomach. However, when Zaldin showed Justice Potts his evidence, Ben said, the judge handed it back to the lawyer dismissively and said he wasn't going to consider some piece of paper that wasn't even witnessed.

■ ■ ■

After the second day of the trial, on Wednesday, Justice Potts adjourned until after the weekend. Thursday was Hallowe'en and Ben had the girls that night. The weekend before he'd taken them shopping for costumes; both planned to dress up as witches. Zoe had selected a huge black hat, cape, and hideous wart-covered hooked rubber nose. Deja chose a black wig with ghostly white strands.

After court that day, Terry had called to say the kids needed their costumes for a school party the next day, and that evening she dropped by Ben's to collect them. It struck me how even in the midst of a custody trial, cooperative parenting was possible – if both parents cooperated. It also struck me that Terry was generally willing to cooperate only when it suited her – as in this case, when she needed something from Ben – and as long as she did not have to be inconvenienced or pay the bills. On Thursday Ben picked up the kids at school and took them trick-or-treating. On Friday, free of kids for that weekend and desperate to decompress before the trial resumed, Ben and I drove up to our friends' farm near Cobourg.

Ben was worried that his testimony had meandered and his story wasn't coming across. He said that Reiter had asked broad, open-ended questions like "Tell me about your marriage," and Ben hadn't known where to begin or end. Then, with Zaldin constantly interrupting and the lawyers getting into catfights all the time, he'd lost his train of thought.

For peace of mind, he wanted us to prepare an outline of his story so the lawyer would have a road map to take Ben through his testimony in a precise, logical manner. We lit a fire, he paced back and forth spewing out the facts, and I sat typing furiously at my laptop. However, on Monday morning, when Ben handed Reiter our notes, he said the lawyer seemed insulted and brushed them aside.

Monday, November 4: court opened at 10:15 a.m. Ben testified, the lawyers made submissions and argued procedural matters. After four hours in session, court adjourned until Tuesday morning.

The paper was mounting. By the end of the third day of the trial, the lawyers had filed twenty-five exhibits: Ben and Terry's income tax returns; four financial statements; two exhibits taken at both parties' cross-examinations; both parties' net family property and equalization payment calculation statements; Master McBride's reasons on Terry's motion for interim child support; Ben's divorce decree from his first marriage; Fanny Applebaum's handwritten letter; a handwritten agreement, dated August 29, 1986, showing Terry and Ben Gordon as debtors to the Nusynas for $20,000; a letter dated October 28, 1991, from ACTRA regarding the value of Ben's RRSP at March 31, 1989; a file card about the Morris Nusyna and Fanny Applebaum loans; a scrap of paper about Fanny Applebaum's $15,000 loan and the Nusyna $20,000 loan; Fanny Applebaum's passbook, January 31, 1984; Ben Gordon's Rogers Cable account for Fanny Applebaum; two ACTRA letters dated November 1, 1991, about Ben Gordon's March 31, 1982, RRSP balance (and insurance policy); August 14, 1990, recommendations of Dr. Irwin Butkowsky; September 5 and 6, 1990, correspondence between Ronald Zaldin and Judith Beaman (three letters); March 31, 1991, Nesbitt Thomson statement regarding Terry's self-directed RSP; a $6,000 cheque from Ben to Terry, dated March 1, 1989; Jules Gordon's $10,000 cheque contribution to Ben and Terry's home, dated June 6, 1986.

Tuesday, November 5. Court did not resume at 10:00 as scheduled. Justice Potts, apparently irritated that the lawyers had made little effort to settle, shooed them away to give it a try. Discussions broke down. Court reconvened at 2:34 p.m. Zaldin began to cross-examine Ben. The registrar noted that the judge had to rule on a number of occasions due to "considerable interruption [by Reiter] throughout the examination." After two and a half hours in session, court was adjourned until 10:15 Wednesday morning.

During their negotiations in the courthouse cafeteria on Tuesday, Terry had proposed Butkowsky's recommendations, but without any mediator/arbitrator. If they couldn't agree on decisions, "the parent maintaining the primary residence of the children" would make them. Ben had proposed joint custody – either Sara's schedule or alternating weeks with each parent, vacations and holidays divided equally and alternating yearly, all major parenting decisions made as per Butkowsky's plan, and a mediator/arbitrator other than Butkowsky.

Ben had proposed Sara's schedule because Terry had flatly refused to consider alternating weeks, arguing that a whole week was too long for the children to be away from their mother. Ben believed (as did I) that the kids would cope just fine and that Terry was projecting her own insecurities, but he could only respond to her stated concerns and thought Sara's schedule might allay them. With this arrangement, five days was the longest stretch the girls had to be away from either parent. This idea was tagged the "5:2 plan" because every week the kids spent two weekdays with each parent and every two weeks they spent a five-day stretch with each.

Ben liked the schedule because he'd observed it working well for Sara. It was a vast improvement over Butkowsky's arrangement, and it would be easier for us to have a family life if all three kids were on the same schedule. (Under an alternating-weeks schedule, on the other hand, we would be able to spend some time with Sara only and other days with just Ben's daughters.) Ben had proposed the "5:2" schedule at the trial, but he'd been careful not to identify it as Sara's. We believed that any proposal enabling us to be a family would threaten Terry, and she'd automatically veto it. We also believed that Zaldin would accuse Ben of proposing the idea strictly for his own convenience, not for the children's good.

As it turned out, these concerns were irrelevant. Ben said the idea died before anyone bothered to consider it seriously. Because the arrangement was an unfamiliar one, everyone became confused about how it worked. He offered to draw the mechanics on paper to demonstrate its simplicity, but according to Ben, the judge, the lawyers, and Terry reacted as if he'd suggested the most complicated arrangement imaginable. Terry refused to consider exposing her children to such a schedule without an expert opinion, while Justice Potts pronounced it a crazy scheme and dismissed it out of hand. And that was that.

On Wednesday, November 6, court did not reconvene. It is unusual for a judge to recess in favour of settlement negotiations during a trial unless there is good reason to think a deal can be achieved, but Justice Potts sent the lawyers away a second time. It seemed as though he was just fed up with their bickering. Ben was furious. If he had to pay a lawyer $350 an hour, he didn't want to spend it engaging in more futile negotiations with Terry and Zaldin. The court was the last resort. If he and Terry – or Reiter and Zaldin, for that matter – could talk they wouldn't be there. He wanted the judge to hear evidence and decide. Wasn't that what judges were supposed to do?

They spent Wednesday and Thursday negotiating in the hall and cafeteria. Zaldin's associate, Clive Algie, counselled Terry. Ben's friend Mark

Anshan came to offer moral support. Ben found the negotiations frustrating and chaotic and the dynamic between Terry and himself tiresome and predictable: they'd engage for a while, then the talks would grow heated and break off. Terry would accuse him of doing this or that. Ben would say, "Okay, fine, I'm the biggest ass in the world. Think what you want of me, but we have these kids. What about Deja and Zoe?" Terry would say her back was against the wall, she didn't know what she was doing, she had to support herself. Ben would say, "Forget about the money. The court will look at our financial statements and decide. Let's worry about the kids." Terry would say she wouldn't discuss the kids until she knew how much money she was going to receive. Ben would ask whether she believed in joint custody. Terry wouldn't answer. Ben would get upset and walk away. After going around in circles like this for hours, they abandoned talks on custody and tried to settle the property issues.

Ben and Mark were sitting in the cafeteria when Zaldin approached and handed them a draft copy of minutes of settlement. Ben went out in the hall to look for Reiter. The document went back and forth. They dickered, made changes, then initialled the changes. In the end the document was virtually indecipherable with their chicken scratchings.

By Thursday afternoon they had succeeded in hammering out the following terms on property issues: the house would be sold according to Justice Walsh's order of April 1991, "except as to Master's involvement." For the first ninety-day listing period, Terry would choose the agent. If it hadn't sold, Ben would pick the agent for the next listing. They'd pay Terry's parents $20,000 off the top. From his share, Ben would owe Terry $35,000 as an equalization payment, but would retain $5,000 (the costs Terry had been ordered to pay for abandoning her appeal on the house). Terry would pay the back realty taxes on closing. Mark Anshan would handle the legals on the house sale and closing and they'd split his fee. (Anshan said he'd charge them only disbursements and a minimal fee for his services.) They'd each keep whatever possessions they'd owned before marrying or had received as gifts while married. The rest would be split. They would pay their own legal costs on the settled issues.

Ben was wary of any document drafted by Zaldin. He asked Reiter to review the wording closely. Were there any hidden traps? Would he finally get his belongings? Would the house go on the market right away? And what did it mean that it would be sold according to Justice Walsh's order "except as to Master's involvement"? He didn't want any loopholes left open for Zaldin to manipulate.

Reiter assured him the document was in order. It was standard for masters to deal with the minutiae; judges didn't get involved in "pots and pans" issues. He'd get his property. The house would go on the market immediately. Terry was willing to sign and Reiter pressed Ben to sign, too. He told him it was cheaper to settle than to litigate over the amounts in question, especially since his share of the Nusyna "debt" represented such a small portion of the money Ben would clear from the house sale. Signing would finalize all the issues except the parenting schedule.

Ben was reluctant to sign the minutes. Once again he believed he was being taken. It still rankled him to pay Terry's parents $20,000. He viewed a $30,000 equalization payment as grossly unfair, considering what Terry had cost him on the house. But if another $50,000 was what it took to give Terry a sense of financial security and the feeling she'd won, it would be worth it. It's only money, he sighed. He signed.

He was happiest about the house. Despite several hundred thousand dollars of lost equity, it was still worth a substantial amount of money. If it sold quickly he could clear his debts. But what truly elated him was the psychological impact he'd always believed that selling the home would have on their joint custody arrangement. Terry would have to move on with her life. At last the spell of that house would be broken.

■ ■ ■

On the weekend the lawyers hit the warpath again. "Your client's steadfast refusal to consider anything other than this recent '5 and 2' plan, is not in the best interests of the children," Zaldin wrote Reiter, "and Mr. Gordon's inflexible attitude on this point has not advanced matters any." Two days later Reiter retaliated with a three-page missive decrying Zaldin's latest avalanche of faxes and insisting that Ben had tried to compromise while "it was your client who took the inflexible and steadfast position."

Among the documents Zaldin had faxed to Reiter's office over the weekend was Terry's latest settlement offer: $958 a month, "one-half summer camp fees and orthodontic expense not covered by either party's orthodontic plan," Butkowsky's report, and, if they couldn't agree on an alternative, Butkowsky as mediator/arbitrator.

Terry had moved from asking for $2,500 monthly child support ($2,000 as an "interim" figure), to winning $958, to losing an appeal for more, to offering to take $1,500 the week before trial, to proposing $958 now. One possible explanation for Terry's willingness to settle for the $958 Master McBride had awarded her in February was that she'd been cross-examined since she'd won that amount. In a couple of days, Justice Potts would learn that she'd won it by filing false financial information. Suddenly her chances of retaining what she had seemed poor.

Significantly, too, although Terry had never liked the idea of having an overseer to help them resolve their difficulties (none of her settlement offers had proposed a mediator/arbitrator), her latest offer gave her the power to veto anyone other than Butkowsky. There was now a compelling reason for Terry to hang on to Butkowsky. If the court decided on joint custody, it would almost certainly appoint a mediator/arbitrator to govern the arrangement. However, the court would be reluctant to appoint someone unless both parties were happy with the choice, the logic being that the process would have little chance of succeeding otherwise, and Ben had already testified about his utter lack of faith in Butkowsky. But Butkowsky had given Terry a lot, and another authority the court appointed might give her less. Therefore, she'd be wise to try to settle that issue out of court by offering to keep Butkowsky on board, and retaining veto power over anyone else. That way she could stick with the devil she knew.

Tuesday, November 12: court opened at 2:41 p.m. The lawyers discussed mechanics for the sale of the home, then fought over Butkowsky. Reiter argued that the assessor's recommendations were outdated and that he'd failed miserably as a mediator/arbitrator. Zaldin fought to keep Butkowsky. They argued back and forth. Then the incomprehensible happened. Justice Potts refused to rule on custody recommendations that were a year old, decided he wanted more expert evidence, and ordered another assessment.

Reiter had never even hinted to Ben of the possibility of this turn of events when they'd talked about knocking out Butkowsky. In his worst nightmares, Ben had never imagined that the judge would refuse to judge and put them all through another assessment.

139

A million questions raced through his mind. What assessor would be thrust upon them now? How much time would another assessment consume? Who was to pay? Who'd monitor their joint custody arrangement in the meantime? How long would it take to get back to trial a second time? What if the status quo had changed by then? What if Terry was unhappy with the outcome and litigated over that assessment too? Did the court just keep ordering assessment after assessment?

He looked at the judge, searched his face for some indication he had an inkling about the consequences of his decision. The stress. The uncertainty. The cost, financially and emotionally. He looked at the lawyers, but neither gave the slightest indication that they considered the judge's decision to be unusual, surprising, or inappropriate in any way. The only people in that courtroom with horrified looks on their faces were he and Terry.

When Ben reported the events at the trial that day, I too was stunned by the court's callous indifference. But I didn't have the luxury of indulging my feelings. Before adjourning, Justice Potts had instructed the lawyers to return the next day with a list of candidates to conduct the new assessment. Ben had overnight to come up with a name.

Reiter had no suggestions. Ben called Susan Himel, the lawyer who'd recommended Ken Cole and Judith Beaman. Himel spoke highly of a child psychiatrist named Sol Goldstein. Ben remembered Cole mentioning Goldstein's name during the search for the first assessor. Goldstein too was considered a top name in the field. I knew him as the author of a book on divorced parenting, one that I'd read when David and I were in the process of splitting up. Reiter had heard of Goldstein but knew nothing of his reputation and couldn't advise whether he was the best person for this particular case.

Our priority was to find a professional astute enough to see through Terry's act and strong enough not to pander to her or be manipulated by Zaldin. Time was short and our alternatives were limited. Reiter called Goldstein. He was available. Then, saying he didn't know anybody else to suggest, Reiter advised putting the psychiatrist's name forward.

Wednesday, November 13: court opened at 10:37 a.m. According to the trial transcript, discussions eventually turned to orchestrating the new assessment.

"As far as you are concerned and your client, you are prepared to go along with the recommendations of the existing expert [Butkowsky]?" Justice Potts asked Zaldin. Zaldin confirmed that was his client's position.

The judge then stated Ben and Reiter's position: that the circumstances required an updated assessment by another expert. There followed some squabbling about who might or might not have changed his mind about Butkowsky, which Justice Potts eventually cut off, saying, "I made it clear that if either one of you had reservations about the existing expert, then the only answer for the best interests of the children was to have a brand new person doing an assessment. So now the question is whether you gentlemen have been able to agree upon a new assessor."

Zaldin had brought three curriculum vitae for the court's consideration. Reiter proposed Goldstein. He argued that Goldstein was a psychiatrist with psychoanalytic background, lived in the same neighbourhood as the litigants, was "of the same faith and social stratum, and understands the criteria," and had a conveniently located office. Zaldin objected. He'd heard that Goldstein took too long to do assessments. He told the court he was worried about delay.

Worried about delay, are you? thought Ben. He wondered how the man could look himself in the mirror every morning.

"I have heard quite the reverse from judges and lawyers," exclaimed Reiter. "I want it on paper, that is a calumny, said in a courtroom, he's free from prosecution, My Lord, but I want him to be responsible for that statement ... That is attacking a man's professional standing and reputation."

"May I go on, My Lord? ... I am just unable to work with Dr. Goldstein." Zaldin told the judge that Goldstein was chasing him for money that one of his former clients owed the assessor. He noted the judge had said he would not impose an assessor who was not trusted by one of the lawyers or litigants. On that basis, Zaldin said, "my client has reservations."

Potts replied, "I have to tell you quite frankly that I have only got the best interests of the children in mind. Because Dr. Goldstein may think you owe him money, or something like that, is absolutely and utterly irrelevant." He was "fully aware of Dr. Goldstein's competence" and of his "track record."

Zaldin cooled it for a moment and returned to his candidates: a social worker, a psychologist, and a psychiatrist. The judge preferred a psychiatrist;

in his words, a psychiatrist was "one jump ahead of a psychologist." Zaldin argued hard for his psychiatrist over Goldstein.

Reiter piped up that he had never used Goldstein on a case before. "I have met Dr. Goldstein once," said Reiter. "My client has never met him. I wanted a total stranger to my practice in the proceedings." He was trying to impress upon the judge that Goldstein was their pick not because they were confident he'd come up with the recommendation they wanted but because he was the best person for the job.

"On balance, it is a difficult choice," said the judge, "but I am familiar with Dr. Goldstein's handling of matters such as this and that judicial notice tips the balance in his favour." He appointed the psychiatrist to do a full assessment and make recommendations on the future parenting arrangements affecting "the best interests of the children."

Zaldin was not about to give up yet. He tried another tack. In case Goldstein couldn't complete the assessment on deadline, would Potts appoint his candidate in the alternative? "I don't want to . . . lose another two or three weeks," he said.

Justice Potts moved on and asked the lawyers for proposals on costs.

"The normal order [would be] for costs to be shared, subject to adjustment by the trial judge," said Zaldin. "I would normally make that suggestion to you."

Ben sensed where Zaldin was going and felt his heart pound.

"I don't want you to overreact to this, but my client hasn't received . . . any child support for five months, she is in extreme financial circumstances, she has to pay the mortgage, the unpaid tax and so on. I am asking, then . . . that the husband pay for the report, subject to readjustment by yourself. My client just doesn't have the money, because she hasn't been receiving anything . . . And if she can't pay Dr. Goldstein, he won't start."

Reiter went nuts. "The lady didn't pay Dr. Butkowsky for a year. She paid him for one and a half appointments, as I understand it. The grounds were poverty . . . She came before [Master McBride] in February of 1991 and said she was making $27,000 gross a year."

"I don't want to get into that," said the judge.

"What I'm getting at, Your Lordship – "

"What's your bottom line?" asked the judge.

"The parties – they are really in exactly the same position at the moment, at the very best for the lady – the worst position for Mr. Gordon in terms of the perception of the court. They are really equal. However reality is that she has the extreme advantage at the moment."

"What is your bottom line?"

"My bottom line is fifty-fifty," said Reiter, "and the court can ... adjust it later down the line. I'm really quite sick and tired of having to walk in here and for every time be told, not just here but everywhere how she doesn't have, she doesn't have, then the children, she's got two-thirds more income than she admits."

"To me, this one is very simple," replied the judge. "Mr. Zaldin is going to be surprised, I am agreeing with him. This assessment is really at your client's request."

"Yes, sir," said Reiter.

"And therefore ... I think your client should pay for the cost of the assessment, subject to being reviewed by me."

Justice Potts ordered Ben to pay for the assessment. He also ordered him to pay interim support payments of $750 monthly and $2,200 in back support, and he instructed him to continue paying for the kids' extras. Potts promised to review the allocation of expenses and Ben's allegations of Terry's financial misrepresentation, a review that Ben hoped would lead to a fairer division of ongoing responsibilities and some reimbursement for past inequities. The judge did not order Terry to pay for anything. Then he granted a divorce judgment, formally dissolving the marriage but leaving unresolved many of its legal repercussions. He adjourned the eight-day trial to await the results of the new assessment. His parting words were: "At least we've made some sense having regard to the best interests of the children, and that's all I really care about."

It had now been two and a half years since Ben and Terry had decided to divorce. Their home had yet to go on the market, their possessions had yet to be divided, and the issue of custody was back to square one.

CHAPTER SEVEN

ASSESSMENT AGAIN

November 1991–March 1992

IN the weeks following the trial that fall of 1991, all Ben and I could do to keep from losing our minds was to avoid looking too far down the road. We tried to tell ourselves we had cause for cautious optimism. At least Butkowsky was out of the picture. A new assessment might mean a more favourable outcome on custody and more time with the kids. And it was becoming increasingly obvious that we desperately needed more time with the kids. They were acting out more, especially Zoe, who was a porous little sponge for the white heat of the conflict, and whose nightmares and tantrums increased in direct proportion. Once when Ben sent her screaming and kicking to her room, I saw a rage so ferocious and profound in the clench of her jaw and the bulge of her eyes that it frightened me. But at least Zoe expressed her anger. Deja just shut down.

Meanwhile, our lives swerved from crisis to crisis. I had come to expect at least two or three disturbing incidents a week from Terry. There were the constant phone calls like the first I'd witnessed, with the shrieking on the other end. "You don't pay for anything, Ben, period. I've been supporting the kids. I had to pay for skates!" The hanging up, calling back, putting the kids on the phone to plead with Ben to pay for their lessons or lunch program, coaching from the sidelines, then blaming Ben for getting them upset. There were the disturbing remarks from the kids, whom Terry involved in every detail of the court conflict and who, more and more, were parroting their mother: Zoe telling Ben she knew he couldn't go on her field trip that day because he had court, Deja mouthing the Butkowsky assessment, "It's okay. You get to see us ten days during the holidays, and weekends and PD days. That's good enough." Deja told me, speaking of the furniture Terry had dispensed with when she met Ben and moved into his apartment, "My mom says my dad probably knew they'd split up when he married her and so he told my mom to get rid of her stuff." (When I asked Deja whether that seemed reasonable to her, she gave me a sheepish look, suggesting she sensed the accusation was absurd but feared being disloyal to her mother or believing she'd lie.) Then there was the day Zoe announced, "That night-light is Mommy's and she should have it back," or "Mommy can't even think about moving because she has too many stresses."

It seemed to me that Terry viewed the children as mirrored extensions of herself and that she was determined to keep them under her thumb lest they develop minds of their own. She parented through fear, guilt, and intimidation, so that the children were terrified to express their true feelings. She often operated subtly, professing motherly concern and sugar-coating her words to mask the clawing need in their subtext, which made it that much more difficult for the children to counter her manipulations. One day when I drove past Dewbourne with Deja, she remarked, "You know, when we're with my mom, she says that's when her friends ask her out. But when we're away, that's when she's home alone."

There was nothing to be done about Terry. There was no way to reason with her or appease her. She perceived any attempt Ben made to phone the kids, make arrangements for them, or share in their lives by attending a recital or school event as harassment and interference. Hers was a black-and-white universe that admitted none of the normal ambiguity to be found in human relationships. "You're not paying a penny. You're never with the kids. You don't have a clue about anything. If it weren't for me, nothing would get done." Pointing out that her accusations were absurd and lacked any basis in reality was a useless exercise.

It had become clear to me that Terry was deeply threatened not only by Ben's fathering of the girls and their obvious attachment to him but by the fact that they greatly looked forward to being with Sara and me, and our family and friends. Which was why I knew we were in for more trouble the day Terry called Deja – not Ben, as she should have – to say she wanted to rearrange the schedule so the three of them would be together on the same weekend that her sister and her niece, Alyssa, were together. "Then we won't

145

see Wendy and Sara," said Deja. "Lynne and Alyssa are our family!" declared Terry. Deja grew defiant and refused to budge. "So are Wendy and Sara," she said. "They're our family, too." Then she rolled her eyes and handed the phone to Zoe.

We weren't competing for the children's love, or seeking to interfere in their relationship with their mother. We were just trying, against the odds, to build a family life of our own. I feared that the more the children expressed their desire to be with us, the more Terry would step up her campaign to extinguish the bonds we shared.

Our fate was now in Sol Goldstein's hands. Once again, we could do nothing but wait.

■ ■ ■

On November 20, 1991, the house finally went on the market at $665,000. The listing described an "immaculate Lower Forest Hill Village family home, gracious principal rooms, stunning gourmet kitchen with walk-out to beautifully landscaped yard," a living room with fireplace, dining room, kitchen with built-in stove, microwave, and dishwasher, instant hot water, garburator, panelled family room with built-in bookcases and walkout to the yard, master bedroom with three-piece ensuite bath and walk-in double closet, three bedrooms in addition to the master, two more bathrooms, and a finished basement. Among the extras offered prospective buyers were window coverings, broadloom, an automatic garage door with remote control, underground sprinkler, cedar closet, Jacuzzi, recently done baths, decking, and landscaping. In the year and a half that Terry had been refusing to sell the house, its value had declined by almost half a million dollars.

In their settlement, Ben had conceded that Terry could select the real estate agents for the first listing period. Although he'd never heard of Barbara Consky and Richard Pinelli of Sadie Moranis Real Estate, he assumed they were Terry's friends and figured the process would go more smoothly if she felt secure with the agents. Now he discovered Terry had never heard of them either. Zaldin had suggested the pair.

The agents recommended market-testing the property at $665,000, then meeting two weeks later to reassess the price. After two weeks, they recommended reducing it. Their research showed that, in a rapidly declining market, only a significant reduction would fetch an offer. Terry refused to cooperate.

At the trial, Justice Potts had given Ben until the first of the new year to arrange financing so he could meet the latest financial burdens placed upon him by the court. He now had about $190,000 in debts and no further borrowing power. He applied for a line of credit at the bank. The only way he could secure a line of credit was by putting a second mortgage on his share of the house, using his equity as collateral. Because Terry was a co-owner, he needed her signature on the mortgage documents. Without her signature, Ben couldn't secure the mortgage or the line of credit. Without that, he couldn't pay Goldstein's $6,000 retainer. And without a retainer, Goldstein refused to begin the assessment. Terry wouldn't sign.

Despite having signed an agreement to divide their possessions, she also refused to commit to a date when Ben could enter their house. Although their settlement was to have finally resolved the house and property issues, and Justice Potts's order was to have initiated the assessment so custody could be resolved, Terry was now effectively obstructing the resolution of all three issues. Once again, she left Ben no option but court.

The week before Christmas, on December 18, Reiter brought a motion saying Terry had refused to enable the mortgaging, accept her chosen real estate agent's advice, or catalogue the house contents in anticipation of the release of Ben's belongings. He asked the court to let Ben put a $50,000 collateral second mortgage on his equity in the home, reduce its listing price from $665,000 to $599,000, and order the cataloguing of possessions.

Ben reviewed events in his sixth affidavit: at the trial his lawyer had explained why he needed the mortgage; he'd sought Terry's cooperation but "received no useful response" until his lawyer had threatened to take her back to court. Zaldin had then responded that Terry would sign and asked for mortgaging details to see if her title or liability would be affected. Reiter had provided the information that day and stressed urgency. Zaldin hadn't returned his calls. The court's deadline was only two weeks away, with Christmas intervening. Unless he could arrange the mortgage, he'd default on a court order, be unable to pay his debts or retain the assessor, and be "put to great disadvantage and embarrassment, if not rendered functionally insolvent."

As for the property issues, at the trial Ben had requested a time to catalogue the possessions but had heard nothing. With respect to the house, Ben included with his copious documentation the lawyers' correspondence and a letter from Richard Pinelli.

December 12, 1991

Dear Ben:

As per your request, I am summarizing the listing progress of your property at 24 Dewbourne Avenue.

When the listing was taken, both you and Terry were advised that the list price of $665,000 was somewhat high given that the property has the major locational problem of being only two doors in from Bathurst Street. But, because of a shortage of good available properties . . . it was worth testing the market response at that price; provided vendors and agents met within two weeks to evaluate the results. Both you and Terry agreed to do so.

You attended the meeting. Terry cancelled out and has not rescheduled, but did say that she is absolutely opposed to considering any price change. Her decision was made without benefit of any of the market feed-back discussed in the meeting.

At the meeting you stated that you understood and agreed with the recommendation to adjust the list price from $665,000 to $599,000 based on negative market response. You agreed that it is time critical to make this change, and that every day counts if you are to exploit your current competitive advantage (before we draw closer to January when more competition may come onto the market).

The economy is worrisome. Even with falling interest rates, it is very difficult to motivate buyers unless a home offers good perceived value. While we do not guarantee it, we feel that a $599,000 price is far more likely to generate offers.

Sources for the enclosed data are the Toronto Real Estate Board's statistical data base and the Board's publication entitled "House Price Trends". Comments regarding 24 Dewbourne were obtained from agents who showed it. They were asked about buyers' reactions to both the property and pricing. As well, a more general commentary was gleaned from the 38 agents who attended the agent open house.

Sincerely,
Richard Pinelli,
Sales Representative.
cc: Ms. Terry Nusyna
Mr. Moishe Reiter
Mr. Ronald Zaldin

Appended to Pinelli's letter were seventeen pages of documentation, including anecdotal comments from agents and potential buyers, data on the number and average price of MLS sales by district between 1987 and 1990, and a ten-page MLS summary of the selling prices of homes in the area. Overwhelmingly, the agents who'd been through the house remarked that they might credibly show the property only if it were listed under $600,000.

Terry contested the motion. She called Ben's motion to collect his belongings "abusive" and claimed to be "agreeable to the cataloguing." She'd allow the mortgage, but "what if Mr. Gordon defaults? I am subject then to foreclosure or Power of Sale proceedings. Mr. Gordon's track record on the interim support payments is abysmal and I am very fearful that the property will be sold out from under me if he defaults ... I have no funds to pay if he defaults." She wanted "appropriate safeguards," full indemnity, and a $10,000 holdback to ensure her child support payments. "If Mr. Gordon defaults *even once* [emphasis hers] under this new mortgage," Terry wanted the right to return to court immediately for an order declaring her sole owner of their home.

Justice Potts ordered the mortgage documents signed immediately. Ben was to assume all payments and indemnify Terry against any damages. Terry's signing of the mortgage application was to be kept confidential, as she had requested. If Ben defaulted on his child support payments, Terry could return to court on seventy-two hours' notice.

On the listing price, Terry opposed any reduction but presented no evidence to support her view. Instead she argued that the listing was only a month old, sales would naturally be slow over Christmas, and any "'panic'

149

reduction now will only lead to 'low-ball offers.'" She claimed two other agents had confirmed this opinion to her (Bruce Smith, of Bruce Smith Realty, the agent who'd appraised the house for $1.1 million in the summer of 1989; and Lynn Kay of Canada Trust Realty, who, according to Ben, was a friend of Terry's). According to Terry, Smith and Kay believed "the requested reduction would be 'disastrous at this time' ... especially because there have been many interested persons through the home." Without letters or affidavits, however, the agents' opinions were just hearsay.

"I am not aware of 'many interested persons' having been through [the] home," deposed Richard Pinelli in his affidavit for Ben's motion. According to Pinelli, "eleven prospects" had seen the house, and virtually all had rejected it because of its proximity to Bathurst Street or because it was greatly overpriced. In Forest Hill, thirty days was "more than enough time" to read the market on a given house. Protracted selling tended to diminish the price and the ability to sell a property. It would face steeper competition in January. The listing had been circulated to all members of the Toronto Real Estate Board; realtors had been invited to the agents' open house, and to show the property – and they "have reported back to us ... I am not aware of any showings by agents with Bruce Smith Realty or agents with Canada Trust Realty. Therefore I am not aware of where Terry ... Gordon could have got the information or the opinions referred to in her material. I am ... confused by the unwillingness of Terry Gordon to meet with us to discuss our selling efforts and possible revisions of selling strategy."

Pinelli concluded by reminding the court that since 1989 the house had "already dropped in value by approximately $435,000 ... not unusual in the current market," where the number of buyers prepared to commit to houses in the over-$500,000 range was "extremely limited. The number of houses that are being sold in distress conditions ... is proportionately sizeable. This is what is called a buyers market and hesitation, or unwillingness to face the realities of that buyers market, may well have a detrimental effect on the sale prospects of this property."

Justice Potts decided not to decide about the house price. He instructed that the cataloguing proceed but adjourned the part of Ben's motion related to the listing price and told the lawyers to resolve the matter.

Then Ben encountered another glitch: the bank wouldn't grant the mortgage unless the back realty taxes were paid up. But Terry wasn't obliged under the settlement to pay the taxes until the house sold, and she argued she couldn't afford to pay them sooner. Once again the mortgaging ground to a halt. And despite her sworn assurances, Terry refused to commit to a date when Ben could go back into the house. Over fifteen days in late December and early January, Reiter wrote Zaldin seven letters seeking Terry's cooperation to move these various matters forward. Zaldin's few replies contributed little to their resolution.

On Friday, December 27, Reiter wrote three letters on various aspects of the file. The first proposed a collaborative approach to the listing problem and suggested a couple of dates for Ben to complete the property inventory; the second suggested bringing in an outside accountant to help resolve other financial issues.

Reiter's third letter that day took up Ben's predicament as the deadline for making his court-ordered payments approached.

December 27, 1991

Dear Mr. Zaldin:
... As part of the Minutes of Settlement ... Terry Gordon had undertaken to pay all outstanding taxes on the residence.

Now it appears ... Terry Gordon has apparently not paid the taxes ... The mortgage lender will be unable to approve the advance of funds to Mr. Gordon in time for him to meet the January 1, 1992 deadline ...

This delay is virtually unavoidable, even if your client pays the outstanding taxes immediately. However, if she does not pay them immediately, the delay will be even greater and there is always the possibility that the mortgage lender will revoke its commitment ...

In addition, it would appear appropriate for us to agree on an extension of the January 1, 1992 deadline ... Failing agreement ... I will have no option but to bring the matter on before His Lordship ...

Yours very truly,
Moishe Reiter

December 30, 1991

Dear Mr. Reiter:
Further to your fax received at 2:07 p.m. today, I see no alternative but to extend the time for payment and there is no need to bring a Motion...

May I suggest that the issue of outstanding taxes of $7,100.00 be solved in the following manner, since my client has no monies to pay them at this time.

Mr. Gordon could borrow this additional amount ... and this amount (plus interest) would be deducted from the equalization payment he owes my client out of the net proceeds of sale of Dewbourne... I have spoken at some length in the last week to the listing agent who advised me that some other agent has an interested buyer and is being worked on to present an offer... within the next week, and we shall see where it goes from there...

Yours truly,
Ronald V. Zaldin

December 27, 1991

Dear Mr. Zaldin:
I have your Facsimile of December 30, 1991 and am extremely distressed by your suggestion.

If Mr. Gordon were now to seek to enlarge the borrowing, he would have to make a new Application and go through the entire process again, thus protracting the problem for at least 30 days. There is no assurance that the enlarged loan would be approved.

...If you will refer to the Financial Statements of the parties, you will note that Mr. Gordon has debts exceeding $150,000.00 ... In contrast, Mrs. Gordon has virtually no debt position and the taxes have and continue to be her responsibility...

To seek to place this burden on Mr. Gordon is, in the circumstances, to add the final straw to his burden. Your client will have to pay...

Thus far, at every turn, Mr. Gordon has been called on to come up with monies to pay the psychiatrist $6,000.00 in advance, to pay the children's camp, to pay a variety of other expenses, and to pay the support claimed by Mrs. Gordon for the children, purportedly out of real need. Of course there is talk of reallocation down the line, but there is no certainty when this will happen and to what extent. In any event, the well is dry ... Your client will have to meet her responsibilities.

As to the ... real estate sale ... I have heard nothing from Mr. Pinelli ... that he has changed his view about reducing the listing price. My concern is [that] the situation not be allowed to deteriorate further by reason of unnecessary delay.

I look forward to hearing from you.

Yours very truly,
Moishe Reiter

January 2, 1992

Dear Mr. Reiter:

Thank you for your letter backdated to December 27, but received in my office by fax at 1:59 p.m., Tuesday, December 31, 1991...

Because Mr. Gordon wants to mortgage *his* interest in the property for $50,000.00 to pay some of his debts (probably including some of your legal fees), does not impose on my client any acceleration of her obligation...

Further, you didn't even think to raise this with Mr. Justice Potts on December 19, 1991 when your Motion was heard and disposed of...

If the arrears are not paid and the January 1st payment is not made on time, I shall move before Mr. Justice Potts to strike out Mr. Gordon's claims ... Just because we gave you some cooperation (in consenting to Mr. Gordon mortgaging the property) does not mean that you can start demanding fresh and new obligations of Mrs. Gordon *after* your Motion is fully dealt with.

Please tell Ben Gordon to go ahead with the mortgaging

financing if he wishes, and tell Mr. Anshan to courier the mortgage papers to me for Terry Gordon to sign, but don't send me self-serving letters attempting to impose fresh and unreasonable obligations on my client...

> Yours truly,
> Ronald V. Zaldin

January 3, 1992

Dear Mr. Zaldin,
I acknowledge your letter of January 2, 1992 and extend the thanks of both my secretary and myself for drawing an obvious typographical error to our attention. We are jointly embarrassed to have made a slip any idiot could have spotted...

Failure to raise the issue before Mr. Justice Potts surely does not absolve your client of a responsibility not to obstruct the mortgaging. It is the height of gall to block the mortgaging by refusing to pay the taxes and, at the same time, to threaten a motion ... for non-payment of the arrears which can be financed only through the mortgaging that is being so obstructed.

I had hoped that the game playing in this matter was over. Obviously it is not. I am going to ask Mr. Justice Potts to hear us one more time...

I cannot imagine that Mr. Justice Potts would ... allow this kind of oppression of Mr. Gordon.

> Yours very truly,
> Moishe Reiter

January 9, 1992

Dear Mr. Reiter:
... My client is *not* obliged to pay the taxes until the *sale* of Dewbourne ... It is not "the height of gall" for Mrs. Gordon [not] to pay these taxes when *both* agreed to that time frame and your rhetoric of January 3, 1992, is ill conceived. There is no "oppression" here.

I intend to bring a Motion to strike next week ... if the arrears [of child support] are not paid promptly...

Further, Dr. Butkowsky advised Mrs. Gordon that Mr. Gordon has not yet paid his retainer...

I received a letter today ... from Mr. Anshan enclosing the mortgage documents signed by Mr. Gordon ... and [my client] has now signed them, but I will only return them to Mr. Anshan if Mrs. Gordon's arrears are "guaranteed" out of the mortgage proceeds ... Accordingly, please have Mr. Gordon sign the enclosed irrevocable direction and fax and mail it to me and I will courier the mortgage documents to Mr. Anshan immediately.

Yours truly,
Ronald V. Zaldin

January 10, 1992

Dear Mr. Reiter:

I am writing to respond to your enquiry regarding the "inventory" of assets in the matrimonial home.

The "inventory" can proceed once Mr. Gordon complies with Mr. Justice Potts' Order ... regarding the ... arrears ... and he pays the overdue January 1, 1992 payment of $750.

Yours truly,
Ronald V. Zaldin

At this point, having tried but failed to work matters out with Zaldin, Reiter informed him that he'd had enough and was going back to Justice Potts. To ensure that Zaldin got the message, he wrote two more letters on January 10, one of them eight pages long. Three days later – exactly two months after the trial had been adjourned – Reiter served Zaldin with a notice of motion.

For the second time in two months, Ben had to ask the court to address issues the court had already resolved. In December, Terry had forced him into court for an order permitting a mortgage the court had already allowed him to arrange. In January, she forced him into court for another order to implement it.

In yet another affidavit Ben recounted the wild-goose chase Zaldin had sent him on and sought an order compelling Terry to deliver the mortgage documents, pay the taxes, reduce the listing price, and divide their property: "I respectfully request an Order ... to permit me to do that which I have always said I was going to do, which the Court directed that I might do, and which the Respondent has promised she would not obstruct me from doing." Having lost all faith in Terry's assurances that she would honour their settlement and divide their possessions, he asked for an order that Reiter had advised him the court sometimes made in property disputes: to have Waddington's auction them off and split the proceeds.

It did not take Zaldin long to fire a return salvo.

January 14, 1992

Dear Mr. Reiter:

My client sees no need for an immediate release of funds of $50,000 to Mr. Gordon, other than her strong suspicion that a large portion of this is to pay a substantial amount of your fees in this matter.

She is of the view that there is no reason why Mr. Gordon cannot pay overdue municipal taxes now to be deducted (with interest) from the net equalization payment that he owes her out of the proceeds of sale.

Accordingly, in order to determine *why* ... Mr. Gordon needs this money in such a rush ... enclosed herewith is a copy of a Notice of Examination of Mr. Gordon for 2.00 p.m. on Thursday, January 16, 1992 at Rosenbergers main office, served pursuant to the Rules...

Yours truly,
Ronald V. Zaldin

Zaldin tried to have Ben's motion adjourned on a technicality: in her affidavit for the motion, his client said she had seen Ben's motion record only at noon that day and needed more time to review it. To "get the *full* story" and "*properly* defend this very important motion," Zaldin would have to cross-examine Ben on his affidavit.

Terry wanted Ben ordered to pay immediately the child support he owed and would owe on February 1. She couldn't pay the taxes – her money was tied up in a term deposit and "not available to me now." She'd deliver the mortgage papers, but only if Ben signed a document promising to pay his child support arrears "off the top." Then, in a burst of righteous indignation breathtaking in its affrontery, Zaldin's client accused Ben of failing to play by the rules: "Mr. Gordon did *not appeal* from this (Consent) Judgment but he now seeks by *Motion* (not even by Court Application or Court Action) to *vary* the terms of a Consent Judgment. This is unconscionable!!"

At the trial Zaldin had expressed solicitous concern about more delay. Yet he was taking a tack that, if successful, would expand the litigation and prolong the conflict indefinitely. He maintained that the court should reject the evidence of the real estate agent he'd recommended because his evidence was unsworn. He'd need to cross-examine the real estate agents as well. He contended that the court lacked jurisdiction to intervene in a listing agreement.

Terry had agreed to divide their property in November. In December she had assured the court she was "agreeable" to doing so and accused Ben of bringing an "abusive" motion. It was now mid-January. Terry was "ready to proceed" but she had conditions. Now she'd only honour her word if "Mr. Gordon complies with the payment of child support arrears."

Justice Potts ordered Terry to pay the realty taxes by noon on January 17. Once Ben had obtained the mortgage, he was to pay Terry child support. That done, he was to give Terry forty-eight hours' notice and then they were to divide the contents. For the second time, Justice Potts refused to make any decision about the listing price.

Again Terry had failed to honour an agreement, this time to divide their property, had obstructed the sale and diminished the value of a jointly owned home, and had forced Ben into court. Again the court was indifferent. For "preparation and attendance on a motion," Ben's lawyer billed him $4,140.

On January 17, Reiter notified Zaldin that Ben and Mark Anshan would be at the home at 10:00 a.m. on January 22 to catalogue the property; in an earlier letter he'd put forth Ben's proposal that Terry also have a witness present during this process. Reiter proposed that the property be divided five days later. On January 22 Reiter wrote again: "As I understand it, it is not convenient to your client to attend within the 48 hour period provided for in the Order of Mr. Justice Potts. You have now rescheduled for 12:00 noon on Friday, January 24, 1992. Mr. Gordon has instructed my office that he has spoken to your client and she has told him that January 24, 1992, at 12:00 noon, will be 'OK, as long as nothing else comes up' … The prospect of having to go back to Mr. Justice Potts for yet another order, in these circumstances, is utterly ludicrous."

On January 24, the couple went through the house with witnesses, cataloguing their belongings. Each signed a list identifying personal, jointly owned, or disputed possessions. Ben assumed he'd be able to pick up the items Terry had conceded were his, and, in accordance with their minutes of settlement, the master would divide the disputed property. But that was not how events unfolded.

On January 30, Zaldin wrote Reiter seeking to "further the division of contents." However, before this process could be completed, Zaldin wanted more paper. First, he wanted Ben to supply copies of the three lists that he and Terry had compiled while going through the house. Then he wanted six more lists: the items Ben had brought into the marriage, and the items Ben conceded that Terry had brought into the marriage. Next, a list of what Ben had taken from the home at separation, and things Ben had removed "following the separation in a series of attendances (about which complaint was made to Judith Beaman)." Zaldin wanted to know what items (except gifts or inheritances) both parties had acquired from marriage until separation. And he wanted a list of gifts both parties had received from others or inherited from marriage until separation. "I will shortly deliver my client's 'lists' as enumerated above," Zaldin promised, "along with a list of items that *she* brought into the home post-separation … Upon exchange of the aforementioned lists, we can discern the disputed items and move this issue forward."

The Toronto real estate market was a deepening sinkhole. The house sat on the market at $665,000, and the day Ben had proposed to divide the property came and went. On February 3, for the third time in as many months, he went to court. This time he wanted Terry ordered to give up the property she'd agreed was his; he wanted the rest auctioned; and he asked the judge to reduce the listing price and establish mechanics for responding to house offers so they didn't have to keep returning to court.

Ben filed a six-page affidavit. It recounted the lawyers' several meetings with Justice Potts; Potts's instructions that everyone should meet to discuss reducing the price; Terry's agreement, then refusal to attend a meeting on December 9; the various attempts to set up another meeting, which eventually took place on January 22; Pinelli asking Terry why the other agents on whom she was relying for advice had expressed such strong views but hadn't contacted either him or Barbara Consky, arranged for showings, or taken any steps to sell the property; Terry replying that Smith and Kay weren't the listing agents, Consky pointing out that any Toronto agent could show or sell the property, Terry stumped for an answer but insisting there hadn't been offers because the house was so close to Bathurst Street and when purchasers adjusted to that idea offers would come in at the right price; everyone pointing out to Terry that her thinking was completely illogical since the house had been on the market for ten weeks and none of the prospective purchasers who'd seen it had expressed any further interest; Consky finally asking Terry point blank whether she really wanted to sell the house and Terry replying that "of course" she did.

"I am informed by Richard Pinelli and Barbara Consky ... that a $632,000 listing price [the less than 5 percent reduction to which Terry had consented after their meeting] will achieve nothing," Ben deposed. "I believe that ... Terry Gordon ... does not wish to see the property sold, that she is obstructing the sale, and that she is not acting in good faith... Unfortunately, neither of us can afford to maintain the property, and unless it is sold, I am probably ruined financially." Once again, Ben furnished corroborating evidence, another letter from Richard Pinelli.

Pinelli wrote that he and Consky had read Ben's affidavit and "state unequivocally that it is an accurate rendition of what was said" at the January 22 meeting. As he had done several times already, Pinelli explained the condition of the market and the damage that had been done by overpricing the house at a level that had been "soundly rejected for 67 days and is rapidly losing credibility in the eyes of the buying public." The recession was forcing more power-of-sale offerings in Dewbourne's price range. "Nobody knows where the bottom of this market is or when it will come." Pinelli said it was truly in the best interests of both vendors to put a "stop-loss on the situation," and recommended a price of $585,000 to generate a sale between $525,000 and $550,000.

"Mr. Gordon is wrong when he says there is little interest in the property at ... $665,000. Further, Mr. Pinelli is wrong when he says that the listing price 'has been soundly rejected' and is 'rapidly losing credibility in the eyes of the buying public'," contended Terry in a responding affidavit. There'd been eight showings that week. Interest rates had fallen considerably recently. The house would probably sell. She claimed a third agent had advised her not to reduce the price, and Bruce Smith had told her $599,000 was "much too low" and "would only attract a lower (class) calibre of purchaser." But Terry produced no evidence. The opinions of the agents on whom she was now relying for advice were still hearsay. Reiter had asked Zaldin for documentation from them, arguing it was unfair to expect the agents she'd chosen to sell the property "to answer third-hand accounts of purported expert opinions." But Zaldin had never responded to the request.

Instead, as before, Zaldin argued the court had no right to interfere with a listing agreement. This time he tried another technical argument: Pinelli's evidence wasn't sworn. Finally, he insisted that the inventory of possessions was proceeding. The only order necessary was one "today" requiring Ben to deliver the lists Terry had requested through her lawyer on January 30, and permitting her "to attend at Ben Gordon's residence and office to inventory the numerous items Mr. Gordon took from the matrimonial home following the separation (for which I have yet to receive a list and an accounting or inventory)."

Zaldin succeeded in keeping the list price high. Justice Potts ruled that he had no jurisdiction to intervene in a listing agreement. He dealt with Ben's request to establish the mechanics for its sale (mechanics which Reiter could have ensured were spelled out carefully in the minutes of settlement) by instructing the master to set the conditions for selling the home in accordance with Justice Walsh's order – an order the court had made almost a year before. The following day Zaldin wrote Reiter: he had a trial and wouldn't be available to see the master for another two and a half weeks. If Reiter scheduled the matter before he was available, he'd send an associate to seek an adjournment and ask for costs.

It had taken two months of legal shilly-shallying since the trial had adjourned for Ben to arrange for a second mortgage, secure a credit line, and pay Terry the support he owed for the months during which she and Zaldin had obstructed the mortgaging. On February 3, the day Ben learned the court had refused a third time to reduce the price of the home to a saleable level, Zaldin brought his third motion to have the court throw out Ben's case. On that day, Ben was two days late with his February child support payment. He "continues to flout the Support Orders," declared Terry, "despite the indulgence by me ... to mortgage his half interest in the matrimonial home."

Justice Potts does not appear to have dealt with this motion.

■ ■ ■

In January we met with Sol Goldstein, a balding, bespectacled man with the worn Wallabee look of the rumpled professor. He wore the remnants of his hair in a bushy fringe reminiscent of the Christopher Lloyd character in *Back to the Future*, but his manner was dour, and he lacked that nutty professor's cheerful, manic energy.

His office was situated in a rambling old house on Spadina Road just south of the cluster of shops and restaurants of Forest Hill Village. He ushered us from a small anteroom furnished with a worn couch and some out-of-date magazines into a cavernous, cluttered, dimly lit room. In the centre was a conversation area with chairs and a coffee table, in one corner stood an imposing wooden desk littered with papers, and in another was a doll's house surrounded by raggedy puppets and dolls that seemed to have been played with by a thousand children, then left abandoned in scattered disarray on the floor of this gloomy chamber. My first thought was what a scary place it must seem to children.

In that meeting, Ben said he wanted Deja and Zoe to have two involved parents, but – as he'd argued to Butkowsky – he'd come to believe the only way to ensure this would happen was to give him custody. Goldstein looked at him quizzically. Ben made his pitch: he'd always believed in the idea of joint custody, and had tried in vain to make it work. But without Terry's cooperation, they'd be constantly in conflict. Without her consent, they couldn't make decisions. We'd be forced to live, day in, day out, skidding from one crisis to the next. Deja and Zoe would be caught forever in the crossfire.

He still wanted to co-parent, he told Goldstein. He still wanted the kids to live with both of them. He preferred Sara's schedule since it worked well and would make it easier for us to have a family life, but alternating weeks would be okay, too. One parent had to have the custodial authority, though. Why should it be him? Because the record showed that he'd behaved responsibly, that he put the children first, took his parenting responsibilities seriously, and would not abuse the power of custody. With Wendy's help, and support from family and friends, he'd ensure the kids were well looked after.

Ben acknowledged he wasn't a perfect parent. He knew he'd made mistakes. He'd blown up in front of the kids. He'd said things about their mother that he later regretted. But it was hard to convey the brutality and injustice of the court process, what it was like to go broke just trying to stay a father, to be criticized for it all around and then have your kids attack you, too. He told Goldstein about Terry ostracizing him at Deja's religious-school consecration, and the time she called Deja, who was feverish with flu, to say the cats missed her and she really should be home with Mommy. He believed Terry's campaign to alienate him from the children was more damaging than the one she was waging in the courtroom.

He didn't want to fight with Terry. He'd done everything possible *not* to fight with her. In spite of how she and her lawyer were characterizing him, he didn't want joint custody to punish her or to reduce his support payments. It had already cost him more money than a lifetime of support payments could make up for. He had wanted joint custody because he thought his kids needed and deserved two parents.

If he had custody, Ben assured Goldstein, he'd operate as if they had joint custody. He'd continue to consult with Terry and respect her mothering role. He knew the kids were attached to their mother. But they were also attached to him, and if Terry had custody, he desperately feared what she'd do. Deja and Zoe were nine and seven, and their mother was forcing them to collude in her hatred of their father. That psychic damage would last a lifetime. What chance did they have of emerging unscathed from such emotional brutality? What chance did he have of protecting them? If he had sole custody, Terry would have to cooperate. It was, he believed, his children's best hope.

I told Goldstein what I'd observed of Terry's behaviour, said it was difficult to convey its insidiousness to someone who hadn't witnessed it, and echoed Ben's views about the perils of a joint custody recommendation in this particular instance. I explained that David and I had a highly contentious joint custody relationship but had somehow managed to shield Sara from our animosity and disputes. A year ago I would have argued for a similar arrangement, assuming that if David and I could make joint custody work, then anybody could, but that was before I'd seen the heart-rending effects of Terry's conduct on the children.

I told him I'd been critical of Ben's behaviour when I thought it was unfair to Terry or damaging to the kids, and that he too had been guilty of using the kids to transfer information but had been receptive to my counsel. I couldn't stress enough that Terry did not seem to rely on anyone for such advice, nor did she accept it when offered.

I now believed the children would be in jeopardy unless Ben had the ultimate authority to make judgment calls when he and Terry couldn't work matters out jointly. I was convinced she would continue to sabotage any co-parenting arrangement because she believed that doing so would win her custody. Whatever my complaints about David – and I had many – I did not believe he'd deliberately use Sara as a pawn in his battles to try to control me. Terry, however, would never stop. Ben's only option to spare the kids more pain would be to step back and let the kids live with Terry. Then he'd have to rely on her good will to see his children. If that happened, I believed, those kids would be lost.

I spoke, too, about why I agreed with Ben that it was vital that their home be sold. Children moved all the time, whether their parents were married or divorcing. All that would make it difficult for two kids like Deja and Zoe to move to another home was a deeply threatened mother who communicated to them in one way or another every day that her survival depended on remaining there. I believed that to Terry, 24 Dewbourne Avenue was not just a pile of bricks and mortar to be sold for another, or a house with bad memories best left behind. It seemed to mean a great deal more to Terry. Ben had told me she'd lived in a grand home in her first marriage but had come away from that marriage with almost nothing. Like him, I conjectured that he was now being made to pay for the lifestyle she

163

thought she'd been robbed of when that marriage failed. Dewbourne seemed to be the towering symbol of the status she'd achieved in her life, all of it through men. Without it, where would she be? Who would she be? I shuddered to think of the role model she was offering her daughters, the messages she was teaching them about men, women, and the relationships between them. Her ambitions seemed to be based entirely on what she could "get" from others, not what she could achieve through her own hard work, and I found it disturbing to see that attitude echoed in the children. And I was seeing it, especially in Zoe.

Goldstein listened intently, took notes, asked a few questions, and said little. He struck me as a thoughtful, intelligent man. But I feared the inadequacy of words to convey the experience we were living through. I wondered how much any assessor could ever really know about the truth of our lives. And I deeply resented having to convince this aloof stranger, practising his inexact science in that eerie room, of why a man I knew to be an extraordinary father should be allowed to continue parenting his own children. Would he distinguish the Nusyna-Gordon file from the many others scattered across his desk? Or would he just take the easy way out and average the blame between the two of them?

Ben's prior experience with the assessment process wasn't the only reason for my wariness that day. By then I'd spoken to enough lawyers, heard them gossip about assessors, handicap them, and trade scuttlebutt about their biases and bunglings, to be on guard. Furthermore, as a journalist, I had a healthy scepticism for all authority. Because I often wrote about social and psychological issues, I'd interviewed many experts. I'd been in therapy and marriage counselling, too. It had been my experience that only a few professionals who came highly recommended lived up to their reputations. Over the years I'd crossed paths with a handful who were superb. Most, however, were blandly mediocre, and a few, blatantly stupid. In a couple of cases, I'd fled from their offices. I'd encountered practitioners with frightening biases and interviewed people with scary stories to tell about their experiences with the experts. I was disinclined to have blind faith in any, and my antennae were up.

Goldstein gave me no particular reason to worry that day. But I was intensely aware that he was just a fallible human being, and I was both terrified and appalled at the power he had. That power felt hugely intimidating, and I wasn't the one at risk of losing my child. How, I wondered, did Ben endure this?

■ ■ ■

Ben thought Goldstein ought to meet Terry's new boyfriend, Randolph Steepe. We'd finally met Steepe in November. He'd turned up at the courthouse for the first time on the last day of the trial, shortly after Justice Potts had adjourned. As Ben and I stood by the elevator waiting to leave, the doors opened and out stepped a boyishly handsome man in his forties wearing black leather pants, a silk shirt, and a jangling gold bracelet.

Wishing to cultivate a friendly relationship with any man who was spending so much time with his children, Ben extended his hand in greeting. Steepe shook Ben's hand warmly, turned to me, and, gazing intently into my eyes, flashed a Tom Cruise smile. Then he went to look for Terry and Zaldin. In that brief encounter, every female alarm bell in my body went off. In January Ben asked Goldstein to interview Steepe, but when the psychiatrist asked Terry about him, she said they were no longer involved, and he did not pursue the matter.

Meanwhile, Ben had a few questions about Terry's latest job. On the eve of the trial Zaldin had informed Reiter that Terry had left the credit reporting company where she'd been employed for just over a year and had just begun a new job working for a company called Environmental Campaigns, earning $48,000. Zaldin had forwarded Terry's letter of resignation but, since he wasn't obliged to do so, provided no further details.

From Terry's letter, she appeared to have resigned overnight. If this new job turned out to be short-lived, Ben feared she'd come after him for more money again, using the children's best interests as a smokescreen. However, if she'd exercised poor judgment in leaving secure employment, there was a chance the court might be less inclined to make him pay for her foolishness. He decided to see what he could find out.

In January he did a computer search at the Ministry of Consumer and Commercial Relations and learned that the company Environmental Campaigns existed only on paper. The name listed as company president was Jackie Izzard. If Terry was so worried about money, Ben wondered why she'd leave a secure job with an established company like Creditel of Canada to work for an outfit that seemed, at least on the surface, to be more tenuous.

In February Ben learned more about Terry's relationship with Randolph Steepe. Reiter received a call out of the blue from Jacqueline Izzard, who identified herself as Steepe's business associate and said she had some information about Terry. Izzard claimed that shortly after the trial, Steepe had broken up with Terry, and afterwards she'd pressed charges of threatening against him and Izzard. In her sworn statement to a justice of the peace, Terry alleged that she'd broken up with Steepe in early December and since then his threats had made her "increasingly fearful for my safety and that of my children." She claimed he'd repeatedly phoned her home, telling her to come to Centro to see his "next victim," threatening, among other things, "We're gonna get you, you fucking bitch... The gloves are off... You're gonna lose your children." On one occasion Terry alleged he'd pointed his finger at her as if it were a gun in a restaurant called Peppinello, saying, "I haven't finished you yet." She claimed Steepe had reported her to the Jewish Family and Child Service as an unfit, heroin-addicted mother who beat her children, but an agency social worker had interviewed her and the kids and had confirmed the allegations were false.

Reiter met with Steepe, who eventually signed a statement containing numerous allegations about Zaldin and Terry. Steepe claimed that Zaldin had told him to move out of Terry's house during the trial and "not to show my face at court," or he'd jeopardize her chances for custody. (Zaldin allegedly told Steepe he could move back in after the trial.) Steepe said that on Zaldin's recommendation, he'd moved out the day before the trial. Terry had begged him to return, but he'd refused. (He later said she began behaving like the Glenn Close character in *Fatal Attraction* and followed him to the ferry docks at nights when he was returning his daughter to her mother's home on Toronto Island.) He alleged she'd shown up at Peppinello and told his date there was a contract on his life and that when they got him, she'd go, too. Steepe also alleged that when they were still together, Terry had said she wanted to use him to "wind up" Ben and had taken him on a week's vacation to St. Lucia. There were other allegations that were particularly damaging to Zaldin.

Ben felt his first impressions about Steepe had been confirmed. He speculated the guy was a gigolo and small-time hustler who'd picked up

Terry at Centro, lived on her tab for a while, then dumped her and moved on to greener pastures. Jilted, Terry had exacted revenge by pressing charges.

He suspected that a handful of Steepe's allegations were true, others half-true, and the rest nonsense. Steepe professed to be coming forward out of concern for the kids, but Ben figured he was just retaliating by jeopardizing Terry's chances for custody and hitting her where he could hurt the most. These two deserve each other, he thought.

Nevertheless, the whole sordid business was troubling. Steepe had been living with Ben's kids for months, and Terry was claiming she now feared for their safety. Whatever the truth, he didn't want Deja and Zoe exposed to Steepe or his ilk. Furthermore, a social worker had interviewed the kids to investigate Steepe's allegations of child abuse, and, according to Terry's statement to the JP, all of this had been going on for the past three months. Yet, when Goldstein had asked Terry about Steepe, she'd denied any current involvement with him.

Reiter was salivating over the Steepe allegations. Whether they were true or not, Ben knew the landscape of their conflict had shifted because of them. Any way you looked at it, Randolph Steepe was bad news for Terry. Goldstein's job was to make the best recommendation for the children. If the assessor viewed Steepe as a lying low-life who was merely out to seek revenge, he'd question Terry's judgment in exposing the girls to a man like him. However, if he believed Steepe's allegations, he'd be obliged to call the police and the Children's Aid Society. If the assessor had been told about Steepe but declined to meet him, or did meet him but recommended that Terry have custody anyway, and then something awful happened to the kids, Goldstein's reputation would be on the line. Terry's bad judgment had finally caught up with her and Ben wanted the court to know about it through the assessor it had appointed.

I had the same impression of Steepe, and I too could only speculate about his allegations. More important, however, the Steepe affair confirmed a pattern in Terry's behaviour. In the three relationships that I knew about – her two marriages and the relationship with Steepe – Terry had claimed to be the victim of abusive men. In the latter two instances, she'd pressed criminal charges. I had no way of substantiating her claims about her first marriage. What I did know from my own experience – and the evidence –

was that Terry imagined many things to be true that weren't, that she lied about many others, and that she was far more the provocateur than the victim.

In the seventies, when Terry's first marriage ended, it wasn't yet fashionable for women to claim to be victims. By the time Terry's second marriage and her relationship with Steepe had soured, however, she was living at a particular moment in the evolution of gender politics when the Victimized Woman had become an archetype of our age, when public opinion held that wife batterers and child molesters lurked in every household, when all a woman had to do was say that a man had hit her and that idea was sold. Women good. Men bad.

According to Ben, Terry's father was a Little Lord Fauntleroy, and her mother a nice but spineless woman who'd suffered in silence catering to him. Ben believed Terry's behaviour could be understood in the context of a father she detested but emulated, and a mother she was determined never to become. He thought she projected her anger towards her father onto all men but identified with her mother's victimhood. I was curious to see what Goldstein would make of her.

■ ■ ■

My unease with the assessment process did not diminish over time. There was a disconcerting coldness about Sol Goldstein, a heard-it-all-before arrogance that did little to inspire comfort or confidence. He rarely gave overt clues about his thoughts, but from time to time I sensed his scepticism at what each of us was saying. Occasionally, when he did express an opinion, it worried me. He didn't see why it should matter at all, for instance, that the house be sold. That he gave no indication of his intentions made the process all the more nerve-racking. Moreover, I did not know if Goldstein had ever been a divorced single parent, and that concerned me. Divorce, like parenthood, is a great divide; those who have crossed it have lived an experience ultimately unknowable to those on the other side, and I worried about such a person, however learned or expert, standing alone in judgment.

His attitude troubled me, too. Once, I mentioned some comments I'd heard about Butkowsky from lawyers. One had guessed his recommendation the moment Ben mentioned his name, claiming the assessor always made the same recommendation; the other told me that her firm had stopped using him because "we were paying for custom assessments but getting off-the-rack ones."

I didn't expect Goldstein to criticize a colleague, but I thought he might be interested in the observations, particularly since they echoed Ben's experience. After all, the court – and the entire future lives of many children of divorce – depended on Butkowsky's opinions, and if the criticisms had any merit, perhaps someone ought to begin questioning them. Goldstein waved his hand dismissively. "Don't believe everything you hear," he said in an irritated voice. "All the lawyers say I only recommend joint custody." I suddenly understood why Zaldin had been so eager to prevent his appointment. Still, I felt patronized. As a journalist I was unlikely to believe everything I heard and had merely reported observations from two sources I considered reliable. Another time I asked how he expected us to make a go of joint custody with Terry. I was looking for some words of wisdom. "Stop fighting," he replied casually, as if the solution were obvious. I bit my tongue, but his answer and his arrogant manner infuriated me. How, short of utter capitulation every time, were we supposed to stop fighting with someone who did not want to stop?

As part of the process, Goldstein had told us that he wanted to meet at McDonald's with each parent and the kids to observe the family interaction. And so, one day around 4:00 in the afternoon, we found ourselves under the golden arches, wolfing down Chicken McNuggets and fries, while a psychiatrist whose view of us would determine the most critical aspect of our future sat beside us, silently staring.

I asked Goldstein once if he ever worried he might make a mistake. Making a mistake could have such shattering consequences in so many lives. No, he said, he didn't worry about making mistakes. Because emotions ran so high in the work he did, he worried someone might show up with a gun one day to harm him or his family. I wondered if it had ever occurred to him how desperately we feared his power to harm ours.

■ ■ ■

Until Goldstein came up with new recommendations, and both parents agreed to support them or the court endorsed them, Butkowsky's plan remained in place. At some point during the summer, with Terry refusing to cooperate and Butkowsky refusing to arbitrate, Ben had given up on the so-called mediation/arbitration sessions, particularly since he was paying for the entire cost of them.

In the new year, Ben had sweet-talked the school bus driver into bending company rules and stopping at his place when he had the kids. He'd also hired a babysitter to meet their bus and stay with them until he finished work. Those two changes returned some normalcy to his life, relieving him of the burden Butkowsky had placed on him of having to collect the kids from school.

I'd noticed a sea change in Ben, and I liked to think that I was in some small way responsible. He no longer felt so urgently compelled to counter Terry's propaganda campaign by "proving" to Deja and Zoe how much he loved them and wanted to be with them. He'd finally begun to realize that no matter what he did, Terry would never be satisfied. He couldn't spend the rest of his life jumping through hoops to avoid her ire or catering to her so that joint custody could work. Nor could he waste emotional energy trying to prove to the powers that be that he was a worthy father. He just had to live his life and parent his kids the best way he knew how.

The new arrangements had been in place for about a month when one day Zoe was riding the bus home without Deja, got confused about her destination that afternoon, and asked the driver to drop her at Ben's. When she found no one home, she stood on her lunch box and retrieved the key Ben had left in the mailbox for such emergencies. Then she called Terry, who picked her up.

Shortly after this incident, Ben heard from Terry. She wrote that his "constant meddling" with things like the kids' bus schedule was "upsetting to the children and unnecessary." She'd expressed concern a month ago about the second drop-off location, which she had learned about "by accident." When she'd called the school principal, "he was surprised to hear I had not been informed or consulted. He told me that if I was custodial parent, then he would have taken the extra precaution to get my approval before allowing any changes. With no stipulation of roles, he assumed there was co-operation and I had approved."

"When are you going to stop?" she signed off. "Your attempts to interfere with a smooth running system, so you can feel a sense of power and control, is sabotaging the children's everyday activities, and causes upsets and problems that I constantly have to fix. Can't you just let us all get on with our lives?"

That January marked one year since I'd met Ben. Crisis had telescoped the stages of our intimacy. We'd travelled relationship light-years each week. The two of us had been through so much as a couple in so short a time that whenever anyone asked how long we'd been together, Ben would say drily, "Twenty-five years."

But Ben's were not our only troubles that year. I was coping with troubles of my own. The year before I'd met Ben, my beautiful, vital, youthful, seventy-three-year-old mother had been operated on for cancer; in the fall of 1991 she'd begun chemotherapy, and for the balance of that year she had required care. I'd also been trying to finish writing a first book, which was slated to be published in the spring. In February, burned out and desperate to escape to some sun and relaxation before I had to set off on cross-country promotional tours, Ben and I hopped a plane to spend a few days with his dad and stepmother in Florida. Two days later I got a call, and we flew home for my father's funeral.

For any child, at any age, the loss of a parent unleashes a torrent of complicated feelings. But my father's death, coming as it did, unexpectedly, in the midst of Ben's struggle to remain a father to his daughters, prompted me to reflect on a father's role in his daughter's life. My father was a moody, charismatic, and often difficult man. Life with him was emotionally taxing, and all three of his daughters had complex relationships with him. So too did my cousin, whose parents were divorced and who came to live with us after her mother died; he mentored her as a daughter of his own. His life ended sadly. But there was no doubt he'd had a profound effect on shaping the women we'd all become. My mother was the centre of our household, but it was to my father that I turned for lessons in achievement. It was my father who helped us with our homework and walked me through math. It was his opinion about what I wrote that mattered to me most. His were the made-up bedtime stories that held me in thrall. And it was my father's sense of humour and imagination and passion that I wished to emulate. How bereft I would have been, I realized, had some assessor or judge evicted him from my life and ordered my relationship with him bound by the straitjacket of weekend "visitations."

171

By the end of February, Goldstein was preparing to release his recommendations. Uneasy about the outcome, I asked him to hear me out one more time, not in my capacity as a partisan supporter of Ben's point of view but as an observer of what the kids had been through in the last year, and a loving adult in their lives. It was my final attempt to influence his decision. Now I was the one writing letters to an assessor.

I reiterated what we wanted and why, and listed several examples of demonizing-of-Ben comments we were hearing from the children. I asked him again to speak to Brenda Spiegler, who now assessed children at the Hospital for Sick Children. If Ben were forced to compete for a full-fledged parenting relationship with his kids, I didn't think he would, because it would mean exposing them to more conflict, and then the girls would lose him. "It breaks my heart to think that Deja and Zoe might lose their dad as a mentor and anchor in their lives. I have no doubt that they will eventually come back to Ben. That is where their safety lies and one day they will be old enough to understand and make their choices. But in what state will they return? As angry, disturbed adolescents? And what difference will Ben and I be able to make in their lives at that point?"

■ ■ ■

The house was still sitting on the market, attracting little interest. On December 12, 1991, Richard Pinelli had recommended listing at $599,000 to generate a sale of $585,000 – and backed up his opinion with reams of market research and evidence. In December, January, and February, Ben brought motions to reduce the price, but Justice Potts refused to deal with the matter. On January 31, Pinelli wrote a letter describing a market deteriorating rapidly, stressed that there was "absolutely nothing on the horizon to suggest that time is on your side," and advised the court to list the home at $585,000. When Paul Slavens assumed the listing on February 19, however, he advised listing at $632,000. On February 28, Master Ross Linton ordered the home listed for ninety days at the price Slavens had suggested. The master, however, threw Ben a bone. If he wanted the price "amended to better reflect the ... prevailing market reality," he could always keep coming back to court. At "reasonable intervals." On March 19, Slavens advised reducing the price to $619,000. Unlike his predecessor, he did not provide any evidence to support his opinion about the price other than his observation that the property was not selling because of its proximity to Bathurst Street. Nevertheless, on March 23, Master Linton took Slavens's advice. As a result, the house remained grossly overpriced and no offers came in. All of Pinelli's dire warnings had been borne out.

In late March, right on schedule, Goldstein released his assessment. In thirteen typed, single-spaced pages, he wrote a report based on a "compilation of impressions" gained over three months from meeting once with the lawyers, two visits to McDonald's, a series of interviews with Ben, Terry, the kids, Sara, and me, and a double session with Randolph Steepe, arranged at Ben's and Reiter's insistence. Goldstein's associate, a social worker, had taken histories of each parent; Goldstein had read some of the letters exchanged between Ben and Terry and had reviewed Butkowsky's recommendations. "Although both parents had requested that I speak to many people who had been involved with them in the past," he'd chosen to speak, on the telephone, "to only two" (whom he did not name). After spending several pages reporting on each parent's perception of the issues in their marriage and divorce, he gave his opinion.

In Goldstein's view, both Ben and Terry had "considerable problems as individuals" and were capable both of manipulation to gain their own needs and of "using the children to undercut the authority of the other parent and ... to gain from each other financially." Both were self-interested, "capable of placing financial interests above ... the needs of their children," and capable of "distorting the truth in order to advance their own interests." He recommended therapy for each.

Mr. Gordon, he wrote, "presented as an intelligent, determined, charismatic and very theatrical man who claims to have difficulty in expressing himself clearly but who seems to have no difficulty whatsoever in his attempts to portray himself as sincere, honest, and well meaning while at the same time being misunderstood, mishandled, and victimized by a system which lacks understanding and empathy."

Ms. Nusyna-Gordon "presented as a pleasant, intelligent, lady who is intent on getting her point across. She, too, is quite theatrical, is disparaging of her husband, and seems to have very little insight into her contribution to the struggle which rages between them. In many ways she is a mirror image of her former husband, with each of them intent on stating their case in such a manner that it leaves very little room for any insight into their own contributions to the war which rages between them."

The lawyers, he worried, were escalating the conflict. But, significantly, the assessor diplomatically avoided blaming his employers, whom he addressed directly: "Both these parents are quite theatrical in their presentations and capable of provoking a great deal of empathy on the part of their audiences," he wrote. "It is little wonder that there is so much material travelling to and fro between the two of you. I am worried that the empathy which each of you has towards your client forces you into positions which are more adversarial than necessary." The fight, he was concerned, would "escalate as a result," and each issue would be "blown out of proportion, leaving the main difficulty between the two of them unresolved." The main difficulty, as Goldstein saw it, had nothing to do with the lawyers. Rather, it was "the inability of either [parent] to let go of the other and the need for each to control and defeat each other."

The psychiatrist chose not to repeat Steepe's "very serious accusations," which Steepe had made while "claiming to do so" for the children's sake. Nevertheless, Goldstein stated he had "grave concerns" after speaking with Steepe, who "apparently was very much involved with these children." Then he handed the hot potato of the allegations to the lawyers. His first recommendation was for them to investigate the allegations to determine if they had merit or were "simply manipulative and in bad taste." If the allegations were true, then "proper precautions" had to be taken "to make certain that these children are protected from what has been going on in their lives." If they weren't true, and "one does not take this man seriously and sees his eagerness to talk with me as an opportunity to serve his own needs, one must question what type of person he is and, therefore, the judgement of Ms. Nusyna-Gordon as to the type of people with whom she associates and to whom she exposes her daughters."

According to Goldstein, I "presented as a warm, giving, empathic and intelligent lady who is sensitive to these girls as well as to her own daughter," who had difficulty understanding why Ben and Terry needed to fight with each other but was nevertheless "solidly" in Ben's corner "in his battle with his former wife. It seems that she has worked out her own dealings with her former husband in such a way that Sara is benefiting very clearly from the parenting which she receives from both of them."

From his observations at McDonald's, the psychiatrist concluded that Ben and Terry had contrasting parenting styles: he considered our interaction with the kids as "comfortable, pleasant ... free flowing and spontaneous," while Terry and the girls were "more formal with each other and related around tasks, teaching, and learning." Ben, he said, was "sensitive to the needs of the children and intent upon fulfilling these." Terry, on the other hand, tended to point things out to the girls and involve them "in helping her."

The girls, he found, had no difficulty sharing their dad with Sara and me and, despite all their difficulties, were "coping very well." Both were bright, alert, verbal, self-reliant, and "rather calm." They spoke to the psychiatrist about enjoying times with both sets of grandparents and "how much they enjoy spending time with Wendy and Sara... It is clear that Wendy Dennis is a very important person in their lives and that she supplies them with an island of sanity in an area which is otherwise tumultuous, stormy, and really unheeding of their basic need to have their parents get along with each other."

Deja and Zoe saw "their mother and father as being quite different, with each being involved with them in different ways." Deja – who, the psychiatrist noted, seemed to be the spokesperson for both – said they'd become used to the schedule but their parents didn't like it. Both were "very aware of what is going on." They "tolerate" their parents and "the games" they played with each other; they knew each parent spoke disparagingly of the other, each used them in the battle with one another. They were, nevertheless, "unblaming of their parents and are attached to both of them. They recognise that their parents fight over many issues which are not really important and that if their parents would truly wish to serve them well, they would learn to get along with one another... They have adapted to this chaotic world around them and have learned to extract the best from any adult with whom they are in contact and to use this for their own personal growth." Nevertheless, "they have a rather jaundiced view of how people treat each other and the value which one places upon the feelings and the needs of the other."

The psychiatrist thought each child was likely to do well individually, but he had deep concerns about how they might treat other significant people in their lives, and he worried about their ability to sustain a healthy relationship. "On a more optimistic note, I would hope that they would have the supreme strength to learn from the mistakes of others and to search out whatever warmth and positive interpersonal relationships to which they are exposed – to use this to learn how to get along with other people. In this regard, I think that it is particularly fortunate that they have been exposed to Ms. Dennis and Sara, both of whom seem to supply these girls a great deal in the way of friendship, understanding, and empathy. I would only hope that they are not disappointed in this relationship and that they are allowed the benefit of an ongoing positive exposure to these people."

And then, while retaining some of the details in Butkowsky's report, Goldstein made his recommendations.

"What would best serve these children," he concluded, "would be a cessation of hostilities and manipulations between these two people." He recognized the potential for an "ongoing vitriolic struggle" and despaired of the conflict ever ending. Nevertheless, unwilling to entrust either Ben or Terry with official power over the other – whether through a sole custody or primary residence/secondary residence recommendation – he proposed that "the parenting plan should involve the children being one week with each parent" and conflicts arising from their co-parenting were to be overseen by an "astute and strong" mediator/arbitrator. "If possible," he wrote, "the label Joint Parenting or Joint Custody should be attached to this plan."

CHAPTER**EIGHT**

THE TRIAL RESUMES

March 1992–June 1992

Goldstein's assessment was difficult reading and we absorbed it with mixed feelings. Despite overwhelming odds in Terry's favour, two assessors had declined to recommend that Terry have sole custody. Viewed from that perspective, Ben had "won." He was relieved to have clarity on custody and more time with the kids. But he had hoped for a better outcome, reasoning that with me in his life he'd have more credibility as a good parent, since in the court's eyes fathers had none on their own. That, coupled with the girls' affection for Sara and me, had led him to hope he had a decent crack at achieving the recommendation he'd asked for. A year ago he would have been elated at this result. Now, when he read the report, all he could think was, They just don't get it. (I found it unutterably poignant – and profoundly disturbing – that although Ben had nurtured his children from infancy, he reasonably concluded that his best chance of being allowed to continue parenting them resided in the serendipity of his having met a person with more impressive credentials: she was female and a mother.)

I too was deeply worried about joint custody, for all the reasons we'd explained to Goldstein, even though I'd never seriously expected him to do what we'd asked. Although I'd hoped for a miracle, I believed that even if an assessor viewed Ben as the more stable parent, he'd be unlikely to make the controversial recommendation of sole legal custody to a father. Nevertheless, I continued to believe that was the only decision that would guarantee the children a relationship with both parents and protect them from a life of tortuous conflict. For those reasons, I thought Goldstein had made the wrong call.

I was disturbed, too, by Goldstein's assessment of Ben. In his review of the marriage's history, he seemed to see him as an insincere, manipulative man who professed to be a victim of an unjust system. The report was cleverly written, and the shots he took at Ben were subtle and subtextual, but they were there in phrases like "presented himself as," or "claims to have … but seems to have…" The implication was that Ben was a phoney. Any self-critical admissions he'd made, such as confessing his guilt on some counts about the struggles between himself and Terry, Goldstein positioned as a manipulative attempt to impress upon the assessor how honest and self-aware he was. The fact that Ben had a mea culpa tendency, was insecure about rambling when he became emotional, and felt compelled to apologize for his inarticulateness at such times, Goldstein seemed to view as a theatrical attempt to portray himself as a sensitive, emotional man. Ben was not a saint, nor had he attempted to depict himself as one, but he was not the man Goldstein portrayed, either.

I found it particularly offensive that he'd equated Ben and Terry in character and behaviour and had likened their situation to a *War of the Roses* in which two disturbed people were locked in a pathological struggle to control and defeat each other. Given the history and evidence in the case, I believed that to be an unsupportable view, and about as accurate as Judge Marshall's casual observation that Ben and Terry were "both basically decent people." I was angry, too, at how Goldstein had let the lawyers off the hook for the conflict, even though by then I had come to realize how the game worked and whose favour assessors were wise to curry.

Ben didn't care what Goldstein thought of him, nor did it bother him to be equated with Terry. He said he'd been judged and misjudged so many times he was beyond caring what another assessor had to say. Based on what he'd seen of the depth and standard of their investigations, he didn't think any of them was in a position to judge. All that mattered to him was the result, and he was relieved about that, although he too had deep concerns about trouble down the road.

Sara and I were the only ones to receive good notices. (His characterization of me as an "island of sanity" in the children's "tumultuous existence" prompted Ben to remark that now he was worried I'd get custody.) While I appreciated the assessor's generally complimentary evaluation, I worried that his comments would cause Terry to crank up her efforts to distance the children from us. Most significantly, however, I believed that Goldstein had missed the mark on two vital issues: Terry's character and behaviour, and the degree to which the children were at risk because of it. His assessment of her had been unflattering but hardly damning, and his depiction of a "pleasant, intelligent, lady" suggested she'd presented herself well. While he didn't trust her enough to recommend sole custody, he gave no indication of concern that she was subjecting the children to mind control.

Like his predecessor, Goldstein was considered one of the best assessors in the business. And like his predecessor, he had failed to uncover the truth, in my opinion. He'd seen two equally blameworthy people with axes to grind and had never managed to penetrate the subtle undercurrents of their story. I viewed that failure as a reflection not necessarily of his ability but of the limitations of the process. Everywhere in the court system the pretence existed that assessments could be relied on as accurate indications of the truth, even though authorities acknowledged privately that was often not the case. Not that assessors were incapable of getting it right; rather, even the most skilled were only human and therefore capable of bias and errors. From the start, I'd been uneasy about Goldstein's lack of humility, and worried about an assessor who conveyed no empathy and admitted no doubt. Notwithstanding his cavalier lack of concern about making mistakes, Goldstein's comment that all we had to do to get along with Terry was to stop fighting revealed a staggering failure to grasp our predicament. Given the nature of assessors' investigations – they were basically limited to what they saw in their offices – they couldn't really know the truth, and it simply wasn't cost-effective for them to conduct the kind of inquiry that would have been necessary to uncover it.

Goldstein spoke to only two other people besides the principals, and he did not read any of the mediation reports, affidavits, legal correspondence, or cross-examination or criminal court transcripts. He did not see the lawyers in the courtroom, witness any scenes involving the children, or view them being parented, other than that surreal visit to McDonald's where he observed us like laboratory rats. Without independent corroboration of at least some of the "multitude of allegations and counter-allegations" he was hearing, how could he possibly know the truth? (Terry's perception, reported by Goldstein, that the police hadn't charged Ben because he was "such a good actor," as opposed to the truth – that there was no evidence to warrant a charge – was a prime example. Without seeing the trial transcript, how could he evaluate the validity of her account?)

Furthermore, it struck me that parents forced to endure an assessment were caught in a terrible bind. First they were made to engage in an adversarial contest where the prize was the right to continue parenting their own children. (Goldstein's boxing-ring imagery about me being "solidly in the corner of Mr. Gordon" underscored that idea.) Having been thrust into that forum, they were then forced to argue their case to an assessor with the power to play God. With so much at stake, a parent's natural inclination was to use his precious time in the assessor's office to get his story across. He had to make him understand. The consequences were too awful if he didn't. Yet how to convey all the nuances of the story?

Because of his theatre background, Ben was often a colourful storyteller, but in Goldstein's office I'd watched him become frustrated at sensing he wasn't being understood. He'd grow more intense then, his tone increasingly urgent, his recounting of events more impassioned and physical. I had sensed Goldstein's disdain when Ben became worked up, and I realized that to someone with no real appreciation of what he'd endured, Ben would have seemed merely melodramatic or self-serving.

It was in these moments that I realized how flawed the assessment process was. A thousand such stories begin to sound tediously similar, and an assessor might simply hear both parties' urgent pleas for understanding as the yada, yada, yada of yet another pair of hostility junkies. Mark Anshan said that, during their interview, Butkowsky struck him as someone with "pat answers" for a problem, and "if it didn't fit into a box, he'd make it fit. It was as if he'd decided, 'You're a category D family, and here's what you do with a category D family.'" Lacking independent evidence or a macrocosmic view, how different, really, was the assessor's vantage point from that of a judge who peers down from the bench and sees two crazy people? ("You'll never convince a judge that the two people fighting in front of him aren't both crazy," a family lawyer told me. "Both clients get tarred with the same brush.") Likewise, the assessor might easily conclude that both parents were self-interested and locked in a pathological control struggle.

How much, I wondered, did judges really know about the assessors on whose opinions they relied? Justice Potts, for instance, had insisted on appointing Goldstein over Zaldin's vehement objections. Had Potts ever seen his office, or asked any children how they felt about him? (Deja and Zoe considered his office "spooky," and Goldstein "kinda weird.") Justice Potts had taken "judicial notice" of Goldstein, but had he ever read his book? Who assessed the assessor, I wondered, or followed up on his assessment to find out if he got it right? But such thoughts had to be put aside. The assessor had spoken.

■ ■ ■

Master Linton's March 23 order setting the price for the house at $619,000 should have taken effect immediately. But Zaldin argued that Terry had a right in contract law to restrict the master's discretion to reduce the price. Although Terry had signed an agreement giving the master that jurisdiction, and in February – claiming the desire to avoid frequent, unnecessary, and costly appointments with the judge – she'd obtained an order confirming it, Zaldin now wrote to Justice Potts seeking to impose new conditions on the master's jurisdiction. Zaldin was unsuccessful, but the move ensured another month's delay before the new price was advertised. The order was effectively meaningless anyway. The real estate market had continued to nosedive. Under the circumstances, a 2 percent price reduction was far too little, too late, to attract interest.

Since January, no progress had been made dividing the contents, either. Shortly after he'd accompanied Ben to the house in January to help the couple catalogue their possessions, Mark Anshan had faxed Reiter the lists they'd compiled. The lists revealed they'd agreed on who owned about half their belongings; the balance was disputed. To signify she'd conceded 102 of the 303 items to Ben, Terry had signed her initials beside those items. But just as Zaldin had succeeded in stalling a price reduction on the house by seeking to impose new conditions, Terry succeeded in delaying the return of Ben's belongings by imposing new terms on a done deal. She wanted to examine Ben's apartment and office, and she had changed her mind about some previously conceded items.

January 24, 1992, was the first day Ben had been allowed back into his house since he'd moved out on October 12, 1990, the day Terry had changed the locks and pressed a third assault charge. Although the first charge had been Askoved and the other two dismissed, Terry had walked out of criminal court with a peace bond that prevented Ben from returning to his home. And therein lay the rub. Once a woman had banned her husband from the house and had a document to prevent him from returning without an agreement through counsel or a court order, she had dictatorial powers. If he wanted his property, the onus shifted to him to bring motion after motion. Eventually he'd be the one abused and beaten – by the system. I watched this happen to Ben. Terry may have signed a settlement agreeing to divide their property and assured the court she intended to cooperate fully to see that it was, but neither she nor her lawyer honoured their word about cooperating. Ben was frustrated that the court had never held either Terry or Zaldin accountable for their behaviour, but he had neither the strength, the will, the funds, nor the faith in the process to return to court for the umpteenth time seeking its help to collect his property.

In any event, Ben's immediate concern was the resumption of the trial as quickly as possible. Not until then could Ben obtain a joint custody order and a new parenting schedule based on Goldstein's recommendations. Until we had the kids for a week at a time, we couldn't begin to parent them. Until the trial was over, we couldn't get on with our lives.

The courts were heavily backlogged and trial dates weren't easy to come by. To arrange a date, the lawyers consulted each other and the judge about availability and requested a date from the trial coordinator. Because the process moved so slowly, clients often had to complete new financial statements prior to the trial. But each time one side introduced new evidence, the other side had the right to cross-examine on it. Furthermore, if one party furnished a new affidavit, that evidence remained the only evidence the judge saw on that issue unless the other party furnished a response. In that way, the process pitted divorcing spouses against each other in a never-ending battle of duelling affidavits. Once forced to engage in this blood sport they then had to endure a slew of paternalistic authorities who profited from their break-up, all the while scolding them for their inability to "let go of the conflict."

Goldstein had stressed that ending the conflict was of paramount importance, although one hardly needed to pay a psychiatrist several thousand dollars to reach that conclusion. Resolving custody had always been Ben's first priority. As soon as the assessment was delivered, Ben urged Reiter to write to Zaldin about a trial date.

Resuming the trial quickly, however, was not in Terry's best interests. The longer Zaldin could delay, the longer his client would continue to receive interim support payments. (By June 1992, when the trial did resume, Ben had paid more than $13,000 in interim support to Terry, in addition to the $10,000 a year he was paying directly for the kids' extras, on an annual income of about $50,000.) Terry could also avoid Justice Potts's promise to review the allocation of the children's expenses. Even more significantly, the greater the delay, the longer his client could avoid sharing the kids' time equally with their father and taking the stand to answer questions about her finances, her lies, and Randolph Steepe.

In the months following Goldstein's assessment, the lawyers busied themselves writing letters. Ben continued pleading with Reiter to wind things up. In May he faxed his lawyer, "Attached copy letter rec'd from Slavens. Any word from Potts? What do we do after Slavens listing expires? I cannot continue paying interim support of $750. Can we get at least a custody ruling from Potts? Something? When does Steepe go to trial? Have charges been dropped? Please respond, Ben." Another three months and twenty-seven lawyers' letters would bring the issues no closer to resolution.

If professional collegiality had ever existed between Zaldin and Reiter, Ben had never witnessed it. Their animosity was so pronounced, they could barely communicate. Lawyers typically conferred on a case by telephone and correspondence, but Reiter said he'd deal with Zaldin only by letter, and even then, presumably to watch out for hidden agendas, he had to read all Zaldin's letters twice.

Zaldin had controlled the litigation from the outset. Once Reiter had Goldstein's assessment in hand, he saw an opportunity to score a direct hit on his opponent. On April 21, professing to have taken "very much to heart" Dr. Goldstein's "implied recommendation" to cool the "adversarial atmosphere" between them, Reiter suggested they collaborate by having the Official Guardian's Office investigate Steepe's allegations, some of which, if true, could be highly damaging to Zaldin.

Ben had been urging Reiter all along to have a lawyer from that office represent the kids; Reiter had earlier deemed the idea inappropriate. Goldstein too had suggested they consider appointing the OG's Office to represent the children's interests. (He'd also recommended the possible involvement of the Jewish Family and Child Service, the agency Ben had fruitlessly begged for help during the Butkowsky assessment.) Concern for the children's welfare, however, did not seem to be the main motivation behind Reiter's sudden enthusiasm to involve the OGO. Instead, Reiter seemed gleeful at the prospect of torturing his adversary a little. He wrote to Zaldin, "As I understand it, Mr. Steepe's allegations are quite serious and, to a certain extent, they involve you ..." Goldstein's report, he said, has "effectively ended this case, other than the interesting areas that he has suggested be investigated."

His letter went on to say that since their clients' incomes were approximately equal and since Goldstein had recommended joint physical custody, Terry had no claim to child support, so they should resolve that issue without troubling the judge. He sought Terry's cooperation to stop further "bloodletting" on the house and honour her agreement to divide the possessions. He suggested that the question of allocating responsibility for the lost equity in the house could be "resolved by direct discussions." Reiter also wrote to Justice Potts that day to request a trial date within three weeks.

Two days later, Zaldin wrote to the judge. He wasn't ready for trial. Declaring that his intention was "to save trial time," Zaldin sought to reopen the entire case. He wanted the lawyers to exchange updated financial statements, then cross-examine on the latest figures, on custody, and on the Goldstein assessment, "so that counsel are not cross-examining blindly at ... trial."

The following day, Reiter wrote to Zaldin that Justice Potts had asked him to canvass Zaldin about available trial dates "within the next short period." He'd scheduled an appointment with the judge the following Tuesday to resolve the matter, and he listed various dates through May when he was available. Reiter declared that reopening the case "would be to continue the very war of attrition that Dr. Goldstein's report recommended be terminated... This matter has got to end sometime."

Justice Potts cancelled the Tuesday appointment. Before they met he wished to review the file and Goldstein's report. Reiter wrote to the trial coordinator to say that Justice Potts had instructed him to seek a trial date as soon as possible after May 25. "So far as I am aware," he wrote, "Mr. Zaldin ... and I are available commencing May 27, 1992."

May 1, 1992

Dear Mr. Sheehan:

Further to Mr. Reiter's letter to you dated April 29, 1992 ... please do *not* arrange the resumption of this trial at this time.

I am currently attempting to arrange an appointment with Mr. Justice Potts ... to "speak to" this matter in his Chambers.

There are a number of issues that I wish to address with His Lordship *before* the Trial is scheduled to resume...

Thank you in advance for your anticipated cooperation.

Yours truly,
Ronald V. Zaldin

May 4, 1992

Dear Mr. Zaldin:

...It was my understanding, from Mr. Justice Potts' secretary that His Lordship wished the date for the resumption of trial to be scheduled in June, so as not to lose the time.

You indicated to me today that you would be in touch with me, by telephone, between 2:00 p.m. and 2:30 p.m. today. It is now 4:30 p.m. and I have not heard from you. I have, however, received a copy of your letter to Mr. Sheehan telling him *NOT* to arrange the resumption of trial at this time.

If this is going to be a matter of controversy and dispute, and if the likely upshot is to cause a delay of the trial's completion into the fall of 1992, then I suggest you make yourself available for an immediate meeting with Justice Potts...

Please confirm, by return facsimile, that you have arranged a meeting and ... your proposed agenda... Apparently you do not think there is any merit in a meeting between us. If we are to trouble

185

Justice Potts, perhaps we should know in advance what we are going to trouble him about.

Yours very truly,
Moishe Reiter

May 5, 1992

Dear Mr. Reiter:
Further to your fax of yesterday received at 4:40 p.m., I did not tell you that I would be in touch with you by phone between 2:00 p.m. and 2:30 p.m. I told you that I could call you then *if* I got back to the office, which I never did.

I would be happy to meet with you and Mr. Justice Potts at 9:00 a.m. some morning and am now available on May 11, 20, 21, 27 and 28...

If you care to arrange such an appointment... then please do so and let me know immediately of the date... Thank you.

Yours truly,
Ronald V. Zaldin

"Thank you for your letter in which you acknowledge that Justice Potts wants us to get together," began Reiter's latest missive. "Thank you also for your prior letter in which you advised that you did not tell me what you told me." He offered to meet with Zaldin any time "between this moment and May 11th." He found it "odd" they had to delay until that date. He was "getting the feeling" Zaldin was "in no rush to get this case on for completion."

Although Justice Potts had the discretion to limit the proceedings, he allowed further cross-examination and instructed the lawyers to exchange their clients' financial statements by June 2. Zaldin was granted permission to cross-examine Ben again on June 4, and the trial was scheduled to resume on Monday, June 22.

A few weeks before the trial, Reiter heard from Jackie Izzard again. This time the information she had to impart related directly to Terry's financial affairs. Terry, Reiter learned, was suing Steepe and Izzard in civil court, where she was claiming breach of contract of employment. In her affidavit in that action, Terry claimed that a detective at 52 Division had told her Steepe was a convicted fraud artist breaching his probation. She alleged that shortly after meeting Steepe in May 1991, he'd urged her to quit her job and work for his company, Environmental Campaigns, and in mid-October she started to work for him full-time from home as a general sales manager. She claimed to have had a one-year contract guaranteeing her a $96,000 salary plus 20 percent of Canadian gross sales revenues (on one deal alone, she said he owed her $120,000 in commission), but she had never seen a penny of her earnings. "Unfortunately," she said, "I have been unable to locate" a copy of the contract.

Terry also alleged that Steepe had fathered the child of a woman who was suing him for child support and, "to prove that he was penniless, asset-free and judgment-proof," was trying to hide his assets. To help him dodge a support order, she'd let Steepe pay her partially through an outside company.

Steepe (who had children with at least three women) had also fathered Izzard's child. In her affidavit, Izzard denied threatening Terry, but she acknowledged Steepe "may have misrepresented ... his position with both [Izzard's] companies in an attempt to portray himself to her as occupying positions of control and authority which he does not in reality enjoy." She believed Terry had left the credit reporting company to avoid being fired. Izzard noted that Terry had made her charges through the same justice of the peace whom she'd used "on numerous occasions in the past to charge her ex-husband." Izzard said a sergeant at 52 Division had advised her that the police were considering charging Terry with public mischief.

Steepe denied owing Terry money. He contended in his own affidavit that because he'd broken up with Terry and refused to sign false affidavits for her, she'd "started a systematic approach to seek some sort of revenge by charging me twice with threatening and commencing a false commercial suit to extort funds from companies I am involved with as a consultant." His version was that Terry and a co-worker at the credit reporting company were about to be fired, and Zaldin had said that would look bad in court – unless she had a letter demonstrating she was going to another job. To help Terry out, Steepe had asked a friend who owned a promotion and advertising firm called SRG to draft a letter saying that Terry was one of his sales reps, and the next day Terry quit her job. Steepe claimed that Terry had never worked for him, or any of his companies, and was using the letter to extort money from him.

Again, I could only shake my head at the allegations and counterallegations that Terry and the cast of characters she kept company with were flinging at one another. But on one issue there was absolutely no doubt: two weeks before the trial in October 1991, Terry had quit her $42,000-to-$44,000-a-year salaried job with Creditel believing she was going to a job where, according to her own sworn evidence in her civil suit, she expected to be earning a salary of $96,000, and at least another $120,000 in commissions. As a party to an application in the family court, Terry had a legal duty to advise the court about any significant changes to her financial situation. However, on the financial statement she'd filed with the court on October 29, Terry reported that her new salary was $48,000. Once again, Terry had lied. Reiter could hardly wait to get her on the witness stand.

■ ■ ■

Pursuant to Justice Potts's instructions, Zaldin served Ben with a notice of examination to cross-examine him on his third financial statement. Completing a financial statement was an enervating chore that involved poring over chequebooks, invoices, credit card statements, and accounting records, then number-crunching, guestimating, and tracking down documentation to back up all the figures. If filled out properly, the eleven-page document often took days to complete, even if one kept organized records, as Ben did.

The lawyers had last exchanged their clients' statements seven months earlier. Each time he'd turned over reams of verification to Zaldin, and each time Zaldin had demanded more. Zaldin could never get enough paper. He requested so many documents, and tied up Reiter's fax machine serving so many of his own, that Reiter once called him an "independent forester."

Ben brought his accountant, Sheldon Derrick, to this cross-examination. He'd have to pay Derrick, but he thought his presence might save them time in the end. Zaldin had questions about a tax shelter; Derrick could explain its financial implications and answer Zaldin's endless queries about his income better than Ben. His latest financial statement showed that in seven months his debts had increased by $66,000, but Terry was still insisting he was flush. Despite all his prior interrogations, Zaldin had never uncovered a secret stash. (Ben was so broke that whenever Zaldin worked him over, I used to joke that for my sake I really hoped he would find something.) Maybe Derrick would finally convince Zaldin that his client was hallucinating. Not that it mattered; we suspected Zaldin would advise litigating as long as there was money in the file.

Ben went through the routine again, but like a man who'd been pistol-whipped so often he no longer felt the pain. I'd observed his transformation from someone who believed that if he was forthcoming and cooperative he would speed matters along, to someone with utter contempt for the judicial process. By then he'd been in court often enough to know that many judges didn't even look at the materials and that disclosure just gave a lawyer like Zaldin the chance to go on another fishing expedition. Ben would tell the truth, but he would not volunteer one iota more than he had to.

Zaldin grilled Ben about his finances and stamped several more documents as exhibits: financial statement sworn June 2, 1992, by Benjamin Gordon; 1991 income tax return of Benjamin Gordon; financial statement for September 30, 1991; Canadian Imperial Bank of Commerce account statements from October 4, 1991, to May 6, 1992; CIBC personal chequing account ledger for Mr. Gordon; statements of CIBC account number 4000110 for Ben Gordon Enterprises Inc.

When Zaldin had finished cross-examining on financial issues, he turned to custody. Reiter stopped him cold.

"I hear what you're trying to do," he said. "You're not going to do it. If you want to cross-examine on anything beyond the financial statement, you have a duty to notify me in advance. Simple as that."

Zaldin protested, but Reiter said, "Good night," stood up, gathered his things, and walked out of the examination. Feeling mortified and exasperated, Ben followed.

The lawyers ran to Justice Potts again. Zaldin accused Ben of refusing to disclose his legal fees, give a "straight answer" about how he'd spent the second-mortgage money, or answer questions about custody. Reiter argued that Ben didn't have to disclose his legal fees or state his position on Goldstein's report until the trial. "I also thought it odd," he added, irrelevantly, "that

Mr. Zaldin would bring his 18 year old son to sit in on the examination of Mr. Gordon."

The judge ordered Ben to answer the questions. Reiter forwarded to Zaldin yet another breakdown of Ben's income and expenses. Then he presented Ben's position on custody. By this point Terry had indicated her willingness to accept Goldstein's recommendations.

> 1. ... Mr. Gordon is prepared to ... accept ... the recommendations of Dr. Goldstein on the condition that Mr. Justice Potts ... incorporate those recommendations as to *true* joint custody, mediation arbitration by Dr. Goldstein, on an ongoing basis, in a Judgment of the Court. Mr. Gordon is not prepared to deal with this matter, in future, on anything but a very clear and officially sanctioned basis.
> 2. If Mrs. Gordon is not prepared to stand by her earlier position, as expressed by you to us, and wishes any ... deviation from Dr. Goldstein's total report and recommendation, Mr. Gordon reserves the right to ask the Court either to implement those recommendations ... by Court Order or to seek such variations as may be appropriate in the context of Mrs. Gordon's changed position.

Having forwarded written responses to the questions Potts had ordered Ben to answer (as was sometimes the practice), Reiter concluded the letter by saying that he trusted Zaldin had completed his cross-examination. Reiter would start cross-examining Terry at 10:30 the following morning.

That Friday, June 12, while the lawyers jousted over procedural issues, Ben and I went to criminal court to see Steepe stand trial for Terry's threatening charges. The week had been a busy one for Terry. One day she'd testified in the proceedings she'd launched against her ex-boyfriend in criminal court; the next, she'd been cross-examined in the proceedings she'd launched against her ex-husband in family court. At least one of Terry's lawsuits would soon be over: on June 18 she filed a notice of discontinuance in her civil action against Steepe.

As we sat in the courtroom waiting for Steepe's trial to begin, Terry entered through the rear doors and glanced around, as if looking for someone. She spotted her girlfriend seated a few rows ahead of us. "Come to watch the show?" she asked as she brushed by. We had. And quite a spectacle it turned out to be.

Terry gave a reprise of her last criminal court performance as the poor single mother just trying to protect herself and her children from a beastly man. She played the role powerfully, with great conviction, but it was the conviction of someone who has told a lie so often she believes it to be true.

"Wow, she's good," Steepe declared afterwards, high praise indeed, coming from a con artist. On the stand he openly admitted he was a gigolo and generally behaved as if the trial were a farce. Doing his best to keep straight all the women in Steepe's life, the judge remarked that he did seem to be a busy man. "Hey, it's the nineties!" said Steepe, smiling broadly and playing to his audience. The charges were dismissed when he agreed to sign a peace bond.

On Saturday morning, the cross-examinations in the divorce case resumed. First Zaldin suggested they try to settle custody, but negotiations went nowhere. "After 1.5 hrs. of negotiation," Reiter wrote in his notes that day, "RZ tries to flim-flam us on terms of custody settlement." Zaldin continued to cross-examine Ben. At 12:30 Reiter began his cross-examination of Terry, and Ben learned that she had been out of work for six months.

Terry testified that after she'd quit her job with Creditel of Canada, her income had consisted of $336 weekly UI benefits, Ben's $2,200 back support payment, his $750 monthly support payments, and $10,000 borrowed from her mother. Nevertheless, in the eight months since filing her previous financial statement, Terry hadn't incurred any new debt. Nor did her financial statement make mention of the "job" with Environmental Campaigns. Furthermore, in the sections of her June 1 financial statement specifically designated for such disclosures, she'd failed to disclose both her UI benefits and the $10,000 loan.

While out of work, at home, and on UI benefits, Terry had continued to maintain a $600,000 Forest Hill home, retain the full-time services of a nanny/housekeeper for $800 a month, spend approximately $800 to clothe herself at Holt Renfrew, and dine at Splendido, one of the city's finest restaurants. She had paid a $1,750 retainer to Irwin Butkowsky to testify on her behalf at the trial (he returned the retainer when dismissed from the case) and voluntarily paid $900 of her own money (above the $8,000 assessment fee Ben had paid) to meet with Goldstein. She testified that she'd met with him to discuss why she hadn't learned of Steepe's role in the assessment until receiving a copy of Goldstein's report, and because, as Terry put it, "the children requested a meeting . . . and I fulfilled that."

According to Terry, she'd arranged to meet Goldstein because the girls wanted to attend a Passover seder, but Ben had refused to let them go or to discuss the matter, and the kids had asked to see the assessor about it. What Terry didn't say at her cross-examination was that their parenting plan decreed it was Ben's turn to have the kids the first night of Passover that year. Terry had told them that if they went with their father they'd miss seeing all their cousins at her family's seder; then she'd had the kids beg Ben to let them go with her. When that tactic didn't succeed (such tactics had worked well on Ben in the past), she'd talked to Goldstein and tried, but failed, to manipulate him into changing the rules.

At the trial in the fall, Zaldin had argued that Terry couldn't pay any portion of the assessment because she "just doesn't have the money." Now, Terry's credit card statements and bank records revealed that twelve days before Zaldin had told the court that his client was "in extreme financial circumstances," Terry had purchased a $9,432.29 GIC. Furthermore, two months before the trial began, she'd spent $3,417.98 on a trip to St. Lucia, which suggested there'd been truth in at least one of Steepe's allegations. Finally, with the $2,200 back support payment the court had ordered Ben to pay her – and which he'd had to second-mortgage his share of the home to come up with – Terry had paid her divorce lawyer.

Terry testified that about a month earlier she'd landed a sales position through an advertisement in the *Toronto Star* and was currently working for a company called ASE of Canada Ltd., selling advertising space at $18 a week per ad for a Mississauga-based promotional publication called *Health and Home*. The job paid strictly commission. She estimated her income to be $36,000 a year but couldn't explain how she'd arrived at that figure. She remembered signing "something" but didn't have it, or any documentation to substantiate her earnings. (Later she produced an "independent contractor" agreement with Mobile Media Inc.)

Reiter asked why she'd neglected to record on her most recent financial statement that she had anticipated earning almost a quarter of a million dollars working for Environmental Campaigns. "Is that relevant to this?" Terry asked. The matter was "still very much in question." Anyway, she didn't think it was something to be "included in that statement." Her lawsuit to recover that money was not something Terry had felt it necessary to discuss with her divorce lawyer until "last night actually. I hadn't talked to Ronald about that action. It's a separate action from this ... I told him that I felt there was something owed to me but the details of which we never got into."

Reiter was anxious to determine how much Zaldin had known about Terry's lawsuit against Steepe when he let his client swear a financial statement claiming her income was $48,000. If Zaldin had knowingly allowed his client to swear false affidavit evidence, he would be open to disciplinary action by the Law Society. But the moment Reiter started down that road, Zaldin made noises about leaving. It was the weekend. He had family commitments. Reiter pressed on. As her lawyer, Zaldin had a "responsibility to make full disclosure."

Zaldin cut him off: "The discussions we had were with respect to the criminal trial yesterday and [that] there was an outstanding action between them." Then, advising of his availability Monday night, he announced, "I have to go, Mr. Reiter," and left.

Two days later Zaldin wrote Reiter: when Reiter had "adjourned" on Saturday, he'd agreed to come back Monday night. But his secretary had called Reiter's office and learned that Reiter didn't plan to attend any more cross-examinations unless Justice Potts ordered him to. So Zaldin wouldn't be showing up.

Reiter wrote to Zaldin, saying, "We did *not* adjourn the examination ... You arbitrarily terminated it by walking out at that time. The entire day had been designated and committed." He detailed Zaldin's bobbing and weaving that morning in the custody discussions, which "effectively wasted three hours of Saturday." As for resuming on Monday evening, he pointed out that Zaldin had "arbitrarily decreed" such an appointment, but that time was "utterly impossible" for Reiter. Finally, Reiter said he was seeking not an "order" but "some direction from His Lordship" to prevent them from getting "bogged down in these obstructionist manoeuvres."

As the second part of the trial drew closer, Terry suddenly became anxious to settle. In mid-May, before her cross-examination, she'd called

Ben, sounding contrite and amenable to working things out between them. According to the notes Ben kept of that conversation, Terry said she'd realized a lot about herself and her first marriage, that David wasn't "half as bad a guy" as she'd thought, that neither was Ben, that they'd lost enough, that they were robbing the children, that it was stupid to go back to court, that a fifty-fifty time-share would be too tough on Zoe, and that she needed to talk with him.

Ben figured he was being conned. He didn't think Terry was contrite, or that she'd suddenly done a 180. Now that they stood to wind up with joint custody, and he was in a position of power, he thought she was simply trying to talk him out of the Goldstein recommendations and into agreeing to a better deal than she was likely to get in court. Still, he indulged her. He listened, remained low-key and non-committal, and didn't tip his hand. He would see how things played out. He'd reserve judgment until he saw how she intended to prove her sincerity.

Three weeks before the trial resumed, in her Rule 49 offer, Terry said she'd accept "custody/access to be joint custody" according to Goldstein's report, and $750 a month child support. Master Linton would still handle property matters. (From Terry's perspective, custody and child support were the only outstanding issues. She made no proposal regarding financial restitution to Ben for overpayments he'd made in child support or the staggering equity losses he'd suffered on her account.) A week before the court date she tried to settle again. This time she offered no child support paid in either direction, but they'd both be obliged to exchange their tax returns each year.

Ben was also hearing from Paul Slavens that Terry was suddenly being very cooperative about the house. In May, Slavens had prepared a report on the property's selling progress. Although he'd noticed "increased buying activity" in the neighbourhood, he believed clients were still objecting to the Dewbourne house because of its proximity to Bathurst Street, and he suggested sticking with the $619,000 price but meeting at three-week intervals to discuss further reductions. Now Terry had reportedly told Slavens she wanted to avoid more court costs and appearances and was considering reducing the listing price to $598,000. She was also offering to share the kids' camp costs with Ben. "Let's get back to court before she's sainted," Ben told Reiter.

Ben believed Zaldin was doing everything possible to keep his client off the witness stand. Her latest cross-examination had turned up another heap of damning evidence that could well make her look like a liar. And then there were the Steepe allegations, which also involved Zaldin. If any of those allegations were true, Zaldin would have even more reason to keep Terry from testifying. But for Ben, there was far too much water under the bridge to consider settling out of court now. He'd lived through too many of Terry's and Zaldin's "agreements." Justice Potts had been cunningly shielded from the facts. Terry still hadn't testified. At the trial, the truth would surely come out, Terry would finally be held accountable for her actions, and he would get the court order he needed.

The week before the trial was set to resume, Zaldin tried another tack. He wrote to Potts seeking an appointment in chambers on Friday morning, June 19, to argue a motion for "Judgment on the custody issue (joint custody per Dr. Goldstein's recommendations), which Motion, if successful, will severely restrict and reduce the amount of Trial time which must be allocated to this case next week." He claimed that the custody issue was settled, that the only outstanding dispute between the parties was who the mediator/arbitrator should be, and he argued that "a trial of custody should not proceed on such a narrow basis."

Zaldin served Reiter with his motion for a pre-trial ruling on the most vital issue in the case on short notice, when he knew Reiter was in the midst of another trial. He told the court that he had to conduct further cross-examinations, and that he wanted Ben ordered to answer questions still outstanding from his earlier cross-examination – or have his case thrown out. Justice Potts adjourned the motion until trial.

Meanwhile, Steepe was playing a game of cat and mouse with Reiter over the Zaldin allegations. One minute he'd claim to have tapes of conversations between Terry and Zaldin. Then he'd turn coy about producing them. Next he'd claim he'd accidentally erased key exchanges but would have the tapes restored. Then he'd say they couldn't be restored. Ben wanted nothing to do with Steepe. He hardly promised to be a credible witness. Furthermore, although he believed Steepe's allegations against Zaldin should be examined, our focus was Ben's case. We couldn't see how Steepe could possibly help that. We also thought it unwise for Ben to be associated in the court's eyes with a con artist and gigolo. But Reiter insisted on keeping Steepe on standby as a "scarecrow" for Terry.

When the trial had adjourned in November 1991, Zaldin had told Justice Potts, "If we're not back to you before next summer, there is something wrong with this system." The trial finally resumed on Tuesday, June 23, 1992. Court opened at 11:40 a.m. I attended the proceedings, since I was allowed to be there until Ben testified again. Justice Potts had to rule on custody and child support and conduct his promised review of the allocation of children's expenses. He had also said he would investigate Ben's allegations that Terry had fraudulently misrepresented her financial circumstances, and Ben wanted him to determine whether she should make restitution to him for overpayments in child support.

The session began with technicalities. Reiter addressed Justice Potts. There was confusion over whether witnesses had been excluded, how many exhibits had been filed. No one could find the trial record.

Then Zaldin spoke. For three years Terry had claimed to be destitute and battled relentlessly for more money. But just as Zaldin had unexpectedly abandoned Terry's appeal on the sale of the house in November, now he announced that Terry was dropping her claim for child support. The judge appeared puzzled at this development but seemed relieved to have one fewer issue to resolve and did not question it. Ben and I, however, smelled a rat – Zaldin's latest ploy to keep Terry from having to answer some very awkward questions about her finances.

Custody was next. If either Ben or Terry refused to accept the Goldstein recommendations, Justice Potts would have to hear further evidence. Terry would then have to testify and be cross-examined. Terry had fought bitterly for sole custody. Zaldin now told the court that she was willing to accept joint custody, but on one condition only: the court had to appoint a mediator/arbitrator other than Goldstein.

Under no circumstances did Ben want Goldstein dismissed. Despite our feelings about his assessment, and the children's about Goldstein, we believed him strong enough to resist manipulation by Terry or Zaldin. Furthermore, Ben didn't want to impose yet another prying professional on the kids, and we couldn't bear the thought of living through another chaotic year while another "expert" went through the learning curve, perhaps grasping the situation or perhaps not.

Justice Potts instructed the lawyers to meet over lunch and try to sort out some of their differences. Reiter asked permission to tape their conversation. Zaldin objected angrily, but Justice Potts agreed it was a good idea. Court let out at 1:05 p.m.

Two hours later, the proceedings resumed. Justice Potts adjourned Zaldin's latest motion again, allowing him to bring it back on a later date. The lawyers argued over witnesses. At 4:25, after some three hours in session, court adjourned. No evidence had been called.

Reiter had faxed his witness list to Zaldin that morning: Mark Anshan, who'd testify about Terry's obstructiveness dividing the possessions and her shifting positions on selling the home; Sheldon Derrick, Ben's accountant, who'd testify about Ben's finances and dealings with Zaldin at Ben's cross-examination; Jackie Izzard, who'd testify about Terry's civil suit and criminal charges against her and Randolph Steepe; David Byers, Izzard's lawyer in Terry's civil suit against Steepe, who'd testify about the connection between Terry's claims of anticipated income in that action and the contradictory evidence she'd sworn about her income in family court; and Randolph Steepe, who'd testify about Terry's criminal charges against him, her claim to recover a quarter of a million dollars of income from his company, his relationship with her and the girls, and his contact with Goldstein. "It is entirely possible that ... additional witnesses may be called," wrote Reiter. "Their identity and the substance of any evidence they may give is not presently known. As and when that information comes to hand, it will be given to you. This is unavoidable because of the fact that the information was not previously disclosed to us." According to Ben, Reiter was making a veiled allusion to the possibility of calling other witnesses arising from the Steepe allegations. His jerking of Zaldin's chain achieved the desired effect.

June 24, 1992

Dear Mr. Reiter:
Your witness list suggests that you intend to pursue issues at this trial that are not properly before the Court.

I insist therefore that you fax me *immediately* (before the trial can proceed) a list of the issues you say are still outstanding before

197

Justice Potts and which you intend to pursue at this trial...

In any event, because of your uncertainty as to witnesses, even now, I shall be requesting ... that this trial be adjourned until all the witnesses and the nature of their evidence be revealed and examined upon.

Yours truly,
Ronald V. Zaldin

Wednesday, June 24, 1992. Court opened at 11:40 a.m. Zaldin told Justice Potts that Reiter's letter had caught him by surprise. He no longer had any idea what the issues in this case were. Everything had come unglued. The trial had gone off the rails. Justice Potts simply had to adjourn it.

Steepe had been hanging around the courthouse. Zaldin asked if Reiter intended to call him. He didn't see Steepe's relevance to the trial. He was just a boyfriend Terry had broken off with before Goldstein's assessment began. Reiter said he might call Steepe and he might not. If he did, he added offhandedly, then Zaldin might require a lawyer of his own. Zaldin exploded in fury at Reiter's implication that he had something to fear from Randolph Steepe's testimony.

The lawyers went at it. Every now and then, totally fed up with their antics, Justice Potts looked over at their clients and exclaimed, "You two people are crazy!" At 12:10 the court reporter threw down his pen in exasperation and stopped taking notes. No evidence was being heard, only endless lawyers' argument. Sighing, he sat back in his chair and left on his tape recorder to record the judge's comments.

The Steepe evidence spoke volumes about Terry. Ben knew that if he refused to accept the Goldstein plan, he could force Terry to testify and be cross-examined on the custody issue, which would necessitate her having to answer questions about Steepe, questions that went straight to the core of her character and judgment as a mother. They could also call Steepe as a witness, and the court would hear that while pleading poverty she was not only keeping company with a self-confessed gigolo whom she'd taken to St. Lucia but had involved the children with a man she'd charged with threatening her, leading her to claim she feared for their safety.

But Ben had never been interested in "getting" Terry. All he'd ever wanted was joint custody and for this nightmare to be over. He accepted Goldstein's plan, provided the court spelled out exactly what the assessor's recommendations meant. Under no circumstances did he want a repeat of the Butkowsky fiasco, when Terry had agreed to support recommendations but then litigated over their interpretation.

Once Terry and Ben had agreed to accept the Goldstein recommendations, Justice Potts had to appoint the "astute and strong" professional Goldstein had recommended to monitor the joint custody arrangement. Reiter argued that Goldstein was already up to speed on the case, his office was well located, and involving a third professional would be disruptive for the children. Zaldin countered that the children had no confidence in Goldstein, and Terry didn't think he'd given her a fair assessment. Unwilling "to force Dr. Goldstein on Mrs. Gordon," Justice Potts instructed the lawyers to return after lunch with some names of new candidates.

Ben stormed out of the courtroom, took the escalator steps two at a time, and waited impatiently for Reiter in front of the courthouse. "He out-argued you!" he shouted when Reiter caught up. Ben's face was contorted with fury. Reiter's face was twisted in a bulldog scowl, his chest puffed up belligerently. The two of them stood inches apart, glowering at each other. I pulled Ben aside and told Reiter to go on ahead to the Holiday Inn, where we'd meet him for lunch.

I was just as furious as Ben about Goldstein being dropped. I believed Terry wanted Goldstein turfed because she hadn't been able to control him. But, just as Justice Potts had dumped an assessor about whom Ben had expressed reservations the year before, now he did the same for Terry. However, I didn't see the situations as precisely analogous. For the children's sake, Ben had lived for a year with a professional in whom he had little faith and recommendations about which he had grave and — as it turned out — well-founded reservations. Since then and despite his sacrifice, the family had been through another year of litigation and a second assessment. Terry hadn't yet made any concessions for the children. Nevertheless, all Zaldin had to do was say his client was unhappy and the squeaky wheel got greased.

Ben found himself in exactly the same position as he'd been in the year before. The court had given Ben and Terry mere hours to find the professional who'd be empowered to make all the future parenting decisions they couldn't make jointly about their children's lives. We began calling around frantically to find someone willing to take over the case. We'd heard of a social worker named Helen Goudge. Reiter knew the name but little about her and couldn't suggest an alternative. I called a friend for whom Goudge had done marriage counselling, and my friend spoke well of her. We had no time to meet with her. Reiter called Goudge to see if she'd take the case, and the social worker agreed.

Court resumed at 3:25 after a twenty-five-minute delay while Zaldin photocopied candidates' résumés. At our insistence Reiter tried to persuade Justice Potts to reinstate Goldstein. But the judge wouldn't hear of revisiting the issue. After twenty-five minutes he recessed, advising the lawyers to settle on the new candidate. Court adjourned at 4:45 after three hours in session. No evidence had been called.

Of the four candidates, Goudge and three proposed by Zaldin, Reiter argued that Goudge, at $90 an hour, "given the costs consideration," was most appropriate. "Your main objection to Helen Goudge," he needled in a letter to Zaldin that day, "appears to be that she is a social worker and [unlike one of Zaldin's candidates] does not have a string of degrees in psychometry, the importance of reserpine and sex hormones in psychological function in the aged."

June 25, 1992

Dear [Mr. Reiter]:
...You told Justice Potts yesterday in Court ... that your witnesses would only be Mr. Gordon himself, Mr. Byers ... and possibly Mr. Gordon's Accountant. I will be objecting to any *other* witnesses being called.

You informed me, however, just before we left the building yesterday afternoon around 4:20 p.m., that you "might" still call Randolph Steepe. Again, I will be objecting. He has no relevance, but if I am wrong, he is properly a reply witness, and, in any event, you have not advised me except in the broadest of terms ... what evidence he has to offer and by dodging my question when I cross-examined ... I am still in the dark ... what evidence he would be offering. Your refusal to advise me ... leaves me *still* guessing as to his evidence and accordingly I am unprepared to deal with him as a witness...

I see this trial now (on financial matters) to be a non-emergency, unnecessary at this stage and wasteful – because the parties will no doubt be back in Court litigating the issue of child support once Dewbourne is sold, and each receives his or her share of the proceeds, and purchases alternative accommodation and there is now a new financial structure. I hope that you will agree with me that enough money has been spent in this proceeding on legal fees, without unnecessarily increasing this burden by litigating child support *now*, and then having to *review* the situation *again* after Dewbourne is sold.

Zaldin advised that he'd ask the court to adjourn the trial until after the house had been sold.

Thursday, June 25, 1992. Court opened at 11:05. Justice Potts wanted to know why Zaldin had asked that court be delayed until 11:00 a.m. so he could photocopy documents. Zaldin made excuses and apologized. The lawyers addressed the court. Zaldin asked for a recess. His client wanted to consult Dr. Butkowsky before agreeing to Helen Goudge. Twenty-five minutes later Terry consented to the social worker's appointment.

Justice Potts now had to deal with Ben's condition for accepting the Goldstein report and pin down the meaning of the recommendations. He told the lawyers to prepare a draft of the report's key paragraphs which he'd include in his judgment. If they couldn't reach a consensus, he instructed them to ask Goldstein for clarification.

Then Zaldin tried to adjourn the trial. He told the judge that the issues were a little clearer now, but the court should resolve custody before the trial proceeded.

"Custody is done! decided! finished!" bellowed Justice Potts in exasperation. "If you can't agree, then I will decide!"

Unfazed, Zaldin pressed on. The outstanding financial issues weren't urgent. Once the house sold in the fall, their clients would only be back in court.

"Don't tell me they're not urgent," the judge admonished him.

Reiter read Zaldin's letter demanding to know what witnesses he intended to call. He'd call Steepe, he said, but since custody had been decided, Steepe would testify only on financial issues. The judge ruled Reiter didn't have to disclose what Steepe would say. Zaldin wanted Ben's receipts for the kids' extras. After two hours and ten minutes in session, court adjourned. Again, no evidence was called.

The trial didn't resume on Friday. Ben had advised the court he'd be in Boston on business from early Friday morning until Sunday evening. On Friday Zaldin wrote Reiter two letters. The first confirmed his request for Ben's receipts. The second raised the matter that seemed to be very much on his mind.

June 26, 1992

Dear [Mr. Reiter]:

... I need to know ... what facts are alleged (and the details of the conversations) between my client and myself, at which meetings Randolph Steepe attended.

I also need to know ... posthaste the precise details of the conversations and facts surrounding what Randolph Steepe alleges I told him (and vice versa) at the aforementioned meeting.

I further need to know ... the facts and details of the allegations of "fraud" and "misrepresentations" that you have made against my client in open court for the past three days.

You stated at the trial that I would need Counsel in view of what Mr. Steepe is alleging against me (and Terry Gordon) at these meetings, and I will be requesting an adjournment of the trial (and possibly further discovery) on the aforementioned allegations, which you have steadfastly refused to provide despite the fact that we are in the midst of trial and I still do not know the case my client (and now I) have to meet in this regard.

I submit that "Trial by ambush" has been abolished, and I demand these particulars, without delay, by fax *today*.

Yours truly,
Ronald V. Zaldin

"It was reassuring, after a bleak morning without a fax from you, to receive two faxes at noon today," Reiter replied. Ben was compiling the requested invoices, although, during Zaldin's "various cross-examinations," Zaldin had never asked for them. Justice Potts had already settled the Steepe question. Reiter denied saying Zaldin might need counsel. According to Reiter, whose recollection differed from Ben's and mine, it was *Zaldin* who'd raised the possibility of needing a lawyer, and *Zaldin* who had said that he "may need to have counsel"; Reiter had simply concurred that "that may be the case."

"You seem to be extremely sensitive to Mr. Steepe's testimony," Reiter continued. "The evidence will be directed to financial issues only, to show that Terry Risa Nusyna-Gordon did not make full and accurate disclosure as required by the Rules. If the cross-examination proceeds as I expect it will, there may be no need whatever to call Mr. Steepe."

Ben returned Sunday evening. On Monday morning, he discovered that Zaldin had faxed Reiter yet another avalanche of paper.

June 29, 1992

Dear [Mr. Reiter]:
I still do not know the case that I have to meet and accordingly, I enclose herewith Notice of Motion for this morning, served pursuant to the Rules.

Yours truly,
Ronald V. Zaldin

A dolly large enough to carry a refrigerator was now required to transport the half-dozen boxes of documents in court file ND 180329/91Q – *Nusyna v. Gordon*. Nevertheless, Zaldin's latest motion declared there hadn't yet been enough "pleading and discovery and disclosure" in the case. His client was therefore seeking an order requiring Ben to furnish another affidavit in which he was to set forth the balance of his claims, and the "material facts" on which they were based. Then his client required an opportunity for her lawyer to cross-examine Mr. Gordon on his affidavit.

His client also wanted costs. She alleged that Reiter had refused to identify his witnesses or summarize their evidence, and accused Ben of a "steadfast refusal to disclose" his receipts for the kids' extras. (The receipts Ben was guilty of a "steadfast refusal to disclose" by Monday were the same ones her lawyer had requested Thursday afternoon when Ben had told the court he'd be away until Monday.) "It is respectfully submitted," wrote Zaldin, "that 'trial by ambush' is no longer tolerated."

Monday, June 29, 1992. Court opened at 10:10 a.m. Justice Potts dismissed Zaldin's motion. He instructed both lawyers to provide their interpretation of Goldstein's recommendations to him for clarification during the week of July 9. (In his first gesture of financial equanimity, Justice Potts instructed Ben and Terry to split any fee Goldstein might charge to write a clarification letter.) Then he called a thirty-minute recess, after which Ben took the stand to pick up where he'd left off eight months earlier. During his hour and a half of testimony, Zaldin objected numerous times. At 4:40 p.m., court adjourned.

Tuesday, June 30, 1992. Court opened at 10:10. Ben testified for another hour. Reiter finally concluded his examination. Zaldin preferred not to begin his cross-examination. He had a bad back. He wouldn't be able to conclude it that day. Reiter filed Ben's receipts: Exhibits 37 and 38. Shortly after noon, after court had been in session for two hours, Justice Potts again adjourned the trial without setting a date for its resumption.

At the pre-trial conference in June 1991, Reiter had estimated the trial would take two days. By June 30, 1992, the trial had lasted thirteen days and was still not over. After thirteen days, only Ben had testified. Terry hadn't testified, no witnesses had been called, and several large issues remained up in the air. Reiter's bill for services at trial was $44,835.

In 1991–92, the cost of operating the Ontario civil courts was $1,002 an hour. By June 30, 1992, Ronald Zaldin had brought ten motions in the case of *Nusyna v. Gordon*, Moishe Reiter had brought eight, and there had been fourteen adjournments. Not counting court time for hearing those motions, the trial of one couple's divorce had already cost the taxpayers of Ontario $24,549.

CHAPTER NINE

THE SETTLEMENT

July 1992–January 1993

WE headed into that summer of 1992 exhausted but hopeful. It had taken Ben more than three years and financial catastrophe to get the words "joint custody" on paper. But he finally had a court order enshrining his right to be a parent and a court-approved recommendation that gave us the kids for a whole week at a time. The success of the new arrangement depended on Terry's cooperation, and about that we were less optimistic. Helen Goudge was the linchpin.

Her first task was to cobble together a parenting plan based on Goldstein's recommendations and the rules concerning holidays, birthdays, and so forth that Goldstein had retained from Butkowsky's plan. Then she could begin to mediate or, if necessary, arbitrate disputes. However, everyone had to be clear on the new rules before she could troubleshoot.

Goldstein had written that the mediator/arbitrator's job was to "oversee the parenting of these children [and to] work with both these adults on a regular basis and be available to them to deal with all of the struggles in which they involve each other … help them deal with the school, extra curricular activities, camp, and general health and welfare of these children … also be available to them on an adhoc basis for any other difficulties which arise between [them]." Terrified of any ambiguity after the Butkowsky experience, Ben and I wrote out four pages of clarifications for a report with only two pages of recommendations. Our understanding was that both parents had fully equal status, were to collaborate and share information regarding the children, and should continue living within a reasonable distance. Neither was to make unilateral decisions (except on daily matters during

205

each parent's time) or withhold clothing or possessions – which had been an ongoing problem. We also stressed that I was to play an *in loco parentis* role with the kids.

We could foresee problems with Goldstein's recommendation that the weekly transfer occur after school on Fridays. In this scheme the children would come home on Friday to the same parent they'd spent the week with, then be ferried from one house to the other. I knew from common sense and eight years' experience watching Sara travel between households that when kids had to disengage from one parent and go directly to the other, particularly in the vulnerable first year after their parents' separation, each transfer was akin to reliving the trauma of the divorce. After seeing Sara suffer through a few exchanges, I realized it made more sense for us to pick her up at the end of the day from her after-school program. After the first six months or so, for youngsters content in each parent's care, as most children are, the parent out of sight was largely out of mind. We suggested that if Deja and Zoe said their weekly goodbyes to Ben before boarding the school bus on Monday morning (or Tuesday after a long weekend), then returned to Terry by bus at the end of that day (and vice versa), they'd escape the upset of a physical separation with each transfer and their parents could avoid contact, as both assessors had strongly recommended.

Goldstein's recommendation also caused Ben unnecessary inconvenience and pain. While Terry had a housekeeper to receive the kids after school, Ben would have to hire a sitter or leave work at 3:30 to be home by 4:00. Having raced home to greet the girls, he'd then have to say goodbye for the week and be left standing in his apartment, bereft. Goldstein's transfer time may have been a good idea in theory, but it created so many headaches in practice, Ben and I were hopeful that he'd see the wisdom of altering that recommendation.

After the trial, Reiter forwarded our interpretation of the recommendations to Goldstein, requesting a "clear statement" to avoid misunderstandings. Zaldin wrote him too, outlining Terry's chief issues.

> Firstly, Terry found herself purchasing virtually all of the children's clothes, which would then be sent with the children to their father's and which would not be returned to her. She cannot afford this and

simply requests that each party purchase clothes for the children separately ... to remove any area of potential strife between the parents that would undoubtedly affect the children...

Secondly, Terry is opposed to any division of children's furniture almost two years post-separation, especially where Deja's bedroom set (except the bed) was Terry's which she had as a child and Zoe's furniture was a gift from Terry's parents. Terry feels that any division of furniture at this time is simply divisive and would only serve to reinforce to the children the separation and their parents' continuing squabbles.

Zaldin's letter implied that the children were Terry's main concern, but anyone with the slightest experience with the system would recognize in it an attempt to manipulate an expert into expressing an opinion on the record to advance his client's interests. How to divide the chattels was Master Linton's problem, not Goldstein's. However, if Zaldin could elicit agreement from the assessor that dividing the children's furniture would upset them, he could use a "best interests of the children" argument in court to win Terry more of the chattels than she was legally entitled to keep.

Goldstein charged $500 above his $8,000 assessment fee to write a clarification letter. In the main he agreed with our reading of his recommendations, with one maddening exception: he refused to alter the transfer time to the first morning of a new school week. He was of the view that transferring the kids after school on Fridays would allow them to "'settle in' prior to the commencement of the school week ... This would alleviate ... struggles resulting from school holidays which frequently occur on a Monday." Unless Goudge and both parents agreed to change the time, he advised letting it stand and mediating "the transportation of the children, the holidays, or anything else arising from the new 50/50 time split."

He wished for me to be as involved with the kids as we'd suggested, and he hoped I'd continue "to remain as constructive an influence" in their lives, adding that he hoped when Terry had someone who "could equally be a positive influence" on the girls, that person would play a similar role. Furthermore, while he saw as "ideal" our view that the kids' possessions should travel freely between both households, he foresaw that policy becoming an "attractive vehicle" through which to continue what he viewed as the "pathological dynamics" between Ben and Terry. Carefully sidestepping any opinion as to what distress it might or might not cause the children to divide their furniture, Dr. Goldstein recommended that "each home have a set of furniture and sufficient clothing for both children, so that they arrive at each home with nothing more than 'the clothes on their backs and their books in their arms.'"

The new alternating weekly schedule began on Friday, July 10. For the first time in almost two years, except during holidays, Ben had the kids for seven consecutive days. A whole week! It was like a honeymoon. Suddenly there was time, delicious time, to hang out, stroll across the street to the park, laze on a bench, and watch the girls playing on the swings. To play catch, amble to the corner store for Freezees, rough-house and sprawl on the couch to watch a video.

There was no longer any need to shoehorn every household task, meal, chore, and pleasurable moment with the kids into the few hectic hours before bedtime, one night a week or on a frenetic weekend. It was the first time since I'd met Ben that our time with Deja and Zoe flowed to the natural rhythms of family life.

The new arrangement delighted Ben, but there was sadness for him, too, that summer. Earlier that year, anticipating the kids' departure for camp on June 26, he'd written in his appointment diary, "Kids to New Moon." But as we stood with the other parents, hugged Sara goodbye, and watched her vanish with paddle and knapsack into a bus teeming with chattering children, I saw the pain flicker in his eyes. He'd have been seeing his own children off, too, were it not for all the debts arising from his matrimonial litigation. Instead, he'd enrolled them in a day camp at Forest Hill Public School. He tried to think positively. Deja and Zoe seemed happy in the program, and with Sara gone for six weeks we could devote our attentions exclusively to them.

Until the house sold, our lives were still effectively on hold. Any expectation that the court would deal fairly or intelligently with its sale had been dashed too many times. Instead we lived day to day, occasionally surrendering to the luxury of imagining what life would be like if we could make plans to live together in one place, like a real family.

From time to time we looked at homes for sale, but that quickly became a depressing exercise. Buying an appropriately sized house in central Toronto, where we'd both grown up and all three kids were at school, was beyond our means. We considered renting, but until Ben's house sold, we wouldn't know what we could afford. All we could do was wait. Given Terry's crusade to stay in that house at whatever cost, Zaldin's manoeuvres to keep her there as long as possible, and the court's nonchalance about it all, the picture wasn't likely to change soon. Instead, we devoted what little energy we had to an endeavour we considered likelier to reward our efforts: having a family life.

The additional time with the girls helped in a thousand ways, and we made progress, palpable daily progress – as long as we were left alone to parent. But we were rarely left alone. Either we had to endure another legal attack, or our efforts were sabotaged in more subversive ways. With Goudge drafting a parenting plan, we had to deal largely on our own that summer with any confusion arising from the new schedule. It wasn't long before trouble arose.

At the end of our first week with the kids that July, we had planned to spend the weekend with friends in the country, leaving on Friday morning after dropping the kids at day camp. They had to be picked up at 3:30. Since they were going to Terry's for the next week, Ben assumed it was her responsibility to collect them. His reasoning was that both Goldstein and Butkowsky had recommended that pick-up and drop-off occur at school, to minimize conflict. Without bus delivery, Ben assumed that Terry was obliged to pick up the kids at camp, just as he'd always been obliged to pick them up at school. Since he'd enrolled the kids in camp and Terry didn't know their schedule, he had faxed her early that week to let her know the pick-up time.

Then Reiter heard from Zaldin.

Dear Sir:
Your client seems to be insisting that Terry pick up the children from Forest Hill Day Camp at 3.30 p.m. this Friday July 17th.
Mr. Justice Potts was very clear when the trial adjourned ... that during the school year "changeover" time on Friday was to be after

209

school, but during the summer, commencing Friday July 10th, the "changeover" time was 6.00 p.m.

My client is attempting to work and support herself and she is unavailable this Friday July 17th until 6.00 p.m. at which time she will attend at Mr. Gordon's Relmar residence to pick up the children.

Yours truly,
Ronald V. Zaldin

Here we go again, thought Ben. He had no idea what Zaldin was talking about. And in the absence of any documentation of Potts's supposed decision, all they had to go on was what Goldstein had said. Unwilling to pay his lawyer to deal with a petty custodial matter, he replied and copied Goudge. Ben told Zaldin he was unaware of any "decision or order made by Judge Potts concerning a variance in the normal pickup time of the children throughout the summer months." He quoted Goldstein's recommendation that any changes to Butkowsky's parenting plan were to be mediated and said Terry was free to seek alterations to the rules through that process. Until Goudge took over, he and Terry were obliged to follow the rules of the past year and a half. He'd told the camp Terry would be picking them up; if she planned to send someone else (Ben was thinking of her housekeeper), she had to let him know before 8 o'clock Friday morning so he could tell the camp; otherwise, they wouldn't release the kids.

> Both Dr. Butkowsky and Dr. Goldstein strongly recommend that on all matters relating to the children, Mrs. Gordon and I should communicate, either orally or through correspondence... Involving lawyers in this discussion is inflammatory, costly and totally contrary to the spirit of co-operation necessary for joint custody – an arrangement that Mrs. Gordon has presumably agreed to. If this is how she intends to participate in joint custody, then I think it important that Helen Goudge understand the depth of her commitment to the process from the beginning.

At 8:30 in the morning on pick-up day, Zaldin faxed Reiter.

July 17, 1992

Dear Sir:

Further to your correspondence of yesterday, firstly you will instruct Ben Gordon not to write me directly again. I will not be responding to him at all.

He will write to you or he will write to Terry, but he will not write to me.

Secondly, Mr. Justice Potts said 6.00 p.m. changeover during the summer and my client will *not* be attending at the camp at 3.30 p.m. If Ms. Dennis is involved in Ben Gordon's corner, then she can back him up *if* he is too busy to be there as Mr. Justice Potts directed.

Mr. Gordon has been picking up and dropping off the children at Terry's house since school ended and he can keep to the Goldstein times. At the end of the Trial on June 30th before adjournment, he tried to unilaterally change Dr. Goldstein's Friday changeover to Monday because it was "more convenient" to him, but "convenience" will not fall here either in the face of Justice Potts ruling.

Accordingly, Terry advises that she *cannot* pick up the children at 3.30 p.m. today and that she has no-one else to substitute today in any event.

Finally, your client's attempts to back Terry into a corner and to make her look like the "bad guy" here in correspondence to Helen Goudge, is wholly transparent, and I am confident that Helen Goudge will see through this ruse and continuing attempt by your client to manipulate and control the situation and "dictate" when and where and how to his ex-wife. Some day he will simply have to accept that he has lost control of her and that he should put an end to these machinations and ongoing struggles on his behalf to control Terry post-marriage.

Yours truly,
Ronald V. Zaldin

In the beginning, when Terry had dug in her heels, denounced Ben to the children, and hurled them into the fray, Ben had almost always given in. If he had to rearrange his plans at the last minute, or pay for the kids' activities because Terry refused, he almost always did so, reasoning that it was better for him to take the hit than the girls. That had been the pattern on every single issue, both in court and out: as long as he capitulated totally to Terry's demands, no problem. The moment he spoke up and asked for some cooperation the other way, all hell broke loose, and he was perceived to be the troublemaker. Then, for the kids' sake, he'd back down. We both knew, however, that he couldn't let that dynamic continue. If he did, he'd never be free of debt and we'd be forced to live forever at Terry's mercy, on red alert, ricocheting from crisis to crisis. Ultimately she'd destroy our relationship.

I believed that was exactly what she was trying to do, whether consciously or not. It hadn't escaped me that my relationship with Ben probably threatened Terry, too. A mother with any wisdom or maturity would eventually have realized that I could be another loving adult in her children's lives. But I'd long since abandoned any hope of expecting either from Terry.

Under the circumstances, all we could do was set our boundaries. We believed it crucial to send Terry a message from the start that we were no longer prepared to give in to her demands. We'd play by the rules, ignore her to the extent that was possible, and try to get on with our lives. Before leaving town that morning, Ben faxed Zaldin. In a style he'd picked up from the lawyer, Ben wrote that it wasn't our job to pick up the kids during Terry's time and unless he had documentation indicating a change in the arrangements, he'd no longer engage in correspondence. Ben left his cell phone number and three others with the camp staff. Then, our stomachs turning somersaults, we hit the highway. Around 3:30 we waited anxiously for the call, but it never came. Later we learned that Terry had collected the kids. The first crisis had passed, but we had no doubts that it would not be the last.

■ ■ ■

Earlier in July, Ben had faxed Terry about his vacation plans and consulted her about sending the kids to camp. Ben was entitled to two weeks' vacation with the kids. We were planning to spend one of those weeks at a friend's cottage in August. David and I had worked out Sara's summer plans, but to make that week happen for all five of us, Ben needed Terry's cooperation on the timing.

Ben wrote to her that he felt strongly the kids needed to get away from all the tension. A couple of weeks of camp would "provide them a much-needed break from us and a chance to feel good about themselves," and would be "a good alternative to having them hanging around the house all summer." He'd investigated some excellent, moderately priced programs and believed Terry should pay since he'd paid the previous two years. "Please let me know ... your thinking ... so we can put our heads together and try to come up with a workable solution that will serve the kids' needs."

Nine days passed without any response. Then Terry wrote back but totally ignored his questions. She wanted the kids to study piano that fall. She was offering to split the cost of lessons. She accused Ben of giving Deja "phoney excuses," then not taking her to the first few Saturday lessons the previous fall, and she said Deja had called her in tears asking Terry to take her "if you continued to be so obviously and unnecessarily obstructive." "Eventually [Deja] won her way and thoroughly loves her piano studies and takes to it quite naturally as I did in my youth." According to Terry, because Ben had refused to discuss enrolling Zoe last year, her friends were all ahead of her, and "it would be very upsetting for her to miss out on another year because of your stubbornness and empathy." (In a subsequent letter, Terry said she'd meant to accuse Ben of "apathy," not "empathy.")

Half the summer passed before Terry answered Ben's letter about vacation and camp.

July 31, 1992

Dear Ben,

I consider your sudden anxiety to discuss camp, highly suspicious.

I am hoping for the day when you are motivated by the needs of the children rather than what suits your convenience...

I realized that since the children were primarily living with me and only visiting you, you could avoid any responsibility for their time out of school. It wasn't until July [and] the new 50/50 schedule ... that you realized you too would have to deal with their summer time. Suddenly you were including ... camp in your barrage of letter writing. [By then] I had found it necessary to make my own plans.

Your first suggestion that we need to give the children a break from us, concerned me. Here it was your first week on our new schedule and instead of relishing in the time to finally be a full week with your children on a regular basis, you were anxious to send them out of town away from us both.

Then on your first weekend of the new schedule, you sent the children up north with friends and had your girlfriend meet them there. You refused to allow them to return home a day early on Sunday in order to be present at their great grandmother's headstone unveiling. Instead, when they did arrive they were severely sunburned. I wonder who was watching them all weekend since your girlfriend didn't even have a tan and you were in Boston since the previous Wednesday or Thursday.

The next weekend you once again, had the children sleeping at friends' homes. It seems to me they are getting plenty of time away from you already ...

For the time being, the kids are having a great time with my plans and if that situation changes, then maybe we will have some time left for camp.

The ten-day vacation schedule Ben had "demanded" would mean too long a time "for the children to be away from their mother."

It is unfortunate that because of the length of time of the trial you insisted upon conducting, in spite of my offers to resolve matters, I am now unable to afford more time without working in order to appreciate a vacation with Deja and Zoe. It is so fortunate that you can afford all this time without working as well as for so many other occasions.

Seeing as we are now in the joint parenting position you wanted, perhaps in the future you will also consider discussing matters that *I* feel are important as well, rather than just demanding your way on all matters that are of significance to you.

I see more need for co-operation now that the children no longer have a home base that they have always had in their lives before.

She ended the letter asking for an "immediate response" about piano lessons. Ben replied he couldn't afford lessons, and proposed another vacation schedule. Terry accused him of "a new unilateral creation" and refused to consent.

> If you can afford to rent a cottage and be absent from work for 2 weeks, as well as for half the week of July 27th, and at so many other times, then surely you have to reconsider your priorities, for the best interests of the children, since it now means you cannot afford piano lessons for them. I'm sorry you refuse to take Deja and Zoe to classes ... I know they would be willing to sacrifice another sprint at a cottage this summer if it means not having to lose the opportunity to play piano. The piano is much more important to them, especially in light of the fact that they have spent a good percentage of their summer at cottages.
>
> I can see, now that the children are going to be spending so much more time living in your care, they will have to give up all extra-curricular activities.

We were supposed to go on vacation in a couple of weeks, but none of Ben's proposals had met with Terry's approval. We decided I'd go up north with Sara for the week on Sunday. When the kids came home to Ben's on Friday, he'd bring them up. That meant the five of us would spend only the weekend together. It also meant Terry had accomplished what I believed had been her goal from the start: to frustrate another opportunity for us all to be together. The kids were terribly disappointed, but short of abducting them for a week so they could have the vacation they were entitled to have with their dad, Ben had no other choice.

August 6, 1992

Dear Terry
Okay, let's stick to the week on/off schedule as per your letter yesterday:

215

Aug 7 Pick-up Ben
Aug 14 Pick-up Terry
Aug 21 Pick-up Ben
Aug 28 Pick-up Terry

Ben

■ ■ ■

Meanwhile, Helen Goudge was working out the new parenting plan. During July, she'd spoken to both assessors, read their reports, and met once with each parent; by the end of the month she'd distributed a draft of her "best understanding (occasionally amplified) of the parenting plan as per Butkowsky/Goldstein/Court," and a letter outlining her powers, asking for feedback from lawyers and clients. This was disturbing. Ben didn't want the lawyers anywhere near that process. They'd only complicate matters, and all he needed was to have to start paying fees on both ends, to Reiter as well as Goudge. As he reviewed Goudge's parenting plan, his anxiety mounted. Ben thought it contained several sloppy mistakes and potential minefields that any experienced professional ought to have foreseen.

Why, for instance, were the parents to alternate authority for decisions about camp each year? That might be fair to the parents, but it precluded continuity for the kids. She'd also meddled with some of Butkowsky's rules for no good reason. Ben didn't think the changes were serious, but he was troubled that she'd made alterations at all. They already had rules and recommendations. Goudge's job was to implement those recommendations, not to start messing around with them.

The last item, however, truly alarmed him. Goudge had decreed that after a year either parent could have her replaced. Ben feared that Terry would dump Goudge if she couldn't manipulate her. Then we'd be back at square one. Deeply agitated, he resolved to speak to Goudge as soon as possible.

I met Goudge for the first time in mid-August, when Ben and I went to her office, a sunny space on the fourth floor of a midtown medical building. She was a cheerfully scattered woman with a singsongy voice and the ingratiatingly empathic manner of the social worker. Brightly coloured drawings depicting a child's view of divorce were tacked to the bulletin board on the wall beside her desk.

We went into the meeting warily. Goudge's letter had not inspired confidence, although by that point we would have been distrustful of any family court professional. The social worker's warmth was a welcome change after Goldstein's dour and distant manner. But she'd taken on a difficult case. She would have to bring more to the challenge than a sunny smile. We did our best to seem enthusiastic that she was aboard. We could not risk alienating her. Like her predecessors, Goudge had a staggering amount of power over our lives, and we knew that if she felt like it, she could easily turn them upside down.

Before long, that's exactly what happened. Although I believed we'd offered several compelling arguments to demonstrate why Goldstein's Friday transfer time had been a bad call in our case, Goudge flatly refused to do anything but monitor the situation for the next four months and decide by Christmas if there was to be a change. In the draft parenting plan she'd distributed (she hoped to formalize it during the summer so that it would take effect at the start of the school year), the transfer time was 6:00 on Fridays. We'd argued that although we still believed the first day of the school week was the optimum time, if it had to be on Fridays, as Goldstein had insisted, then 4:00 made more sense than 6:00. Deja and Zoe would go straight home to the other parent by school bus, and in summers their parents could avoid contact by collecting them directly from their activity. We'd also explained that during the school year we often had Friday-night dinners with family or friends; in summers we headed north to friends' cottages. Being forced to linger until 6:00 or later was annoying and unnecessary when the problem could so easily be remedied. Not to mention that if either parent turned up late, the other would be in a venomous mood and the kids would absorb the tension. However, if our protests at having to endure four more months living with an ill-conceived rule that made life worse for everyone in the family registered with the social worker, she gave no indication. Our opinion didn't count. We were there to be listened to, patted on the head, and ultimately ignored. Dr. Butkowsky and Dr. Goldstein and Helen Goudge were the experts, and the experts knew best.

Having dispatched our concerns, Goudge turned to Terry's. Ben was to have the kids for March break that year, but Terry wanted to take them to visit her parents in Florida. Would Ben consent to give up that time? Ben said if he didn't have any significant arrangements he wouldn't deny the kids a

217

chance to visit their grandparents. However, since Terry's plans often didn't materialize, he suggested she call when she wanted to book flights; by then he'd know his intentions and could give her an answer.

Next was piano. Ben told Goudge plainly that he was $250,000 in debt. Right now it was a struggle for him to pay for the kids' most basic needs, like their food, clothing, and shelter. Under the circumstances, he couldn't consider spending money on pianos or lessons. If he could scrape together money for extras, his priority was to spend it on camp, since camp would at least give the kids a break from all the fighting. Well then, asked Goudge, since Ben had purchased coverage for the kids on his ACTRA dental plan, could he get Terry coverage, too?

Ben and I exchanged horrified glances. He told Goudge in no uncertain terms that she wasn't to involve herself in their financial matters. Nowhere in Goldstein's report was there any indication that she had that authority. That was Justice Potts's domain. Her job was to implement the joint custody recommendations and to help them resolve parenting disputes.

I left that meeting enraged. Helen Goudge seemed like a very nice person, and I had no doubt that she wanted to help. But I had the feeling that she was in over her head. Like all the professionals we'd encountered in that process, Goudge was off in one corner of the room, playing with one piece of the puzzle. After three years, two assessments, and a thirteen-day trial, not one of them had heard the whole story or come anywhere close to the truth.

Watching Ben tell his story that day, growing agitated and upset, trying to make that woman understand our frustration, it struck me again that he must have seemed to her like every other emotionally overwrought divorced spouse whose tale of woe echoed within those four walls, just as he'd seemed to Butkowsky, who'd censured him for being so worked up, and Goldstein, who'd lectured him that his problem was his inability to "let go" of the conflict. But Ben wasn't telling someone else's story. He was telling his own. It couldn't be made to fit into some expert's neat little box. Sadly, he might as well have been Galileo trying to convince his inquisitors that the earth revolved around the sun.

The following week, consumed with similar worries, Ben wrote to Goudge, saying "some history is pertinent." Fearing the worst on the question of the piano – that Goudge would ignore everything he'd said about his desperate financial situation and rule that the kids were to have lessons – Ben argued that past history and present financial circumstances dictated that Terry should pay. "I have exhausted all my financial resources. I have no property or assets . . . My debts exceed $250,000. My yearly income is about $50,000 or less. Meanwhile, Mrs. Gordon, according to her own financial statement, is debt free." Terry's June 1, 1992, financial statement had disclosed no new debt other than her legal fees. "She has significant savings (over $20,000)," and she had recently inherited at least $5,000 from her grandmother's estate.

Since Terry still had the $4,000 Young Chang studio piano that he'd bought for Deja to begin lessons, where were they to get a second piano? He made three proposals: sell that jointly owned piano and he'd buy one for his place, in which case Terry could borrow her parents' piano and his would become the property of the kids; sell the piano and they'd each purchase keyboards; or let Terry buy out his share of the piano for $2,000 and he'd buy one for his place.

Again, Ben strongly warned Goudge not to involve Terry in his dental plan or finances: simply "confirm the parameters of your mediation/arbitration for now" and let Justice Potts settle the financials "whenever that might happen." "I know much of this missive constitutes the ravings of an irate ex-husband with a strong sense of being victimized – but that's exactly how I feel. At this point I'm not looking for vindication or revenge, merely for some relief. I do hope this letter conveys how desperate the situation for us (Wendy, me and the kids) really is."

Goudge released her parenting plan on August 24. She handed March break that year to Terry, neglected to arbitrate a change (if any) to the transfer time by Christmas, as promised, and involved Terry in Ben's financial affairs, opening another forum for conflict. It was unclear whether Goudge had been careless, confused, or oblivious, or had simply ignored us, but it hardly mattered.

Goudge ruled that Ben was to cover Terry on his dental plan and the kids were to have piano lessons. Both parents were to submit proposals for camp for the following summer and Goudge would rule by March 15. Ben was to arrange and pay for the dentist, orthodontist, and religious school lessons. Terry was to arrange and pay for piano lessons. Both parents were to submit receipts to Goudge for a twice-yearly accounting. Within two months, Ben was to provide the children with "an instrument on which to practice" and Terry was to pay $900 towards its cost. Ben was to keep the piano as long as either child took lessons, then give it to the kids or sell it and hand the proceeds to the mediator, who'd deposit the money in an interest-bearing account for the kids until Zoe turned twenty-one, when the girls would split the money. Goudge would review the Friday 6 o'clock transfer time not in four months, as she'd promised, but in six months.

It was as if she'd heard nothing we'd said, as if nothing that had happened before she'd been parachuted in to take over the case was of the slightest consequence. Terry wanted piano lessons. Ben wanted camp. Terry wanted dental coverage. Ben wanted a new transfer time. Helen Goudge liked to mediate. So Helen Goudge would mediate. Every problem could be solved by listening to both sides and finding a nice, neat compromise in the middle. No history. No context. No understanding.

Before Goudge had formalized her plan, Ben had asked Reiter to write to her about the provision that she could be replaced in a year. To promote "continuity" and avoid "game-playing by either side," Reiter had argued that she should be able to resign only for good reasons of her own, or, failing agreement between the parties, be replaced by court order. Presumably because a lawyer had made that particular request, it was honoured. In a letter written to the lawyers (and copied to the parents), she noted she'd "changed the terms of reference of my involvement," and that clause had disappeared from the official document. Now Ben was kicking himself that he'd asked for that change. He scrawled a big "No" beside the Expenses section, wrote "Authority?" under Jurisdiction, then threw down the letter in disgust. He didn't have the strength to deal with Helen Goudge right now. He had too many other problems.

■ ■ ■

Paul Slavens's listing on the house had expired during the trial. Shortly afterwards, Reiter wrote to Zaldin, threatening a motion if Terry wouldn't review the price. "Since the outcome of such a motion is an obviousity, I should think that we would all be better served and our clients exposed to less expense, if an agreement can be reached in advance." Zaldin replied on

July 3 that a motion was unnecessary. He expected "some agreement" between the parties and admonished Reiter not to arrange motions on short notice. "I am not available this afternoon as I am going to physiotherapy which I arranged for my sore back."

The next day, on Slavens's advice, Terry signed a new listing for sixty days at $569,000. Ben had been furious with Slavens ever since he'd assumed the listing in February and recommended a $619,000 asking price. Until late May the agent had advised sticking with that price in defiance of common sense, the market research, and the virtually unanimous opinion of other agents who'd seen the property. Almost seven months had passed since Pinelli had stressed the urgency of listing below $600,000.

Slavens was a major Forest Hill realtor who sold a lot of properties in the area, and whom Ben knew because he'd valued their house in the past. The agent was also a good friend of Reiter, who'd recommended hiring him. Slavens later maintained that while he understood that Ben wanted to cut his losses and sell at any price, he had a responsibility as the agent to both clients to list at the highest possible price to attract the highest dollar. If he recommended a lower price, he wouldn't be doing his best for Terry.

Ben believed that while Slavens's stated position was entirely defensible and kept him clean for the record, it flew in the face of reason, and in fact Slavens was serving only Terry's interests. Because of his desperate need to realize his equity, Ben could not dawdle, waiting for a buyer to show up at a high price. Terry and Slavens, however, seemed to have all the time in the world; selling at the highest possible price was all that mattered to them. Just like almost every other professional Ben had encountered in that process, Slavens had a vested interest. The higher the price, the higher the commission.

Burned once too often by Terry's manoeuvring and by the court's refusal to intervene in a listing agreement, Ben refused to sign the new listing unless Terry agreed that they could lower the price during the listing period. He told Slavens to advertise the house in the meantime, but Slavens said he couldn't put it on MLS without Ben's signature. Ben refused to sign unless Terry agreed. Terry wouldn't agree. Ben instructed his lawyer to seek a court order to auction off the house.

I faxed Reiter with Ben's instructions:

The house has been on the market for 9 months without any offers. Ben is desperate for money. He wants you to impress upon the Master that Terry should not be able to have it both ways. If she refuses to do whatever is necessary to sell the home, then she cannot also enjoy the benefits of it while Ben continues to live in much reduced circumstances at a much greater monthly cost. Please let Zaldin know as soon as possible that this is Ben's position.

Also ... Ben wants you to ask the Master to assign a day on which the chattels that are *not* in dispute (Ben has a signed and initialled list from Terry) can be removed from the home, as per Judge Potts' order of eight months ago. Surely, since there is agreement, at least this one small matter can be resolved and scratched from the list right away.

On July 16, Reiter wrote Zaldin on the matter of Ben's belongings: "At the very least, Mr. Gordon would like to attend at the matrimonial home to remove ... those items which she does not dispute are the exclusive property of Mr. Gordon ... I would appreciate a prompt response."

■ ■ ■

By early August, with the house at a stalemate and Terry refusing to part with any possessions, Reiter began making noises about a motion. Reiter's nephew Paul Bercovici, a young lawyer who'd worked in the taxation field but had no background in family law, prepared the motion. (Reiter ran his firm like a cottage industry. His wife, Carol, handled the firm's finances and his daughter, Naomi, worked as the receptionist.) On August 5, Bercovici faxed a draft notice of motion to Zaldin's associate, Clive Algie, seeking Terry's consent on the house and chattels issues, or they'd have to go to court on August 10.

Ben drove downtown to sign another affidavit. He'd lost count of how many he'd signed. He bristled at handing the parking lot attendant twenty bucks, knowing he wouldn't see change. Upstairs he read over the document in Reiter's office. How many times did the court have to hear the same story? How many affidavits did it take for the "learned judges" to get the picture?

The document told of Walsh's order to sell the house sixteen months before, Terry's appeal of that order, then her abandonment of the appeal. Her refusal to listen to her agents' advice and reduce the price. The five motions he'd had to bring to reduce the price. His consequent refusal to sign another listing unless they could lower the price during the new listing period. "I am content with a reduced listing price of $569,000.00," read the affidavit, "but have no real expectation or hope that the property will actually sell at that price." He asked the court to put the house up for auction. The balance of the document recounted what he'd been put through trying to collect his possessions.

On August 10, Master Linton ordered Slavens's listing extended at $569,000 until September 8. Then he had to rule on Ben's property claims. It had now been two and a half years since Ben and Terry had separated, and almost a year since Terry had agreed to divide their property. Zaldin told the court he needed more time to review the matter with his client. The master gave him three more weeks.

August 21, 1992

Dear Mr. Zaldin:
On our attendance before Master Linton [on August 10] and upon the adjournment of the portion of the Motion dealing with the division of chattels, you indicated that you wished an opportunity to review the matter and discuss it with your client. It is now almost two weeks since you advised that you were prepared to consider consenting to the Order for the division of chattels and I have heard nothing from you.

May I have your response so that we can know whether we have to go through the wasteful exercise of continuing with our Motion to obtain an Order ...

I look forward to hearing from you by return mail.
Yours very truly,
Moishe Reiter

Zaldin forwarded an affidavit. Terry viewed Ben's motion to collect his belongings two years after he'd moved out of their home as "just another example of my ex-husband's desire to litigate this matter at every possible opportunity."

She accused Ben of having taken "numerous items" from the house but failing to list them "in his various lists." Among the thirty-nine items which she now wanted "factored in" to the total were two Mickey Mouse watches (according to Ben, Terry was referring to two Ronald McDonald watches he'd received for hosting a fundraiser at Sunnybrook Hospital), a (stale-dated) weekend for two at the Sheraton Hotel, a Dustbuster, two king-size pillows, an ice chopper, extension cords, TV and stereo adaptors and wiring, a VCR, and six bottles of Dom Pérignon.

Terry wanted back the Fisher-Price child monitors, queen-size sheets, baby crib, wicker rocking chair, and seat covers that she and Ben had handed down to Mark Anshan and Brenda Spiegler when they were expecting their first child. Terry had also had second thoughts about returning several items she'd already initialled and conceded were Ben's. She'd colour-coded the lists to reflect her latest position on what was hers. And, presumably on Zaldin's advice, she'd also decided not to turn anything over before consulting another expert. "It would be wrong to release the property," she wrote, "without first getting an appraisal."

The law was clear that divorcing spouses were entitled to keep whatever property they'd brought into the marriage or had received as gifts during the marriage. Terry demanded the two "fish ashtrays" Ben had given her. She conceded that their bedroom and dining room furniture was Ben's before marriage, but reasoned she should be entitled to keep that, too: Ben "told me that he had in effect gifted this to the two of us," she told the court, "because he persuaded me to give away or sell my bedroom furniture and dining room suite because we had his." Therefore, it was "patently unfair ... for him to keep the furniture that *he* brought into the marriage without compensation." She also claimed that Ben had bought her another gift that should be hers to keep: the piano.

On August 31, Master Linton ordered Terry to make available for Ben to pick up "forthwith" the items that Terry had admitted belonged to Ben. In other words, the court ordered Terry to turn over whatever she felt like turning over. With Zaldin's participation, Terry breached that court order, too.

September 14, 1992

Dear Paul [Bercovici]:

On August 31, 1992, Master Linton made an Order ... making those items which Terry Nusyna has admitted belong to Mr. Gordon available for him to pick up forthwith.

My client wishes no more "scenes" at the matrimonial home and, accordingly, she has arranged to deliver those undisputed items to Mr. Gordon at 21 Relmar Road, Toronto, by her renting a truck on September 19, 1992, to arrive at Relmar Road at approximately 12 noon.

There will be arriving that day some cumbersome furniture items which may require storage. Please advise your client of this fact as he may want to make *his own* arrangements for the storage of these items *on that day*.

> Yours truly,
> Ronald V. Zaldin

Ben was outraged when he saw Zaldin's letter. It reminded him of the infuriating letter advising of Terry's so-called agreement to the Butkowsky recommendations, providing Ben vacated his own home according to Zaldin's schedule. Who does he think he is? Ben wondered. Were there no standards to which family lawyers had to adhere? Here was a so-called officer of the court telling him that his client had decided not to obey a court order, that she would be delivering his property at her convenience and as she saw fit, and that he'd better make arrangements to receive it when she dictated. Ben viewed Zaldin's letter as just another in a long line of contemptible actions by a contemptible man.

Saturday mornings the girls had religious school from 9:00 until 11:30, then piano lessons in Forest Hill Village at 1:00. Ben made them lunch at the apartment or took them around the corner to the Village Restaurant for "strangled eggs," one of their favourite rituals. The court had ordered Terry to make Ben's property available for him to pick up. Terry, however, had unilaterally decided to arrive at Ben's place when she knew the kids would be there, at high noon that Saturday, riding shotgun on a truckload of his belongings. In July, Zaldin had told Goldstein his client was concerned that dividing the children's furniture would be too "divisive" for them. Now he again insisted her intentions were strictly honourable: she was only trying to avoid a scene. But it was clear to me that Terry's actions were those of someone deliberately looking to provoke one.

Zaldin's letter did the trick. It launched us both into combat mode. Ben faxed Goudge. Then he sent Zaldin an angry fax. He told Zaldin not to make inflammatory statements or unilateral decisions about his property. Saturday was neither convenient nor appropriate. "Nevertheless I'm sure that a time convenient for both parties and taking the children into consideration, can be arranged."

September 16, 1992

Dear [Mr. Reiter]:
I am returning your client's letter to you unanswered. I will *not* respond to letters from Mr. Gordon. You are his solicitor of record and I will only respond to letters from you on your letterhead and not from Ben Gordon.

Please instruct him not to write me again directly or indirectly ...

Yours truly,
Ronald V. Zaldin

On Friday, Reiter wrote back: "Your ultimatum and threat to take the matter back before Mr. Justice Potts is a good idea. Please make an appointment ... so that His Lordship can get a clear picture of how this situation has degenerated ... I will be bringing a motion on at the same time."

That Saturday morning, Ben and I ran around trying to dodge Terry's and Zaldin's latest bullet. I was furious at yet another demonstration of their wanton contempt for a court order, disgusted at the lawyer's pouring of fuel on the fire, and worried about the kids witnessing an ugly scene. I imagined Terry arriving with Ben's stuff just when he returned with the girls from religious school and dumping it on the lawn if he refused to take it in the manner she'd dictated. His only way of averting a confrontation, short of scrambling to make storage arrangements and capitulating, yet again, to her unilateral actions, was to secure a letter from his landlord saying he didn't want her on his property. His landlord, an old family friend, lived in the neighbourhood. On Saturday morning, after dropping the kids at synagogue, Ben called him to explain the situation. Then we drove to his house while he typed up a letter. After religious school, Ben dropped the girls off at the Village Restaurant to keep them out of the fray, told them to order, and said he'd be along shortly. Then he came home and posted the landlord's letter on the front door, and we waited. Around 12:30, Terry rounded the corner in a van, accompanied by a man. I watched from the front door. Ben went outside and handed her a copy of the letter. Fearing another incident or criminal charge, he snapped a few photographs of her, her sidekick, and the van, then went inside. After a while, Terry climbed back inside the van and it pulled away.

We'd survived another crisis – for now. But the cumulative damage of the assaults we'd endured from all quarters was taking its toll. Although I did not speak of my feelings to Ben, I did not know how much longer I could go on like this.

After the weekend, the letters started flying again. Monday, Ben faxed Terry proposing Wednesday morning to deliver his property. Tuesday, Zaldin accused Ben of frustrating Terry's delivery. "Perhaps Mr. Gordon does not wish his items?" he asked, enclosing a letter from Terry "attesting to her efforts to comply with the Court order."

According to Terry, she told Ben she'd deliver his belongings but since he didn't give her a reason why she shouldn't, she arrived at noon as planned. When she asked Ben where he wanted his stuff, he handed her a letter. Then we'd shut the door in her face. That made it "impossible for me and my 3 strong helpers to complete our delivery." She returned to the truck and Ben came outside snapping photographs. She "carefully placed" his belongings in a storage locker, but was no longer "prepared to go through any more humiliation or expense." The locker key was with the letter. Also attached was a list of the things Terry had delivered. According to Ben, there was nothing of value. Most items were odds and ends he'd accumulated prior to their marriage that had been in storage in the basement, things Terry had never had any interest in: an antique globe, some posters, a reel-to-reel tape recorder. It was as if Terry had simply swept the last traces of him from "her" house.

■ ■ ■

Since the motion before Master Linton in August to auction the house and retrieve his property, Ben had been pressing Reiter for some action on the file. Aside from the unresolved property matters, he wanted Justice Potts to deal with his outstanding financial concerns, which had been left hanging after the second part of the trial in June. Ben was still hoping that Potts's review would allow him to recover overpayments he'd made to Terry in child support because of the false financial information she'd submitted to the court. (Not only on her financial statements and child care budget, but because of her failure to report the substantial income she'd anticipated earning from Steepe – money she was suing to collect. At that point Ben didn't know Terry had dropped that action or if she'd settled with Steepe.)

No progress had been made towards compensating Ben for the money that had gone down the drain while Terry had held up the sale of the house. Ben was also now considering claiming child support from Terry. Based on the evidence that had emerged, he believed she had the greater income. He could use support to provide for the kids, and it would be satisfying to reclaim some of the money he believed she'd been unjustly awarded, but he wasn't counting on it. Still, just suing Terry for child support would force her to provide financial information; making that claim might finally uncover the truth about Terry's finances – a truth Zaldin had managed to conceal at the trial.

After Reiter's most recent failed attempt to get the master to reduce the price of the house, Ben found it harder and harder to reach Reiter, and, when he did manage it, he felt their exchanges were increasingly unsatisfying. Whenever Ben asked Reiter to outline his strategy, it seemed Reiter didn't have one. Eventually – some time in September, as Ben remembers it – the lawyer stopped returning his calls. Around the same time, however, Carol Reiter was phoning Ben frantically late at night to say they couldn't make the rent on their Scotia Plaza office, and pleading with Ben to let her pick up a cheque. Ben had already paid Reiter $80,750 and the lawyer had billed him for another $94,635, but Ben had no more money to give him.

Ten months had passed since they'd supposedly settled the property issues and Reiter had declared in his notes: "House going to be sold now!!! got rid of that club now!!!!!" But Terry was still in the house with their property. Ben believed that because the money had stopped flowing and Reiter couldn't do anything more for him, he'd lost interest in the file.

It seemed Reiter had hit a brick wall. Ben was stuck with Master Linton. He'd gone to the master umpteen times with stacks of data, market research, expert opinions, affidavits from Pinelli – overwhelming and incontravertible evidence proving why a house that had been ordered sold because of a desperate financial situation more than seventeen months earlier had to be sold. But he'd gotten nowhere. The master, it seemed, didn't want to make a decision or effect any change to upset the status quo. Ben had been in court on every motion before the master, and every time he'd felt the weight of the system's biases. He had the distinct impression that Master Linton had been reluctant to move a mother and children from a home and, because Ben was a husband forcing the sale of the matrimonial home, seemed to view him as a man just trying to get his money out at the expense of the children. So Linton had rejected the evidence, adopted a wait-and-see attitude in a crashing market, and, as Ben saw it, denied him justice.

From Reiter's perspective, Ben theorized, Gordon was just calling again with some other trite problem outside the legal arena that he couldn't do anything about. Reiter wasn't going to get paid until the house sold, but he couldn't make that happen, so why bother returning his calls?

Ben thought back to his first meeting with Reiter, what a mess he'd been when he'd walked through his door, how desperate he'd been to find a lawyer who could deal with Zaldin, how Reiter had given him the impression that he knew Zaldin's tricks, that he could play the mongoose to the snake and close the file in a couple of weeks. Now he felt as if his lawyer had taken him on a ride through the system, led him to a dead end on the house, bled the file dry, moved on to other, still lucrative files, and abandoned him to wait for the master to realize that the house was listed way over market value.

Ben finally caught up with his lawyer the first week in October and pinned him down to a meeting. He refused to go downtown again and asked Reiter to meet him at a restaurant one morning on the way to work.

According to Ben, Reiter arrived about forty-five minutes late, accompanied by his daughter, Naomi, made no apologies for his tardiness, and behaved as if it was a great imposition for him to be there. When Ben asked Reiter pointedly what he was doing for him, Naomi Reiter told him he had no right to talk to her father that way, Reiter said he didn't have to listen to criticism, and they left. (Reiter later denied the exchange had been heated.)

We couldn't worry any more about a judge labelling Ben "crazy" because he'd had so many lawyers. We no longer had the strength to care what a judge might think. We couldn't imagine the situation being any worse than it was. Reiter had to go. My cousin Joyce suggested we consult Julie Hannaford, a partner at the downtown firm of Borden & Elliot. Joyce characterized Hannaford as smart, sensible, and tough enough to deal with Zaldin. Hannaford agreed to take the case. On his forty-first birthday, Ben finally fired Moishe Reiter.

October 9, 1992

Dear Moishe,
It has been apparent to me for some time that communication between us has been strained. It has become increasingly difficult to discuss legal matters with you, and our last meeting on Monday, October 5th went very badly. In addition to the fact that we both left feeling frustrated and angry, none of the issues we'd come together to discuss were any closer to being resolved. Consequently, I am writing to inform you that I have lost confidence in your ability to satisfactorily represent me and will no longer require your services as counsel. I have retained the law firm of Borden & Elliot to act on my behalf. I also wish to inform you that, among other things, I will be disputing your fees charged to date.

Borden & Elliot will be contacting you shortly to request my file. Since you informed me that I am on the list for continuation of the trial during the week of October 19th, which is only 10 days away, I would ask that you ensure that the complete file be transferred immediately in order that the trial may proceed at that time. Obviously, Borden & Elliot will require as much opportunity as possible, within a very tight time frame, to familiarize themselves with the reams of material pertaining to this lengthy and convoluted case.

Sincerely,
Ben Gordon

P.S. Attached please find direction authorizing you to release my file to Messrs. Borden & Elliot.

That day Hannaford sent Reiter a notice of change of solicitors and requested Ben's file. Reiter refused to release it unless Ben agreed not to mortgage his house further, and to apply any money he received from its sale towards his outstanding fees, after an assessment. (Disputes over legal fees are resolved through a trial proceeding called a fee taxation assessment.) In the meantime, Hannaford could review the file at his office. Reiter also said the case wasn't on the trial list for next week, and "given the circumstances, it is very unlikely that Mr. Justice Potts will accept it for that date. The urgency Mr. Gordon refers to may be considerably more apparent than real."

We met with Hannaford after she'd reviewed the file. Careful to avoid making any comments about Reiter, Hannaford strongly advised Ben to challenge his fees. Then she asked Ben what he wanted. Ben said he wanted closure. Hannaford advised agreeing to Reiter's terms. Then she said that whatever financial losses Ben may have suffered at Terry's hands, he could forget about getting any money back: the court wasn't big on retroactivity. He should also forget about the court ordering Terry to pay him child support. The evidence didn't warrant such an order. She asked about the chattels. Were there any valuable antiques or works of art at stake? Ben said no. Hannaford advised him to forget about his belongings, too; it would cost him more to pay her to fight for them than they were worth. "I advise you to capitulate," she said. "In this legal system, a spouse who feels wronged can carry on a court battle indefinitely – as long as there's enough anger and money to fuel it – and so far Terry has demonstrated no shortage of either." She advised drawing up an offer to settle. Her fees would be about $30,000, to wrap things up.

I believed Hannaford's advice was sound; still, it rankled me to hear it.

By that point, however, Ben was too beaten up and dazed to have much of a reaction to the advice, or to the fee she'd quoted. The amount he'd lost was so astronomical, the legal fees he'd been charged so outrageous that money had ceased to have meaning for him. Ben told Hannaford he wanted to think about what she'd said. The only remark he made afterwards was that he'd have thought it should cost less than $30,000 to give away everything he owned.

■ ■ ■

Since Goudge's parenting plan had become official on September 1, we were encountering even more headaches than anticipated with the transfer time. Goldstein had seen the Friday after-school transfer as a way for the kids to say goodbye to the parent they were leaving, and then "settle in" with the new parent before the new school week on Monday. In practice, his recommendation had exactly the opposite effect. The kids came home around 4:00, spent a few minutes packing up their stuff, then waited for the next two hours. It was like sitting through two hours of dead air. They didn't know what to do with themselves. They became agitated and irritable. Anticipation of the impending separation hung in the air like a toxic odour. If the table was set for guests that evening, or we had a dinner invitation, the kids would become upset about missing out on the fun. We could easily have avoided those problems if they'd returned to Terry's by bus after school as we'd suggested.

Meanwhile, several of Goudge's other rulings were causing conflicts and confusion. Shortly after she'd released her parenting plan, Ben had written Goudge reiterating his many warnings not to enter off-limits territory. The court would deal with financial issues. "In the interim it doesn't make sense for me to buy a piano when I already own one."

Nevertheless, he was cooperating with Goudge's rulings to the extent that he could. Both kids had begun piano lessons in September. Unable to afford $1,800 to buy a piano, and doubtful he'd see Terry's share even if he could, Ben borrowed his dad's studio piano when he left for Florida that winter. Angry, though, that another authority had ruled in a vacuum and saddled him with all the responsibility and inconvenience, while for Terry nothing changed, Ben sent Goudge a $900 invoice for the "rental fee" to include in her reckoning of expenses.

That autumn, our only pleasure was having the kids for week-long stretches. The new routine had begun in July, but Sara had been away most of the summer and the Jewish high holidays had disrupted the schedule in September. It wasn't until October that the new arrangement began to take on a fluid rhythm. With the ground constantly shifting below us, the fall finally gave us the continuity we needed, and the girls began to settle down.

Goudge had spent the summer assembling the new parenting plan. She had met with both parents but did not meet the children until the fall. On October 19, after her first meeting with the kids at Ben's apartment (she'd already met with them once at Terry's), Goudge announced that she was considering altering the schedule: Zoe was expressing some "attachment issues" to Terry, was "stretched" by the current schedule, and would need more time with her mom. Ben and I were stunned. It had taken two and a half years in court, tens of thousands of dollars, and two child care professionals to achieve a stable parenting plan. After two half-hour interviews with a seven-year-old child, Goudge was now considering changing it.

Ben told Goudge that she had no authority to tamper with Goldstein's schedule and that under no circumstances would we support any decision to do so. We weren't seeing any signs of Zoe's "attachment issues." The kids rarely called Terry, although Terry sometimes called them four and five times a day, and they were finding her calls extremely intrusive. Deja had taken to rolling her eyes whenever her mother called. If anyone had "attachment issues," it was Terry. We had noticed Zoe becoming uncharacteristically clingy around Ben, however, although it was no wonder the poor kid was hanging on to her dad for dear life: Terry was telling Zoe how lucky she was that her mommy let her see her daddy, since some kids never got to see their daddies at all. Goudge said she would "monitor" Zoe's "attachment issues" for a few months before making her decision.

That night, Ben and I put the kids to bed biting back a murderous rage. Whenever I thought about Goudge's casually heedless announcement, her cheerful certainty that she knew best, her awesome power yet stupefying ignorance of the path she was headed down, I felt a fury unlike any I'd ever known. Still, we had to tread carefully. We knew only too well how the game worked by now. We had to make nice with Helen Goudge.

Goudge had reported to us that when she'd met with the girls she'd found "warmth and responsiveness" to the kids in both households. She said that Zoe told her "sometimes my dad settles me down," and that both girls had said it helped when I talked to them about their problems, particularly Deja, who'd been very "positive about Wendy" but was "probably not relating her feelings to Terry."

Goudge had also reported to us that she'd asked the girls to tell her stories, because storytelling was a good way for kids to express the "emotional junk" they were carrying around. Deja had apparently told "boring stories," although Goudge thought she had a good sense of humour. Deja had found the old schedule confusing and, except for the transfer time, was "perfectly happy" with the new one. Her main issue was the conflict between her parents. Deja was "absolutely preoccupied" with it. After a half-hour, the social worker had concluded Deja was "just about perfect."

Zoe, whom she described as "expressive" and "spontaneous . . . not a suppressed child," had reportedly told stories all about a "mommy who gets a police hat and a gun to go after the person who took her baby." In Zoe's stories, a man had hidden a baby from the mommy, or a "bad Bart Simpson" had taken the mommy's baby away. The mommy had tried to rescue the baby, but by the time the mommy got the baby back, she was too old. Zoe had reportedly told Goudge that she thought boys should be with their daddies and girls with their mommies. Zoe had also said she liked the schedule the old way and wanted to see her mom during the week.

Goudge told us the themes in Zoe's stories revealed a child who was "very attached to . . . misses [and] feels for her mom" and who "feels the need to protect a mother who can fall apart." She theorized these themes meant Zoe had "anxious attachment issues" to Terry, and the best way to resolve these "attachment issues" was for Zoe to spend more time with her mother.

It was obvious that Zoe's stories revealed a child who felt burdened with the inordinate responsibility of taking care of a needy mother. The problem was where Goudge went from there. I was not an "expert." I did not have a degree in psychology or social work. I was only a mother, with a daughter of my own, who'd developed certain insights from being a parent and from having spent a great deal of time with Ben's kids. Zoe struck me as a highly impressionable seven-year-old who was locked in an unhealthy bond with a mother preying on her needs and insecurities. It was Terry's script I recognized in Zoe's stories – the line about girls needing to be with their mommies and boys with their daddies had her imprimatur all over it, as did the story about a bad man stealing a baby from a victimized mother who tried righteously but helplessly to protect it. I believed that Zoe, fearing her mother's reprisal and needing her approbation, had learned her lines well.

Zoe had told Goudge that she missed her mom and liked the schedule the old way. Goudge's error, I believed, was taking what Zoe said at face value. Goudge seemed to equate sympathy for Zoe with acquiescence to her request, while failing to identify the greater evil that had prompted it. Instead of empathizing with Zoe, explaining gently that her mom was unfair to burden her with adult needs and problems, confirming the new rules – and then telling Terry in no uncertain terms that such a destructive pattern would not be tolerated – Goudge, like Butkowsky, just pandered to it.

At our meetings, we tried to explain all this to Goudge. We warned her, too, about destroying the continuity it had taken so long to achieve, setting us up for more conflict, and directly contradicting the main intent of Goldstein's recommendations: that the joint custody agreement was to be scrupulously equal in every respect to avert one parent attempting to assert primacy or control.

Our concerns fell on deaf ears. When we told Goudge she was upsetting joint custody, she told us that Goldstein's term "joint custody" was a misnomer, and that the reality in this case was that *she* had custody of Deja and Zoe. That remark rendered us speechless, and Ben and I just stared at her. We didn't have the strength to argue. Anyway, we knew we'd only be barking at the moon.

Meanwhile, in counterpoint to Ben's worsening troubles, we had mine. Since the spring my always uneasy truce with David had grown increasingly fragile. From the start, our joint custody arrangement had been fraught with controversy. In addition to the carton of legal documents left over from our first go-round, I'd accumulated a thick file of faxes we'd exchanged about this issue or that, and a lawyer's letter David had sent me over one of them. Nevertheless, as I'd explained to Goldstein, who'd remarked that Sara was a terrific kid, we'd somehow managed to shield her from our acrimony.

By the fall of 1992, however, David and I were arguing about everything, and our disputes weren't being resolved. Now that Sara was an adolescent, she was understandably eager to play a role in decisions about her life. Matters had come to a head the previous spring when Sara was graduating from Grade 6 and we had to choose her new school. As was our practice, David, Sara, and I had gone together to check out various options. Sara's first choice was a Toronto Board of Education alternative school with a superb academic reputation. Sara was interviewed and accepted, and she was thrilled. Her teacher and the principal who'd known her since junior kindergarten concurred that the choice was a good one for her. But then David had second thoughts. At the time he said he was unhappy about the distance Sara would have to travel by public transit to the school, and he refused to consent.

Sara had always been mature for her age – since childhood, she'd been mistaken for being two years older – and as a city kid, she was used to subway travel. She assured David she'd manage the forty-five-minute commute, but David wouldn't budge. When he began talking about schools we'd all rejected, Sara became distraught. Because we had joint custody, if David withheld his consent, the school Sara wanted to attend couldn't legally admit her. Her only option would be for me to obtain a court order. I told Sara I believed her schooling was important, important enough that if her dad forced the issue I'd go to court. (What I didn't tell her was that I couldn't possibly afford to go to court, that because I couldn't, her father could wield the power of joint custody like a club, and that even if I could afford to go to court, his resources far outweighed mine so it would never be a fair fight.) Fortunately, shortly before Sara left for camp, David relented. But the months of worry and uncertainty took their toll on her.

Although David insisted that his main reservation about the school had been Sara's travelling time, I suspected something else was going on. I'd always feared Sara would encounter problems with her father when she hit adolescence and began to assert her female autonomy. I believed that Sara's choice of an alternative school that none of his friends' children attended, located in a modest neighbourhood far from his, signalled to David that Sara was leaving his world and drawing closer to mine. Because of his need to control, he was trying to pull her back.

The problem was exacerbated because I was encouraging Sara to learn to make her own choices, while David was communicating to her that he was the parent, she was the child, and she was being disobedient. I saw it as my job to encourage her developing autonomy; David said we should maintain the "practices and protocols" that had been in place in the past. Sara felt insulted by her father's refusal to recognize her own voice – and caught in the middle. Her adolescence, then, became the catalyst for a whole new set of problems between David and me, problems in which, for the first time, she became embroiled.

Sara had moved happily between two households since she was four, but that fall she began to express reservations about returning to David's. She reported feeling isolated, ganged up on by him and Jan, having terrible, unresolved fights, and sitting through dinnertime with an unsettled stomach. She said that if she expressed a view that contradicted her father's, he'd insist that I'd manipulated her into it, get mad, give her the silent treatment, withhold his approval, and make her feel guilty until she capitulated to his will. She began to call me surreptitiously from his household, and to express recurring anxieties that I'd be killed in a car accident or plane crash. I watched helplessly as my once happy-go-lucky daughter became anxious, confused, and depressed. That autumn and early winter, I spent most of my time with Sara either trying to comfort her before she left for her dad's or picking up the pieces when she returned. For the first time I worried about her when she was living with her father.

The behaviour Sara was reporting was behaviour I knew only too well. I did my best to reassure her that her dad loved her, that it was just his way, and I tried to give her strategies to protect herself. But I was furious at David, and frustrated that I couldn't protect my daughter when she needed me. Sometimes, with all the pressures of Ben's situation – and now my own – weighing me down, my volatile anger at David exploded irrationally in front of Sara. Ben, however, never wavered in his calm. He did for Sara what he wished someone would do for his kids. He held her close and talked to her for hours about how she might try to work things out with her dad, and told her over and over again how much her father loved her.

That autumn was an endless blur of trying to cope with the ongoing litigation, fend off ex-spouses, put out fires set by Helen Goudge, and shore up three increasingly battle-scarred children. Meanwhile, Ben was still going to auditions, trying to be funny, and I was still promoting my book, trying to deliver bons mots about sex on national television. By November we were running on empty. I had a speaking engagement in Buffalo that month, and we seized the opportunity for a family outing in Buffalo and Niagara Falls. And so one Saturday morning we piled into the car and headed west on the Queen Elizabeth Way.

November was a strange time to visit the falls – the weather was cold and damp and blustery, and the place was like a ghost town – but we were happy for the escape and strolled the strip in our ski jackets and toques, exploring all the kitschy museums and souvenir shops. Later we checked into a honeymoon motel with a waterbed and hot tub, and we all climbed into the tub for a bubble bath. The girls put on their pyjamas and jumped on the waterbed, and Zoe said it was the best time she had ever had in her whole entire life.

In Buffalo we went shopping at the Gap, and everyone ran in and out of fitting rooms trying stuff on. Heading home on Sunday night we stopped in St. Catharines at the Big Wheel, one of those restaurants where families go for Sunday dinners. We were all giddy that night, and I don't recall exactly how it started, but we began spoofing ourselves, pretending to be the all-American family, Sara playing the big sister, and the girls making faces and acting silly and pretending to be bad and spill their Cokes, and me pretending to scold them, saying if they didn't settle down their father would be cross, and Ben play-acting the stern, overbearing fifties father, announcing, for my benefit, that if the kids didn't settle down they wouldn't be able to watch the Beatles on *Ed Sullivan* that night. When it was time to go, we climbed into the car, adults in the front, kids in the back, and because it seemed the capper to the evening, I suppose, Sara pulled down her pants and hung a moon between the two front seats. We all died laughing then, and I remember thinking on the drive home, listening to the gentle breathing of the kids by then asleep in the back seat, that we could do it, we could really do it, if only someone would help, or just leave us alone.

■ ■ ■

In October, Ben had agreed to Reiter's terms and Hannaford had initiated the settlement process with Zaldin. On October 27, she proposed that she and Zaldin each draw up an agenda and offered to shuffle her schedule to meet at any time to work out a deal. She arranged an appointment with

Justice Potts to secure a trial date. If negotiations failed, they'd go to trial.

Zaldin responded to her invitation that day. In a letter crowned with the words "WITHOUT PREJUDICE," he proposed that they meet alone first, then with their clients, to settle the property issues, assuming they could work out the remaining financial matters as he proposed. "Without Prejudice, I think that both parties should simply walk away at this stage and stop the erosion of the declining equity that each party has in the matrimonial home."

On November 4, Hannaford forwarded to Zaldin a signed draft of minutes of settlement. Ben had taken Hannaford's advice and abandoned all his outstanding financial claims against Terry. They would have full joint custody. Neither would pay child support to the other. Goudge would resolve their disputes. Master Linton would continue to deal with all matters related to selling the home and dividing the possessions.

The following week Hannaford sent a current statement of Ben's income, assets, and liabilities. Because Ben had asked her to take one more shot at negotiating the return of at least some of his belongings, she'd also attached "a list of the contents which Mr. Gordon would like your client to consider returning to him." Ben had abandoned most of the household goods but had told Hannaford that Terry's claim to their bedroom and dining room furniture was "ridiculous" – he'd owned that property before marriage – and her claim to the kids' furniture and the piano "indefensible" – those were family assets. He also wanted her to return his grandmother's furniture.

The next day, Hannaford proposed a selection process that some couples used to divide their property: they would take turns picking from a list of property they agreed was jointly owned. The lawyer also apologized for having "misstated" Ben's proposal on the chattels: "Please stress to [your client] that any over reaching which she may have inferred from those lists would result from my error and not from the actual instructions of Mr. Gordon." Before signing off, Hannaford apologized again: "Once again, please convey my apologies to Ms. Nusyna, for any misunderstanding of the lists."

The apologetic tone of Hannaford's letter made sense in light of her client's desire to settle. After Reiter's long-winded pomposity and Zaldin's inflammatory, emphatically underlined righteous indignation, Hannaford's style was refreshingly professional. Nevertheless, I found that letter almost unbearable to read. In spite of all the lies Terry had told, property she'd withheld, deals she'd broken, court orders she'd ignored, and damage she'd wrought, Ben had to grovel to her.

Negotiations proceeded throughout November. Terry wanted a provision obliging them to split the kids' extras. I suggested drafting that clause so they paid their shares directly to the payee, a fairly standard alternative for couples who could not deal with each other without wrangling over money. When camp or piano lessons rolled around, they'd each mail in a cheque for their share to the camp or piano teacher, they'd each be liable to the payee, and there'd be no need to join battle.

Discussions went smoothly as long as Ben was willing to give Terry everything. The moment he asked for a concession – that she hand over some of his belongings, for instance – she refused to settle. On November 10, Hannaford wrote to Zaldin that she'd advised Ben "your client was reviewing the chattels issue and would be delivering instruction to you imminently in this regard." Two days later Zaldin wrote back: "Terry assures me that she is working on the lists and I expect to have them in your hands next week. Her lists will include a short reason for Mr. Gordon if she is in disagreement with any items on his lists."

Hannaford wrote to Ben that Zaldin had said Terry was delivering her chattels list on Sunday. She hoped to produce the finalized minutes of settlement and have Terry's chattels list and financial information by Monday. Then she warned Ben that minutes of settlement were only as effective as the good faith of the two parties who signed them.

> The type of resolution, calling as it does for joint custody and negotiation around a number of issues, will never put an end to negotiation or conflict between you and Terry. There are many "holes" in the Minutes which by definition cannot be satisfactorily shored up so as to prevent discussion. One example of this is of course issues surrounding the children such as the type of education they will receive, the type of extraordinary medical or other treatment they may receive, and so on. Because this agreement calls for joint custody, it assumes that all of these types of issue will be the subject

of ongoing discussion. Thus the expense sharing issues will similarly be the ground for ongoing discussion. These Minutes of Settlement cannot guarantee any end to conflict. But they do put an end to the ongoing litigation ... More importantly, if Terry wishes to be unco-operative, then Minutes of Settlement can only provide a backdrop against which subsequent behavior can be measured and dealt with.

■ ■ ■

On Sunday, November 22, the first two offers came in on the house. The best offer was for $470,000. It was presented by an agent in Slavens's office and expired at midnight Monday.

When Hannaford had taken over Ben's file in October, she'd agreed the house was unlikely to sell at $569,000. Earlier in November, on Slavens's recommendation, Ben and Terry had agreed to reduce the price to $549,000. But when Slavens's listing expired in December, Hannaford planned to bring a motion asking the master to reduce the price further. To that end, she'd asked Ben to secure three opinion letters on the property value. The agents' estimates were between $450,000 and $500,000, but Slavens recommended countersigning the offer at $539,000. Ben signed. Terry refused.

On November 23, Hannaford wrote to Zaldin that she was having "significant difficulty" explaining to her client why his client had yet to complete her financial disclosure or her contents list, "especially since I insisted that he complete financial disclosure and contents list within 3 days." She advised that if the minutes weren't finalized, she'd deliver a formal offer to settle and request "the earliest possible trial date" since "it is unreasonable to protract the proceedings into a pre trial."

> I have learned that two offers were presented on the home. I learned that Mr. Paul Slavens communicated with both your client and mine. My client was prepared to rely on the expertise and recommendations of Mr. Slavens, and thus authorized Mr. Slavens to sign back the offer at $539,000.00. To my great surprise (and disappointment) your client has refused to do so. Mr. Slavens has expertise in the field of real estate. He is under significant difficulty in dealing with this

situation. My client agreed to abide by Mr. Slavens' expertise, and is somewhat concerned that your client is refusing to do so.

My client had been instructed by me to obtain further opinions of value in respect of the home. These pre date the offers, and are in the range of $450,000 to $500,000. There are three such opinions.

Please speak to me about this. I trust and hope we can work this out. There should not have to be a motion in respect of the sale of this home, but I am concerned in that regard.

Yours very truly,

JKH

On Monday the purchasers increased the offer to $485,000 and agreed to change their closing date to suit Terry. "To my knowledge & belief," advised Slavens, "this is the best offer" they were willing to make. Nonetheless, the next day he recommended playing hardball and counteroffering at $539,000 "with the expectation of increasing [the] offer to possibly the $500,000.00 range." That offer expired midnight Wednesday. Ben signed. In case Terry refused, Hannaford prepared an affidavit. Then we waited. But Terry took Slavens's advice and signed back the offer.

On Wednesday the purchasers raised their offer to $490,000. To help close the deal, Slavens threw in the cost of a survey and the GST on his commission, "thereby providing you with $465,500.00 net after deduction of our commission of $24,500.00 (based on 5% of selling price) . . . This offer is not negotiable," he added. Ben signed. Once again, we waited to see what Terry would do.

That same day Terry signed the minutes of settlement. "*This case is now settled* (save and except for the two References before Master Linton)," wrote Zaldin. Linton still had to wind up the house sale and the division of property. "Terry is still working on her 'contents' list and *promises* them to me by the middle of next week," Zaldin assured Hannaford, "at which time I shall fax it to you and perhaps we could spend an hour by phone or in person putting that aspect of the case to rest." The house offer would expire at midnight the next Monday. By Thursday, Terry hadn't signed. Then we had another crisis on our hands.

Earlier that week, Terry's Aunt Rose had called Ben to ask if the girls could attend a family Friday-night dinner. Ben said sure and faxed Terry to confirm arrangements.

November 26th, 1992

Terry,
This letter is to inform you that your Aunt Rose called me and asked if you might have the kids this Friday evening so that you could bring them to her home for a family dinner. You have my permission to do so and I will pick them up Saturday morning at 9 a.m. at Dewbourne Ave.

Ben

November 26, 1992
Ben:
My Aunt Rose called me the other day and informed me of your telephone conversation in which you agreed to let her have the girls for dinner. She asked me to bring them to her house at 6:00. She assured me that she, or someone would safely deliver them to your place ... at around 8:30 p.m. Friday Nov. 27. Please be sure you are at 21 Relmar Rd. where someone will be delivering Deja and Zoe at 8:30 p.m. Friday night.

Terry

Ben read Terry's fax and felt the anger welling up inside of him. The whole pattern of their dealings was captured in that fax. Terry had asked him for an accommodation. He'd agreed. But he'd asked her for an accommodation in return this time. Although Terry had promised that the girls would be delivered at 8:30, he knew from experience it was likelier they'd show up at 9:30 or 10. So he'd said the kids could go to dinner if Terry took them for the night and brought them back Saturday morning. That way he wouldn't have to hang around all evening killing time, waiting for them to return, just so he could put them to bed and say goodnight. If Terry was already spending the evening with the girls, then he thought it made more sense for her to take them back to her place afterwards. And he could make his own plans for the evening, too.

In effect, he'd said to Terry that if you want something, then once in a while you have to be prepared to give something in return. But Terry had plans, too, and she didn't want to be inconvenienced. Terry wanted the kids to go to Aunt Rose's while she went out for the evening, and Terry wanted Ben to hang around all night to receive them. In court or out, whenever a situation arose requiring cooperation or compromise, ninety-nine times out of a hundred, the pattern was the same. Terry wanted, Terry wanted, Ben conceded. He was the one who gave in, who made the sacrifices for the children's sake.

But he just didn't feel like conceding at that moment. He was too damn tired. Nor did he feel like trying to "negotiate" with Terry. He'd had his fill of that charade, too. And he was far too angry about everything else that had gone on, everything that was still going on, her refusal to sign back the house offer, to part with his property. He just didn't have the desire to accommodate or appease a woman who was unappeasable, who was utterly unwilling to accommodate him in any way in return. It occurred to him that he should call Aunt Rose and ask if he could bring the kids for dinner himself – he had a good relationship with her and Uncle Percy – but he wasn't in the mood for that either. He was sorry the kids would have to miss a family dinner, but it was just a dinner, no particular celebratory event, nothing special, and he knew there'd be others.

November 26, 1992

All changes to the schedule are off and our regular schedule stands. As usual, you're obliged to deliver the kids to 21 Relmar at 6:00 p.m. I've informed Helen Goudge of this matter and have told her that I'll be expecting the kids at 6:00 p.m. so that we can now have our usual family Friday night dinner together.

Ben

November 27, 1992, 12:15 p.m.

I discussed this with Helen Goudge. She says that from 6:00 pm tonight the children are in your care and responsibility. I am sorry I cannot babysit them tonight following Rose's affair. I will deliver the children at 6:00 pm unless you can arrange something different with Rose.

    I think that Rose is still expecting them at 6:00??

Terry

Ben called Aunt Rose to apologize for disappointing her, but said he'd been unable to work out suitable arrangements with Terry. He faxed Terry.

November 27, 1992, 12:50 p.m.

I have spoken to Rose and she knows that the kids will not be there tonight. I will be expecting the kids at 6:00 p.m. as per your fax.

By Friday, Terry still hadn't signed the offer. Slavens had advised that the $490,000 offer was non-negotiable. Terry signed at $500,000. Master Linton would have to rule on whether to accept the offer. All we could do was wait out the weekend and see what the master would decide on Monday.

    Around 4:00 that afternoon, angry at Terry and with worries about whether the house would finally sell very much on his mind, Ben came home to do some shopping, make dinner, and await the kids. He found it relaxing to work in the kitchen. He especially liked making Friday-night dinners; they were an opportunity to reconnect with Deja and Zoe after their week away. Ben was in the kitchen when the phone rang. I was sitting on the living room couch. He came out of the kitchen to answer the phone with a chef's apron tied around his waist and a dishtowel slung over his shoulder. When he picked up the phone a grave expression crossed his face.

    I motioned to him to put the phone on speaker. Zoe was screaming hysterically. "I want to go to Aunt Rose's for dinner," she howled. "I'm going, and you can't stop me. Grandma has a present for me. She bought me a Super Mario. I want to get my present." I could hear Terry in the background, egging her on.

    In a clipped, barely audible voice, Ben told Zoe he expected her at 6:00 and he wasn't going to discuss anything while she was having a tantrum. They'd discuss it at home later when she'd calmed down. Then he said, "I'm going to hang up the phone now, Zoe." And he did.

Zoe called back. She was still screaming. Terry was still coaching her in the background. "Mommy knows the rules," Ben said. "She called Helen and Helen told her the rules. It's my decision and I've decided that you're to come home for dinner." "I don't care about Helen," Zoe wailed. "I can do what I want." "Oh, let her go, Ben," said Terry.

Zoe called back several times. Eventually Ben stopped answering the phone. It rang and rang. Then it stopped. We had no idea what to expect. Around 7 o'clock, Terry's car pulled into the driveway. Deja came into the apartment looking miserable, dropped her knapsack at the front door, and without a word went to her room. Ben went out to Terry's car. Zoe was coiled angrily in the back seat. He extended his hand, gently asked her to come inside. Zoe would have nothing to do with him. "Don't tear her away, Ben," Terry snapped. Ben ignored her.

Ben told Zoe we were going to have dinner and she could join us when she was ready. Then he went back inside and we tried vainly to salvage the wreckage of our evening. The three of us sat down to dinner. After a while Zoe came inside, stomped down the hall to her bedroom, and shut the door. Later, Ben asked Zoe why she'd decided to come home. "Because Mommy phoned the lawyer," she spat angrily, "and the lawyer said I had to."

I had my own theory about how events had unfolded when the kids returned from school that day. I believed that Terry had called Goudge about the dinner, that when Goudge had told her the decision was Ben's she'd gone to work on the kids, told them how bad their father was to make them miss a family dinner, worked them up into a lather about having to miss Grandma's presents; then, having made Zoe hysterical, she'd put her on the phone to plead with Ben, and when that tactic failed, she phoned her lawyer, who told her what she'd known all along – that Goudge had the last word. At that point, because Terry had plans for that evening and her various manipulative schemes had failed, she'd had no option but to deliver the kids to Ben's.

And all of this had happened during the golden hours after school that Goldstein had insisted that the children have before their weekly transfer. I'd made notes about the incident. If nothing else, perhaps my notes would convince Goudge to change that dreadful recommendation. Maybe my record of the incident would also give Goudge a flavour of what we were dealing with. Maybe the social worker would realize that her assessment of Zoe's "attachment issues" was somewhat more complicated than she'd imagined, and that there were more constructive ways to resolve them than by giving Zoe more time under Terry Nusyna's motherly wing.

Before the lawyers got to court on Monday to argue about the house offer, the purchasers had withdrawn it. Terry had succeeded in scuppering an offer it had taken a year to attract. Ben's only recourse to prevent a similar scenario in future was to have the court set terms for dealing with subsequent offers. Zaldin and Hannaford agreed to three conditions: they'd both see copies of all offers; the offers had to be irrevocable for three business days so the lawyers had time to see Master Linton; and either party had the right to bring a motion before Master Linton on twenty-four hours' notice. On Monday, November 30, Master Linton formalized the agreement between counsel into a court order.

Three weeks later, another offer came in on the house. This time the offer was for $450,000. But, unlike the previous one, this offer came through a competing real estate agency. Slavens recommended against accepting. He told the master he could do better, and Master Linton gave him another sixty days to try.

Christmas holidays were approaching. Ben had faxed Terry his proposed holiday schedule late in November.

November 26, 1992

Dear Terry,
I've spoken with Helen Goudge to confirm holiday arrangements with the kids...
    This letter is to inform you that I'll be taking my Christmas holiday week with the kids from Monday December 28th until Monday January 4th. I propose that we adjust the regular schedule to accommodate the holiday break in this manner:

Friday December 18–Friday December 25: Kids with Terry
Saturday December 26 and Sunday Dec. 27: Kids with Terry

Monday December 28–Monday January 4: Kids with Ben, holiday week. Terry delivers kids to Ben at 8:15 a.m. on Monday December 28.

Monday January 4 to Friday January 8: Kids with Ben

Friday January 8: Ben delivers kids to Terry at 6 p.m. to begin regular week on/week off schedule.

The holiday week is my choice. If you wish to suggest any changes to the schedule I've proposed, please inform me by December 4th so we can discuss the matter. If I don't hear from you by then, I'll assume that the schedule is acceptable. Should you neglect this matter now, but wish to discuss it after December 4th, please note that I won't be obliged to adjust the schedule at that time. Ben.

Terry didn't like Ben's proposal. With the holidays two weeks away, he faxed Terry again: "Let's keep the holidays real simple and stay on our regular schedule throughout, uninterrupted ... Still awaiting your list re chattels," the letter ended.

At around 3:30 on January 7, 1993, Goudge phoned me, looking for Ben. She opened with "I understand your last week with the kids was a disaster." The holidays had been uneventful. I hadn't a clue what she meant. "Wendy," she asked, "did you know Ben hit Zoe?" Then it began to dawn. Goudge said Terry was bringing the kids in at 4:00 to tell her "the story." She was calling Ben, a half-hour before Terry and the girls were scheduled to arrive in her office, to hear his version. Ben was out on an errand. Taking a deep breath to stay calm, I told Goudge what Ben had told me.

During the holidays, nine days earlier, Ben had left work around 3:30 to pick up the kids from the Jewish Community Centre on Bloor Street, where he'd enrolled them in a holiday program. He'd parked in a no-parking zone in front of the building on Spadina Avenue, then dashed inside. Zoe wanted a treat. Ben said not today, he didn't want to get a ticket. Zoe got mouthy and threw a fit. Back at the car, horns were honking. The kids started squabbling over the front seat. As usual, Deja gave in and let Zoe sit up front. Ben started the car, did a U-turn on Spadina, and began to drive home. Zoe refused to buckle her seatbelt. With one hand on the wheel, Ben reached over with the other, swatted Zoe on the back of her head, and barked, "Do up your seatbelt!"

When they got home, Ben sent Zoe to her room. Later, he said he was wrong to have swatted her and apologized. Zoe agreed her behaviour was out of line, too. Ben had promised to take the kids to see *Aladdin* that night but told Zoe her punishment for misbehaving was that she couldn't see the movie. He took Deja to the movies. Zoe stayed home with a sitter. The next morning, the incident was over and Zoe was cuddling in Ben's lap as usual. That last fact I could attest to myself.

Goudge told me Zoe had "reported" the incident to Terry, who'd then "reported" it to Goudge. On the basis of Terry's call, Goudge had arranged for Terry to bring the girls in to tell her "all about it." The three of them would be in any minute.

I told Goudge that taking into account Zoe's behaviour that afternoon and Ben's stress level these days, I considered his reaction understandable, although not excusable. Considering the circumstances, any parent might lose it for a moment and swat a defiantly misbehaving child. I told her I knew many decent parents under far less pressure who'd done the same. I wasn't proud to admit it, but I was one of them.

Goudge ignored my words. She asked whether Ben would get therapy to deal with his anger. She asked if he'd pledge not to hit the kids again. Otherwise, she'd have to "do something about it."

"You'll have to ask Ben that question," I replied.

I said all this in a flat tone, but I was enraged. I had my own explanation for Zoe's sudden enthusiasm to tattle on Daddy nine days after this non-event had ceased to be a matter of any consequence in the household. I believed Zoe was a victim, but of a far more insidious form of child abuse than a momentary swat. During the holidays she'd said to Ben, "Mommy says you're bad, Daddy, for not letting me see *Aladdin*, but I'm not worried because Mommy says she'll take me to see the movie herself." That Terry had used the kids as weapons again was despicable, but it was Goudge's role in the episode that I found truly terrifying.

It seemed obvious to me that Goudge was investigating an allegation of child abuse. If the social worker had good reason to suspect Zoe had truly been the victim of abuse, she was obliged to make a report to a child protection agency, which would then conduct an investigation. It struck me as precipitous, however, for Goudge to lend credence to a mother's serious allegation in the midst of an acrimonious divorce before even soliciting the father's account of what had happened that day. That she'd agreed to interview the kids on the strength of Terry's word alone and then come to a conclusion was stunning to me, considering the source. But that the social worker had set up an appointment for Terry to bring the girls into her office before even contacting Ben to determine if there was a "story" to investigate took my breath away.

Goudge's actions were particularly hard to excuse since it was widely known within the legal and social service community that false assault and abuse allegations during divorce proceedings were a rampant problem. Any professional monitoring an acrimonious arrangement ought to have been extremely alert to the possibility of such allegations and exceptionally cautious about handling them. Yet that Terry's call might have been motivated by anything other than motherly concern did not seem to have crossed Goudge's mind. Worse, she seemed to have no idea of the harm she was causing: that by encouraging Terry to march the children into their social worker's office to "report" about how bad their daddy had been, she was confirming in their minds precisely the message their mother wanted confirmed.

The scenario was eerily reminiscent of what had transpired when Terry had claimed to be the victim of "abuse." Although police had found no evidence to lay a charge, on the basis of a woman's word, the entire machinery of the state had whirred into action. The same was happening again. Without even hearing from the father, an authority was threatening ominously to "do something about it," if "it" happened again.

Goudge called at 9:30 the next morning to report on her interview with the kids. We made notes. She reported that Zoe had been very big on wanting her to know "all about the incident," about how wrong Ben was to have hit her and make her miss *Aladdin*. She said Zoe "didn't feel good about staying in her room and not going to see the movie." Zoe thought a better punishment would have been for her to miss watching TV. (According to Goudge, restricting television was Terry's discipline of choice.) Zoe had reported that the rest of the holidays were "fine." Deja had confirmed that Zoe had behaved like "a maniac" in the cafeteria and car that day, and (as

Goudge put it) "deserved to be clobbered." Deja had also confirmed that Zoe deserved to miss the movie and was fine the next day.

"I told Zoe I didn't think that hitting was a good way of looking after kids because then they respond to fear," Goudge said. She made this remark as if this was a novel idea that might not have occurred to us before.

I spoke next, calmly, with controlled, deliberate politeness. I told Goudge Ben wasn't in the habit of hitting anyone, nor did we need to be educated that hitting was an inappropriate way to discipline children. I said it was nice to hear that Zoe thought having to miss the movie was an unduly harsh punishment, but that, being a seven-year-old child, Zoe wasn't in charge of the disciplinary decisions in our family. Nor, for that matter, was Terry. I told her that by encouraging Terry to keep the incident alive in Zoe's mind long after it had ceased to be an issue of any significance for her, Goudge had caused great harm.

"We have some issues to deal with around Zoe's provocative behaviour," she said, changing the subject. "It might be a help for you and Ben to come in with the kids to talk about what should happen when Zoe goes out of her mind."

I wanted to scream at her then. I wanted to shake her, do anything to jolt her into awareness, make her understand. You think what this family needs is a little session on how to handle Zoe, do you? Helen Goudge's Top Ten Parenting Tips for Divorced Families. Our situation desperately needed drastic intervention, but Goudge was only treating the symptoms of the problem while in our view remaining heedless of its cause. For the first time I truly understood the depth of the anger Ben had described feeling in Butkowsky's office.

She steered the conversation in another direction. In their interview, she'd asked Zoe to tell her another story. This time Goudge reported that "everything seemed fine," and Zoe "didn't seem to be missing her mom." So at the end of the interview, the social worker admitted, she'd asked the seven-year-old a leading question: "Do you still miss your mom?" And Zoe had reportedly replied, "I feel the same way as before. I need to have more time at Mom's. I liked it better the old way."

Deja had reportedly said she didn't need more time with Terry and could "adjust" to the new schedule. Then, Goudge said, Deja had added, "But it does feel like I need my mom a bit more, especially as I get older." Goudge believed Deja tended to say what she thought others wanted to hear and to some extent was identifying with Sara, whom Deja had raised as an example of a daughter needing her mother more as she grew older. Overall, if the schedule did change, Goudge said Deja wanted to be with Zoe, "although she did have some ambivalent feelings in this regard." Then Goudge dropped another bombshell. She'd monitor the "theme" of both kids' "attachment issues" until the end of February, then decide about changing the schedule.

Then she decided it was time to wrap up the conversation. "I'm satisfied that you're both cognitively aware that hitting out of anger is inappropriate," she pronounced. Nevertheless, she wanted some "reassurance from Ben" that it wouldn't happen again. She repeated her threat about having to "do something about it" if there was a next time, and asked for Ben's promise that if it did, he'd discuss hiring an "anger management consultant."

I put down the phone shaking with rage. Goudge was a great one for getting the kids to talk about their feelings, letting them vent. But she seemed to have no idea there might be another reason why the children were saying what they were saying. She was turning two scared, confused kids into the centre of power in a bitterly charged struggle, and leaving us to pay the price.

On January 12, in desperation, we wrote her a lengthy but restrained letter encapsulating recent events, offering our insights about each kid's needs and behaviour, and summarizing our objections to her handling of matters. Our purpose was twofold. We were still trying to make her see the folly of her ways, hoping that maybe if we walked her one more time through our concerns she might finally understand them. We also wanted the facts on the record. Nevertheless we knew deep down that we had no realistic hope of getting through to Goudge. It seemed that we would be living under a microscope to an even greater extent than before, and that Ben's parenting of the kids would be subject to the manipulations of a clever and "highly expressive" seven-year-old child who desperately needed attention and had learned how to manipulate to get it, a child who was herself being manipulated by a mother who'd never supported joint custody, who'd stop at nothing to subvert the mediation process, alienate the children from their father, and win control of their hearts and minds. It was clear to me that Helen Goudge would be Terry Nusyna's unwitting accomplice.

CHAPTER TEN

CATASTROPHE

January–May 1993

Throughout the fall and winter of 1992, the troubles with David continued to increase exponentially. Sara's adolescence had brought with it one new set of problems; Ben's arrival in my life the previous year had brought another. In September, before heading for New York to begin my book tour, I asked Sara where she wanted to stay while I was out of town. In the past she'd always elected to be with her dad. This time she chose to stay with Ben. David insisted to Sara that she stay with him and demanded that I tell her to do so. Sara was terrified of disobeying her father but remained resolute. Sara and Ben had developed a close relationship by then. Not only did he counsel her through her difficulties with her dad, he became the voice of reason if she and I were at loggerheads, and when he felt it warranted, he acted as her ally.

I reminded David that Sara's caretaking arrangements during my custodial time were my call and that unless he had well-founded concerns for her welfare, he was out of line. He expressed no specific concerns about Ben, but simply said Sara's preference was "inappropriate." In December he sent me a fax demanding that I agree in writing not to let Sara stay with Ben – a demand I ignored.

Then came the Bat Mitzvah armageddon. In October David and I had agreed to hold separate evening celebrations for Sara's Bat Mitzvah in the spring. In November he changed his plans to a luncheon at an elegant restaurant following the Saturday-morning service. Sara was happy with the new arrangements, which were proceeding smoothly until he insisted she leave the synagogue immediately after the ceremony. In addition to the party we'd planned at a downtown disco/diner for Sunday evening, Ben and I were hosting a kiddush buffet luncheon for family and friends in the sanctuary afterwards. I'd always assumed that David and Jan would co-host this traditional event, which typically lasts about forty-five minutes to an hour immediately after the service. When David switched his arrangements, I argued there'd be perhaps three days in Sara's life – her Bat Mitzvah, college graduation, and wedding – when she'd have the opportunity to celebrate a special occasion with both of her families and all her friends. I didn't think it fair to her, us, or the guests that she be whisked away immediately following the ceremony. Sara agreed. She wanted to mingle for a while and receive congratulations.

David insisted she leave right away. Between mid-November and the end of December, he and I exchanged a flurry of correspondence over this picayune issue. I offered various compromises – including reducing Sara's stay to thirty minutes and offering to pay for food and drink for his guests – all of which he rejected. He suggested I take my guests elsewhere. When I refused, he threatened to cancel his restaurant luncheon altogether – a threat which made Sara distraught.

In the same period our money tangles heated up. A classic example was the bike fight. According to our agreement I had to buy Sara's recreational equipment – so I bought her a bike. David interpreted that clause to mean that I had to buy two bikes – one for his house, one for mine. He bought her a second bike and sent me the bill, which I ignored.

The gap between Sara's standard of living in David's household and in mine had always been wide, but by 1992, it had become a chasm. I didn't expect to live David's lifestyle, nor did I covet it. But I was finding it impossible to provide for Sara at the level we both wanted without indebting myself. I raised the issue of increased support, but he refused to discuss it. He said he was paying more than enough. (Unlike many divorced couples, we didn't disagree on the lifestyle we wanted for Sara. David happily took her on vacations to resorts like Aspen and expected her to enjoy all the amenities like camp, concerts, theatre excursions, ski equipment, art classes, etc. He just didn't want to pay me more to underwrite their cost. Unlike many divorced husbands, David didn't think I spent his child support extravagantly on Sara. He claimed the opposite: that I had lots of money but refused to spend it on her.)

When we'd separated, I'd verbally agreed to reimburse David for any expenses he incurred for Sara that I was required to cover, and since then I'd paid him back for every bill he sent me, however nominal, although not legally obliged to do so by our agreement. That fall, however, I ran out of money – and patience. With David sending me the bills not only for major items but for five-dollar pairs of socks, and at the same time refusing to discuss an increase in Sara's support while my debts were growing, I stopped reimbursing him. That angered him. Then we had a skirmish about Sara's weekend schedule, her vacation plans, and a bank account that I was administering in trust for her. By December we were faxing each other almost daily. After eight years, our precarious joint custody arrangement had broken down. Late that fall I wrote David twice, asking him to enter mediation to resolve our disputes. He refused. Then he threatened to take me to court.

Because Sara felt hopelessly torn and was in an impossible position, I asked her if she wanted to talk to a therapist who'd offer her a neutral ear. She leapt at the suggestion. Since David had to consent, I suggested she talk to her dad before I did. The day after she spoke to him, David left me a voicemail message saying he'd met with an "excellent" child psychologist, Dr. Berenice Mandelcorn. I knew of Mandelcorn's reputation and reasoned that David would be likelier to accept the advice of a professional he'd selected, so I too met with her right away. She explained to me, as she'd already told David, that she'd assess Sara to determine whether she needed individual therapy or whether we all needed to enter family therapy/mediation. I told her I'd already implored David to enter mediation, and wholeheartedly concurred with her suggestion that we needed "some methodology for conflict resolution."

■ ■ ■

By January, making camp arrangements was top of Ben's mind. Deja was abuzz with talk of camp, and Zoe too was showing interest in going away for a month. Determined to find the money, Ben had been busily researching programs. The popular ones filled up quickly, and most required deposits by March.

Sending the kids to camp wasn't one of Terry's priorities, if she had to split the cost. According to Ben, Terry figured she was already paying a full-time housekeeper who could look after the kids during the summer. Why spend more? Whenever Ben asked the kids if they were keen on camp, they'd say, "Mommy can't afford it, Daddy. She says we'll have to get you to pay if we want to go." In the past, the kids had gone only if Ben paid. This year, however, they had an agreement and Terry was obliged to split the cost. Goudge had told us that Deja had raised the issue with her and asked her to make sure her parents would send in her camp application in time. It was Goudge's job to decide whether the kids would go to camp, and if so, where they'd go, and for how long. Hoping to set that process in motion, Ben faxed Goudge.

Jan. 18/93

re: Deja & Zoe Summer Plans

After investigating several summer camps and programs, interview-ing camp directors and numerous discussions with the kids – I am suggesting the following arrangements for the 10 week summer holiday '93.

Deja is keen on going to Camp Tamakwa, a sleepover co-ed camp in Algonquin Park. Wendy's daughter Sara is going. We know a number of other families who go and the camp director is Jeffrey Wilson (a cousin of Wendy's ex-husband). She will likely want to go for the full 8 week term, though we might be able to commit for 4 weeks and see if she wants to continue.

Zoe feels she's ready for sleepover camp as well. She'd like to start at "New Moon" (where Deja went her first summer). She's visited the site, knows several kids who are going and again could commit for the first month and if she's happy, continue for another 3 weeks.

The remaining two weeks (or in Zoe's case three weeks) of summer could be shared one week each with Terry and I.

If the kids choose not to stay at overnight camp there are two day camps available both of which they have attended before and enjoy. They are the YMCA and JCC programs. Each are 2 week programs.

There is also an Olympic sports camp (sleepover one week sessions available) for Deja's age group which Deja is enthusiastic about (2nd to her preference for Tamakwa).

Costs are significant, especially for New Moon and Tamakwa but considering how important this time away from home and in the company of other kids in a camp setting is to Deja and Zoe – it's a financial sacrifice well worthwhile.

Have all kinds of brochures, videos etc. about the camps to show you when we discuss the matter further.

Thank you and regards,

Ben Gordon

Ben attached information on the various programs' costs. Goudge would have to take it from there.

■ ■ ■

On the morning of Monday, January 18, I answered my doorbell to find a man standing on my porch holding a thick manila envelope. "Are you Wendy Dennis?" he asked. I nodded. "I have something for you," he said, handing over his package. I knew instantly that I was being served with a legal document. "Thank you," I replied, in that idiotic way one politely thanks a police officer who has just handed over a traffic summons.

Sara had the day off from school. "What's that?" she asked, sensing my anxiety. I work at home and often receive courier packages. I mumbled something about a business delivery. But my upset was palpable and she knew something was amiss. I opened the envelope upstairs in my office. David was suing me over five issues: "Bat Mitzvah," "Weekend of January 22-24," "Ben Gordon," "Trust Account," and "Summer Plans – 1993."

That afternoon Sara was scheduled to see Mandelcorn for her first appointment. Privately, I told Mandelcorn the news. I said David didn't appear to see any connection between Sara's complaints and our disputes, or his desire to engage me in a court battle over them, and the impact of that decision on his daughter's emotional state. Judging by his actions, he seemed to believe that he could dispatch Sara to therapy where Mandelcorn would take care of her problems, then declare war on me to take care of ours. The psychologist shook her head and said she'd speak to him.

■ ■ ■

The next day another offer came in on the house. This offer, which came through Slavens's agency, was for $455,000, and the purchaser subsequently increased it to $470,000. Slavens had brought in the promised higher offer. Master Linton would almost certainly order that it be accepted.

At around 4 o'clock on January 21, the fax machine began rumbling in Julie Hannaford's office. Zaldin was serving her, on short notice, with what he called an "emergency motion" on the sale of the home. The motion was scheduled to be heard at 10 o'clock the next morning. Among the documents Hannaford received was a competing offer, which would expire at 11:59 a.m. the next day. It was signed by Terry Nusyna.

Zaldin was violating virtually every term of the deal he'd made with Hannaford in November for handling offers. He was also breaching a court order respecting that agreement. He'd failed to give twenty-four hours' notice of his motion. His client's offer was not irrevocable for three business days. And, although Hannaford didn't know this yet, he was bringing the motion on a day when Master Linton was unavailable to hear it.

Ben was leaving his office for a night movie shoot when he heard the news. Because he'd be filming at a hotel downtown until 3:00 that morning, he'd have no chance to read Terry's affidavit or file a response to it. Hannaford was scheduled to fly to Ottawa the next day on another matter. She advised Zaldin that Ben intended to contest Terry's motion to purchase the home and asked him to reschedule the motion for Monday. His client wouldn't be prejudiced, she argued; Terry could extend the expiry time on her offer to any date she chose. Zaldin said his instructions were to proceed "regardless."

Hannaford rearranged her plans and told Ben she'd seek an adjournment. If she failed, his only chance of averting Terry's purchase of the home was to make a competing offer, in the hope that Master Linton would cast a curse on both their houses and take the third party's offer.

Hannaford called first thing next morning. She'd just seen Terry's affidavit. She was on her way to court so had time to give Ben only the highlights. It wasn't until after the court had ruled that Ben saw Terry's affidavit.

Since our separation, I have always "wanted" to retain (and remain in) the matrimonial home for my two young daughters ... but I could not afford it.

Indeed, I "wanted" to purchase Mr. Gordon's interest in Dewbourne in December ... but I could not afford to do so at that time either ...

Just this week, I got a new job with Bates Printing (a Chicago company) at a draw of about $50,000.00 per year (U.S.) against commission, plus expenses, and, as a result of my new employment, I looked around for financing to purchase the home (in the best interests of my children) and I have been successful in securing financing to match (and "better") the [third party] offer.

Regrettably, however, Mr. Gordon is refusing to accept the offer (and he is unreasonably withholding his consent thereto), and for his own subjective reasons, which resistance I believe is intended to "punish" me for my decision to leave the marriage.

I verily believe that Mr. Gordon's unreasonable attitude and vendetta against me will have the effect of forcing our girls to move to a new home, about which prospect they have always been fearful and extremely anxious.

I am at a loss to understand why Mr. Gordon would continue his personal vendetta against me (which would deny the children the chance to remain in the only home they have ever lived in, with the same schools and neighbourhood friends). Accordingly, I am requesting that the Court override Mr. Gordon's bitter personal feelings and approve my ... offer.

I know that Mr. Gordon thinks that I have schemed to drive down the price of the home and then purchase it ... I categorically deny any such intent.

Court opened at 10:00. That morning we ran around trying to put together an offer on a house we had neither the money nor the slightest desire to buy. On the remote chance that the court would order the home sold to Ben, we planned to sell it to the prospective purchaser who had increased his offer to $475,000 the previous evening. We came up with the deposit by borrowing it from my credit line. Then we drove downtown.

Justice Edward Eberle heard the motion. He had had no previous involvement in the case. He refused to grant an adjournment and heard the motion in chambers with only the lawyers present, the way motions often were heard in family court. When we arrived, the motion was already in progress. Terry, who had not attended court for any other motions, sat on a bench outside the judge's chambers, talking on a cellphone.

Ben knocked on the door of the judge's chambers. The judge beckoned him to come in. Both lawyers were sitting in front of the judge's desk. Hannaford looked grim. Ben gave her our offer. Justice Eberle stared at us, a hard, cold stare. We left.

After hearing arguments behind closed doors for two hours, Justice Eberle ruled that Ben was obstructing the sale of the home. He allowed Terry to buy it for $475,000.

Jan 22/93

Offer by wife ... approved, with following amendments:
(1) price $475,000.00
(2) closing date Apr 13/93
(3) deposit $20,350.00

Consent of husband is hereby dispensed with. If he refuses to execute deed and/or any other necessary documents, wife is hereby authorized to execute on his behalf.

In so ordering, I have considered a competing offer received this morning from husband, on same terms substantially as wife's first offer. I am prepared to assume husband would, given time, be prepared to raise his price to $475,000, and move closing date to Apr 13/93.

But husband's offer, coming only after he learned that wife has made an offer, and matching her offer almost word for word, suggests strongly that he is merely trying to be obstructionist about the sale; and merely trying to prevent the wife from purchasing. He could have made an offer at any earlier time for there were no restrictions upon the parties making offers. The wife explains her timing, in reference to a new employment which enables her to manage the financing now.

The wife's offer meets the outside offer ...

The property has been on the market for well over a year, and listing price has been lowered. The market exposure appears quite adequate. The current outside offers have the disadvantage of being subject to conditions; the wife's offer is not. Acceptance of the wife's offer obviates the expenses of moving for her. Acceptance of an offer from husband would presumably require the expense of two moves. And it is possible that it is better for children to continue to reside in existing home, although of course I can not and do not make any decision about that.

I am told that the present legal proceedings have been long, acrimonious and expensive; but that the disposition of the home and division of chattels are the only remaining issues. It is highly desirable to bring one of those issues to a close without further delay. I am told that offers submitted were to be open for 3 days; the one I have accepted falls short in that respect. In all the circumstances, I think it is proper to overlook that. I do not think the husband has been at all prejudiced in the shorter time for considering the wife's offer for he has been able in a few hours to prepare and submit an offer of his own with a certified cheque for deposit.

"I strongly advise you to appeal," said Hannaford. This from the lawyer who, two months earlier, had advised capitulation. Hannaford was furious at Zaldin's tactics and believed Ben had been denied a fair hearing. Furthermore, she was so disturbed by the judge's behaviour behind closed doors that morning that she'd returned to her office and immediately recorded the details in a memo. Ben took his lawyer's advice and instructed her to seek leave to appeal the decision.

In the first few weeks of the new year, a court-appointed social worker had treated Ben like a child abuser, and a judge had accused him of obstructing the sale of the home that he had desperately sought and successfully secured a court order to sell two years before. It was impossible to forget the countless times Terry had refused to sell while the price plum-meted and how the court had indulged her. I observed what the court had done to Ben on the single occasion he refused. Then I recalled Goudge's declaration that what he needed was an anger management consultant, and I could only shake my head in disbelief.

Justice Eberle's decision dealt Ben a devastating blow. He had always believed that in their particular case, selling the house was essential if joint custody was to work. Terry now had the court's blessing to tell the kids what she'd been telling them all along: that she was their parent, that her house was their home.

The kids were coming to Ben's that evening and I dreaded their arrival. I had little doubt they'd be full of the news of their mother's "victory," and I feared I'd lack the strength to contain my feelings if either one opened her mouth. But whatever they knew, they instinctively sensed they should not repeat it. Ben said nothing to them of the events of the day. There was nothing to say.

■ ■ ■

"I felt your letter was remarkably accurate," Goudge said when she met with us in late January. "There were just a few minor things." She was referring to the comment she'd made about Goldstein's term "joint custody" being a misnomer. Uncomfortably, in a manner suggesting she didn't wish to be seen discrediting a colleague, Goudge explained that the words "joint custody" can mean "anything to anybody" and are defined by what's speci-fied in the settlement agreement. "What I meant to say was that as the final decision-maker, I have custody. I don't know what I meant saying Goldstein used an inappropriate term," she said, hurrying to change the subject, "but I don't think we need to get into it."

She agreed she could do only what she'd been mandated to do, but since Goldstein had said her job was to "oversee the parenting of these children," it "seemed" she had the authority to alter his plan. However, because, in her opinion, the report was "diffusively written," and "it would appear that there's a good chance [Ben was] right," she advised us to call Goldstein for clarification. She intended to call him, too. She also intended to get her own legal advice.

"If, at the end of February, it's my best opinion that the kids should stay in the plan as is, they'll stay," she said. If she thought there should be a change, then the matter would go back to the lawyers for clarification. Until then, there was no point in making a "tempest in a teapot." If there was a dispute about her powers, Ben could simply subpoena Goldstein. She made this last suggestion offhandedly, as if re-entering the court system was like visiting the chiropractor.

We were both dumbfounded. "Do you have any idea what we've been through?" Ben asked. "Do you have any idea what I've spent in court?"

"How much?"

"Around a quarter of a million dollars!"

"Oh, that's the highest I've heard yet!" she chirped, as if hearing this news for the first time. But beyond a prurient fascination with the figure, its import did not register. His voice crackling with outrage, Ben told her about the house. We waited for a glimmer, a clue, something to make us feel she comprehended the enormity of what was happening. But Goudge didn't understand why Ben was so angry. "I don't happen to think kids get so wedded to a house," she said.

Ben and I left that meeting sickened. Now the mediator/arbitrator, whose job was to defuse the conflict, was bringing yet a third lawyer – her own – into the fray and advising us on whom we should subpoena if, as a direct consequence of her involvement, we had to go back to court. But after years spent with only devastation to show for it, going back to court was out of the question.

■ ■ ■

The next day David and I met with Berenice Mandelcorn. Sara, she explained, felt caught in the middle and was trying hard to please everyone, but that burden was an inordinate one for her to bear and would undoubtedly begin to affect her school performance and self-esteem. She also told us that Sara had requested a meeting with her parents, her stepparents, and Mandelcorn (or another professional), and she hoped her dad would go to that meeting. Mandelcorn endorsed Sara's right to participate in the decision-making process and recommended family mediation. In no uncertain terms, she told David that pursuing a court action was the worst way to go about solving our problems.

■ ■ ■

Two weeks later, Ben heard from Goudge again. She planned to do her reckoning of expenses. She wanted receipts. By March 1 she'd also be making her "determinations regarding how the time-sharing is to be exercised for this current school year," and she asked Ben and Terry to contact her immediately, or have their lawyers do so, if they had any "questions or concerns."

Ben and I had told Goudge our concerns a thousand times. There was neither the will nor the money to have a lawyer walk her through them again. So we prepared ourselves for the worst. All we could do was try to minimize the damage we firmly believed her ham-fisted meddling with the schedule would cause. We decided to agree to a change in the schedule, but on our terms only.

February 14, 1993

Dear Helen,

This letter is further to our conversation last week about various matters concerning the kids, and further to your letter of February 11th.

It's our understanding that you'll be meeting with the kids again this week and will then be making recommendations by March 1st regarding Zoe's desire to be with Terry one night a week, the kids' camp plans, and the new changeover time.

ZOE

You have been monitoring Zoe for almost six months and throughout that time have been concerned about her expressed need to see Terry during the week that she is with us. Although we have yet to experience any of these requests from Zoe, or have yet to see any evidence that she is missing Terry when she's with us, we will accept your suggestion and agree to the idea of Zoe temporarily spending one night a week with Terry.

We think that Tuesday night is the best night because it falls mid-way through the week, and because Sara is with us on Tuesday nights. That way, when Zoe is with Terry, Deja will have the opportunity, as she has repeatedly requested, to spend some independent time with us and with Sara. Deja has made it clear that she feels no need to spend an extra night with Terry and we feel strongly that she not be made to accommodate Zoe's needs in this regard, as Deja often goes well beyond the call of duty accommodating Zoe's needs as it is. Furthermore, if Deja is required to spend that extra night with Terry, it will defeat the purpose of allowing Terry to give Zoe some undivided attention on that evening. Deja has made it abundantly clear that she wants to stay with us during the night that Zoe goes to Terry, so that she can have that time with us and away from Zoe, and extra time with Sara.

This week, following her meeting with you, Zoe expressed to us, for the first time, that she also wanted to spend one night a week with Ben on Terry's time. We think it's significant that Zoe is now suddenly asking for one night a week with Ben even though she has not expressed any need to you or to us in this regard before. We think that she is now attempting to manipulate the schedule so that she gets special treatment on both ends, and we feel strongly that it would be unwise to accede to this latest demand of Zoe's since it will only perpetuate her manipulative behavior. We've seen repeated behavior from Zoe where she seems to gain a misplaced sense of her own identity from demanding special treatment. We think that acceding to her wishes in this regard would merely reinforce for Zoe the fact that all she has to do is make demands, and they are granted. We will, of course, continue to give Zoe lots of love and positive reinforcement for her appropriate behavior and to discipline her for her inappropriate behavior so that she continues to improve as we feel she has been doing.

We think the best arrangement is to tell Zoe she will be spending Tuesday nights with Terry, and that this arrangement will stay in place until the summertime. After the summer, we'll re-evaluate the situation and decide whether it should continue.

We suggest the following arrangement, as it is the most expedient: Zoe comes home to Ben's on the school bus at 4 p.m. on Tuesday. Terry can pick her up at 4:30 and take her for the evening.

265

The next morning, it will be Terry's responsibility to drive her to school.

We are willing to go along with your suggestion that Zoe temporarily spend one night a week with Terry, so long as the above-stated conditions are met, and on the understanding that this arrangement in no way alters Dr. Goldstein's 50-50 joint-custodial parenting plan. We are willing to go along with your parenting recommendations in this regard, but, in doing so, we are in no way endorsing your authority to arbitrate in this matter or to make any decision which violates the recommendations of Dr. Goldstein's report, parenting plan and schedule.

We would remind you that both parents and the Court, under the auspices of Justice Potts, accepted the recommendations of Dr. Goldstein based on his detailed assessment of the children and the parents. It was only because Terry objected to Dr. Goldstein personally that he was not instituted to implement his own recommendations. You were appointed in his place as a neutral person to better mediate issues arising from the implementation of Dr. Goldstein's report, and not to provide another assessment and/or subsequent recommendations.

THE SWITCHOVER TIME
When Dr. Goldstein first instituted the 6 p.m. Friday switchover time, we expressed our fears about the problems such a changeover time would create, and there have been numerous incidents over the last several months where our fears have been validated. We have given the 6 p.m. changeover time a fair try, as you requested, but we now reiterate our concerns about this transfer time and feel strongly that the time has come to move the transfer time to Friday morning, when the kids leave for school on the bus ...

That way we can see the kids off on the bus in the morning when they go to school, wish them a good week, and they return directly from school to Terry's. That way there is virtually no opportunity for contact and the inevitable anxiety or conflict. All this means is that one night a week – Friday nights – Terry and Ben have to be home by 4 p.m. or have to arrange for a babysitter to greet the kids at that time. Since Terry works from the house, that really shouldn't be an inconvenience.

CAMP

We had Jeff Wilson, the director of Camp Tamakwa, over to the house on Tuesday night to make his presentation. We also invited Sara's friend Calen Freeman and her brother Jed, who is Zoe's age. The kids know the Freemans well, as they are our best friends, and we often spend weekends together at their farm and Saturday evenings at their home.

As a result of Jeff's visit, Zoe now wants to go to Camp Tamakwa. We spoke to Deja about this, since she wanted to go to a different camp than Zoe, but she says she's okay with it. Since Sara and Calen and Jed will also be going to Tamakwa, we think that Deja feels that there will be enough kids around whom Zoe knows so she won't have to feel responsible for playing with Zoe all the time or taking care of her.

We've also assured Deja that we can speak to Jeff Wilson, whom Wendy knows well since he's a cousin of Sara's – to ensure that Zoe does not become a problem for Deja at Tamakwa. On Friday after school we had the director of Camp New Moon over to the house for a presentation as well, after which time Zoe confirmed her desire to go to Tamakwa as opposed to New Moon.

We're delighted that Zoe now wants to go to Tamakwa and that all the kids can be together. We're confident we can monitor the situation for Deja because of our close relationship with the camp director.

We don't know if Terry has any objections to Camp Tamakwa. It has been her pattern in the past (except where music lessons are concerned) not to do any research on her own and then to object to any suggestions that Ben makes on various irrelevant grounds. She did call Ben on Friday claiming that she couldn't find Camp Tamakwa in the phone book. Lest she registers any financial objections to sending the kids to Tamakwa (which costs, by the way, slightly less than the other camps) we ask you to keep in mind that she has just made an offer to buy Ben out of the house on the basis of her new job. (The Court accepted her offer, although it is currently under appeal by Ben.) That means that she is claiming that she is capable of buying out his quarter-million dollar share in the home, and of maintaining a half-million dollar home on her own.

The children are very excited about camp now, and very keen to go; obviously we think it will be a wonderful experience for them. They both need time away from their parents and the conflict, and time to develop independently. The applications must be sent in very shortly, so we'd like to be able to tell the kids that they're going to Tamakwa by March 1st, so we can all start looking forward to the summer.

> Sincerely,
> Ben Gordon
> Wendy Dennis

■ ■ ■

Ben's motion seeking leave to appeal the court's decision on the house was coming up in a few days. He had to prove that the court had erred in law and that the issue was sufficiently important to the administration of justice for an appeal court to hear the matter. Zaldin's underhanded tactics had prevented Ben from seeing or responding to Terry's affidavit before the court ruled. Hannaford could not argue the case because she planned to furnish an affidavit herself; a colleague of hers would argue that Ben had been denied natural justice. Their case was that the court was setting in motion a financial catastrophe for which Ben could later be made to pay. Ben had stumbled across information suggesting that Terry's new job might be less solid than it looked; the court would hear an outline of Terry's checkered employment history and the dubious circumstances surrounding her latest career move. If this job blew up, too, Terry could come after him for money, claiming she needed to maintain the home "in the best interests of the children." But it was hardly in the children's interests for Terry to overextend herself financially when she could easily purchase more modest housing.

Ben also wanted the judge to know that Zaldin had breached an agreement and court order; furthermore, he considered it a distortion for Zaldin to say that it was in the children's best interests for Terry to buy the house. Ben believed Zaldin was merely playing on the court's prejudice about keeping mothers and children in the matrimonial home. In fact, Zaldin's argument was specious since they had a fifty-fifty joint custody arrangement and the children divided their time equally between the two households. Ben also insisted that Hannaford set the record straight about Terry's ridiculous allegation that he was punishing her for leaving the marriage. It was he who'd initiated their separation.

The court had ordered the house sold on a Friday. On the Monday, Hannaford heard from Reiter. He was writing to remind her of Ben's promise to pay his house proceeds into court and ask for the return of the file.

Hannaford replied crisply, and with some indignation, that she did not need to be reminded. Decision had been reserved on Ben's motion for leave to appeal, and once that was dealt with, there was still the issue of chattels to be resolved. Reiter would have to wait.

On February 19, Justice James Southey of the Ontario Court of Justice was "not persuaded that the issues that might be raised ... would be of sufficient public importance." He dismissed Ben's motion and later ordered him to pay $1,500 of Terry's costs.

■ ■ ■

David's lawsuit was hanging like a sword over my head. After meeting with Mandelcorn he'd agreed to negotiate terms for entering mediation but said he intended to proceed to court if negotiations failed. Greg Cooper, a family lawyer of David's vintage, was representing him. My cousin Joyce Harris offered to represent me. Had she not done me that favour, I would have had to represent myself. I was told that because I owned a home and some RRSPs, I did not qualify for legal aid. In case we had to go to court, she told me to prepare an affidavit telling my story. Now I was composing affidavits.

Although I knew the court was the worst place to resolve our problems, I was sceptical about mediation succeeding in our case. I'd been in mediation with David during our first imbroglio to formalize our separation agreement, and for many of the same reasons that the process had failed in Ben's case, it had been a complete waste of time. Nevertheless, my options were limited: either David agreed to enter mediation or he took me to court.

Unlike parents in an intact marriage who can lobby for a child while disagreeing between themselves, I couldn't advocate for Sara when I believed she deserved a hearing. David didn't respect me or my point of view. And when we had fights about her, my ability to counsel Sara was limited by the fact that she understandably felt caught in the middle and perceived me to be part of the problem. Since my goal was to find Sara a forum where her dad and I could resolve disputes without having them tear her apart, where she'd have a voice in decisions governing her life, a neutral ally to advocate on her behalf, and a mediator to help her work out her differences with her dad and Jan (and with us, if any arose we couldn't resolve) and help her develop a satisfying, age-appropriate relationship with her father – something she desperately wanted – I believed I had an obligation to try everything.

David and I had to agree on the mediator and the terms of the process. He proposed a social worker named Robert McWhinney. I checked his references scrupulously and interviewed him by phone. McWhinney said he'd mediate our issues and his associate, a social worker named Diane Moody, would counsel Sara. Sometimes Moody might want to meet with each couple, or together with Sara. McWhinney's rates were steep – $185 an hour – but he sounded like a pro. I agreed.

We hit a wall negotiating the terms. David would enter mediation only with a specific list of issues, which he reserved the right to dictate. I thought his terms were outrageous. If David had the sole right to determine the issues we'd discuss, how were we to resolve any issues Sara or I wanted resolved, or any new issues that arose, as they seemed to every day? Most significantly, however, David's rigidly controlled terms would prevent us from devising a methodology to resolve conflicts, something we obviously needed and Mandelcorn had advised. I called McWhinney. Couples often had difficulty agreeing on terms, he explained, and he could always mediate/arbitrate the terms of the process before we embarked on it. He suggested we get started anyway. I thought this made sense, and agreed. David refused. Then, on February 20, he told Sara he was going to court.

I'd asked David to enter mediation. Sara had asked him. Ben had called him and spent an entire Sunday one weekend trying to talk him out of litigating, attempting to explain how he could be David's ally: they both loved

Sara, I was receptive to his counsel, if he thought I was being unreasonable in one of our disputes he could talk to me and help mediate it. The psychologist David had chosen for her excellent reputation had told him that going to court would only hurt his daughter. The mediator David had picked had encouraged him to enter mediation. Friends and family had counselled him to reconsider: Ben's college roommate, a lawyer who golfed with David; my sister, also a lawyer, who'd maintained a relationship with David after we split up. But David knew best. And, in that system, David could do whatever he pleased.

In our system, it takes two to tango but only one to tangle. One spouse can try, in every way imaginable, to avoid a fight, but if the other is spoiling for a battle, the spouse who seeks to negotiate is defenceless. That spouse's only option is to capitulate or scramble desperately to defend himself or herself in a process that promotes hostility and discord every step of the way. Which was why, whenever I heard a judge lecture two spouses and blame them both, as Justice Potts had done when he called Ben and Terry crazy, or whenever I heard some relative or casual observer who didn't know any better remark, "Isn't it a shame you two people can't get along?" – that most detestable of divorce platitudes – or whenever I thought about Goldstein's offhand comment that all we had to do to make joint custody work with Terry was "Stop fighting," I wanted to pummel them all.

Like Ben, I'd done everything possible to avoid a fight. But, like him, I had an ex-spouse drawing me into battle. An ex-spouse whose mentality was such that no matter how many concessions he was offered he always believed he was being taken, and if he played hardball he could wear me down and win another. I was tired, so tired of fighting, but David had attacked. Now I had to defend myself, play the game, think tactically, out-manoeuvre my adversary. I'd been thrust into a world with a logic unto itself, a world where morality, as I understood the word, did not exist, where rules and evidence were often ignored, where decency was dangerous and expecting it, naive. I was now at war. It just so happened that the enemy was my daughter's father.

David had practised family law on occasion and had an insider's knowledge of the court's sensitivities. In his affidavit he'd acknowledged that Sara seemed to have a close relationship with Ben but said he knew "very little" about him and thought it "inappropriate for a 12 year old girl to be staying unaccompanied with an adult male other than her father." He seemed to be implying that Sara was unsafe in Ben's care. There was nothing direct, for there was not a shred of evidence and nothing to allege, but there was just enough insinuation to raise questions in a judge's mind and leave a misleading impression, as I'd seen lawyers do. Unlike Ben, who had legitimate reasons to be concerned about Randolph Steepe and no way of learning more except by hiring an investigator, David had no legitimate cause for concern about Ben and many people in his immediate circle to whom he could turn for information. (Not only had my sister Joan confirmed Sara's affection for Ben, but Ben had invited David to meet with him, and David's parents' closest friends were deeply fond of Ben – he was their granddaughter's godfather. If he truly had concerns about Ben, he could easily have put his mind at rest. But David, it seemed, didn't want to inform himself. He wanted a weapon. If he was willing to sink to that level, I reasoned he was willing to do just about anything.)

I believed David was using the court process to bully me. Having met many litigation lawyers over the years – not only did I marry one and socialize with others, but there are several in my family – I believe certain of the breed are simply deeply insecure people who have turned their insecurity inside out into aggression and become professional bullies. While I do not think this is true of all litigation lawyers, of course, I believe our adversarial legal system is a perfect forum for the bully pathology because it rewards intimidation tactics handsomely with power, money, and prestige. Membership in an elite club notwithstanding, however, bullies are merely scared little people. Which is why I have always believed the best way to deal with a bully, if reason fails, is to stand up to his intimidations.

Unlike Terry, I'd encouraged joint custody from day one and had spent nine years trying to make it work with a difficult man, for our daughter's sake. Unlike her, I'd implored my ex to mediate our differences. But without anyone willing to force mediation on him, or hold him accountable if he refused to cooperate, I had only one tactic available to me. The weapons at David's disposal were his pocketbook and an inside knowledge of the system. The weapon at mine was the system's prejudice. The last thing I wanted was a custody fight. But if push came to shove, David knew the odds. I was the Mother.

Losing custody was the only outcome I believed he truly feared. So I called David's bluff. In March, hoping this tactical move would force him to abandon his lawsuit and enter mediation, I countersued for sole custody on the grounds that our agreement had broken down and a joint custody arrangement no longer served Sara's best interests. Despite my fury at David for taking us down this road, my intent was not to wrest custody from him or to drive a wedge between him and his daughter. It was just the opposite. The towering irony – and idiocy – was that although I had always been profoundly supportive of joint custody, my only remaining option in that system was to counterattack on that issue.

■ ■ ■

On Monday, March 1, Goudge released her arbitration. The transfer time was to be Fridays at 4 p.m., "delivery by school bus." Tuesdays, both kids were to have a midweek overnight with the other parent. The kids were to have phone extensions installed in one of their bedrooms in each home "in order that they may call their non-resident parent as they wish and in private." Neither parent was to phone the children in the other parent's home unless there was an urgent question regarding "instrumental" issues (such as a birthday invitation that needed a reply), or to call them more than once a day. Deja would go to Camp Tamakwa for two months, Zoe to an unspecified day camp for a month. Ben and Terry would split the cost. Both parents would follow Goudge's "Guidelines on Behaviour":

a) Neither parent will interfere with the relationship between the children and the other parent. (eg Terry amplifying Zoe's concerns about leaving her thermos at her Dad's)

b) Neither parent will involve the children in his/her views on adult issues (eg Zoe reporting to me that she and her mother agreed that Ben was trying to take their house away from them)

c) Both parents will make every attempt to encourage/not undermine a) the children's relationship with the other parent and b) this parenting plan.

d) Both parents, in consultation with Helen Goudge, will

immediately embark on psychotherapy programs in order to get help in dealing with this situation and these guidelines.

The balance of the document outlined the reckoning of expenses. According to Goudge's calculations, Terry owed Camp Tamakwa $1,112.98 by May 15.

Goudge's rulings, which were to take effect immediately, came out during a week when the kids were at Terry's. When they arrived at his apartment that Friday around dinnertime, Ben greeted them enthusiastically. "Deja," he said, "isn't it great that Helen has decided that you'll go to camp for two months?" But Deja fell silent, looked away. "Well," she said, "I'm not sure if I want to go to camp."

"What are you talking about?" Ben asked. "You've been dying to go to camp."

"Well, who's going to pay for camp?" Deja fired back. "I think you should pay for camp. Mommy pays for a lot of things, you know, and the house is more important than camp, and anyway camp's not that good because you have to do stuff you really don't want to do, and if you stay home you can do just what you want to do, like go to Ontario Place. Anyway, I think you just want me to go to camp to get rid of me. Well, I'm going to stay home to see if that's true."

Ben called Goudge on Monday morning. He told her about Deja's sudden about-face on camp. He asked sarcastically if she was getting the picture yet. Goudge told him not to worry. The matter was decided: Deja was going to camp. If she didn't go – well, then Goudge would have to resign.

We met with Goldstein and begged him to intercede. The ship was sinking. The kids were drowning. In despair, Ben saw only one way left to end the conflict: let the kids live with Terry. The psychiatrist emitted an alarmed "No!" But he was out of the loop now. He told us that Goudge had an excellent reputation and suggested we have her call him. Beyond that, there was nothing he could do.

In our February letter, attempting to cooperate with Goudge, we'd agreed to a temporary Tuesday visit for Zoe alone, under certain terms and on the understanding that we did not accept her authority to change

Goldstein's recommendations. When Goudge ignored our terms in her arbitration, we told her all bets were off.

In a detailed letter on March 23, Ben spelled out his response. On the financial side, Ben figured that Terry owed him about $5,600. In future, he said, he would be sticking to the terms of the minutes of settlement: equal sharing of the kids' expenses, with payment directly to the dentist or other supplier. Ben would buy outerwear and equipment such as skates for the girls to use at his home only.

Deja's change of mind about camp, Ben wrote, could be traced to her mother. Ben said he knew Goudge could not stop Terry from "cruelly working on the kids so that they wind up feeling that they will betray their mother if they dare to express what they truly need." But he asked Goudge to take this burden off Deja by telling her "that it is your decision that she attend camp" and that the decision was final, no matter what Terry said. In any case, he remarked later in the letter, camp might soon be out of the question unless Goudge could get Terry to pay her share of the deposit, now past due, to hold Deja's place. "When Terry refuses to pay, as I have no doubt that she will, I leave it to your professional expertise to deal with the matter, and to explain to Deja why she will not be going to camp."

Goudge had altered the changeover time to 4:00 p.m. on Fridays – an improvement over the 6:00 p.m. mess – but her revision was not the one we'd asked for and it failed to address the difficulties of days when the school bus did not run. Ben repeated our proposal that the changeover time be Friday morning, on both school weeks and holidays. On days without school, the parent who would be taking over for the new week would be responsible for picking them up by 9:00 a.m. "This is crucial, since it has been our experience that when it has been Terry's responsibility to deliver the kids, they usually arrive at her convenience (around noon) as opposed to the appointed time, so she can effectively screw up any plans we have made for the day."

Ben reiterated that he would not support Goudge's decision on midweek visits, "as you are not empowered to make it." He would continue with Goldstein's schedule, but "if either Deja or Zoe specifically requests to spend some extra time with their mother because they miss her or need to be with her, I will make the arrangements for such a visit." As for her

"Guidelines for Behaviour," Ben said they were "lovely, lofty ideas but are virtually useless in any practical way." He noted that Terry was already ignoring them.

Zoe would not be going to overnight camp, a decision Ben strongly disagreed with but would accept "under protest." He asked for details of the day camp plans and volunteered to register Zoe once Terry came up with her share of the fee. "Once again, if Terry is not forthcoming with the cheque, I leave it to your professional expertise to explain to Zoe why she will not be going to day camp."

A week passed before Ben heard from Goudge. "You're quite right on the changeover time," she admitted, "but once a decision has been arbitrated, it's hard to change, because then everything is up for grabs." Goudge said she'd ask Terry for permission to make the change. Then Goudge admitted she'd meant to say the Tuesday overnight visit could be cancelled by the resident parent, not non-resident parent, as her arbitration actually read. That mistake, however, she was willing to correct.

Ben told her coldly that he wouldn't support any changes to Goldstein's plan. Obliquely, he raised the possibility of her resignation. "Resign? You want me to resign?" she asked. Ben told her he thought that would be a good idea. Goudge said she'd been speaking with Zaldin, and Zaldin had told her Terry had been on his doorstep complaining about her, too. Goudge said she'd need notice in writing if he wanted her resignation.

■ ■ ■

A week after David learned of my countersuit, Joyce called. David had "virtually capitulated." He'd enter mediation with Robert McWhinney, and Diane Moody would counsel Sara. My high-stakes gamble had paid off. But I felt no sense of victory, only relief at having dodged a bullet and deep resentment at what Sara had suffered and what I'd had to go through to accomplish what I believed should have been mandatory from the start. What were our problems doing in an adversarial arena? Why had lawyers been involved at all? Why wasn't David told that he had to participate in mediation/arbitration or some other form of alternative dispute resolution, and that if he refused to cooperate, he'd be at risk of losing his custodial rights?

For the moment, one fire had been put out. But on another front Helen

Goudge skipped obliviously about sprinkling water on the violets while the house burned down. We had avoided involving Hannaford in our problems with Goudge because of the cost, but now it seemed the only remedy. I wrote to her on April 1, asking her to call Goudge about the legal matters only. Goudge's lack of authority to allocate payment of expenses, for one thing, badly needed clarification. "She thinks that her 'formula' for payment takes precedence over the Minutes of Settlement, and her refusal to follow the Minutes of Settlement concerning financial payment is wreaking havoc."

I proposed a review of all expenses since September and informed Hannaford of our intention to follow the minutes of settlement from then on. In the meantime, I explained it was urgent that Helen get Terry's share of Deja's camp deposit now, even while the payment formula remained in dispute.

Goudge's authority to order the Tuesday visits was another issue I asked Hannaford to take up. And her contention that she could not unilaterally make changes to her own arbitration was puzzling. Since Goudge agreed that her decision on the changeover time was a mistake, I wrote to Hannaford, could she not just make an addendum?

"We'd really appreciate anything you can do here, Julie," I wrote. "I think she needs to hear ... from a lawyer. But I advise you to follow up anything you discuss in writing."

The same day, Ben and I wrote Goudge again. We had no reason to think that a fifth letter would help more than the previous four, but writing gave us an illusory sense of control over a situation that had spun out of control. This time our fury was palpable on the page. We both believed that Goudge truly cared about the kids and was doing her best to help them. But ironically, we found Goudge's cheerful niceness far more infuriating than the detached condescension of the assessors, whom we viewed much more as jaded consultants processing a file.

We outlined, in strong words, the many reasons we believed she'd mishandled Ben's case, including her failure to report to us, despite repeated requests, the evidence on which she'd based her opinion that Zoe had "attachment issues." Her involvement, we told her, had only led to conflict, instability, and chaos for everyone concerned.

The letter ended:

Once again, we urge you to consult with Julie Hannaford concerning this matter as soon as possible, as it's clear, with all parties
unhappy with your handling of this case, Deja unsure and confused
about what's happening this summer, the changeover time in a state
of disarray, the whole matter of finances and payment for the kids
in chaos, you're ensuring that you will be the catalyst for a tragic
ending to this situation.

 Although we raised the matter of speaking to Deja and Terry
about summer camp in our last letter, and impressed upon you the
urgency of doing so, you have so far done nothing. Given that you're
supposed to be overseeing the welfare of these kids, and given that
Deja is in a state of extreme distress because of what Terry has told
her about camp, perhaps you could devote some of your energies
more constructively to helping Deja through that crisis.

 Finally, until you deal with [these urgent and pressing issues]
and demonstrate that you are able to restore some order to this
situation, as you have been paid to do, we find it difficult to justify
engaging your services to deal with any new issues.

 ... Please call us on Monday to let us know what you intend to
do about these matters and about the other matters which you have
so far failed to address from our previous correspondence.

Sincerely,
Ben Gordon
Wendy Dennis

We heard nothing on Monday or Tuesday. On Wednesday, Hannaford
called Ben. She'd just spoken with Goudge. The call lasted an hour and
fifteen minutes. During their conversation, which Ben calculated had cost
him about $300, Goudge had asked Hannaford to explain why Ben was
so angry.

 "Ben is extremely frustrated by this whole process," Hannaford told her.
"It can't work if whoever is going to yell and scream the loudest simply gets
their way." (Goudge had characterized Terry to Hannaford as a "screamer.")

Hannaford said her greatest concern was that the whole situation would end with Ben giving up. Had Goudge ever considered the possibility that by catering to the children's every whim and making them the centre of power, she was entrenching the conflict rather than helping resolve it?

"Oh, now that's an interesting issue!" Goudge reportedly replied.

Hannaford told Goudge how upset we were about Deja's sudden turn-around on camp, and that we were anxious to know how she planned to handle the crisis. Goudge replied that if Deja didn't go, she'd resign.

Their conversation turned to money matters. Hannaford told Goudge she was mistaken in thinking her arbitration took precedence over the minutes of settlement. Goudge replied she thought her parenting plan was the same as the one in the settlement.

"I'm not sure that's true," Hannaford told her. "The minutes say the kids' expenses are to be split fifty-fifty, and each parent's share is to be paid directly to the payee."

Goudge wasn't clear on the meaning of the word "payee."

"Well, Camp Tamakwa, for instance."

"Oh, so they pay directly? That's a better system!"

"Yes."

Goudge said she'd never heard of that kind of arrangement, thought it was a great idea, and became very interested in learning how it worked.

Ten days passed without a response to our letter. On April 12, we wrote Goudge again.

April 12, 1993

Dear Helen,

It's been ten days since our last correspondence to you and although we impressed upon you the urgency of the matters requiring your immediate attention, you have once again failed to respond.

In our telephone conversation last Wednesday March 31st, you agreed that the proposed changeover ... was the best idea ... You told me you would discuss it with Terry to determine if there was any objection to this arrangement. We assumed that you did so. Terry neglected to collect the kids at 9 a.m. to begin her week ...

Consequently, we delivered them to her home.

I still have not received Terry's deposit for Camp Tamakwa ... Julie Hannaford ... reported that you said you would resign if Deja didn't go to camp this summer ... I can only assume that you are preparing to tender your resignation. I spoke with the camp director today and it's not likely that there will be room for Deja as per your determination in your "Arbitration" letter of March 1/93. The camp is having a special function next week for all the new and returning campers (information attached). This would have been a perfect opportunity for Deja to meet everyone and begin to feel a part of the Tamakwa family.

We have informed Deja that she will be attending camp as per your arbitration but we have also told her that she cannot be enrolled until her mother fulfills her financial obligation to pay for 1/2 of the deposit and fees. She knows that if Terry delays sufficiently and/or refuses to pay, she will not be going to camp at all. Since this now seems to be the case, we leave it to you to explain to Deja why she'll be spending the summer in the city...

Your inability or unwillingness to deal constructively (or deal at all) with our situation is tragic. This may be a difficult "file" for you, but it is our life.

We think you are a very nice person, Helen. However, this case requires someone who will not simply try to be nice and placate whoever makes the most noise, creates the most chaos or panders to every one of the children's whims ... ensur[ing] the collapse of the joint custody "agreement."

...We have been more than patient in awaiting your response on these and other matters. Please contact us today especially with respect to the camp matter.

Ben Gordon
Wendy Dennis

P.S. I still have not seen copies of the [receipts for] expenses Terry is claiming.

That day Goudge finally responded. She wrote to the lawyers, asking them to clarify her jurisdiction on money matters. She also wrote to Ben and Terry.

Ap 12/93

Dear Terry and Ben,

Enclosed is a letter to both lawyers regarding the question of my doing the accounting for you both regarding parenting expenses.

Regarding expenses, this is to clarify that (as per the arbitrated ruling of Mar 1), Ben is to pay Deja's camp $3,108.02. Terry pays $1,112.98. Ben is responsible to cover initial costs and Terry's payment is due May 15.

Ben – With regard to your statement of expenses, thank you for submitting them (as per request in the arbitrated ruling of Mar 1). They will be assessed and dealt with in the Oct 15 reckoning.

Regarding summer camps, I understand the children have attended the YMCA and JCC programs. I would ask you both to please mail me details of programs and your preference if you have one. This is to be mediated/arbitrated by May 1.

The day camp time should be distributed equally between the households as it is not meant to be babysitting time. If either parent wants the whole camp time or none of the time to take place during his/her periods, that parent should propose to me regarding compensation regarding babysitting costs lost/gained.

If either parent wishes to leave town early Fri. either during the summer or during a PD Friday during the school session, that parent should phone me and I will mediate/arbitrate that request.

Yours sincerely,
Helen Scott Goudge

Across the bottom of the page, in pen, Goudge had scrawled: "Ben: Please call Julie & ask her to clarify re: the Accounting jurisdiction ASAP!! Thanks, Helen."

In spite of everything we'd endured with Goudge, that letter took my breath away. The social worker's "solution" for having messed up on the transfer time was to turn the resolution of that issue into a make-work project for Helen Goudge and force us to debate the issue every weekend. Moreover, if there was any intelligible explanation for her camp/babysitting compensation ruling, it utterly escaped the two of us.

The following afternoon, Ben spoke with Goudge. He thought she was going to ask for Terry's permission to change the transfer time. He guessed that plan hadn't worked out too well. No, said Goudge. Terry had "flatly refused." Then he asked about her plans to ensure that Deja went to camp. "If the kids don't want to go to camp," Goudge answered, "we'll have to deal with it." Ben asked her if she'd bothered to ask Terry what they'd do in the city if they didn't go to camp. Goudge said she hadn't.

Three days later Hannaford faxed Goudge, confirming what she'd explained already: the minutes of settlement were pre-eminent in governing the parties. Four days later she wrote Goudge again: "In our view ... the expenses and method of payment for same should be dealt with in accordance with the Minutes of Settlement." Then Zaldin faxed Goudge to say he wasn't acting for Terry on the mediation/arbitration. She should get Terry's instructions directly.

On Wednesday, April 21, Goudge called. She was trying to work out the finances, but it was "very complicated." Actually, she was calling on Deja's behalf. In her arbitration, Goudge had decreed the kids' overnight visits were to take place Tuesdays. But Ben had a weekly hockey game on Tuesdays, and the previous evening Deja had preferred to go to Ben's hockey game instead of going to Terry's. That morning, however, Deja had called Goudge. Could she spend tonight – Wednesday – with Terry instead? Goudge told Deja it was up to Ben, but she'd call him to put in a good word for her. Since Ben wasn't around, Goudge asked me brightly whether Deja could go to Terry's tonight.

My voice went icy. We had no intention, I said, of disrupting our lives even more by getting involved in weekly schedule negotiations with the kids through Helen Goudge. This week Deja wanted to go to her dad's hockey game on Tuesday and visit her mom on Wednesday. Next week she'd ask for another alteration. Then Zoe would start. Goldstein's schedule was the simplest, cleanest arrangement, the one the court had ordered, and the one we intended to follow.

"Do you mean to tell me that these visits aren't happening and you're not supporting my arbitration?" she asked sharply.

"That's right," I said. "As we've told you in numerous meetings and letters, we believe you've overstepped your powers."

"I need it in writing," she said crisply.

"You have it in writing," I said. "Many times."

I heard her shuffling for a few moments among the papers on her desk. Eventually she spoke.

"It's a very serious thing to defy an arbitration," she said. "If it's not honoured, I'll have to resign."

"I think that would be a very good idea," I said.

Then we said curt goodbyes and hung up.

Hannaford called Ben. According to the lawyer, Goudge had met with Terry at her own expense. The purpose of her meeting was to tell Terry she shouldn't amplify Zoe's "attachment issues" or try to use her ordained overnight visits to get more time with the girls than Ben had with them. Hannaford reported that Terry had told Goudge she had no intention of listening to her.

On April 22, Helen Goudge resigned.

■ ■ ■

The house sale was supposed to have closed on April 13. Ben had furnished his documents, but Mark Anshan had heard nothing from Terry. The day before the deadline, Anshan heard from another lawyer whom Terry had apparently retained, in violation of the minutes of settlement, to act for her. He asked Anshan to forward the necessary documents when he received them, but Anshan didn't hear from Terry, so April 13 came and went without the deal closing.

Hannaford called Zaldin to find out what was going on. On April 19 she received a handwritten letter from Terry. Yes, she wanted the sale to close, but she "was under the impression that Mark Anshan had already prepared the proper documentation as per court order. If he has not already done so, he has my permission to do so. However, I do not want Mark Anshan to act on my behalf." Terry wanted all documents forwarded to her new lawyer.

Meanwhile, Paul Slavens had retained his own lawyer to make sure he got his commission. On May 5, Gary Shiffman wrote to Hannaford to find out what was holding up the sale. "My client's concern is that the parties now don't seem particularly concerned with closing this transaction, as evidenced by their cavalier approach herein. My client's position is that they are entitled to treat the transaction as completed and to [disburse] the deposit immediately toward commission."

Slavens intended to take a commission when he'd sold the house to Terry. Slavens argued he was entitled because there wasn't a clause in their listing agreement to cover a sale between spouses. Ben responded that there was no such clause because that possibility had never arisen – Terry had always claimed to be destitute. At the very least, he argued, Slavens should take a commission from her only. Ben was furious with Slavens. As he saw it, first he'd been screwed on the sale of his house, and now he had to pay the real estate agent for the privilege.

The next day Hannaford fired off a pointed reply, setting the record straight. She reminded Shiffman that Slavens had dealt with Terry directly on the purchase and had "apparently informed Ms. Nusyna" that he was willing to adjust his commission to "close the deal." She refused to accept any suggestion that Ben had impeded the closing, stressed Terry's violation of the minutes of settlement, advised Slavens to contact Zaldin or Terry "with respect to her actions, or, perhaps more properly stated, her inaction," and strongly censured Slavens for instructing his lawyer to send his correspondence to her alone. She considered the lawyer's allegation "purely inflammatory" – and directed at her firm. Unless otherwise informed she would assume Slavens had instructed him to make the allegation and, unless it was withdrawn, she intended to proceed further with respect to it. Shiffman replied that he'd been unaware of the facts and offered an apology.

Paul Slavens wasn't the only one who hired a lawyer to make sure he got his cut of the Nusyna-Gordon divorce. On April 14, the day after the deal was to have closed, Reiter swore an affidavit for a motion he planned to bring on May 3 seeking an order confirming the pledge Hannaford had already given him in writing to have "$94,635.44 plus applicable interest" from Ben's house proceeds paid into court. He also wanted an earlier date to assess his fees. (On November 6, 1992, shortly after firing Reiter, Ben had applied for a date to contest the lawyer's billings. The first two available were February 2 and 3, 1994 – then fifteen months away. They still had nine to go.) As well, Reiter wanted to force Ben's compliance with a direction in which Ben had agreed to pay a portion of his fees when the house sold. (Ben said Reiter had pressed him to sign the direction under duress during negotiations for the first minutes of settlement.)

On May 5 Justice Heather Smith ordered $94,635.44 plus interest paid into court pending the fee assessment, and the hearing advanced if dates became available and the lawyers ready. Practically, the date was unlikely to change.

In fact, Reiter was on the brink of bankruptcy. The previous month he had filed a proposal to his forty-one creditors, to whom he owed more than three-quarters of a million dollars. Ben first caught wind of this situation shortly after Justice Smith issued her order.

On May 18, 1993, Terry bought 24 Dewbourne Avenue for $475,000. She financed the purchase with a $300,000 mortgage guaranteed by a man named Michael Ostro, whom Ben did not know. Of the $454,650 proceeds Terry took $30,000 off the top and her parents $20,000. (Ben had conceded those amounts in the first minutes of settlement, signed at the trial in November 1991, only because Reiter had advised him the house would sell immediately.) After fees, taxes, Ben's $30,000 equalization payment, and repayment of the first mortgage, Terry received $219,317.24 and Ben $159,317.24. From his share, Ben paid $50,500 owing on his line of credit, and Anshan paid $98,553.63 into court pending the assessment of Reiter's fees.

When Ben and Terry had separated in March 1989, their home was worth $1.1 million. When it finally sold four years later, he netted about $10,000. Paul Slavens cleared $19,000. It remained to be seen how much Moishe Reiter's piece of the action would be.

■ ■ ■

Through the whole sordid process Ben had kept hoping that someone would help. He'd prayed for a King Solomon, but there were no King Solomons in the family court, just beleaguered judges running a clearing-house for divorce, high-priced lawyers living off the avails of human misery, and the tell-me-how-you-feel brigade, who thought they were getting it but weren't getting it at all. Far too often the arbitrators of the family court catered to the shrillest voices or assumed that the truth of a matter lay somewhere in the middle. But the truth, as Solomon knew, was more elusive than that.

Terry had said repeatedly that nobody could make her support joint custody, and she was right. Her attempts to alienate the children and interfere in our lives increased in direct proportion to the time we had with the girls and their longing to participate in our family life. And with no one there to help, I knew nothing was going to change. Since the trial we had been buffeted by storm after storm, with countless hurtful incidents in between.

One day Ben came across a picture Deja had drawn with "Deja Nusyna" scrawled across the bottom. Terry had been working on the girls to go by her last name, and Goudge had told us she'd spoken to Terry about the inappropriateness of that suggestion. For me, it was the most haunting symbol of the crime being committed against those girls. After that discovery I took Deja to dinner, just the two of us. I was hoping to talk to her, maybe encourage her to open up a little, as she'd sometimes done in the past. We went to the BamBoo, a hip, lively Queen Street restaurant. I wanted a special evening. But there was a wall around her a thousand miles high. She was anxious. She couldn't look me in the eye. She was shut down like a house that had been boarded up and abandoned. There was nobody home any more.

"I'm losing these kids," Ben had said to me in anguish a few days earlier, his voice trembling with desperation. Half-heartedly, I offered some reassuring words, but he would not hear them. They were hollow and we both knew it. Deja and Zoe were far too young to understand what was happening. And there was no way to explain without burdening them more. Day by day I watched the girls slipping away, pulled more and more into the magnetic field of their mother's hostility and suffocating need. *I can do what I want and Mommy says I can and you can't make me.* They began to defy Ben's authority, to turn on him, to lie their way out of scary places. What else could they do? The situation had left them no other way to cope. For Ben it was the ultimate indignity, and I could not bear to watch this heartbreaking turn of events at close range.

I loved Deja and Zoe, and I wanted to help Ben parent them well. But

I no longer had any illusions that the family court system would help us look out for the best interests of those children. And so, with no stamina left even for anger, I began to retreat from a situation I now viewed as hopeless. I still spent time with Ben and the kids, but less time. Now, when he had the girls, I stayed at my place more often than not, and Sara and I spent time with Ben when the girls were with Terry. I was no longer prepared to live in the eye of a hurricane, pretending we could build a family together. The family court had taken care of that dream. Although it was too painful for him to speak about, Ben knew what was coming.

It was Helen Goudge's weekly overnight arrangement that triggered the final catastrophe. In her arbitration, Goudge had spelled out the rules: the parent taking the kids on Tuesday was to pick them up at 4:30 at the other parent's place.

Goudge's new regime was to have begun after March break, but on the first two Tuesdays that Ben had the kids for the week, Terry didn't show up to collect them, so they stayed where they were. The first time the ruling became an issue was on April 21 – the Wednesday Goudge had called to ask if Deja could go to Terry's that evening, and I'd told her the visits weren't going to happen. But when Ben arrived at the synagogue around 6:00 to collect Deja from Hebrew school, she had started to cry and plead with Ben to go to Terry's.

Ben knew flexibility was best for everyone. If he'd been dealing with a reasonable person, he'd have called Terry and, if it was convenient for her, dropped Deja off. But he wasn't dealing with that kind of woman. He had to calculate every move, especially because it was hopeless to rely on Goudge for guidance or clarification. Everything was upside down, and no one was monitoring their arrangement any longer. With Terry, even the slightest opening gave onto a slippery slope. Ben cursed Goudge for meddling with the schedule.

With Goudge's resignation expected any day, Ben considered her arbitration dead and Goldstein's schedule and their court order to be the law of the land. That had always been the case, and had Goudge not interfered, the issue wouldn't even be debatable. He didn't seek a legal opinion on the matter. He was beyond broke, and he was no longer prepared to deal with a system for which he had nothing but contempt. Clarifying the rules and the law was irrelevant if Terry could break both with impunity. He had no intention of returning to court again. He was on his own now.

He didn't want to give Terry the impression that Goudge's rules were operational. But if he let Deja go, that was the message he'd be telegraphing. His heart told him to let his daughter go to her mother's, but his head told him that if he did he'd be setting a dangerous precedent. Terry would consider that night "hers." She'd take it as a sign that he was supporting the midweek visits. She'd tell the kids they were to be with her on alternate Tuesdays. He'd be following one set of rules, she'd be following another. The kids wouldn't know where to go or what to do. There'd be more chaos, more confusion. He settled on a compromise. He told Deja she could have dinner with her mom but was to return home at bedtime. Deja said fine.

Ben called Terry. Terry refused to commit herself to bringing Deja back to Ben's after dinner. She'd "see" how she was. Ben could tell Deja that all bets were off unless her mother agreed to play by the rules. Or he could drop her at Terry's and expect the worst. He didn't want to punish Deja for Terry's behaviour, so he dropped her off. He asked Zoe if she wanted to go to her mom's, too, but Zoe said she didn't need to see her mom and preferred to stay with him. After dinner, Deja called. Could she stay over at Terry's? Ben reminded her of their deal. But Terry didn't bring Deja back that night.

Both kids came home on the school bus the next day. That night, Ben talked with Deja. He explained that her mom should have brought her home because that was the deal. He told her that when people made bargains they had to keep them, that going back on a promise was wrong. He hoped she'd understand his reluctance to bend the rules the next time. Deja promised it wouldn't happen again.

It happened again the next Tuesday that the kids were with Ben. It was May 4, Deja's tenth birthday. Zoe had turned eight the week before. On Monday night Ben's mom had called the girls at Ben's to make arrangements to take them for a birthday dinner the next day. She'd meet them at the apartment when their bus came home from school.

The bus never arrived. Frantic that they'd been in an accident, she called Ben at work. Ben called the school. The principal said Terry had picked up the girls. Ben called Terry's. Deja answered. "Deja, where are you?" he asked.

"Why didn't you come home?" "But we're supposed to be here!" Deja wailed. Ben heard Terry yelling at Deja to get off the phone.

The kids came home on the bus the following day. Ben asked if they'd known their mother was planning to pick them up at school. They said yes. Why had they kept their plans a secret, then? Why hadn't they come home when it was their week at their dad's? Why had they made arrangements with their grandmother that they didn't intend to honour? How could they leave her stranded and panicking, worried that something awful had happened, without even bothering to call?

Zoe giggled nervously. Her eyes darted about. Deja spoke. "Because if we'd told," she said, "all the books would have come down." It was Deja's way of saying that there'd have been trouble if she'd told the truth. Her mom would have been angry at her for revealing their secret, her dad would have been upset with her for going with her mom, there'd have been more fighting, more confusion, and the house of cards that was her life would come toppling down around her again.

Ben took a deep breath. He told them that this was probably the most important discussion they were ever going to have in their lives. He told them Helen wasn't in charge any more, and they had to follow Dr. Goldstein's rules. The rules were that they lived one week with Mommy and one week with Daddy. When they lived with Mommy, she was the boss, and when they lived with him, he was the boss. If Mommy came to get them at school again during a week when they were with him, and they became confused about what to do, they should go and find Mr. Mokriy. He would clear up the confusion. Ben asked them if they understood. They nodded and said they did.

He told them that this was their home, and in this home, there were certain rules. The most basic rule was that people had to treat each other with respect. People could not lie to each other. Lying was wrong. If they weren't prepared to live by those rules, he wasn't prepared to pretend that lying was okay. He didn't want them growing up believing that it was acceptable to lie to anyone, let alone to people they loved. He asked whether they understood what he was trying to say. Again, they nodded.

The next day Ben called Mokriy. He told the principal about their joint custody order and Goldstein's schedule, and about Helen Goudge and how she'd put these weekly overnights in place but now she'd resigned and they had to follow their court order. He said that even if Terry believed the overnights were in effect, she knew the rules: for these visits, Goudge had said she was supposed to pick up the kids at his place. Any way you looked at it, she had snatched the children.

Ben said he'd drop by the school with the court order the next day and asked Mokriy to keep an eye out in case Terry tried to take the kids again. Mokriy promised he would.

Tuesday, May 18, breakfast. Ben asked the girls if they understood they were to come home after school. They said yes. He wasn't surprised when his babysitter, Margaret, called around 4:30. Wearily, Ben called the school. Mokriy came on the line. Terry had taken the girls again. He'd just found out. He hadn't managed to stop her in time. He was terribly sorry. Ben thanked him for trying and said he realized Mokriy couldn't possibly monitor the comings and goings of every student in the school.

He knew it was pointless to call Terry's. She'd only hang up. He left work and drove home, where he dialled Terry's number and asked Margaret to ask for Deja. Terry answered. She called Deja to the phone. Margaret handed the receiver to Ben. "Deja, why are you there?" he asked. "Why didn't you come home?" "We're supposed to be with Mommy!" Deja howled. Then Terry shrieked at her to get off the phone, and Deja hung up.

Ben was waiting for the kids the next day. They came bounding off the school bus as if nothing was amiss. Deja dropped her knapsack and wondered absently whether they could have spaghetti for dinner. She did not look him in the eye. She knows she should have come home yesterday, Ben thought. She knows she should have gone to find the principal. She just hopes I won't say anything, or make all the books come down. He said they wouldn't be eating dinner there that night. Zoe cast a furtive glance at Deja. Deja stayed cool. Ben asked them to sit down.

Both kids knew the routine. Dad would be upset. He'd go over the rules. They'd listen solemnly and tell Daddy that they understood. That way the storm would pass, until the next time. But something was different about Dad this time.

Ben looked at his two daughters. They were so beautiful. He closed his eyes. The whole terrible history, all the conflict, was contained in that moment. He knew that he could no longer carry on. The chaos and the pain were finally just too much for him. He no longer had even the basic comfort of knowing that his children would come home from school. And now they were being made to lie, too, just to survive. He couldn't bear to see his children forced to live that way, to see their hearts divided for another moment. If no one had the wisdom of a King Solomon, then he would have to make that terrible choice himself. He took a deep breath. Then he began.

He said that he loved them very much and that he'd tried with all his heart to make a home for them, and that everyone who'd been involved in this dreadful situation had agreed that they should have two involved parents. He said that being their dad was the only thing in his life he'd ever truly wanted to be. But their parents couldn't go on fighting for the rest of their lives. The only thing he could see to do, so there wouldn't be more fighting, was to let them live with Mommy for a while. It would be just for the time being, until he and Mommy could sort out new arrangements. When things cooled down, after the summer, he'd try to work out some new plans with her so they could be together again.

He knew they were too young to take in all of this, but he hoped that when they were older they'd understand his decision. He said that he'd always be there for them, and that he'd call them at Mommy's until things were straightened out, but he hoped they'd call him, too, and not just when they wanted something. If they wanted a relationship with their grandparents, or Wendy and Sara, or anyone else who loved them, they'd have to pick up a phone once in a while, too.

The kids were silent. Zoe's bottom lip trembled. Tears streamed down Deja's face. Then he told them to gather their things and change into the clothes they'd come in, the way they were supposed to when they went back to Mommy's. They dashed into the bedroom. Deja grabbed her stuffed polar bear, Zoe her blanket.

Ben was losing his children and he was on the verge of breaking down. He felt as if he was going mad. He did not want to get behind the wheel of a car. He wasn't fit to drive. He was afraid of seeing Terry, too. No good could come of it at that moment and he knew it. Nor could he bear to bring the children to her, to deliver them up. He wished he had a neighbour, someone to call. But it was 4 o'clock in the afternoon. No one was around.

He called a cab. When it arrived, he took down the driver's particulars and gave him Terry's address. If no one was home, the driver was to drop the kids off with his second cousin Margaret, who lived next door. She was usually home in the day. He told the girls to call Terry's mom from there. He wrote down his phone number and gave it to the driver, telling him to call if there was a problem.

Then Ben bent down and drew his children to him. He gave each of them a long, clutching hug. "I'm sorry," he said. "I tried my best. This didn't have to happen. I love you very much." Then he put them in the cab, closed the door, and stood watching numbly as it rounded the corner and drove away.

CHAPTER ELEVEN

LOSS

May 1993–Summer 1998

Ben knew that by sending the children to Terry during a week when they were supposed to be with him he was altering the status quo, and Zaldin could argue that now, in effect, she had custody. But he didn't care. Legal implications mattered only to someone who planned to go back to court, and he had no intention of participating in that charade any longer.

He was finished taking all the initiative to try to make joint custody work. Now it was over to Terry. He imagined it would turn out as he'd always feared, that Terry would dole the girls out to him at her convenience, use him as a fallback babysitter, call at the last minute and ask him to take them for the weekend. That was the worst-case scenario. But he hoped that once she was dealing from a position of power and could dictate all their arrangements, she would be more benevolent. Maybe once she had the booty – the children – she wouldn't have to use them against him any more. Once she was no longer fighting for her identity, things might settle down. She'd claimed to be the better parent. She'd wanted to call all the shots. Now it would be up to her to ensure that she was the good mother she believed herself to be.

He couldn't bear to talk to her and the situation was far too hot to call immediately; they'd just wind up in trouble. He had to allow some cooling-off time. He'd wait to hear from her. He figured the kids would spend the rest of the week at Terry's and then she'd call and they'd work out some new schedule that suited her, something other than a fifty-fifty arrangement.

That was not how events unfolded. There were no calls from Terry or from the girls. When he called the house to speak to the kids, a machine picked up his calls. His messages were not returned.

In late May, we celebrated Sara's Bat Mitzvah. By then, ten days had passed without any contact. The girls had been eagerly anticipating the event, and Ben was certain he'd hear something, but the day passed without a word from them or Terry, and the party dresses Ben had bought Deja and Zoe for the occasion hung in the closet. Despite the troubles between David and me, it was a wonderful celebration. At our party on Sunday evening, Ben was a charming, funny host. Only our closest friends knew that his heart was breaking.

May turned into June. Still Ben heard nothing. At the end of June he gave up his apartment and moved in with Sara and me. The peace bond, his fear of a scene and of Terry pressing criminal charges again prevented him from going to Dewbourne to try to communicate with his children. His only way of making contact with them was through the school.

Shortly before classes let out for the summer, we went to the school and waited anxiously outside Deja's classroom, as kids spilled noisily into the halls. Deja emerged from class and spotted Ben. She froze. Father and daughter stood staring at each other across an awkward divide. Ben said he'd hoped to hear from her. Deja said she'd waited every day for his call.

Unable to watch a moment longer, I bent down and gathered Deja in my arms, whispered that maybe she could give her dad a hug, since it was obvious they'd both missed each other terribly. Deja tumbled violently into Ben's arms and they clutched each other fiercely. Tears streamed down their faces.

"I want to be with you so much, Dej," Ben told her. "After the summer, we can see how things are going. Then we'll work out new arrangements for us to be together." Deja nodded uncomfortably, hastily gathered her belongings, and dashed for the school bus.

Through all this, Zoe had been peering nervously from behind her classroom door. "Hi, Zoe," Ben said, walking towards his "little fish." Afraid to meet her daddy's eye, Zoe wiggled to escape his hug and, chattering maniacally about a field trip, raced out the door after Deja. Ben followed his daughters across the field and watched them vanish into the school bus.

That summer Ben wrote the kids cards. No reply. Once, he placed a call to the kids from a phone booth out of town and managed to get Terry on the line. He asked to speak to the girls. Terry said they weren't at home. He asked when they would be home. Terry said she didn't know.

Ben's mother called Terry, hoping to see her grandchildren. "Maybe in the fall," Terry told her. "When they're adjusted." By the fall, a recorded message on Terry's phone said that the person at that number did not wish to receive their calls. Ben called, his mother called, I called. We heard the same recording. (Later I discovered that Bell Canada offers a service to "screen out unwanted calls." Call Screen "directs up to 12 numbers ... to a Bell recording that tells the caller you are not available." One of the features of the service is that when a call comes in from a screened number, the phone does not even ring in the home.)

Distraught, Ben's mother called Ruth Nusyna. She hoped Ruth would understand a grandmother's pain at not being able to see her grandchildren. She asked if Ruth would call her when the girls were visiting so she could see them there. According to Ben's mom, Ruth Nusyna said Terry was terrified that Ben would kidnap the children, admitted her daughter could be "irrational" sometimes and that she was "sick" about the situation, but had concluded there was nothing she could do.

Ben's mother joined the G.R.A.N.D. Society (Grandparents Requesting Access and Dignity), a support and lobby group for grandparents whose relationships with grandchildren have been severed through divorce. She was told that grandparents in Ontario had no rights in these situations. She was advised to try sending Terry a registered letter requesting permission to see her grandchildren.

The court order decreed that the children were to live alternating weeks with each parent, neither was to pay support to the other, and both were to split the cost of the kids' extras. Terry was suddenly silent about money, too. Ben heard nothing from her about the kids' extra expenses, nor did she seek child support from him. Attempting to fulfill his obligations, he advised the children's orthodontist and dentist to bill him for half the cost of their treatment, then discovered that Terry had requested that all the bills be sent to her. Concerned only that the children continue to receive treatment, he asked to be contacted if it stopped. Once, he received a bill the dentist had mistakenly sent him for the total cost of a visit. When he attempted to rectify the mistake, the receptionist told him huffily, "Well, they're *your* kids!" He spoke to the dentist about the incident and spelled out the billing arrangements again, but he never received another bill for any amount.

No longer interested in belonging to the synagogue, Ben resigned. He'd kept the membership until then but was no longer willing to pay dues simply because the synagogue was located across the street from Dewbourne and suited Terry's convenience. Terry would have to make her own arrangements. He reasoned that if she was in a financial position to buy the house, then she could afford the dues; otherwise, she could contact him about sharing them or making other arrangements for the kids' religious schooling. He learned that the children had stopped attending, but he received no bills from any other synagogue or program and had no way of learning if they were still receiving a Hebrew education.

In September Ben consulted with Berenice Mandelcorn. He described his visit to the school in June and explained that even in his worst nightmares he'd never imagined not seeing his children again. He said he desperately wanted to see the kids but feared his attempts to contact them would only cause them pain. "I think, in their minds, it's 'No daddy, no problem,'" he told the psychologist.

She told him not to heed what the kids said or did.

"They have no power, and because they're being forced to protect their mother, they cannot call, even if they want to. But it's a horrendous thing for a child to lose a parent, and I think it's important for you to let them know that you're still there. You've been burned. But keep writing. Keep doing whatever you can. If the school is the only place that you can see them, then visit them there, if you can take it. If you can't take it, then write. After that, you can see what you want to do next. It's a process. But don't give up. Keep the door open. It will be difficult, and you may get far less from them than you want or need, but you have to think of what you're doing as an investment in the future. The parent-child bond is a pretty formidable thing, and I doubt that even she is strong enough to break that."

Ben continued to write his daughters letters, asking what they were up to, saying he thought about them every day. I wrote, Sara wrote, the grandparents wrote, our friends wrote. No answer.

That fall Deja, now ten, began Grade 5 and Zoe, eight, entered Grade 3. Ben met with Terry Mokriy and brought him up to date on events since the spring. Mokriy, who was divorced with children, and who had witnessed Ben's close relationship with the girls, offered to help in any way he could. Ben asked him to set up a meeting with the kids' teachers, the school psychologist, and the social worker so he could explain what the girls were coping with. Mokriy arranged the meeting and told Ben that any time he wanted to take the girls out for lunch, he'd be happy to arrange it.

Early in October, Ben went to the school to see if Deja would go to lunch. Fearful, Deja asked if he'd bring her back. Ben said of course he would, but suggested that if she was worried she should call her mom. While Deja vacillated, Leah and Karen, two of the kids' closest friends, jumped up and down yelping, "We'll go, Ben! Take me! Take me!" Reluctantly, without calling Terry, Deja decided to go to lunch. At Harvey's, she told Ben that Mommy had told her and Zoe not to go with their father, because he might kidnap them and then they might never see their mommy again.

Ben asked Deja if she'd like to see him again.

"I think we'd better wait until things settle down," she said. "I want Mommy to have custody. When Mommy has custody, then she says she'll let us see you sometimes."

Ben told her that if Mommy had custody, Deja would never see him again. He told her that she was missing out on having two families to love her.

"I don't want two families," she said. "At Mommy's we can do whatever we want."

Ben told Deja he'd tried to call often, but he could never get through because of the recorded message on the phone. Deja said there was nothing wrong with the phone.

He returned Deja to school and spotted Zoe playing in the schoolyard. "Hi, Zoe. Remember me?" he said. But to Zoe Ben might just as well have been someone else's father. She chattered at him momentarily, then became distracted and returned to her friends.

Ben visited the school periodically. The routine was always the same. He waited in Mokriy's office. The principal went to find the girls, told them their dad wanted to see them. Deja and Zoe cast their eyes downwards, spoke robotically. "We're not ready. Maybe next time." Mokriy returned to his office, shaking his head sadly. He said it was obvious the kids had been put in a terrible bind. Ben continued to drop off letters. His letters said he loved them and missed them and that nothing that had happened was their fault. But his children would not see him or speak to him.

Shortly before Christmas, Ben's mother left Hanukkah presents for the kids with Terry's parents and dropped off giant felt Christmas stockings at Terry's house. Though Jewish, she and the kids had always delighted in this ritual. A courier returned all the gifts to her, unopened. Enclosed were two letters, virtually identical, signed by the children: "Dear Zella, Thanks but no Thanks. Why did you give me a Christmas present when we are Jewish? ... Why didn't you listen to me when I wanted to go to my mommy's house? ... You never cared to hear how we felt, but you did what my dad told you to do."

Occasionally a crumb of information would come our way. An acquaintance I was chatting with at a party said she'd bumped into Terry and the kids on Eglinton Avenue. Another told Ben he'd seen Deja waiting for Terry to pick her up from camp in the summer. Other than such reports, we heard nothing.

Stories drifted back to us, rumours, gossip. I heard that Ben never gave a shit about the kids – he was only fighting for custody to mess with Terry's head. I heard that Ben was refusing to pay a cent for the kids. I heard that Ben abused the children. I heard that when the judge said Terry could buy the house, the next day Ben put the kids into old clothes, stuck them in a cab, and sent them away. I heard that Ben had abandoned his kids, that he never even visited.

Someone we knew heard the word on the street. "I know Ben is heart-broken," he told me, "but there's detaching and then there's detaching. I don't think I would be capable of not seeing my children. No matter how much the kids are being poisoned, no matter how hard it is to see them, as a man and a father, I have difficulty justifying what Ben did."

People asked questions, offered advice: But there must be *something* you can do. Have you thought about getting some professional help? Why can't you go back to court?

1994

Ben and I met with the school social worker, Norma Petitti. She told us Deja was participating in her support group for children of divorce. She

30/12/93

Baba Zell,
Thanks but no thanks.
Where were you when I needed
you. Why did you give me a
Christmas present? I'am Jewish.
"Thanks but no thanks?"
Why did you not help us when
we wanted to be with our mother
most of the time and not
half + half.
You never cared to hear how we
felt, but you did what my dad
told you to do.

Zoe

Dec 30/93

Dear Zella,

Thanks but no Thanks.
Why did you give me a Christmas
present when we are Jewish?
Are these the kinds of things
you think i really need? "How
many day's this week did you go to
church?"
Why weren't you
there when i needed you? Why didn't you
listen to me when i wanted to go to my
mommy's house? Like the time that i
had to go to your house for New years
and i wanted to go to my mommy's
house for New years.

said Deja had told her that her mother had instructed her and Zoe to turn over all their father's letters to her before reading them, and she would decide for them if there was anything in his letters they needed to know. From then on, Ben left all his letters open with unsealed envelopes attached, so the children could read his letters without fear of their mother knowing. Petitti said it was clear to her that the children were being instructed what they were to do and think. "Keep doing what you're doing, Ben," she told him.

Petitti told us Deja was dealing with more complicated issues than the other kids in the group, and she thought she could benefit from individual therapy. Ben asked her to do whatever she could to help Deja. Because she was legally obliged to do so, Petitti canvassed Terry. Terry told the social worker that she was to have nothing more to do with her children. Petitti told Ben that she was terribly sorry, but Terry had made it perfectly clear she was to stay away from her children. She very much wanted to help Deja, but with joint custody her hands were tied unless both parents consented.

We attended a meeting Petitti had arranged for the parents of the children in her divorce group. Terry didn't show. The mom of one of Deja's school chums came that evening. "How's Deja?" she asked Ben brightly. She was unaware of the situation. The girls no longer played together. Ben had developed a way of dealing with such questions. He didn't go into details, but he refused to skirt the issue, pretend nothing was amiss, or participate in the lie. He refused to collude in the crime that had been committed against his children, as he'd seen so many others collude. "I don't know," he said, matter-of-factly. "I haven't seen my kids for two years." The woman was stunned. Later, when it was Ben's turn to tell the group his story, I noticed her weeping silently.

1995

February 14: Ben's mother went to the school with bouquets and valentines. The principal told the girls their grandma had come to see them. The girls refused to see her. They repeated their mantra: "We're not ready. Maybe next time." Ben's mother showed the principal the letters she'd received with the returned presents. No child wrote those letters, he told her.

June: Deja's public-school graduation. Ben hadn't had any contact with

Terry, Deja, or Zoe for almost two years. He ached to attend his daughter's graduation but was concerned that his presence would upset Deja, so he sought Mokriy's advice. The principal advised him to attend. "If you don't, Deja can always say you didn't care enough. But if you go, however she views your presence now, the undeniable fact is that you loved her enough to be there."

Onstage, Deja looked elegant as a swan. Ben beamed at his daughter. He could not believe how grown up she had become. Neither child would meet his eye. The ceremony ended, the kids climbed down from the stage, their mother hurried them out of the auditorium and left the school. Deja never got the chance to join her friends for refreshments and goodbyes. Ben never got the chance to congratulate his elder daughter on her graduation. We drove by Terry's house. Ben laid a bouquet and modest keepsake, engraved for his daughter, at Terry's door.

August 30: In an unmarked van, and without warning, Terry moved. The kids didn't show up at their schools in September. The school secretary told Ben that Terry had called to say Zoe wouldn't be returning, but she'd refused to leave a forwarding address. Mokriy told Ben that if the kids were in school, their records would have to be forwarded "sooner or later."

We called the police and were fortunate to reach a sympathetic officer who told us his wife had moved away with his younger son, and he "couldn't believe that there was no way" for him to get help in the system. A month later his son's principal had called to say his son's records had been transferred to Barrie, Ontario. "The system so favours the mother," he told us. "Dads are just left out, forgotten." He called the Youth Bureau and was told that technically the girls weren't really missing. He gave us a knowing look. "Maybe I had better come over and talk to you in person," he told the individual on the other end of the line. He promised to do whatever he could, "but I have the distinct feeling that the police are going to say there's nothing they can do."

I could hardly believe what I'd just heard. This father had a court order for joint custody. The court order said his children were supposed to be living with him every other week. For the past two years their mother had prevented that order from being followed by alienating him from his children and denying him any contact with them. Now she was breaking the law again by moving away with them and refusing to leave any forwarding address. Why wasn't that considered child abduction? Why wasn't she apprehended and charged with kidnapping? Ben wasn't asking that the order be enforced. He just wanted to know where his children were and if they were safe. He was their father. What did the police need to file a missing person's report?

"There has to be some indication of foul play," the officer said. "Right now, technically, she has the right to be with the kids, and she has the right to go where she wants with them."

"Yeah," said Ben, "but not on the weeks when they're supposed to be with me!" The officer shrugged. "I'll do what I can," he said.

September 7, 1:50 p.m.: The officer called back. He had succeeded in filing a missing person's report but had to pass us on to 13 Division. There we spoke to another constable, who said "no criminal offence has been committed." He asked if Ben had spoken to his lawyer.

Ben told him he had no plans to speak to any lawyers. He'd had his fill of lawyers, thank you very much. He explained to the officer that he had no desire to engage with Terry. He simply needed to know that his children were safe.

We were referred to Detective Constable Michael Polson of the Metropolitan Toronto Police Youth Bureau. He asked us for any information that might lead him to Terry. He warned us, however, that if he found Terry, she didn't have to say where she was living. That was her right.

Polson started checking around. He spoke to the lawyer who had acted for Terry on the house closing. The lawyer said he had no idea where Terry was but would like to know – she owed him money. The detective spoke to Morris Nusyna. He said he and Terry had had a falling-out some time ago and he didn't know where she was living, but he thought maybe somewhere in Thornhill (a community north of Toronto). Polson asked him for the names of some of Terry's friends. Terry doesn't have any friends, her father said.

I called the mother of one of Deja's best friends. I'd seen her taking photographs at the graduation in June. I explained that Terry had taken off with the kids and the police were looking for them. I said we had no recent photographs and asked if she had any pictures of Deja in her graduation photos. She said she'd check and get back to me, but she never did.

Ben called a man who he'd heard had been working with Terry recently on a camp reunion committee. He was shocked to hear that the police were looking for Terry but didn't want to get involved. He said he was aware she'd moved, but he didn't know where. When he'd asked, Terry said, "I'm not telling anyone where I'm living."

September 11, 1:45 p.m.: Detective Polson called. He'd located Terry in Thornhill, but he said Terry claimed Ben was stalking her. Terry also claimed Ben's father and stepmother were stalking her. Ben said nothing. He was dazed. He could feel every alley dead-ending on him again. I asked what evidence Terry gave to support her allegation that Ben's seventy-seven-year-old father and his wife were stalking her. He read aloud from his notes: "I often saw Mr. Gordon's stepmother and father driving down my street." This was Terry's stalking report.

Polson said Terry had told him that Ben deserted his kids ("put them in a cab and that was that"). She also told him that she was afraid of what his letters did to her "kids' psyches." The story Terry gave to police was that her children were so upset by their father's letters that, since the first one, they'd delivered all of them to her, unopened.

Stalking is a criminal offence, Polson said. He didn't "feel comfortable" telling us where Terry was living.

I asked the detective if Terry had provided any evidence to substantiate her stalking allegations. The detective said no. I asked him if he had asked her for any. The detective said no. I told him about Terry's history and explained that, except for their daughter's graduation when he sat several rows behind her and the children in a school auditorium, Ben hadn't been anywhere near them for the past two years. Anyway, I asked, why would a father who allegedly "deserted" his children be stalking them and their mother?

"Stalking is a criminal offence," he repeated. "Based on what she did tell me, I don't feel comfortable saying where she lives. If that is going to be the catalyst for a repeat of what she says occurred before, I don't want to be a party to it."

Apparently Terry had claimed to be the victim of domestic assault;

because of her allegations, the police officer wasn't taking any chances. "You have two conflicting stories and no evidence," I said. "Why are you willing to give a woman's story more credence than a man's? Why, on the basis of a mother's word, are you prepared to deny a father with a joint custody order knowledge of where his children are living?"

Polson repeated himself again. He didn't wish to be a party to a criminal offence. Ms. Nusyna says Mr. Gordon can't suddenly rely on a court order which hasn't been followed for the past two years, and he agreed. Mr. Gordon's court order was unenforceable. I told him we were well aware of all the legalities, but a joint custody order was supposed to mean he was legally entitled to information about his children.

"It's all going to boil down to Mr. Gordon going back to court again," he said. Terry had said she wanted to communicate only through her lawyer, Jack Straitman. "If Mr. Straitman thinks Mr. Gordon has the right to know where his kids are in school, then he'll tell him. Otherwise, your only avenue is family court."

Ben called Straitman right away. "Whatever you're hearing, rest assured you're not getting the whole story," he told him. Ben said he was worried about his kids. He just wanted to know where they were living, who they were living with, and where they were in school.

"I can't tell you right now," said the family lawyer. He asked us to "set out in writing exactly what you need to know." He'd get the requests to Terry immediately, along with any letters for the kids.

"When will I have an answer?" Ben asked.

"I can't tell you ... I can pass along a request immediately and hope to get you a response."

We composed a letter and faxed it to him right away.

September 11, 1995

Dear Mr. Straitman,

I phoned you today on the advice of Detective Constable (5916) Michael Polson of the Metropolitan Toronto Police, 13 Division, Youth Bureau. I contacted the police when I discovered that my former wife Terry Nusyna had moved out of her home on August

30, 1995, and subsequently pulled the children out of their schools, leaving no forwarding address or number.

According to Detective Polson, Ms. Nusyna asked that I speak to you regarding my children. You and I . . . spoke this evening concerning their whereabouts. You told us that Ms. Nusyna had hired you to advise her. I told you that I had serious concerns about my children. You then advised me to put in writing exactly what I needed to know and you would get back to me with answers promptly. Consequently, please inform me of the following:

a) Where are my children living, and with whom? b) Are my children attending school? If so, where?

I am attaching a copy of the court order and Dr. Sol Goldstein's assessment to which the court order refers. As this is a matter of deep concern to me, I would appreciate an immediate response.

Sincerely,
Ben Gordon

Eight days passed. Frantic for some word, Ben called Straitman's office twice and left messages. The lawyer did not return his calls. Desperate to find his children, Ben wrote him another letter.

September 19, 1995

Dear Mr. Straitman,
Over a week ago, I spoke with you regarding Terry Nusyna (my ex-wife), and the whereabouts of my two children: Deja (age 12) and Zoe (age ten).

I explained to you that I had particular reason to be concerned about my children's safety, given Ms. Nusyna's past association with Randolph Steepe, whom she charged with threatening assault.

You asked me to put in writing exactly what information I wanted. I complied with your request immediately and faxed you on the evening of September 11. Since then I have called your office twice, on September 15 and 18, and left messages with your receptionist, but you have not returned my calls.

I don't know if you are a father, Mr. Straitman, but you are a Family Law practitioner. One would think you would be sensitive to the concerns of a parent who had suddenly lost knowledge of the whereabouts of his children.

I would appreciate the basic courtesy of a response.

Sincerely,

Ben Gordon

Straitman called the next day. He'd spoken to Terry, but had no "instructions." The following conversation ensued.

BEN: Let me get this straight. She asked you to communicate on her behalf. But you don't have any instructions to communicate anything.
STRAITMAN: She hasn't given me instructions to release [the information] to you. I don't rule out that she may give out the name of the school and the phone number. Give it another few days. I've been in touch with her. I'm doing the best I can.
B: Are you comfortable representing her?
S: I'm not representing her.
B: You don't mind being associated with her?
S: Sounds like you had a bad experience. Why are you tarring me with that brush?
B: I'm tarring you with your own brush. You wouldn't advise a client to break the law, would you?
S: No, I'd never do that.
B: But you know there's an order and she's violating it and you won't tell me where she is and you're comfortable doing that?
S: I'm like a fax machine. I haven't been instructed not to give you information but I haven't been instructed to give it to you either.
B: Do you know her home address?
S: I can't tell you that.
B: Are you withholding information?
S: I don't view it as withholding. I don't think I'm representing her per se. She's left me as a means of contact. I will certainly confirm they are in school.

B: The police told us that. Are you a father, Jack?

S: Yes.

B: Have you ever heard the expression, "It should happen to you"? God forbid.

S: Yes, I hear you. Your relationship with the kids is somewhat strained, I take it.

B: To say the least.

S: I take it you're saying contact was denied.

B: Yes.

S: So why haven't you done anything about it?

B: Okay, fair question. You're saying if access is denied why haven't you gone back to court. That's a reasonable question and there's a whole long story, and maybe one day you can buy us a drink and we'll tell it to you. But the short story is this: after a quarter of a million dollars, and being reamed by your system, and a mother who simply refused to support joint custody, who brainwashed the kids and turned them against me, and nobody, nobody did a damn thing to help, and everybody made it worse – no thanks. No more money. No more emotional energy. Every professional said the best thing for the kids was to end the conflict. So I let them go.

S: So you stepped back?

B: Yes, but never expecting how insidious this woman would be. Messages on the phone, refusing to take calls, cutting off the grand-parents. You're not representing her, but I was told by the police to call you. You know she's violating a court order but you won't tell me where my kids are. You're playing a game, Jack.

S: No, I'm not.

B: Is there any kind of case you wouldn't take, Jack?

S: Yes.

B: But this doesn't fall within it?

S: No, not yet.

It seemed to me that Ben's conversation with Straitman contained all that anyone needed to know about the pretence and the stench of hypocrisy that rose from the family law system and those who made a living within it. Here was a system that professed to care about children. And here was a father frantic to find his children, calling the family lawyer the police had said was representing the woman who'd run off with them. And here was that family lawyer just doing his job – telling the father he didn't know when he'd be able to give him an answer. Everything he said was perfectly proper and legal. He even sounded like a nice guy.

But for Ben, it was déjà vu. For him, the bottom line was that he was a distraught father desperate to protect his children, and here he was again disenfranchised and at the mercy of a lawyer hiding behind rules of propriety and conduct while playing games with his children's lives. A lawyer equivocating and saying he wasn't really representing Terry, he was only a conduit for information, but had no instructions to impart any, and telling him to "give it another few days." A lawyer asking Ben why he hadn't done anything about it if contact was denied, even though he knew there wasn't a thing to be done about it, that the court would never hold a mother accountable, that, by asking such a question, he was colluding in the pretence that there was something to be done about it, that there was justice to be found in this system and that it protected children's best interests, when the truth was that all "doing something about it" would achieve was to put more money in a lawyer's pocket.

Ben was no longer prepared to collude in that lie. He expected no victory, had no illusions that this lawyer would help him. He just wanted to shake him up a little, challenge him to recognize that he wasn't dealing with just another file. He was dealing with a father in agony because he had lost his children. Which was why he had cross-examined the lawyer and refused to play polite. He would force Straitman to deal with the moral questions, challenge him to answer whether there was any moral standard to which he would adhere. He would not let the lawyer off the hook. Because for Ben, the crux of the matter was that those who earned their daily bread in a world devoid of morality – a moral vacuum where any kind of behaviour, however contemptible, could be justified by saying they were only doing their job, they were only acting in their client's best interests – were no different from those who said they were only following orders.

Ben thought Terry and the kids might be living with an old friend of Terry's named Tom Kirschner. We'd seen Kirschner sitting with them at

Deja's graduation. He was a stocky, overweight man who wore a yarmulke. Ben told me that Kirschner had a crush on Terry and used to show up unannounced and uninvited at their door, then overstay whatever welcome he could muster. He described him as a cloying character whose family had money and who used to brag all the time about his big "connections" and secret wheelings and dealings.

Ben called Peter Israel to see if he had any idea where Kirschner was living. (Israel's and Kirschner's families had known each other for years.) Israel said he'd see what he could find out, but he never called back. Ben called Israel's mother. She too said she'd check. But she never called back either.

I called a private investigator. He told me he'd have taken the assignment over the phone a few years ago, but "with this new anti-stalking legislation, it's not that easy any more. The legislation's really weighted against the man." He explained that as information becomes more centralized, more protections exist to prevent its unauthorized usage.

"We can find it but we can't pass it on. The fact of our having requested the information is recorded. If I then pound the shoe leather, and she finds out, and she complains, then I'm facing a $25,000 fine."

He wouldn't take an assignment for less than a $500 retainer and refused to touch a case if the woman was litigious. "You can call other investigation agencies. They might do it. They'll charge you just as much." Then he said, "I know the frustrations of trying to deal with someone that intransigent. My son was fifteen when we split, and my wife did everything to try to alienate him from me. He was a gifted intellectual who got into drugs as a result and became totally dysfunctional. Even now I can't get any sense out of the situation. Talk about heartbreak. I've been there."

I called Joyce, brought her up to speed, and asked her if she knew of another investigator through her law practice. "How can the police not tell him where his kids are?" she asked me, still trying to process what I'd reported. I told her about Terry's stalking allegations.

"Isn't there an outstanding court order?" she pressed on. I told her yes, but it was worthless. The police wouldn't enforce it. They wouldn't even say where his kids were living. Apparently a mother's unsubstantiated stalking allegation carried more weight with the police than a father's court order.

Joyce couldn't believe it either. "Well, then she should be charged with kidnapping!"

I told her that was my view as well, but not, apparently, the view of our criminal justice system.

Joyce called back later. She'd spoken with an investigator who said he received these requests all the time. Eventually he came up with the location of the rented post office box in Thornhill where Terry's mail was being forwarded.

Ben called the Jewish Family and Child Service and the Children's Aid Society. Neither agency would get involved.

Three weeks had passed since Terry had disappeared with the children. On September 20 Ben faxed the superintendent of schools for the Thornhill Board of Education about an "urgent custodial matter." After providing the background details, he wrote:

> I have reason to believe that Ms. Nusyna is living in Thornhill and that my children are attending school in your district ... I don't know what Ms. Nusyna has told the school concerning our custodial arrangements, but I am attaching to this fax a copy of the court order outlining my rights. The Court has empowered me to participate in all decisions regarding my children's welfare, including which schools they attend. I don't necessarily object to their transfer; however, I would like to know where they are attending school and I would like to meet with the school principal to apprise him or her of the background to this situation. Furthermore, my only means of communicating with my children has been through their school and I have been advised to continue doing so by the social worker at John Fisher Public School and by every other psychological professional consulted.
>
> Mr. Terry Mokriy, the children's former principal at John Fisher, is well aware of the background in this case and would be happy to talk to you should you have any concerns ...
>
> Please alert all the schools in your area immediately concerning this matter. It's possible that Deja and Zoe have been registered under the name Gordon or Nusyna. Their dates of birth are: Deja

– May 4, 1983; Zoe – April 26, 1985. I am very concerned about this matter, so please call me as soon as you've reviewed this fax to confirm its receipt and to advise what steps you will be taking to help me locate my children.

The superintendent left Ben a voicemail message around 5:00 that afternoon. He understood Ben's concerns and would keep him apprised, but before he could initiate a search of their schools, he had to consult the board's solicitors.

Although Ben's court order had proven to be virtually useless, we both knew that the only reason the school authorities were even responding was that the words "joint custody" were on it. Had he not fought to have those words enshrined on a legal document, had he consented to Terry having sole custody, as some criticized him for refusing to do, the school board wouldn't have had to respond to his letter, let alone initiate a search of its schools. He'd have had fewer options than the limited ones he held. And if he'd hired a private investigator and managed to find the children through his own expense and effort, and if he'd gone to their school and asked the principal to pass his letters on, and Terry then advised the school she didn't want them passed on, he'd have been out of luck. Had he lingered in the schoolyard to hand the children the letters himself, he could have been charged with stalking. In the end, he would have had no way of telling two little girls who'd been led to believe that their father had abandoned them and were imprisoned behind a wall of disinformation and lies that he loved them.

Another five days passed before Ben heard from the superintendent. The board's lawyers had confirmed that his court order was the only one on the books. He told Ben that the kids were enrolled at Thornhill Public School and that Ben had the right to meet his children at the school. However, the Freedom of Information and Protection of Privacy Act prevented the school from releasing Terry's new address. Ben knew that unless he could find a private investigator who was willing to follow the children home and risk a stalking charge, there was no way for a father with a joint custody order to learn where his children were living.

September 28: On a Thursday afternoon, Ben and I met with Glyn

Bancroft, the principal of Thornhill Public School. Ben had called earlier to set up this meeting. He wanted to introduce himself to the kids' new principal, provide him with some background so he understood the issues the kids were dealing with, and make sure their new principal would continue to deliver his letters, as Terry Mokriy had done. Classes were in session when we arrived. En route to the office, we happened to see Zoe chatting with another student in the library. Ben gazed longingly at his daughter through the glass, but she didn't see him.

We then spent an excruciating forty-five minutes with Bancroft, who'd already spoken to Terry and who, judging by his inquisitorial and judgmental treatment of Ben, appeared to have accepted everything she'd told him as self-evident truth. Shaken by the encounter, Ben asked to speak to the vice-principal, who was female and Jewish. If the girls wanted to talk to someone, he explained, they might be more inclined to seek her out. Rhonda Polisuk told us the kids had already been to see her. They'd arrived in her office yesterday to say they knew their dad had found them and to ask her not to make them go with him. "Are you afraid your father will take you away?" the vice-principal had asked Ben's daughters. "No, he'd never do that. We just don't want to go with him." Ben explained the situation to Polisuk and asked her to pass on his letters. They were his only hope of reconnecting with his children one day.

Approaching a school exit after the meetings, we almost collided with Deja. Startled, Ben blurted out her name: "Dej!" Less than a foot away, now with the disdainful slouching gait of adolescence, Deja kept on walking, but not before glancing in our direction. In her eyes there was curdled rage.

1996

An old friend of Ben's called. She'd just discovered her daughter and Deja were playing on the same basketball team at the Y. A child of divorce, too, her daughter had called Deja to offer a sympathetic ear if she ever needed to talk. She said her daughter told her that Terry answered and began grilling her hysterically about where she got their number. Her daughter said the coach gave it to her. Terry said he never should have given out their number. Then Deja got on the phone and repeated what Terry had told her: nobody was supposed to know their number. At a subsequent game Terry came over to her daughter, the friend reported, and admitted she had over-reacted, but "it's just that your mom and my ex-husband are such close friends." A few weeks later, Deja stopped coming to the games.

Through the grapevine we heard rumours: Terry was living with Tom Kirschner. Terry had gone Lubovitch (an ultra-Orthodox sect of Judaism) and koshered her kitchen. Kirschner was telling people he was looking after a woman and "her two abandoned children." Terry was "in sales." Terry was looking for work. Terry was at an ad agency. Terry was let go from the agency. Terry was desperate for money. Terry wouldn't tell anyone where she was living. Terry was in hiding to dodge creditors, including Revenue Canada.

We heard from several reliable sources that Terry was estranged from her own family, which confirmed what her father had told police, but we also heard that she had totally isolated the children from her family, too, and was holding them hostage to extort money from her parents. The story was that when Morris Nusyna refused to co-sign the mortgage so Terry could buy Ben out of the house and told her she'd have to adapt to a lesser lifestyle, she refused to let her family see the kids. Someone close to the Nusynas told me that Ruth Nusyna had knocked on the door at Dewbourne one day only to discover another family living there.

That fall Ben heard from his cousin that he'd seen the girls. His children were attending the same school and saw Deja and Zoe playing in the schoolyard. The girls were so tall, especially Zoe. Ben's cousin said they were friendly to him at first – they knew him well – but snubbed him and his kids after Terry learned he was communicating with them. "Zoe won't talk to me any more," his son told him. "We just stare at each other now, Dad."

In September Ben received a letter from the Office of the Children's Lawyer. A letter from Terry's latest lawyer, Barry Greenberg, of Beglaubter, Greenberg & Ernst, was enclosed. It listed various bonds that Terry believed Ben was holding in the children's names: "Our client is concerned that the integrity of the funds be properly maintained on her daughters' behalf," the letter read. Greenberg asked for confirmation of "the nature and extent of funds currently held" and "full particulars and supporting documentation."

"This office represents the interests of minor children, those under the age of eighteen years, in connection with property and estate matters," read the accompanying letter from P. Ann Lalonde, counsel for the Office of the Children's Lawyer. "You appear to be acting as guardian of the property of your children. Please advise me in writing whether you are in possession of a guardianship of property order pursuant to Section 47 of the *Children's Law Reform Act*." Ben was also asked to confirm for their office that he was "in possession of the certificates and bonds outlined in Mr. Greenberg's letter."

Ben wrote back enclosing the only order he had – one for joint custody – and said he'd declared any bonds and certificates that he held in his name, the children's names, or jointly with his ex-wife, when he made full financial disclosure to the court during their matrimonial litigation between 1990 and 1993. He also enclosed a copy of their minutes of settlement, in which they'd agreed to abandon all claims against each other. "It was understood at that time that each of us was to provide for the children from our own income and assets (including any bonds and certificate which each of us held at that time). Consequently, it is unclear to me why Ms. Nusyna is now, suddenly, through the Attorney-General's office, 'express(ing) her concern that the integrity of the ... funds is being properly maintained on behalf of her daughters...' and 'requir(ing) confirmation' respecting same."

Ben said he'd been advised that unless Terry decided to commence litigation, and therefore reopen all matters between them, he wasn't obliged to divulge information about his financial affairs or the savings he might be maintaining for the children. He pointed out that Terry owned their former Forest Hill home, which she'd briefly listed for sale in April for $529,000, but that the property was presently off the market and she was apparently renting it out. He then provided the government lawyer with an account of their story, including the facts surrounding Terry's disappearance with the children, "which may give you some additional background concerning my children's welfare."

"I have no desire to engage with Ms. Nusyna," he concluded. "However, since she has brought to your attention the matter of our children's needs, an issue about which I am deeply concerned, I would be most grateful if, as a government advocate for children's rights, you would inquire after my children's welfare, investigate whether their rights have been violated, and advise their father – who has a joint custody order – where they go to sleep at night."

Ben did not hear from Greenberg or the Office of the Children's Lawyer again.

1997

March: 24 Dewbourne Avenue went on the market again with Spectrum Six Realty Services. The agent was Tony Vaccarello and the vendor was listed as Michael Ostro. Terry's name appeared on the listing as occupant only. Ben and I went through the house during an agents' open house. I'd never been inside and was curious to see the home that had been the scene of so much misery and the subject of so much litigation. Ben walked me through without emotion, pointing out the den where they'd had the fierce argument resulting in Terry's first criminal charge, the front hall and vestibule where they'd had the others, the kitchen desk where he'd found Terry's bankbook. He remained detached until we walked into Zoe's room and he noticed the stars and moon decals he'd glued to the ceiling when she was little.

The house was worn and badly in need of a paint job. A family was renting; things were in a state of mild disarray. How sad it looked, how far from the house I'd imagined, this nice but unspectacular house that had been grossly inflated in price and invested with mythic significance. I thought about the drama that had played out around that house, all the nonsense that had gone on in court, how wasteful and stupid and unnecessary it had all been. On May 26 the house sold for $513,000. Coincidentally, my cousin, who worked as an agent for Paul Slavens Real Estate, sold the property.

June: Rhonda Polisuk called to say that Deja's graduation was coming up. Deja had asked the vice-principal to call her father and tell him she didn't want him to attend. Ben learned Deja was to be named Athlete of the Year. He asked Polisuk to tell his daughter how proud he was, and how much he would like to be there, but that he'd respect her wishes.

That fall Deja, now fourteen, entered Grade 9 at Westmount Collegiate Institute. Zoe, twelve, would begin Grade 7 at Baythorn Public School, a school for the arts. (Both schools were in Thornhill.) Ben had developed a good rapport with Rhonda Polisuk, who'd been passing on his letters to the girls. One day Ben mentioned to her that he didn't know if the kids were reading his letters, and she told him she thought they were. She'd also delivered valentines and birthday cards from the grandparents, and when Ben's mom delivered her cards in person one day, she told the girls their grandma hadn't forgotten them and still loved them. In June Polisuk called the kids' new principals to give them some history, explain about the letters, and smooth Ben's way. When Ben and I met with them they were welcoming and glad to help in any way they could.

More stories: One of Terry's former acolytes called. They'd had a falling-out. He confirmed that Terry had gone kosher and cut off her family, gave us her address, and said she and Kirschner were living in a half-million-dollar house owned by Michael Ostro, the man who'd guaranteed her mortgage on Dewbourne. The caller said he was suing Kirschner over a real estate deal and alleged that Kirschner, Terry, Ostro, Vaccarello (the Spectrum Six agent who'd sold Dewbourne), and Barry Greenberg, the lawyer who'd sent Ben the letter about the children's bonds, were involved.

My friend Judy's daughter Ida reported that she saw the kids one day when Kirschner came into the Thornhill restaurant where she worked. She rushed to greet the girls. "Deja! Zoe! Look at you! You're so tall! So beautiful!" Ida said, hugging them. Zoe was apprehensive, but Deja greeted her warmly. Kirschner wanted to know how she knew them. Ida explained she'd babysat for them when they lived with their dad. "She lived upstairs from him," said Deja. "That fucking asshole," said Kirschner.

Appalled, Ida returned to the kitchen. Complaining of a headache and needing a Tylenol, Deja followed her. "Look," Deja said. "I know you like my dad, but he's being a real jerk right now. He won't sign my passport. I can't go to Florida with my friends because of him." Ida pointed out she didn't need a passport to go to the United States. "Listen, Deja," she said. "There's another side to this story. You'll understand when you're older." She said she'd heard good things about her and that she'd won a big award; she told Deja she was glad to see her looking healthy and gave her a big hug. Ida never saw Kirschner or the girls in the restaurant again.

October 16: Messages from the children. An envelope arrived with no return address and two letters enclosed. The following week copies of the same letters came by registered mail. The letters, written in what Ben imagined must now be the children's hands, were replicas of the angry, accusatory missives his mother had received by courier with her returned Christmas stockings. The purpose of the letters – his first communication from his children in four and a half years – was to demand their bonds. "I am going to make this short and simple so that you can understand," read Deja's letter. "You and I both know that you don't care about me ... I don't want to see you and I don't want anymore stupid letters. To tell you the truth I am ashamed to have the same last name as you. All I want is my bonds ... Just give them back." Zoe's missive, which was addressed "To Ben," accused him of failing to support her and demanded the "money that belongs to me ... At least give me my bonds and the bond money you already cashed."

I regarded these missives, just like the others, as letters written by hostages who had been silenced, brainwashed, and forced to collude in the propaganda of their captor. Ben, however, viewed them as a gift. "Forget about the content," he said. "The content is irrelevant. They wrote the letters. This is their handwriting. This is the paper they wrote on." I found this so sad I turned away.

He wrote his daughters back that day, but he did not mention anything about money. He was unwilling to lend any credence to the notion that these demands had come from them, that in four and a half years the only communication they'd had with their dad was to claim their entitlement to their bond money, something they wouldn't even have been aware of, let alone thinking about. If Terry wanted to discuss the children's bonds, she could get in touch with him directly. Instead he focused on the fact that they'd written.

He told Zoe he'd spent an hour just looking at her letter and said he guessed it had been very hard for her to write it. He reminded her how much he loved her and believed in her and was proud of her. He wrote Deja he was "thrilled just to hold the paper and stare at your handwriting, knowing they came from you," that he cared about her more than she could believe, and he enclosed stamped, self-addressed envelopes so she could write. "Even though I can't be there for you, I am always here for you, whenever you want to write, call or see me."

Then he made an appointment to see Mandelcorn. He showed her their letters and his. She said his were good letters, but it was time to stop writing pussycat cards, to write more about the truth of what had happened. He should still allow them their feelings but tell them how he felt, too, and about the events in his life, a subject he'd avoided. He'd been advised that they might find it too painful to hear about his life with me and Sara, his life without them. Deja in particular, Mandelcorn said, was at an age where she was going to have some questions and would naturally be in conflict with her mother, although, given the situation, it was impossible to know where Deja was at.

Ben wrote Deja's new vice-principal to say he'd received his first communication from the girls in over four years and, "without getting into details and certainly without any expectations of your getting inappropriately involved, I ask you to please check on Deja and, as you have already graciously offered to do, let her know that she can come to you for assistance if she wants to.

"Although the letters seem to be handwritten by the girls, the content is clearly their mother's message. Nevertheless, I still see this communication as a breakthrough and I am happy for it. I am also very concerned. I don't know what circumstance has prompted the kids and/or their mother to communicate with me at this time in this manner but I suspect that they may be under some kind of specific financial, emotional or even legal pressure."

December: The *Toronto Sun* ran a story that Terry had been charged in the theft of $128,000 worth of art "in an apparent landlord-tenant dispute." "Terry Nusyna, 45, was charged with theft ... in the disappearance of paintings and other items belonging to the owner of a home on Braemar Ct. in Vaughan ... Police did not release the name of the alleged victim in the case."

According to the police information, a document on the public record that I secured later, on September 15, 1997, Terry Nusyna-Gordon "did steal Artwork to wit: paintings, the property of Michael Ostro of a value exceeding five thousand dollars contrary to section 334 of the Criminal Code of Canada."

Ben checked with the schools. The kids were still enrolled. He met with

Constable Mike Goode, the officer handling the theft case, and learned that the charge was an indictable offence, carrying serious maximum penalties. The officer couldn't say where Terry was living and told him he could check the police information (which Ben didn't have yet) but added that he doubted it would be much help to him.

The address for Terry on the document turned out to be false. The street was around the corner from Braemar Court, where Terry and the girls had been living in Ostro's property, but there was no such number. Goode told Ben he couldn't divulge the correct address but suggested other avenues Ben might try, all of which turned out to be dead ends. When I called Goode back, he told me, "I had a fat hand that day," implying that his finger had slipped when he'd recorded the address and he had written it incorrectly. Then he sent me on a wild-goose chase through the bureaucracy, where it quickly became apparent that there was no way to get the correct address. When I called Goode again and said I wasn't asking for confidential information – Terry's address was a matter of public record, I'd paid for the document, it had incorrect information, and it seemed to me that I was therefore entitled to the correct information – he refused to provide it. I had the distinct impression that Terry had again claimed to be a stalking victim and again police were protecting her. Only this time, if I was correct, they were affording more rights to an accused thief than to a father with a joint custody order.

We spoke to a private investigator who was willing to follow the girls home from school, for a fee, if Ben identified them, but Ben wasn't even sure if he could identify the kids any more, and the thought of "stalking" his own children revolted him. In the end he had no stomach for it and he remained in the dark about where his children lived. Fearing that Terry might try to leave the country, however, he notified the Passport Office and U.S. Customs and Immigration that he had joint custody of the children.

1998
January 9: I went to court in Newmarket on the day Terry was scheduled to appear to answer the theft charge. No longer the complainant, she stood waiting her turn in a lineup to answer criminal charges with a motley assortment of accused.

That day the matter was put over until February 10. On February 10, Terry advised the court that her lawyer, Randall Bars, was unavailable to conduct her pre-trial proceedings until April, and the matter was adjourned until April 22. On that day the pre-trial was adjourned again until June 16. On June 16, the proceedings were scheduled to continue on August 26. On August 26, the pre-trial was scheduled to continue on October 1. When this book went to press, the matter had not yet been heard. Ben and I knew, however, that even if Terry were convicted, her conviction would be highly unlikely to affect Ben's chances of seeing or parenting his children, unless she was sent to jail for a long period.

May: Temple Sinai synagogue. At a Bar Mitzvah service Ben ran into Terry's Aunt Rose and Uncle Percy. They greeted him warmly. Then Ben went right for it. "How are my kids?" he asked. "Tell me. Tell me." Aunt Rose told him excitedly that the girls were both beautiful and so grown up. Then she looked him in the eye and said, "You go after those kids, Ben. You go after them." I could feel the anger welling inside of me but said nothing, lest I say the wrong thing. "Well, it's not that simple," said Ben, kindly. "I don't want to be arrested." Terry's aunt persisted. "So you'll be arrested, you'll be arrested. You go after those kids, Ben." "Well," he said gently again, "somebody should be arrested but I'm not sure it's me."

They told him there'd been a long period when they hadn't seen the children either. I asked if they knew where they were living, but they said they didn't know. "I'd like to know," said Uncle Percy. "I'd like to know where my nieces are living."

Later that evening, at the festivities, we spoke to their daughter and son-in-law, Nina and Larry, who were also delighted to see Ben. Nina came over during the dinner and plunked herself down in his lap and brought him up to date on the family gossip. Larry told Ben all about Deja and Zoe, how close the girls were, and that Terry had refused to let her parents see them unless they gave her money, and so Ruth had given her money and then had been allowed to see her grandchildren. Nina said Terry was cool to her these days. Ben asked why. "Because I've never forgiven her for what she did to you," Terry's cousin replied.

■ ■ ■

320

Westmount Collegiate, winter 1998: The vice-principal asked Ben if he'd like to see a photograph of Deja. They had pictures of all the students on computer. We stood hunched over a monitor in the school office while a secretary called up the file. Suddenly an image exploded on the screen. We stared at it, stunned. The secretary thought she'd called up the wrong file. "How do you know it's her?" she asked the vice-principal. "Because I know her," he replied. "Well, that's where you've got it all over me," said Ben quietly.

Almost fifteen now, Deja, who strikingly resembled Terry, stared at the camera with the mock-sultry pose of a teenaged girl on the cusp of womanhood. Except for a couple of brief glimpses, five years had passed since we'd last seen her, the years of dramatic metamorphosis between ten and fifteen. The last image we carried of her in our minds was that of a child, and the loss, the terrible loss of all those years, slammed us in the face.

EPILOGUE

One day in the fall of 1993, when it had become clear to us how the story would end, Ben and I sat in my kitchen going over old ground. I wondered aloud whether there was anything more we could do. To my surprise, Ben said he wanted the story told. At least then the facts would be on the record. If Deja and Zoe ever decided to seek the truth about what had happened to their father, they would know where to start. Ben also hoped that once their plight was known, someone in their milieu – a teacher, coach, the parent of a friend – would reach out and offer a sympathetic ear. Because the girls had been forced to collude in their mother's hatred of him, it was unlikely they could express any feelings they still had for him to her. He hoped, too, that although his own children were lost to him, by speaking out he might help others whose children had been similarly victimized.

We discussed the idea of going public. His only hesitation, and mine, was what impact publishing a magazine story might have on the girls. The children deserved only empathy, but we knew that divorce, although common, was still largely viewed as dirty linen best not aired. We imagined they'd feel shame and embarrassment, but we could imagine their discomfort whenever anyone asked about their dad or wondered why he never came to their recitals or games. It was possible they'd despise him more than they already professed and that any chance of re-establishing the relationships between them would be destroyed. But Ben no longer knew their true feelings. He could control only his own choices and live with the consequences.

Ben believed that his children had been silenced and that to acquiesce in their silencing would be wrong. If they did come looking for answers one day, he might not be around to provide them. A published article would remain available and offer a context for understanding what had happened to their lives. Whatever upset they might suffer while the story was on the newsstands paled by comparison with the horrific losses they'd already endured. To expose the truth, he reasoned, the story had to be told. At the same time, neither Ben nor I had concerns about Terry. She'd taken their divorce to court, and almost all of the material needed to tell the story was on the public record. Moreover, we both felt strongly that what the judicial system had wrought cried out for exposure.

There were, however, some writerly issues I had to confront. Because I would be writing in the genre of personal journalism, I would have to overcome the reader's natural scepticism about my ability to be objective. My ethical and legal obligations were to report fairly and accurately and to declare my conflict of interest so readers could determine for themselves if I'd delivered the straight goods.

In addition, although Ben may have lived the tale, I was telling it. The same rules applied to his story as to any other and I could not show it to him before it went to print. I intended to be painfully honest and include information that I knew would reflect poorly on Ben, information on which he would be judged by readers who held deeply ingrained stereotypes about the sexes. Because divorce is high on the list of hot-button debates between the sexes, I also knew I'd be writing on landmined terrain.

The piece would have a strong point of view, as all good magazine stories must, but my perspective had to be firmly grounded in the evidence. Whatever impressions readers formed had to spring from the evidence and my presentation of it. For that reason, and because the focus of my outrage was the legal system and the societal attitudes it reflected, I intended to remain scrupulously neutral in tone, to tell the story in a documentary fashion. In my view, the facts alone were an unequivocal indictment.

I saw this story as the very kind I'd become a journalist to write. I knew that many families were suffering terribly through the divorce process and, in the name of their "best interests," children's lives were being damaged. I did not think Ben's case was typical, but I did view it as a microcosm through which to explore larger systemic issues. Not only would the article be an exposé and anatomy of how the system dealt with the dissolution of one couple's marriage, it would be an indictment of the adversarial process, a cautionary tale for those innocently considering becoming involved with it, and a modern father's story of divorce which, to the best of my knowledge, had never been told. I saw it as a story of our time, one that raised many disturbing questions about the views our culture currently holds about divorce, gender politics, and the roles men and women are expected to play when a family breaks down.

In February 1996, *Toronto Life* published "The Divorce From Hell" to instant and enormous controversy. The reaction was deeply emotional and hugely polarized. The article generated a media storm and more mail than my editor had ever seen on a piece in his thirty-year publishing career.

I was to be pilloried or sainted, depending on whom you spoke to. From readers who'd lived through nightmares of their own, Ben and I received a slew of haunting letters recounting their stories. Those who'd lost relationships with children – and there were many – encouraged him not to give up on the girls; some had heard from their children years later. Many wrote simply to say thanks for making them feel less alone and to salute Ben for having the courage to speak up. One woman told us that her mother had changed her and her sister's last name when her parents divorced, then moved away with them. When she reconnected with her father years later and asked where he'd been all those years, he said her mother had prevented contact despite his efforts to reach them. She told us it would have made a world of difference to her if, as a child, she'd known how much her father had wanted to be with her. Another grown child of divorce, whose mother and stepfather moved away "so that they could put my father out of the picture," wrote to the magazine wondering "how much the complaints of 'one-sidedness' against this article have to do with the fact that there are custodial parents who prefer that their dirty deeds ... never see the light of day." If he had a hand in writing the laws, children of divorce would be "given legal advice and rights to sue for disruption of parental relationship."

Many readers, however, assumed the children would be ashamed to have the story made public and expressed outrage on their behalf. Such readers believed the girls had been exploited because of the publication of their pictures and the reproduction of their letters to their grandmother – the only communication she received from her granddaughters after they vanished from her life. For such readers, the real crime, and a far worse one, was not what had happened to the children, but my revelation of what had happened, along with the faces of the two little girls who were the victims.

This response told me that a significant number of readers were reacting to the story less with thoughtful reflection than with knee-jerk emotion, speculating wildly and then leaping to conclusions that sprang not from the evidence in the story but from their own fiercely held prejudices. The discordance between perception and reality was disturbing. For instance, the story offered overwhelming evidence to demonstrate that one party had driven the litigation and cunningly played the system to advance personal interests while the other had done everything possible to avoid a fight. Furthermore, the record showed that the mother was fighting for the sole right to control the children while the father was seeking only to continue sharing in their parenting – an arrangement to which the mother ultimately consented at trial. In a strictly legal sense, the father achieved joint custody, secured an arrangement whereby the children lived with him half the time, and accomplished his main objective – the right to continue parenting his children on a day-to-day basis, like their mother. Nevertheless, in spite of those facts, many readers incorrectly perceived the story to be a sordid *War of the Roses* tale, told by the husband's girlfriend, about two people locked in a pathological struggle for sole custody, the outcome of which was that the husband won only "access" or had lost custody altogether.

What most astonished me was the number of readers who insisted on seeing the woman as the victim and the man as the villain – in spite of the facts. They seemed willing to ignore and excuse a woman's behaviour, however pernicious, while pointing a collective finger at the faults of the man whom they held to a superhuman standard.

Toronto Sun columnist Heather Bird, who criticized me on ethical grounds for failing to interview the "key people," speculated that Terry hadn't returned her calls because she was above engaging in debate through the media. "A message passed through her lawyer this week was not returned," wrote Bird. "We should respect that. Unlike Lady Di, she has no desire to fire back through the press." Aside from the fact that it's a rather tall leap for any reporter to assume that someone who doesn't return her calls is taking the high road, the only facts Bird knew about Terry were those I'd provided in the story – and there wasn't one to suggest this was a woman who held herself above an unseemly fray. Bird made the requisite calls so she could pat herself on the back for having been "objective" but came nowhere near the truth.

In addition, certain words and scenes became lightning rods for readers' impulse to demonize the male. Although I'd reported the circumstances surrounding the woman's assault charges and their withdrawal or dismissal, many readers insisted on believing the man was guilty. As Bronwyn Drainie, writing in the *Globe and Mail*, trumpeted, "This is a man who was charged three times with criminal assault by his wife during the years of the divorce proceedings and who swatted his daughter on the back of the head in the car one day." Her conclusion? "Gordon emerges as a man with a serious problem of uncontrolled anger and physical violence."

Others accused him of hiring a lawyer to play hardball, even though he'd hired that lawyer in self-defence to stand up to his wife's lawyer – who was playing hardball. Some vilified him for "abandoning" his children when he sent them home in a cab, instead of driving them to their mother's house when he was in a distracted and highly emotional state. Many saw him as a callous aggressor who'd put his children through years of litigation. He was the bad guy in their eyes because he wouldn't just move out quietly and accept the ordained role for divorced fathers.

Finally – and this distortion of the truth truly took my breath away – many women found him guilty on financial grounds, declaring emphatically and definitively, "That guy stopped paying child support!" It would have been considered preposterous to suggest to any divorced mother that she move out of the family home, find an apartment, help maintain her ex-husband's lifestyle in the matrimonial home when she couldn't possibly afford to, willingly hand over her children and all decisions about their future to her ex-husband, write a child support cheque each month, "visit" with her kids one night a week and alternate weekends, find them if their father disappears with them and then send him money she wasn't obliged to send. Yet apparently few readers asked themselves why a devoted father might find those expectations equally outrageous when applied to him.

Almost without exception, the public reaction from the Toronto legal community was defensive and self-serving. Publicly, lawyers insisted the story was out of date and claimed that reforms like case management and alternative dispute resolution speeded divorce cases smoothly through the system. They opined that certain clients were hell-bent on fighting and simply couldn't be helped, that the Gordon divorce was a singular case that went bad – an argument that was not only blatantly untrue but profoundly offensive: it was like saying the public didn't have to be concerned if only two children lost their father.

In a piece titled "Stop the Insults: Lawyers Shouldn't Accept This Kind of Abuse Lying Down," Gavin MacKenzie, later a bencher of the Law Society, editorialized in the *Law Times* that lawyers were blameless for what had happened and called his colleagues to arms to put an end to lawyer bashing. However, reports filtered back to me that, privately, lawyers and judges were saying, "What do you expect with those two lawyers?" After that response, which so clearly demonstrated the profession's denial of the larger systemic problem, I no longer wished to hear from the legal community.

Like the public, the Toronto media were divided down the middle. Several columnists praised the piece, but many of my colleagues argued that I had an impossible conflict of interest and should never have written it. Some claimed I'd abused my access to the media to argue my "lover's" case in the press and vengefully attack his ex-wife. A few insisted that my own bad divorce disqualified me. Still others heralded it as a great story but said someone else should have tackled it.

Of all the pious pronouncements I heard from the media, the latter was perhaps the silliest. Had my editor assigned another reporter to do a more "objective" treatment, it would have been a very different story and it wouldn't necessarily have been any closer to the truth. In fact, it would have been an impossible story to get. Newspaper reporters receive desperate calls about similar stories all the time but can't pursue them unless both sides are willing to talk. In this case, Ben would have been willing to talk to a reporter, but it was a safe bet Terry wouldn't. It was hardly in her interests to talk to the media; she would have had far too much explaining to do. Meanwhile, the lawyers could hide behind solicitor-client privilege and the assessors and mediators behind client confidentiality. The only person who could have written that story was the writer who'd borne witness to it.

It seemed particularly bizarre to me that some journalists would maintain I shouldn't have written the story. I'd had a ringside seat inside the family court system for years – the kind of access few journalists would ever acquire. I'd witnessed all manner of systemic corruption, greed, hypocrisy, sanctimony, arrogance, and incompetence. Unlike a beat news reporter, I didn't have to worry about burning bridges with sources. For me, the question was never How can I write this story? but How can I not?

Clearly, I'd produced a deeply disturbing article that challenged a number of sacred cows in our politically correct culture. The story was saying that the divorce process in this country is a corrupt farce, that not all fathers are "deadbeats" or child abusers, that not all mothers are blameless victims, that men as well as women can get shafted in divorce, and that we live in a society where a mother can poison her children's minds against their father, then steal them away, and nobody will give a damn. I expected readers to feel moral outrage. What I didn't expect was for much of it to be directed at Ben and me.

Upon reflection, I realized many readers simply found what the story was telling them too disturbing. They tried to dismiss it but couldn't because it had the ring of truth. So they shot the messenger, ignored the facts, or twisted them to suit a more comforting or familiar version. This need to reject the reality of the story was well illustrated the afternoon I appeared as a guest on *Jane Hawtin Live*, a national television phone-in show. During a commercial break, Hawtin asked about lawsuits. She'd heard a rumour that there'd been libel actions. I told her no one had sued over the story; the magazine hadn't received so much as a lawyer's letter.

"Well, no wonder! The cost!" sniffed the family lawyer seated to my right.

Not wanting to sound churlish, I refrained from pointing out the irony of this lawyer's indignation that her colleagues could not see justice done because of the high cost of litigation.

"Well," I replied, "it is possible nobody has sued because of the cost. However, everybody I was writing about was highly litigious, and the cost has never stopped Terry from litigating in the past. There is another answer, and I find it striking you haven't mentioned it."

"What's that?" asked Hawtin.

"That nobody has sued because they haven't got a case. The story is true."

From the penny-just-dropped look on Hawtin's face I had the feeling that she'd never seriously entertained that possibility.

Because of the media's navel-gazing preoccupation with whether I should have written the story, the vital issues I'd hoped to raise for debate evaporated without much discussion. However, the reaction, from supporters and detractors alike, persuaded me that the problems were more widespread than I'd realized. I saw how rampant were the myths, prejudices, and sexist biases embedded in our views about men, women, and divorce, how gender politics inflamed and clouded the issues, how a pervasive media bias distorted them, how a blind enslavement to political correctness was preventing justice from being served and the truth from being told. The reaction convinced me of the need to write a book.

■ ■ ■

During the two years I worked on this project, the issues seeped more and more into public consciousness. In 1997 Liberal senator Anne Cools catapulted them onto the national agenda when, allied with Tory senators, she stopped Bill C-41 in its tracks in the Senate. Bill C-41 established federal child support guidelines and introduced punitive measures, such as revoking passports and drivers' licences, for payers – overwhelmingly fathers – who failed to meet their support obligations. Critics (I was one) argued that while uniform child support guidelines were needed, the bill was regressive because, among other problems, it considered only the payers' income, reinforced stereotypical notions about post-divorce parenting roles, heightened the possibility of custody fights because whoever got the children got the money. Most significant, it utterly failed to address the other side of the issue: the widespread problem of custodial parents – overwhelmingly mothers – who denied non-custodial parents contact with their children.

Senator Cools's outspoken refusal to support legislation she called "degrading to fatherhood" precipitated a huge public groundswell of support. Jean Charest's office alone received more than 800 messages running two to one in opposition to the bill. Justice Minister Allan Rock's quid pro quo to ensure the bill passed was a promise to establish a joint

Senate–House of Commons committee to investigate the issues of child custody and access. It began holding cross-country hearings in February 1998 and was scheduled to make recommendations to the government in November 1998. The media were awakened to the idea that there might be another side to the divorce story.

In the United States, the father's version of divorce was also capturing national media attention. The actor John Heard, whose wife won custody of their nine-year-old son and whose parenting role had been reduced to a strict and minimal "visitation" schedule, appeared on *Larry King Live*, his pain tangible on the screen, to describe how he had given up his New York theatre career to move to Baltimore to be closer to the boy. He told King that he had discovered that matrimonial lawyers who didn't advise their female clients to allege violence and abuse against their spouses weren't considered to be doing their jobs.

In June 1998, the *New York Times* ran Gail Sheehy's op-ed piece "The Divorced Dad's Burden." "The cliché is the Deadbeat Dad," wrote Sheehy. "The newer reality is the Deadbolted Dad – locked out of his children's hearts after divorce." According to Sheehy, the greater role fathers are taking in raising children is one of the strongest shifts in the manly ideal. More and more men whose wives work are acting as primary caregivers to preschool children. Yet, when divorce occurs, the courts are still operating in the retro world of *Ozzie and Harriet*.

Sheehy cited the case of a couple who relocated to a new city where the wife took a high-paying job and became the breadwinner, while the husband became the soccer dad. When the wife later asked for a divorce, the husband expected the courts to recognize his desire to continue being a hands-on parent. His lawyer, however, "is trying to persuade him not to fight, because he won't win." Even though the mother intends to hire nannies, the lawyer says she will almost certainly win custody "because it is seen as a social disgrace for a mother to lose custody of a child." Sheehy reported being struck by the stories she had heard about the bias that "post-patriarchal New Men" face in the courts, daycare centres, and their children's schools, "not to mention from punitive former wives."

The tide, it seemed, was turning.

■ ■ ■

According to Statistics Canada, in 1994 mothers were awarded custody approximately 70 percent of the time, and fathers approximately 10 percent. Parents wound up with joint custody 20 percent of the time, and on half the occasions that fathers fought for custody, they won it. These numbers, however, are extremely misleading. Family lawyers point out they often see fathers who want some form of custody but refrain from seeking it because they are advised and are convinced they'll never win, while others embark on the fight but wind up so brutalized by the system that they eventually withdraw. Likewise, many devoted fathers become so frustrated dealing with "access" problems that they throw up their hands. "I can't tell you how many clients I've had in my office who appear to be very decent fathers who have no relationship with their kids," family lawyer Paul Pellman told the *Globe and Mail* in April 1997. "[They've had] access problems and they finally say, 'Piss on it, I've given up.'"

The reality in Canada today is that no matter how good a father a man may be, if his marriage ends and his wife decides she wants custody – a divorce dividend that family lawyers will advise she is wise to go after and that Bill C-41 has turned into a lucrative prize for her to pursue – or if she simply decides to make it difficult for him to see his children, the chances are overwhelming that he will lose the right to parent them.

Yet an impressive and growing body of social science research tells us that fathers are vitally important to children's lives, that they want to parent, that they grieve when they cannot, that children want to be parented by their mothers and their fathers, and that when fathers are absent, a litany of disastrous social problems like poor school performance, drug and alcohol abuse, teen suicide, welfare dependency, and child poverty follow. Fatherless boys become confused about their masculinity and disproportionately become violent criminals. Fatherless girls believe their fathers have abandoned them for not being good or pretty enough, suffer from low self-esteem, and fail to learn how to conduct healthy relationships with men as adults. We also know that there is absolutely no reason to value the contribution of one parent over the other. Mothers and fathers give their children different gifts, but each gives something necessary and valuable.

We know, too, that fathers who live with their children usually work hard to increase their incomes, while fathers who have been banished from the day-to-dayness of raising their children tend to lose the incentive to put more money into their households. This should come as no great surprise. There is no widespread problem in this country of fathers refusing to support their children within marriage. It's unlikely that all of the same men who have supported their children when married suddenly turn into swinish "deadbeat dads" once divorced. The crux of the issue is that when we evict fathers from their children's lives, then tell them their only function as fathers is to pay the bills, we should not be shocked if some of them temporarily withhold support – the only leverage they can use to see their children – or lose heart and drift away.

Significantly, there is strong evidence that the fathers who drive carpools and pack lunch boxes are the fathers most likely to disappear from their children's lives if they are prevented from parenting after a divorce. The sudden amputation of their fathering role – the hurt of truncated "visitations" and partings, the sadness they feel knowing their ex-wives' new partners will see more of their children than they – becomes unbearable for them. So they fade out of the picture and tell themselves it's less disruptive for the children if they do. Often they gravitate towards second families, where they can be fathers again – fathers who have the opportunity to support their children not only in a financial sense, but in an emotional one, too.

■ ■ ■

Like most women of my generation, I was shaped by feminism. Over the years I have worked for feminist causes and written from a feminist perspective. However, by 1998, when I was invited to appear before the Joint Committee on Child Custody and Access as a divorced parent, second spouse, and journalist who had been researching and writing about divorce issues, my views had changed. I testified that I wished to distinguish myself from a segment of the feminist movement that professed to speak for all women but did not speak for me, nor, I believed, for the majority of women who, whether married or divorced, whether in acrimonious relationships with their ex-spouses or not, recognized in their hearts how important it was for their children to maintain relationships with their fathers.

Many feminist academics, family lawyers, lobbyists, and advocates in government-funded women's groups and in the Justice Department as well as some feminist journalists are arguing that what is best for women and children is to maintain the status quo: mothers should be the primary care-givers with final say in all custodial matters. In effect that means that mothers have dictatorial powers regarding the children, that they are not held accountable if they violate court orders or deny their children contact with their fathers, that fathers will see their children at their ex-wives' discretion while providing them with child support on pain of having their wages garnisheed or their drivers' licences and passports revoked should they fail to make their payments.

These feminists, who are largely controlling the debate and the direction in which legislation pertaining to "women's issues" is moving, almost always speak of women and children as one entity, as if the two are inextricably bound, as if what is good for one is automatically good for the other, as if fathers had nothing to do with children nor any place in discussions about them. They argue that child support and access should not be linked because children are entitled to the financial support of both parents whether they are allowed to maintain contact with both or not. And they maintain that there can't be a presumption of joint custody in our divorce laws because of widespread domestic violence.

These ideas were presented forcefully to the government prior to the passage of Bill C-41 and to members of the Joint Committee on Child Custody and Access. They have been used to encourage the government to introduce ever more punitive measures to punish fathers who fail to meet their support obligations and are at the centre of a strenuous lobbying effort designed to prevent any change in the divorce laws that would give fathers a greater role after divorce than they are currently permitted.

We know that some men walk away from their children and support obligations. We also know that, statistically, divorce causes women more economic hardship than men. It is a sad fact that domestic violence goes on in far too many homes. However, with all the selective "abuse" statistics being hurled from both sides of the gender divide, and the media's denigration of divorced fathers through repetition of inflammatory phrases like "deadbeat dad," it's easy to forget that what makes a good parent is character, not gender, and that the vast majority of divorced parents in our communities are decent citizens who don't shirk their obligations and just want to raise their kids to the best of their abilities.

Feminists pulled down the walls of the patriarchy in part to help create the New Man – the dad who's in the delivery room the moment his kids are born, who enrolls them in their classes, reads them stories, nurses them when they're sick. Ironically, the man I wrote about – the kind of man feminists would have celebrated as an ideal father to his children in marriage – was the same man feminists attacked for *not* walking away from his children (except in a bill-paying sense) in divorce. For me, that is the essential bankruptcy of the feminist position – or at least what is being advertised as the feminist position – on these issues. Feminism, as I understand it, is about sexual equality, about mutuality between the sexes, not about replacing one double standard with another or a patriarchal society with a matriarchal one.

The sad truth is that there's a double standard at the heart of feminism today that is as bad as or worse than any it sought to replace. What we see around us is not feminism but bigot feminism. Many feminists who speak out about "women's issues" in general and divorce issues in particular myopically refuse even to acknowledge that there is another side to this story. Or they demonstrate a blinkered, stone-hearted lack of understanding and compassion for what that story might be. What's truly best for the children of divorce is eclipsed, in some cases, by a deep and abiding hatred of men. In other cases, it is overshadowed by anger at ex-husbands and the need to seek revenge against them, an us-against-them mentality based on the notion that men are finally getting what they deserve and that it's payback time for the patriarchy. What most know, but few are willing to acknowledge, is that for the ex-wives who wish to exact revenge on their ex-husbands or extort money from them, the best weapon is their children.

Both sexes play the system using the cards they're dealt, and there is no question that the white heat of divorce and the adversarial process bring out the worst in everyone. But the women to whom I am referring cash in on the perceived moral superiority of women (especially mothers), beat their breasts, and play the victim card. They leap to the moral high ground and appropriate the language of children's best interests to advance their own.

Gender politics and a certain brand of feminist rhetoric have blinded us to the fact that most men are decent, that many make wonderful fathers, that some make far better parents than their partners, and that after divorce, not only do children yearn to continue being parented by both parents – they are entitled to be. Politics and rhetoric have obscured the reality that maintaining involved relationships with both parents is truly best for children, except in the minority of cases where a parent is abusing a child. And, as is well documented but not widely known, child abusers can also be and often are mothers.

■ ■ ■

One of the most startling discoveries I made during the course of my research was a book called *The Parental Alienation Syndrome: A Guide for Mental Health and Legal Professionals,* by Dr. Richard A. Gardner. Gardner is a child psychiatrist and custody expert who practises in New Jersey. He has worked for years with divorced parents and their children and has authored more than thirty books in the field. He is also a clinical professor of child psychiatry at Columbia University in New York.

Gardner was the first to name parental alienation syndrome, a disorder he began to see in his practice in the context of child custody disputes in the early eighties. He claims that the syndrome is now so common that he sees manifestations of it in about 90 percent of children involved in protracted custody conflicts, where it primarily arises. In 1992, after having written scholarly papers on the subject, he published *The Parental Alienation Syndrome* as a manual for professionals who work with divorced parents and children. Since his groundbreaking work, others have begun to address the subject.

Gardner defines parental alienation syndrome as a folie à deux in which the domineering party transmits his or her pathology to the more suggestible one. "Brainwashing," he is careful to point out, is too simplistic a term to describe what happens to the syndrome's victims, because it suggests that one parent systematically and consciously programs the child to denigrate the other. While brainwashing plays a part, Gardner says subconscious and unconscious factors in the "programming parent" also contribute, as do the child's own unjustified and/or exaggerated denigration scenarios "of the allegedly hated parent." Children are easy prey, he says, because they're highly suggestible and have a deep need to ingratiate themselves with adult authority.

According to Gardner's clinical observations, alienators are most often mothers. They, more than fathers, are likelier to use their children to strengthen their positions in custody conflicts, while children are likelier to support them against their fathers. Mothers, of course, are also usually the primary parents and so have more opportunity to influence their children.

Gardner says the alienator perpetrates "a kind of emotional abuse" on the child. In this form of abuse the child does not hate the abuser but instead harbours anger for the "hated" parent, who has done nothing to warrant it. He provides exhaustive examples of parental alienation syndrome gleaned from clinical observations of a parental alienator's modus operandi. Generally speaking, he says the perpetrators like to operate surreptitiously, trying to change the children's last names, making constant, intrusive calls to the other parent's home when the children are there, directly or indirectly campaigning to belittle the other parent in the children's eyes. They do not like authorities looking over their shoulders, they believe that only they are capable of looking after the children, and they demonstrate an unwavering hostility towards their ex-husbands, who, no matter what they do, can do no right.

Furthermore, Gardner says that a mother who alienates her children from their father extends her hatred of him to his family. "Cousins, aunts, uncles and grandparents – with whom the child previously may have had loving relationships – are now viewed as similarly obnoxious. Grandparents, who previously had a loving and tender relationship with the child, now find themselves suddenly and inexplicably rejected. The child has no guilt over such rejection, nor does the loved parent. Greeting cards are not reciprocated. Presents sent to the home are refused, remain unopened, or even destroyed."

Children programmed by a mother in this manner adopt and reflexively support her point of view, learn to excuse and protect her, offer absurd rationalizations for her behaviour, speak with a rehearsed quality, and view any attempt the father makes to contact them as harassment. They do not know the truth and, despite incontravertible evidence, refuse to believe the truth when it's offered. Gardner explains that the hated parent is only ostensibly hated and the loved parent "sometimes feared much more than loved," yet because the father is expected to and usually does leave the house, he is portrayed as an abandoner. The children will view him that way, and because they fear losing their mother's love as well, they will do nothing to risk her rejection.

Gardner's analysis explains the letters Ben's mother had received with the returned Christmas stockings and the ones he had received, a year and a half after publication of the *Toronto Life* piece, demanding the girls' bond money. Although Deja had written the words on the page, they contained her mother's message: "You and I both know that you don't care about me. You proved that by writting [sic] that repulsive, bias [sic] and totally one sided article."

According to Gardner, maternal parental alienators fall into three categories – severe, moderate, and mild. Severe perpetrators are obsessed with antagonism towards their husbands, often paranoid, and willing to use any mechanism, legal or illegal, to prevent the children from seeing their father. Projection is central to their paranoia. "These mothers see in their husbands many noxious qualities that actually exist within themselves. By projecting these unacceptable qualities onto their husbands they can consider themselves innocent victims of their husband's persecutions." They will not respond to reason – even court orders confirming that the father is not guilty of the abominations they have alleged fail to end their hate campaigns. Energizing their rage is the "hell hath no fury like a woman scorned" phenomenon. Children of such mothers are "similarly fanatic" and share their mothers' "paranoid fantasies about the father."

In moderate cases, "the rage of the rejected woman" is central, but these mothers also campaign to withhold the children from the father as a "vengeance maneuver." While severe cases have a "sick psychological bond" with the children, moderate mothers are likelier to have a healthy bond "compromised by their rage." Their children are far likelier to involve themselves benevolently with their fathers when "removed entirely from their mother's purview," particularly when they're with their fathers for long periods. A younger child (according to Gardner, the younger the child, the greater her susceptibility to the syndrome) may need the older one to keep the campaign going because, when the children are with their father, the older child is serving as a "mother surrogate."

Finally, mothers in the mild category are unlikely to engage in litigation to gain primary custody, are more conciliatory in approach, and recognize that alienating the children from their father is not in their best interests. Nonetheless they are capable of programming them to strengthen their positions.

Based on Gardner's analysis and the evidence of seven years' personal experience, I believed I had certainly witnessed the acts of a parental alienator. I found it telling, not to mention disturbing, that of the three "top" professionals who'd handled Ben's case – and to whom we'd reported a litany of like behaviour – not one had identified the behaviour nor done anything to protect the children from it. At least two had directly pandered to a mother who was alienating her children from their father.

Gardner writes that many court authorities fail to recognize the syndrome and are predisposed to take at face value the hatred that alienated children express for the denounced parent. Furthermore, he says he is convinced it is a "widespread phenomenon" for a certain type of female therapist to ally with the alienator's demonizing of men. "Parental alienation syndrome mothers have a way of finding therapists (almost invariably women) who reflexly [sic] join with them in their campaign of denigration of the father ... Typically, these therapists see no need to interview the father, let alone work with him ... Some of these therapists are paranoid themselves. Others harbour deep-seated hostility toward men, hostility so strong that they seize upon every opportunity to vent their rage on them. A parental alienation syndrome provides them with just such an opportunity."

In part, Gardner's methodology to determine the presence of the syndrome is to apply what he calls "grandma's criteria," the things grandma's ghost would consider if it "were free to roam the house and then report her findings to the examiner." Grandmas generally have "very little formal so-called psychological sophistication," and are unlikely to have a string of degrees. What grandmas do have is keen intuition; and they tend to know who is truly looking out for the children. She'd observe the family from morning to night and "would be particularly concerned with which parent is willing to make the most sacrifices on the child's behalf."

In making an analysis, Gardner would be particularly alert for "vengeful maneuvers" such as trying to retaliate in the financial realm or alleging abuse to destroy the father's reputation or have him incarcerated. Because he'd also be looking for certain behaviours that would emerge only when parents are together, he'd insist on an initial joint interview. If the mother claimed fear of physical abuse and refused to be in the same room with her husband, Gardner, who says such women are not truly abuse victims and whose claims fall somewhere between "fabrication and delusion," would tell her an assault was unlikely to occur in his office, but she was welcome to bring a police officer to the interview, or to find a new assessor.

Gardner also recommends interviewing housekeepers, whom he views as excellent sources of information because they witness first-hand what's going on at home. Finally, he is particularly scornful of experts who ask children how they feel, accept as gospel whatever they say, and equate sympathy for them with compliance with their requests.

Even more striking to me than Gardner's comprehensive and common-sensical diagnostic approach are his tough, consequences-for-actions strategies for dealing with alienators, measures he argues can be effective only if the courts back them every step of the way. Generally speaking, he recommends court-ordered family therapy and advising any party who does not comply that the judge will be informed and serious consequences will ensue. (As part of his data collection process, he also reviews court materials.) In severe cases he suggests imposing fines or jail sentences or withdrawing custody.

Gardner's key intervention strategy is to remove the children from the alienator's care and restrict her contact with them until they have been "debriefed" and her hold on them broken. When such measures are imposed, Gardner reports that the animosity towards the father is gradually reduced. "In contrast, if the court allows the children to remain living with such a disturbed mother, then it is likely that there will be lifelong alienation from the father." He adds that judges have been generally unreceptive to his proposals, because "most judges still hold stringently to the traditional view that mothers are generally better than fathers in the realm of raising children." While Gardner says there is sometimes merit in this view, he adds that "there is no question that there are many mothers who are far less capable than their husbands to raise their children. And mothers in the severe category of parental alienation syndrome are likely to be so deficient."

Although he has done no formal, long-term follow-up studies, Gardner says he is convinced that without intervention, most of these children will probably be alienated from their fathers throughout the course of their lives. "A psychological bond can withstand just so much attenuation before it dwindles to nothing. And I hold the courts responsible for this tragedy, a tragedy that could have been avoided."

In Canada, the story is the same. Many judges, assessors, and court authorities are ignorant of parental alienation syndrome and of the basic empirical social science data on the needs of children of divorce. Others are reluctant to contest the court's prejudices about the inviolate mother-child bond. In addition, the idea that women are incapable of wickedness permeates our legal system. In April 1998, Osgoode Hall law professor Dianne Martin, who calls herself "a moderate feminist, not a mingy right-wing one," told the *Globe and Mail* that "the presumption of innocence has taken a major hit in the last fifteen years," in a misguided attempt to show sensitivity to witnesses who are seen as particularly vulnerable. According to Martin, "Children and women are treated as truth tellers for the purposes of their claims."

As a result, the crime of parental alienation – and I believe it to be a crime – is going unpunished. I think of it as a post-feminist crime, women abusing their power over men and children, and part of the fallout of bigot feminism and the noxious gender politics that have so strongly influenced society's current. Parental alienation is also still largely a silent crime, one that exists in the public consciousness precisely where the crimes of domestic assault and child abuse existed fifteen years ago. We once considered those problems private family matters and "dirty linen." Today we know better.

Because of the subtle and sometimes unconscious nature of the programming, parental alienation syndrome is extremely difficult to prove in court. Yet even when the evidence is plain and the syndrome can be proven, the odds are overwhelming the court will do nothing. Although Ben did not intend to pursue the matter, though he had compelling evidence to do so, I consulted two reputable family lawyers about his chances of securing custody of the children if he were able to prove they were the victims of parental alienation syndrome. Both said he'd win the battle but not the war. Having turned a blind eye to the problem while it was happening, the court would most likely say that once the children were programmed to hate their father there was nothing it could do: the kids didn't want to be with him. My subsequent conversations with family lawyers and my reading of the scientific and legal research confirmed that the courts almost never remove a child from the custody of an alienating mother.

It is no longer acceptable to tell women that they belong at home with their children, and yet we continue to insist that children of divorce belong at home with their mothers. This deeply rooted belief that mothers are morally untouchable and children of divorce are better off with them, almost regardless of the circumstances, was articulated by one of the letters from a *Toronto Life* reader. The writer, who was female, was angered by the story on the children's behalf. "Having not seen their father for two years," she wrote, "they have most likely started to settle into a comfortable life. Printing this article will no doubt set them back to square one."

Given the staggering losses the girls had suffered, the traumatic and inexplicable absence of a father who had loved and nurtured them for the first eight and ten years of their lives, the disappearance of his family and friends, the loss of their grandparents, the end of the relationships they wanted and might have had with Sara and me, that argument struck me as truly astonishing. It was no different than asking how police could publish pictures of missing children on milk cartons or on the sides of buses. After all, these children too have most likely settled into comfortable new lives with their abductors.

■ ■ ■

The judicial system tends to hurt men and women in different ways. Because it favours the litigant with the deepest pockets, men are usually perceived to have the upper hand in divorce court in the financial realm, and often that is the case. However, it is also the case that many women can qualify for legal aid while their ex-husbands are driven into bankruptcy battling the infinite resources of the state. Men are at a clear disadvantage in seeking custody through the courts and they are more likely to be held accountable for violating a court order (usually for support). Furthermore, men are far more vulnerable to false allegations brought before the courts.

Many men who wish to protect their rights to a relationship with their children now know they cannot just leave the home when their marriages dissolve. For their wives, making false allegations against them has become an easy way to get them out of the house and gain the advantage in the battle for custody and property. Family lawyers regularly see clients who are using the criminal justice system to help them tactically in family law proceedings. Members of the Joint Committee heard so many horror stories of false allegations that Chairman Roger Gallaway told the *Toronto Sun*, "The Divorce Act is suddenly becoming an instrument of the Criminal Code."

In some reported cases, lawyers coached female clients to provoke an incident: "Can you get him to throw a shoe at you?" "Can you get him to hit you?" Moreover, the word "abuse" is now so broadly defined that a man can be permanently evicted from his home for spitting at his wife in the heat of a domestic argument, behaviour that, while offensive, hardly warrants the state's intervention. For that reason, lawyers routinely advise male clients, particularly those still living in the matrimonial home, to scrupulously avoid situations that could result in a nuisance charge, and to photocopy and keep safely outside the house any documents they might need in a divorce action.

One Toronto criminal lawyer reported to me that in recent years police have responded to complaints of spousal abuse "more zealously," laying charges even in the absence of supporting evidence. He claimed that the police and the Crown are in effect required to proceed on any domestic and sexual assault complaint and that the normal standards of investigation have been suspended. Consequently, he said, "we see many occasions when charges have been brought forward to a justice of the peace and there was really nothing but a vindictive motive [and] in fact no assault."

Many family court judges confronted with abuse allegations have tended to operate on the assumption that it is better to be safe than sorry. Caution prevents potential tragedies and has the added advantage of protecting them from criticism by women's groups or the media. Once charged, a man will generally be handcuffed and removed from his home, often in front of his children, then forced to spend a night in jail, have a restraining order slapped against him, or bail conditions set that restrict him from returning except to collect his personal effects. Although the charges against him may be uncorroborated, he will be guilty until proven innocent. If the charges are ultimately dismissed, the damage to his reputation will be done. The stories are legion of fathers whose lives have been destroyed by malicious allegations, but it is virtually unheard of for the women who falsely accuse them to be held accountable.

This phenomenon has turned out to be a boon for a certain type of woman, not to mention a certain type of lawyer for whom any tactic, no matter how morally rank, is justifiable, indeed obligatory, in the vigorous pursuit of his client's interests. Some women don't need to pay for such advice; they are becoming wise to the opportunities now afforded them in law.

Feminists, for the most part, have been unwilling to admit that such women exist, let alone that their actions cause irreparable harm or that they should be held responsible for reprehensible acts. Instead they attack those who voice contrary views as anti-feminist mouthpieces for the fathers' rights lobby. Even Senator Cools, who helped to found a battered women's shelter, was tagged with the "anti-feminist" moniker.

Fathers' groups have been trying for years to raise public awareness about the issue of false allegations, along with other injustices that divorced fathers and their children face, but the media have been highly sceptical of the claims of men they perceive to be mostly angry, marginalized, and misogynist. It is no coincidence that it took a female senator with a history of feminist activism to bring them to national attention. On these matters men have been silenced in our culture. Men are simply not perceived to have the bona fides to speak about issues of sexual politics even though the debate dramatically affects their lives. And while some fathers' groups attract women-hating extremists just as some women's groups thrive on man-hatred, most of the politically active fathers I have met are dedicated individuals, putting in long hours at their own expense and without funding from any level of government to make their voices heard.

A disturbing recent development is that the rash of false allegations of abuse has initiated a backlash. Judges are becoming jaded, and some family lawyers report that it is increasingly difficult to convince the courts in those cases where a woman has in fact been abused. The sooner that women with no claim to victimhood are outed, the better for women who truly need the state's protection and for society in general.

■ ■ ■

According to MP Paul Forseth, a member of the Joint Committee, the family law system in Canada is a mess. Indeed, the picture that emerged from the committee's hearings was one of a system designed to serve the interests of the legal establishment while treating with contempt the citizens who desperately need its help and are paying for its operation. Committee members learned of a system rife with vested interests, where judicial discretion is often synonymous with judicial bias, where perjury in affidavits is widely acknowledged to be rampant and to go unpunished, where bringing false charges to gain advantage has become the norm and where scorched-earth tactics are so common that lawyers regularly attend professional development seminars on how to combat them. (One course I attended was billed: "Dealing with Dirty Tricks and Borderline Tactics in Family Law: Defeating the Tricksters While Maintaining Your Reputation.")

Richard Gardner, long a critic of the adversarial system, stopped testifying as an expert witness in custody litigation years ago because he'd seen "normal people become neurotic, and neurotic people become psychotic, as a direct result of embroilment in adversarial proceedings associated with their divorces." He writes that he encountered "uninterested, lazy and uncommitted" judges during his years as an expert witness, and while he acknowledges that not all lawyers exploit their clients by encouraging protracted litigation, he says unreservedly that some divorce lawyers are "overt psychopaths" with "absolutely no appreciation of the grief they are causing fellow human beings."

Lawyers are fond of saying that they're only acting on their clients' instructions, and therefore it's really the clients who are to blame when divorce cases turn ugly. (Ronald Zaldin, interviewed by the *Globe and Mail* after the *Toronto Life* story was published, claimed to have no quarrel with how he was depicted, describing himself as "an aggressive matrimonial lawyer who's not afraid to go to court in a hotly contested battle." He said the lawyers were simply carrying out their clients' instructions and added that he'd gained new business because of the publicity.)

While the excuse that "I was only acting on my client's instructions" conveniently lets lawyers off the hook for any conduct, it ignores the fact that people generally wind up in the offices of family lawyers when their lives are in pieces and they are emotional wrecks. Scared and confused, the vast majority do exactly as they're advised to do. They have entered foreign, intimidating territory and much is at stake. Some are hell-bent on revenge for real or imagined marital pain or for all the disappointments of their lives; some are walking time bombs of repressed rage and have finally found the perfect forum to act it out. Those are the clients who go looking for a hired gun. But many others could go either way and in their desperation are highly suggestible and highly malleable. When they are urged on by seemingly helpful suggestions – "You can go after his business, you know..." – it becomes less clear who is giving the instructions and who is taking them. And the longer clients are in the trenches, the more combative they become. The process is so brutal that many are reduced to a dysfunctional state where they become easy prey for those manipulative lawyers masquerading behind fancy credentials for whom the fee, the fight, and the win are all.

Most who turn to the court system at this traumatic time in their lives have little idea what lies ahead. They enter the system as we did, wishing they did not have to be there, but innately respectful of the process and believing that if they have the evidence and tell the truth, justice will prevail. Whether they "win" or "lose" in the end, typically they emerge from the experience unspeakably angry at a process that has little to do with justice and with the feeling that they have been fleeced. How much they spend before the scales fall from their eyes seems to depend on how much they have. A father I met at the Joint Committee hearings told me, "The only difference between Ben and the rest of us is the number of dollars he spent." Said another, "When it's your kids, you spend everything you have."

Case in point: In January 1994, as a last resort, I applied to the court for an increase in child support. I hired a lawyer to advise me and conduct cross-examinations but otherwise acted for myself. A year and half later I won – or so I was told – one of the highest support awards on record for one child. David was ordered to pay approximately four times what he'd been paying. I'd racked up around $25,000 in legal fees despite acting for myself. The court declined to award me costs. Shortly thereafter David appealed. Two years later the Court of Appeal reduced the amount to approximately two and a half times what David had been paying, and virtually the same figure I'd offered him to settle three years before. David then asked the court to reconvene for clarification on the deductibility of his payments, repayment of the difference between the two judgments, and his court costs for the appeal. The court agreed. My divorce has now cost me an amount approximately equal to my gross annual income in an average year. If David is successful, I'll be in a worse financial position than when I sought the court's help four and half years ago. I'd have to apply to the court for an increase in child support based on a material change in circumstances – which is exactly what I did when all this started.

Having acted for myself, I can say that there is absolutely no justification for the costs involved in resolving divorce matters and the usurious fees many lawyers charge. The law may appear arcane and beyond the ken of ordinary mortals, but, stripped of its cumbersome, obfuscating language and forms in triplicate, what family lawyers do is not rocket science and is made to seem far more complicated than it is. The staggering amount of money people are forced to spend to dissolve their marriages is the main reason we are unlikely to see initiatives for reform coming from the family law community. It is they who are the chief beneficiaries of the current system.

We cannot rely on the legal profession to clean its own house nor to protect us from unscrupulous lawyering. The bad apples are known and tolerated. Furthermore, in a world where just about any tactic can be justified if it is deemed to be "in my client's best interests," accountability is largely a moot point.

Lawyers are also fond of saying that the adversarial system is the best system we've got. In fact, it's impossible to imagine a worse system. It should be remembered that a mechanism which was originally designed to determine the criminal guilt or innocence of an accused is being used to choose which parent should care for children after divorce when, in most cases, both parents are equally capable of doing so. Judges and lawyers, by virtue of their background, their training, and sometimes their personalities, are hardly the best professionals to deal with family issues. And the court system, blunt instrument that it is, is the worst possible place to bring a family in crisis.

In the end, practitioners work within systems: many judges, worn down by crushing backlogs and the human suffering paraded before them every day, simply become hardened. After a while every case sounds much like the last. Others are power and control freaks who enjoy issuing orders and meting out punishment. I have seen judges treat decent citizens with such unwarranted cruelty that it reduced them to tears. But even the most compassionate judges are hamstrung by a process that is open to manipulation by those who play the system. Similarly, even the most dedicated mental health and social service professionals must play by the system's rules. And the most ethical lawyers, those who care about their clients' problems and are sincerely dedicated to solving them in the most expeditious manner possible – as most of Ben's lawyers were – are powerless to help within a system that consistently rewards the unscrupulous.

Until we come up with a better method, my fantasy is to put a lock on the door of every family court in the land, send criminal matters to criminal court, and tell divorcing couples to resolve their problems by some other means. I'd tell them to ask the wisest person they knew – preferably a trusted friend or family member, or the best professional advisor they could afford – for counsel during the white-heat stage. If that didn't work, I'd tell them to flip a coin. To those who accuse me of grossly oversimplifying a complex issue, I say this: flipping a coin would be just as arbitrary as the system we have now, it would be far less costly and destructive, and it would be significantly more fair. At least children would have a fifty-fifty chance of living with their mom or with their dad.

Whatever approach legislators adopt, the first order of business must be removing divorce from the hands of judges and lawyers. The judicial system is fundamentally an adversarial forum based on competing rights, where two spouses are forced to duke it out and where one can carry on a personal vendetta against the other indefinitely, given the will and enough cash. Any way you look at it, such a system is damaging to children. So are words like "custody," "access," "visitation," "primary parent," and "secondary parent" – language which only reinforces the terrible idea that children are property and that in divorce one of their parents becomes more important to them than the other.

Canada is seriously lagging behind other Western countries in divorce reform. The trend in other Western countries such as Britain and Australia and in certain American states such as Washington, Florida, and Maine is to get parents out of the courts and around a table where they work out a parenting plan before they divorce. These jurisdictions have shifted the focus of the divorce process from parental rights and wants to parental responsibilities and children's rights – which is the direction in which our thinking must turn. If couples were told that they must come up with a parenting plan that is based on some form of cooperative parenting, and that if they can't, it will be imposed on them, they'd be better served than they are by the options available to them now.

In the first year, when emotions are raw and everyone is learning to adjust, parents need a mediative forum where they can take the ongoing problems that inevitably arise. Fathers who want to co-parent should be allowed to do so, while those who feel insecure about assuming the role should be encouraged to take it on. Keeping both parents actively involved in their children's lives after divorce is not only better for their kids, it's better in the long term for parents. Joint parenting also means that fathers should not automatically be expected to leave the home after divorce.

Any form of alternative dispute resolution will be useless, however, unless it's mandatory and timely, unless it involves binding arbitration and enforcement of decisions, and unless both parents are held accountable, as much for defaults on support obligations as for denying children contact with their parents. Committing perjury and making false allegations should be considered serious offences, too. Parents who are given guidance but continue to demonstrate that they won't exercise their parental rights responsibly should lose those rights. Criminal court is the place to deal with criminal matters – charges of child abuse or domestic violence or parental alienation.

Reforms should be based on what we know the children need. That means paying attention to our common sense, to the social science literature, and to what children of divorce tell us, not what judges with preconceived notions or assessors with vested interests or special-interest groups with political agendas would have us believe children need. The whole concept of child support should be broadened to include emotional as well as financial benefits. Children need parents who support them not only with money but with love. We punish parents who don't pay their child support but do nothing to ensure that children receive the other kind of support they need, even though children are probably far more able to cope with a lower standard of living than with losing the guidance and model of a loving parent.

Finally, the process of divorce must offer fair value for the dollar and lie within the financial grasp of the average citizen. Families suffering the trauma of a divorce are already facing tremendous stresses and downward mobility; they should not have to drain their life savings to dissolve their marriages, nor should their children be robbed of their inheritances.

As a society, we have to face our fears, examine our prejudices, and begin talking about these questions, however disturbing or uncomfortable they may be. These are questions that concern us all, whether divorced or not. In the end we cannot legislate that people be good parents. But we can protect those who want to be and ensure that the children of divorce continue to be nourished by all those who love them.

Divorce is not a gender issue but a human issue. To speak of divorce is to speak about matters of the heart and soul that reside at the centre of everything we cherish most fiercely. They reflect the values we hold as a society, and they distinguish the path we want to establish for the next generation. If we hope to prepare our children well for their journey down that path, we cannot avoid the fact that on this issue we are failing them and that we have to change our thinking and our practices around divorce.

Divorce is about loss, about being cut loose from the moorings of a former life, forced to watch helplessly as the shore recedes, never sure that one will make it back to terra firma again. It is one of the most traumatic alamities that can befall a family. In addition to the sordid, unseemly mess of it, a divorce brings pain, terror, and anger.

We do not have to add to that agony. We do not have to destroy completely a family already crippled by marriage breakdown. We can deal with the devastating realities of divorce wisely and intelligently and compassionately. We owe it to ourselves and to our children to see that we do.

POSTSCRIPT

ON November 6, 1992, Ben initiated the process of contesting Moishe Reiter's fees, legal bills that totalled $175,385.94 by the time Ben dismissed him. The fee assessment – a trial proceeding in which the court's task is to decide whether a lawyer's bill is fair and reasonable – lasted twenty-two days over three years.

Robert Schipper acted for Ben. William Roland acted for the other side. It was unclear who Roland was actually representing: Reiter (who was bankrupt), his trustee in bankruptcy, or the Royal Bank – his only secured creditor. (Reiter owed creditors more than three-quarters of a million dollars – including $400,000 to Revenue Canada. He'd left a trail of credit card debts amounting to $42,577.76; he walked away from $66,375.65 in unpaid rent; and he owed $31,034.05 to his nephew Paul Bercovici. Almost all of his forty-one creditors came away empty-handed.)

On October 29, 1996, the court ruled that Reiter had overcharged Ben and reduced his bill by almost two-thirds, from $175,385.94 to $60,790.94. Ben was entitled to all the money in court (virtually his entire share of the net proceeds, plus interest, from the sale of 24 Dewbourne, approximately $119,433.92). Reiter was also ordered to return $19,958.06 of the amount Ben had already paid him, plus interest. From the funds in court, Ben repaid a loan from his stepmother (money lent to him during the matrimonial litigation) and he paid Robert Schipper for recovering the money his previous lawyer had overcharged him. Ben was left with about $10,000.

The court then had to decide who would pay for driving twenty-two days of litigation: Reiter and/or the Royal Bank. The matter was at issue because Reiter was an undischarged bankrupt when the proceedings began, but became discharged before they ended. After hearing more submissions, the court found Reiter personally accountable for costs, and he was ordered to pay Ben another $72,093.94.

Because Ben had made settlement offers that were far more advantageous to Reiter than the final outcome – and Reiter's bankruptcy made it highly unlikely that Ben would collect from him – Schipper advised opposing confirmation of the costs decision and asked the court to order costs against the Royal Bank. He suspected the bank was the real litigant – Reiter was only the straw man. When Schipper brought a motion seeking costs against the Royal, it claimed it wasn't a party to the assessment and shouldn't be held accountable for costs. In November 1997, Justice Hugh O'Connell agreed with the bank and dismissed Ben's motion.

That left Ben only two options: to try to collect costs from Reiter personally or from his trustee in bankruptcy (or both). Schipper brought a motion to collect from the trustee. That's when he learned that the trustee had declined to participate in the litigation from the start, and that Reiter and his wife, Carol, who owned their home, had made an agreement with the bank: if Reiter agreed to participate in the assessment, the bank wouldn't go after Carol Reiter's guarantee and take their home. Reiter also agreed to indemnify the bank for up to $10,000 if it had to pay costs. Reiter had assured the bank that the objections to his accounts were unfounded, and presumably the bank hoped that by litigating it would get its hands on that money to pay down Reiter's bank debt.

This explained why Reiter had participated in prolonged litigation from which he had nothing to gain directly as a bankrupt. It also appeared from the documentation that the Royal Bank had been more involved in the assessment than it was prepared to disclose, and had been financing the litigation from the start. As Schipper had argued, the documents suggested that the Royal Bank had put forward Reiter, so the real litigant – the Royal Bank – could litigate without consequences.

Schipper advised Ben to ask the court to set aside Justice O'Connell's order on the strength of this new information. The bank, however, strongly contested the motion and indicated it planned to vigorously oppose these new proceedings. That meant more time and money. Ben had no choice but to settle. One of the bank's stipulations, to which Ben agreed, was that the settlement terms remain confidential.

Still unresolved was the issue of whether Reiter would be held personally responsible. That necessitated Justice O'Connell's hearing arguments on whether the costs Reiter owed Ben had survived his bankruptcy. The judge reserved decision, and as this book went to press, the matter was still undecided. By then, it had cost Ben approximately $90,000 and taken the court six years to decide whether one lawyer's bill was fair and reasonable and who should pay court costs.

Whatever the outcome, Ben has almost no chance of collecting the $92,052.00 Reiter owes him. If Ben secures a judgment that survives Reiter's bankruptcy, and if Reiter doesn't have a bank loan, and if he has cleared all his debts – three extremely big ifs – Ben can garnishee Reiter's billings from his accounts receivable, and get a court order directing his clients to pay the sheriff, who will, in turn, pay Ben. But he'd have to bring him in for examination first, and that would entail further costs. Then Reiter could appeal and tie up the matter for two more years. And so on.

Moishe Reiter continues to practise law. His ad in the Yellow Pages reads: "Moishe Reiter QC Barrister-At-Law: 'Certified by the Law Society as a Specialist in Civil Litigation.'"

■ ■ ■

Ben has said that if we split up, he wants me to act for him. I told him I'd take the matter under advisement. I can't represent us both. So I have a dilemma: Do I represent myself and get half of all he owns? Or do I represent him and get it all?

The Cost of Ben Gordon's Divorce

The lawyers' fees

Ken Cole		$2,665.00
Judith Beaman		$3,800.00
Tim Lipson		$2,000.00
Moishe Reiter	(reduced from $175,385.94 after assessment)	$60,790.94
Julie Hannaford	(billed $43,000 but balance forgiven)	$15,000.00
Robert Schipper	(represents approximately half docketed time spent on file)	$90,500.00
Total		**$174,755.94**

The mediators' and assessors' fees

Mario Bartoletti		$1,300.00
Irwin Butkowsky	for recommendations (2/3 of cost)	$3,900.00
	for mediation/arbitration	$1,000.00
Sol Goldstein		$8,200.00
Helen Goudge	(1/2 of cost)	$2,200.00
Total		**$16,600.00**

Total professional fees   *$191,355.94*

Loss on the matrimonial home

July 1989 (appraised value)	$1,100,000.00
May 1993 (sold to Terry)	− $475,000.00
Approximate loss in value	**$625,000.00**

Ben's approximate loss   *$312,500.00*

Total Cost of Ben Gordon's Divorce   **$503,855.94**

SELECTED SOURCES

In addition to the references listed below and many other secondary sources, I relied upon the voluminous documentation of *Gordon v. Gordon* and *Reiter v. Gordon*, particularly the sworn affidavit evidence and testimony contained in dozens of motion records and transcripts, all on the public record. Most of the legal correspondence, both family assessment reports (by Irwin Butkowsky and Sol Goldstein), and virtually all the material pertaining to my own divorce are also on the public record.

Ackerman, Marc J., and Melissa C. Ackerman. "Child Custody Evaluation Practices: A 1996 Survey of Psychologists." *Family Law Quarterly* 30, no. 3 (fall 1996): 565-86.

Advocates' Society. "The Response of the Advocates' Society to the 'Custody and Access: Public Discussion Paper.'" [1994?]

Ambert, Anne-Marie. *Ex-Spouses and New Spouses: A Study of Relationships.* Greenwich, CT, and London: JAI Press, 1989.

Bala, Nicholas. "Assessing the Assessor: Legal Issues." *Canadian Family Law Quarterly* 6 (1990): 179-226.

Bala, Nicholas, and Jane Anweiler. "Allegations of Sexual Abuse in a Parental Custody Dispute: Smokescreen or Fire?" *Canadian Family Law Quarterly* 2 (1987): 343-415.

Bender, William N. "Joint Custody: The Option of Choice." *Journal of Divorce and Remarriage* 21, nos. 3/4 (1994): 115-31.

Bender, William N., and Lynn Brannon. "Victimization of Non-Custodial Parents, Grandparents and Children as a Function of Sole Custody: Views of the Advocacy Groups and Research Support." *Journal of Divorce and Remarriage* 21, nos. 3/4 (1994): 81-113.

Benotto, Mary Lou. "Ethics in Family Law: Is Family Law Advocacy a Contradiction in Terms?" Speech to the Annual Convention of the Advocates' Society, Nassau, Bahamas, December, 1995.

Best, Patricia. "How the 'Divorce From Hell' Pressed All the Hot Buttons." *Globe and Mail*, March 16, 1996.

Bird, Heather. "Love Hurts: The Trilogy." *Toronto Sun*, February 10, 1996.

Blankenhorn, David. *Fatherless America: Confronting Our Most Urgent Social Problem*. New York: Harper Perennial, 1995.

Boyd, Susan B. "W(h)ither Feminism? The Department of Justice Public Discussion Paper on Custody and Access." *Canadian Journal of Family Law* 12 (1995): 331-65.

Bryan, Mark. *The Prodigal Father: Reuniting Fathers and Their Children*. New York: Clarkson Potter, 1997.

Canada. Department of Justice. Communications and Consultation Branch. *Custody and Access: Public Discussion Paper*. Ottawa: Department of Justice, 1993.

Canada. Human Resources Development Canada and Statistics Canada. *Growing Up in Canada*. Ottawa: Statistics Canada, 1996.

Canadian Advisory Council on the Status of Women. "Child Custody and Access Policy: A Brief to the Federal/Provincial/Territorial Family Law Committee." February 4, 1994.

Caplan, Paula J., and Jeffery Wilson. "Assessing the Child Custody Assessors." *Reports of Family Law*, 3rd series, 27 (1990): 121-34.

Cartwright, Glenn F. "Expanding the Parameters of Parental Alienation Syndrome." *The American Journal of Family Therapy* 21, no. 3 (Fall 1993): 205-15.

"Combatting Unfair Tactics in Family Law." Distributed at a seminar of the Canadian Institute, Toronto, March 2, 1994.

Dafoe Whitehead, Barbara. "Dan Quayle Was Right." *Atlantic Monthly*, April 1993.

———. *The Divorce Culture*. New York: Knopf, 1996.

Doyle Driedger, Sharon. "After Divorce." *Maclean's*, April 20, 1998.

Drainie, Bronwyn. "Damn the Ethical Judgments! Full Steam Ahead!" *Globe and Mail*, February 8, 1996.

Dunne, John, and Marsha Hedrick. "The Parental Alienation Syndrome: An Analysis of 16 Selected Cases." *Journal of Divorce and Remarriage* 21, nos. 3/4 (1994): 21-38.

Fife, Robert. "Divorce Law 'Hell' for Dads." *Toronto Sun*, April 12, 1998.

Forseth, Paul. *Child Custody & Access*, no. 4 (May 1998). Report to constituents from MP for New Westminster-Coquitlam-Burnaby.

Gardner, Richard A. "My Involvement in Child Custody Litigation: Past, Present and Future." *Family and Conciliation Courts Review* 27, no. 1 (July 1989): 1-12.

———. *The Parental Alienation Syndrome: A Guide for Mental Health and Legal Professionals*. Cresskill, NJ: Creative Therapeutics, 1992.

Goldstein, Sol. *Divorced Parenting: How to Make It Work*. Toronto: McGraw Hill-Ryerson, 1982.

SELECTED SOURCES

Harr, Jonathan. *A Civil Action*. New York: Random House, 1995.

Harvison Young, Alison. "Joint Custody as Norm: Solomon Revisited." *Osgoode Hall Law Journal* 32, no. 4 (1994): 785-816.

Honywill, Brad. "128Gs Art Theft Alleged: Suspect Known for High-Profile Divorce." *Toronto Sun*, December 10, 1997.

Jones, Frank. "It May Not Be Fair, But Story Useful." *Toronto Star*, February 1, 1996.

Kaganoff, Penny, and Susan Spano, eds. *Men on Divorce: The Other Side of the Story*. New York: Harcourt Brace, 1997.

Kronby, Malcolm C. *Canadian Family Law*, 7th rev. ed. Toronto: Stoddart. 1997.

Kruk, Edward. "The Disengaged Noncustodial Father: Implications for Social Work Practice with the Divorced Family." *Social Work 39*, no. 1 (January 1994): 15-25.

———. *Divorce and Disengagement: Patterns of Fatherhood Within and Beyond Marriage*. Halifax: Fernwood Publishing, 1993.

———. "Grandparent-Grandchild Contact Loss: Findings from a Study of 'Grandparent Rights' Members." *Canadian Journal on Aging* 14, no. 4 (1995): 737-54.

———. "Psychological and Structural Factors Contributing to the Disengagement of Noncustodial Fathers after Divorce." *Family and Conciliation Courts Review* 30, no. 1 (January 1992): 81-101.

Laframboise, Donna. "A Real-Life Divorce Nightmare." *Toronto Star*, February 5, 1996.

———. "Oh Dad, Poor Dad." *Globe and Mail*, April 12, 1997.

LaRossa, Ralph. *The Modernization of Fatherhood: A Social and Political History*. Chicago: University of Chicago Press, 1997.

Levy, Robert J. "Custody Investigations as Evidence in Divorce Cases." *Family Law Quarterly* 21, no. 2 (summer 1987): 149-67.

Maccoby, Eleanor E., and Robert H. Mnookin. *Dividing the Child: Social and Legal Dilemmas of Custody*. Cambridge, MA: Harvard University Press, 1992.

Mack, Dana. *The Assault on Parenthood: How Our Culture Undermines the Family*. New York: Simon & Schuster, 1997.

MacKenzie, Gavin. "Stop the Insults: Lawyers Shouldn't Accept This Kind of Abuse Lying Down." *Law Times*, February 19-25, 1996.

Makin, Kirk. "Lawyer Says Top Court Deserves Tough Criticism." *Globe and Mail*, April 18, 1998.

Melton, Gary B. "Shrinking the Power of the Expert's Word: Who Really Can Determine the Best Interests of a Child?" *Family Advocate* 9, no. 1 (summer 1986): 22-25, 42.

National Association of Women and the Law. "Response to 'Custody and Access: Public Discussion Paper.'" Submitted to the Custody and Access Project, Family and Youth Law Policy Section, Department of Justice, January 1994.

Owen, Ursula, ed. *Fathers: Reflections by Daughters.* New York: Pantheon, 1983.

Parke, Ross D. *Fatherhood.* Cambridge, MA: Harvard University Press, 1996.

Pearson, Patricia. *When She Was Bad: Violent Women and the Myth of Innocence.* Toronto: Random House, 1997.

Popenoe, David. *Life Without Father.* New York: Free Press, 1996.

Secunda, Victoria. *Women and Their Fathers: The Sexual and Romantic Impact of the First Man in Your Life.* New York: Dell Publishing, 1992.

Selick, Karen. "Order in the Court Room." *The Next City*, Winter 1996/97.

Sheehy, Gail. "The Divorced Dad's Burden." *New York Times*, June 21, 1998.

Simpson, Bob, Peter McCarthy, and Janet Walker. *Being There: Fathers After Divorce.* Newcastle upon Tyne: Relate Centre for Family Studies, University of Newcastle upon Tyne, 1995.

"Tomorrow's Second Sex." *The Economist*, September 28-October 4, 1996.

"Violence and Abuse Within the Family: The Neglected Issues." Papers from a public consultation by Senator Anne C. Cools, Toronto, June 9-10, 1995.

Wallerstein, Judith S., and Sandra Blakeslee. *Second Chances: Men, Women and Children a Decade After Divorce.* Boston and New York: Houghton Mifflin, 1996.

Wallerstein, Judith, and Joan B. Kelly. *Surviving the Breakup: How Children and Parents Cope with Divorce.* New York: Basic Books, 1979.

Warshak, Richard A. "Child Custody: Reform Research and Common Sense." Prepared statement of testimony before the U.S. Commission on Child and Family Welfare, Public Hearing on Custody and Visitation, April 19, 1995.

———. *The Custody Revolution: The Father Factor and the Motherhood Mystique.* New York: Poseidon Press, 1992.

———. "Father Custody and Child Development: A Review of Psychological Research." *Behavioral Sciences & The Law* 4, no 2 (1986): 185-202.

Weisman, Norris. "Case Comment on Access After Parental Separation." *Reports of Family Law*, 3rd series, 36 (February 1992): 35-83.

Wente, Margaret. "Chronicle of a Divorce from Hell." *Globe and Mail*, January 27, 1996.

INDEX

abuse, domestic. *See* domestic violence; spousal abuse
affidavits, preparation of, 84
Aiken, Stuart, 15
Algie, Clive, 136, 222
Anshan, Mark, 53, 55, 136-37, 154, 155, 157, 180, 181, 197, 224, 283, 285
anti-stalking legislation, 309, 311
Applebaum, Fanny, 122-23, 133, 135, 214, 219
Applebaum, Louis, 107
ASE of Canada Ltd., 192
assault complaints
    process of lodging, 40. *See also* domestic violence
assessment(s)
    process of, 44, 47, 56, 180-81
    view of by family court system, 179
assessors
    fees of, 44, 46, 129
    relationship of with lawyers, 129
    qualifications of, 44-45. *See also* Butkowsky, Goldstein

Bancroft, Glyn, 312
Barb (friend of Wendy), 11
Bars, Randall, 320

Bartoletti, Mario
    attempts to mediate separation agreement, 24-33
    fees of, 24-25, 28, 353
    hired by Gordons, 24
    on mediation vs. litigation, 32, 33
    neutrality of, 28
    role of, 122
Bates Printing, 259
Baythorn Public School, 315
Beaman, Judith, 135, 140
    as divorce trial witness, 128
    fee of, 43, 353
    on in-house separation, 54
    on joint custody issue, 44
    representation of Ben by, 43-44, 46, 48, 49, 50, 52, 54-55, 64, 65, 66-67, 69, 72-73, 111-12, 158
Beglaubter, Greenberg & Ernst, 313
Ben Gordon Agencies Ltd., 65
Ben Gordon Enterprises Inc., 65, 189
Bercovici, Paul
    and property items, 225
    Reiter's debt to, 350
    representation of Ben by, 222
Bill C-41, 329-30, 331, 333
Bird, Heather
    on *Toronto Life* article, 325-26
Borden & Elliot, 230-31

Bruce Smith Realty, 150
Butkowsky, Dr. Irwin, 161, 180, 235
  assessment by, 47, 48, 49, 50-51,
    144, 184
  Ben's confidence in, 251
  as divorce trial witness, 128-30, 191
  fees of, 46, 84-85, 111, 129, 353
  and Goudge, 201, 216
  on in-house separation, 54
  investigations conducted by, 48, 82
  manner, methodology of, 55, 218
  parenting plan of, 124
  recommendations of, 57, 58, 61-62,
    73, 77, 81, 90, 92, 97, 108-12,
    121-22, 129-30, 135, 136, 139,
    141, 169-70, 173, 176, 199, 205,
    209, 217, 225
  reputation of, 44-45, 168-69, 179
  sessions with, 84-85, 104-105, 106
Byers, David
  as divorce trial witness, 197, 200

Camp New Moon, 256-57, 267
Camp Tamakwa, 256-57, 267-68,
  273, 274, 279, 280
Canada Trust Realty, 150
Canadian Imperial Bank of
  Commerce, 189
Cherry, Alan, 16, 114
child support guidelines and
  legislation, 86-87. *See also*
  Bill C-41
Children's Aid Society, 167, 310
Children's Law Reform Act, 314
Cole, Ken
  fees of, 35, 353
  on Goldstein, 140
  meets with Gordons and Zaldin,
    41-42, 44, 65
  presses for settlement, 37-39
  recommends assessor, 44-45
  representation of Ben by, 34-43,
    56, 66-67
Consky, Barbara, 146-47, 159
Cools, Senator Anne, 319, 343

Cooper, Greg, 269
Creditel, 188, 191
custody
  Canadian statistics, 331
  judges' feelings about ruling on, 129
  men's disadvantage in seeking, 341
  and parental alienation syndrome,
    337
  types of, 73-74. *See also* divorce
    process (sexist biases in);
    Gordon-Gordon custody and
    support issues

deadbeat dad cliché, 330
Debby (friend of Wendy), 11
Dennis, Wendy
  announces break-up to Sara, 8
  Ben's influence on, 170
  David Wilson's (ex-husband's)
    lawsuit against, 255, 257-58,
    269-73, 276
  divorce of, 9-10, 12, 13
  early relationship with Ben, 11-13
  effect of father's death on, 171
  ex's remarriage, 10
  on family law system, 307-308
  financial settlement with ex, 5-7,
    9, 345-46
  and Goldstein, 161-65, 172, 173,
    174-75, 176, 177, 178-79
  and Goudge, 252, 264-68, 274-75,
    279-80, 282-83
  impression of Steepe, 167-68
  impression of Terry, 81-83
  in loco parentis role of, 206
  Joint Committee appearance by,
    332, 345
  joint custody issues (involving
    Sara), 3-7, 212, 235-37, 246-47,
    253-55, 272
  lawsuit against ex, 345-46
  lifestyle of vs. ex's, 91
  and Mandelcorn, 263
  marriage breakdown of, 1-2
  matrimonial home of, 3-4, 6, 9

Dennis, Wendy (*continued*)
  relationship with Ben, Deja,
    and Zoe, 74-76, 80-81, 109,
    145-46, 207, 208-209, 215,
    238, 286-87, 296, 298, 300,
    317, 341
  separation agreement of, 5-7, 9
  Terry's comments about, 214
  and Terry's theft charge, 319-20
  Toronto Life article (ground rules),
    323-24
  writing career of, 237-38. *See also*
    "The Divorce From Hell";
    Wilson, Sara
Derrick, Sheldon
  as divorce trial witness, 132,
    188-89, 197, 200
disciplinary action
  by Law Society of Upper Canada
    (Ontario), 193
Divorce Act, 342
"The Divorce From Hell" (article)
  reactions to, 324-29
divorce process
  sexist biases, stereotypes in, 20, 88,
    89, 103, 117, 126, 128, 129, 182,
    269, 272-73, 301-302, 323, 324,
    329, 332-35, 341, 343. *See also*
    family law
domestic violence, 333
  allegations of, 342-43. *See also*
    spousal abuse
Drainie, Bronwyn
  on *Toronto Life* article, 326
Dubin, Chief Justice Charles, 121
Dunbar Sachs Appell, 43

Eberle, Justice Edward, 260-61,
  262
Environmental Campaigns, 165-66,
  187, 191, 193
Epstein, Cole, 34
equalization payments, 123
Evans family (Alyssa, Brian, Lynne),
  50, 82, 106

family law system (Canada), 343-48
  adjournments, delays, 86
  as adversarial arena, 276, 346
  assessment process, 168-69
  awards in, 121
  Ben Gordon on, 306-308
  cost to taxpayers, 204
  court system, 344-45
  false charges used in, 250, 344
  judge's role in, 124
  litigation alternatives, 36, 38, 271
  recommendations for reform of,
    347-48
  trial process, 126, 182
family law system: components,
    process, terminology. *See*
    affidavits; assault complaints;
    assessment(s); assessors; custody;
    disciplinary action; equalization
    payment; fee assessment; finan-
    cial disclosure; financial state-
    ments; grandparents (rights);
    joint custody; lawyers; legal aid;
    mediation, mediators; minutes
    of settlement; peace bond;
    property division; Rule 49;
    separation date
father(s)
  fathers' groups, 343
  rights of in divorce, 329-30, 331
  role in children's lives, 331-32,
    334-35. *See also* custody
fee assessment, 231, 350-51
financial disclosure requirement, 41
financial statements (completing),
  188
Forest Hill Public School, 83
Forseth, Paul, 343
Freeman, Calen and Jed, 267

Gallaway, Roger, 342
Gardner, Dr. Richard A., 335-39
  intervention strategy of, 339-40
  on judicial system, 344. *See also*
    parental alienation syndrome

Goldstein, Dr. Sol, 146, 246
  assessments by, 173-86, 177-80,
    183, 305
  on Ben-Terry dynamics, 208
  Ben's first meeting with, 161-65
  Ben's and Wendy's responses to
    assessments by, 177
  on custody, 271
  dismissal of, 196, 199
  fees of, 142-43, 147, 153, 191-92,
    204, 207, 353
  and Goudge, 216, 262-63
  and "joint custody," 235
  manner, methodology of, 168-69,
    217, 218
  meets with Terry, 167, 191-92
  observes family interaction, 169, 179
  parenting plan of, 176, 266, 276
  recommendations of, 172, 182,
    183, 189, 190, 194, 195, 196,
    198, 199, 201, 204, 205, 206,
    207, 209, 210, 211, 218, 274-75
  recommends mediator/arbitrator,
    176
  reputation of, 179
  role of, 167
  and Sara Wilson, 235
  scheduling arrangements of, 232,
    275, 282, 287, 289
  and Terry's custody concerns,
    206-207
Goode, Constable Mike, 319
Gordon, Ben
  acting, entertainment background
    of, 14-16, 17-19
  advised to petition for divorce, 83
  in aftermath of May 1993 events,
    293-94
  allowed back into home, 181-82
  attempts to locate Terry and
    daughters, 301-16
  attempts to reach daughters,
    294-95, 296, 298, 300, 301, 312,
    318, 319, 321
  background, 11, 13-14

  begins separation, 36
  and Butkowsky parenting plan and
    recommendations, 55-57,
    58-59, 60, 62-64, 104-105, 124
  celebrates 40th birthday, 119-20
  Christmas week (1992-93) events
    involving, 249
  contacts private investigator, 309,
    319
  cost of divorce to, 353
  daily activities of, 83
  and David Wilson, 257
  debts of, 46, 51-52, 83-84, 114,
    126, 147, 152, 188-89, 219,
    285, 350
  decides to let children live
    primarily with Terry, 290-91,
    292, 293
  described, 10, 74-75
  domestic assault allegations
    against/trial of, 40, 53, 68-69,
    71, 93-100, 101-102 (dis-
    missed), 103-104
  early relationship with Terry, 14-16
  early relationship with Wendy,
    11-13
  effect of stress on health, 120
  extramarital relationships of, 17, 18
  on family law system, 306-308
  feels he is losing children, 286-87,
    288-90
  financial picture of, 21, 48, 218,
    219
  financial statements of, 188-89, 239
  first marriage of, 14, 135
  funds left with after Reiter ruling,
    350
  and Goldstein-related issues,
    161-65, 173, 177, 180, 199
  and Goudge-related issues, 216-20,
    232-35, 252, 264-68, 274-76,
    277-78, 279-80
  hears from daughters (1997), 317
  hears reports of daughters, 298
  income of, 21, 112-13, 183, 219

Gordon, Ben (*continued*)
interpretation of "joint custody," 34
jobs of, 83
joins father's business, 18-19
on judicial process, 189
last conversation with daughters at
home, 291, 292
lawyers of. *See* Beaman, Cole,
Hannaford, Lipson, Reiter,
Schipper
learns of Terry's motion to
purchase home, 258
legal fees, court expenses of, 66,
232, 263
locates Terry, children, 303, 316
Mandelcorn consultation by, 296,
318
marriage to Terry, 16
mediation/assessment costs for, 85,
353
mediators/assessors of. *See*
Bartoletti, Butkowsky,
Goldstein, Goudge
meets with Deja (October 1993),
297
moves from family home, 41
moves in with Wendy, 294
reasons for entering mediation,
23-24, 25
and Reiter fee assessment, 284-85,
350-52, 353
relationship, involvement with
daughters, 17-18, 20, 22-23, 43,
45, 49-50, 57, 77-81, 238, 289
relationship with Sara Wilson, 77,
253, 270-71, 294
rumours circulating about, 298
seeks separation mediation, 21
separation proposal of, 25
settlement proposal of, 36-37
tells daughters about divorce, 22
and *Toronto Life* article, 324-26, 327
uses humour as a means for
coping, 118-20
vacates home, 37

vilification of, 326
work performance of, 45-46
Gordon daughters (Deja Victoria and
Zoe Nicole)
activities of, 45, 49, 68, 75, 105,
109, 110, 134, 213-16, 217-18,
219-20, 225, 226-27, 232,
238, 248
in aftermath of May 1993 events,
293-94
alternating weekly schedule of, 208
"attachment issues" (Zoe), 233, 277
behaviour patterns of, 64, 144,
234-35
Ben's changing approach towards,
170
birth of (Deja), 17
birth of (Zoe), 18
camp plans for, 208, 212-14,
255-57, 267-68, 273, 278,
279, 280
Christmas holiday week (1992-93)
events, 248-52
consecration ceremony (Deja),
105-106
daily life of (separation period), 35
demand bonds from father, 317
discuss Ben with Butkowsky, 106
discuss Terry with Goudge, 251
during last stages of parents'
marriage, 19
effect of move on, 163-64
estrangement from Terry's family,
313
Goldstein's profiles of, 174, 175-76
and Goudge's "Guidelines on
Behaviour," 273-74
Goudge's sessions with, 233-35
graduations of (Deja), 300-301,
308-309, 315
impression of Goldstein, 181, 199
letters to grandmother from, 298,
299, 337
on living in two homes (Deja),
55-56

meet Wendy, 75-76
as messengers, 30, 49, 81, 120, 144-45, 172, 317, 318
missing person's report filed on, 302
privacy of, 324-25
refuse to see grandmother, 300
relationship with father, 20, 77-81
relationship with maternal grandparents, 320
relationship with Sara, 76-77, 78, 177, 265
relationship with Wendy, 80-81, 145-46, 177
school visits by Ben, 294, 297
on selling of home, 105 (Deja)
and Steepe association, 167
support group for, 298, 300 (Deja)
temperaments of, 76, 77-80
told of divorce, 22
use of Nusyna name (Deja), 286
Gordon, Jules, 13, 65, 68, 72, 303, 341
attempts to contact grandchildren, 315
Ben joins business of, 18
as divorce trial witness, 128
gifts, loans from, 21, 123
relationship with grandchildren, 81. *See also* Jules Gordon Agencies Ltd.
Gordon, Nettie, 68, 303, 341
loan from, 350
relationship with grandchildren, 81
Gordon, Terry (née Nusyna)
in aftermath of May 1993 events, 293-95
allegations by involving Steepe and Izzard, 186-88
attempt to change children's last name, 286
bank account of, 29, 30-31
becomes anxious to settle, 193-94
begins working, 45
and Ben's career, 17, 112-14

on Ben's parenting, 2, 46-47
and Ben-Wendy relationship, 109, 212
and Butkowsky recommendations, 67, 73, 104, 121-22
on career, 114
charged with theft, 318
children and Goudge discuss, 251
and Christmas 1992 events, 249, 250
debts of, 115, 122-23
described, 15
discontinues mediation, 48
domestic assault charges, claims made by, 40, 53, 68-69, 71, 163, 179-80, 181-82, 250, 303-304, 315
at domestic assault trial, 93-104
eagerness to settle, 193-94
early parenting role of, 18, 22-23
early relationship with Ben, 14-16
estrangement from family, 302, 313, 316
finances of, 116-17, 189, 191, 192-93, 219, 228
financial misrepresentation allegations against, 142, 143
first marriage of, 14-15, 163, 167, 168
Goldstein assessment of, 173-74, 175, 179
jobs and income of, 15-16, 32, 35, 36, 46, 85, 88, 114, 115-16, 165-66, 187-88, 191, 259
lawyers of. *See* Greenberg, Orbach, Straitman, Zaldin
marriage to Ben, 16
moves from Dewbourne house, 301
parenting by, 145
purchases Dewbourne house, 283-85
reasons for break-up, 24
rumours about (1996), 313

Gordon, Terry (*continued*)
  seeks employment, 21
  seeks interim child support,
    87, 88
  speaks to Ben's mother, 295
  stalking allegations made by,
    303, 309
  Steepe allegations concerning,
    202-203
  and Steepe relationship, 105-107,
    165-68
  at Steepe trial, 190-91
  tells Ben to move, 36
  tells daughters about divorce, 22
  theft charge against, 318-20
  threatening charges pressed by
    (against Steepe), 166, 190-91,
    193, 197
  and *Toronto Life* article, 325-26,
    327
  unknown whereabouts of, 301-16
  on Wendy, 214
Gordon, Zella, 60, 288, 289, 341
  attempts to contact grandchildren,
    295, 298, 315
  grandchildren refuse to see, 300
  grandchildren's letters to, 324-25,
    337
  joins G.R.A.N.D., 295
  marriage and divorce of, 13
  relationship with grandchildren, 81
Gordon-Gordon custody and support
    issues
  alternating weekly schedule begins,
    208
  ambiguity of Butkowsky custody
    recommendation, 73
  Ben clarifies Goldstein plan,
    205-206
  Ben considers claiming child
    support, 228
  Ben and Deja discuss scheduling,
    288
  Ben pleads for Goldstein's
    intercession, 274

Ben suspends payments, 89
Ben's payments, 83-84, 107, 161,
  183
Ben's position on custody, 24,
  57-59, 61, 161-62
Butkowsky recommendations and
  joint custody, 58, 104-105
camp issues, 81, 212-14, 255-57,
  267-68, 274-76, 277, 278,
  279, 281
child support budget, 87
Christmas 1992 schedule,
  247-48
custody issue (assault trial), 98
custody issues, proposals (divorce
  trial), 122, 123, 130, 135-36,
  138, 189
family function conflict, 242-47
financial and scheduling responsibilities (per Goudge), 219-20,
  281
interim-support ruling (appeal),
  88-89
joint custody/joint parenting
  recommendation (Goldstein),
  176, 177
"joint custody" on court order, 205,
  295, 311
minutes of settlement (financial
  claims, joint custody), 239,
  242
Passover scheduling, 192
scheduling and transfer times, 97,
  102-103, 145-46, 170-71, 203,
  206, 209-16, 217-18, 244-47,
  252, 264-66, 267, 273, 275, 282,
  287-90
support order (divorce trial),
  134-35, 139, 143
Terry drops claim for child support,
  196
Terry seeks interim child support,
  83, 84
Terry seeks sole custody, 42, 49,
  70, 72, 73

Terry stops seeking support, 295-96

Terry's claims for support, 87-89

Terry's position on custody, 24, 27, 34

Terry's understanding of custody position, 108-12

Terry's willingness to accept joint custody, 196

weekly overnight arrangement (Goudge), 287

Zaldin on Terry's custody concerns, 206-207

Gordon-Gordon matrimonial home

appraisal sought for, 30

Ben advised to make competing offer on, 258, 259-60

Ben advised not to leave, 35

Ben agrees not to enter, 102

Ben seeks to force sale of, 83, 158-60

Ben seeks mortgage on, 147

Ben vacates, 25, 37, 41, 67-68, 73

Ben's motion to sell, 89-90

Ben's share from sale of, 350

closing of sale of, 283-85

court refuses to lower price of, 161

described, 23, 146, 315

division of proceeds from, 285

effect on children of sale of, 131-32

goes on market, 146-47

issue of at assault trial, 97-98

listing of (Slavens), 172, 173, 220-22, 223

listing agent named for, 64

listing prices of, 146, 147, 148-49, 181, 241, 314, 315

locks changed on, 68

loss in value of, 353

mortgage and tax dispute over, 147-60

motions on, 260-61, 268-69

need to sell, 21, 35, 54, 86

offers on, 241-42, 244, 245, 247, 258

proposed sale of, 26-27

purchase (Gordons') of, 16, 21-22

purchase price of (May 1993), 285

Reiter's payment from sale of, 284-85

rotation plan for residence in, 25-26, 48-49, 54

ruling that house be sold, 89-90

ruling that house be sold (appeal of), 90

symbolism of, 27, 91, 92-93, 138, 163-64, 263

Terry abandons appeal on sale of, 131, 132

Terry fights sale of, 84, 89-90, 209

Terry moves from, 301

Terry purchases, 258-62

Terry seeks exclusive possession of, 70, 71, 72

Terry's financing of, 285

Gordon-Gordon property issues, 123, 147, 148, 221-28

addressed at divorce trial, 197

court appearance on, 158-60

division of property, 23, 157-58, 181, 207, 239-41

Justice Marshall's comments on, 100-101

Terry breaches order and delivers items, 225-28

Gordon-Gordon separation

assessment process begins, 47

confrontation during, 39-40

debts, finances at time of, 25, 27-28, 29-30, 32-33, 35, 36, 59, 88

expense-sharing arrangements during, 37

financial statements prepared during, 35, 36, 65

in-house arrangement's impact on family, 44, 45, 53

mediation of agreement (Bartoletti), 24-33

mediation, arbitration recommended, 19, 62

Gordon-Gordon separation (*continued*)
  meeting of parties during, 41-42,
    44, 65
  parties enter into peace bond,
    101-102
  separation date selection, 48
Gordon v. Gordon (divorce trial).
  See Nusyna v. Gordon
Goudge, Helen, 211, 226, 237, 277,
    282-83
  and assessors, 216
  authority of, 207, 218, 219, 232,
    239, 262-63, 266, 279
  Ben requests resignation of, 276
  on Ben's anger, 278
  and camp arrangements, 256-57
  discusses Terry with children, 251
  fees, 200, 353
  involvement of with Gordons,
    216-20
  issues "Guidelines on Behaviour,"
    273-74
  letters to and from Ben, 264-68,
    274-76, 277-78, 279-80
  manner of, 217
  parenting plan of, 205, 209,
    216-18, 219-20, 232, 233-35,
    237
  resignation of, 283, 287, 289-90
  response of to Christmas week
    events, 248-52
  scheduling and transfer-time
    matters, 217-18, 244-45, 246-
    47, 252, 273, 275, 282, 287-90
  sessions of with Deja and Zoe,
    233-35
  takes on case, 200, 201
  Terry's complaints about, 276
  treatment of Ben by, 249, 261, 262
  on words "joint custody," 235, 262
grandparents
  parental alienation and, 336, 337
  rights of, 295
Grandparents Requesting Access and
    Dignity (G.R.A.N.D.), 295

Greenberg, Barry
  representation of Terry by, 313,
    314, 315, 316

Hannaford, Julie, 278-79, 280, 281
  fees of, 231, 353
  representation of Ben by, 230, 231,
    232, 238-42, 247, 258, 259-60,
    261, 268, 269, 277, 282, 283, 284
Harris, Joyce, 117, 269, 276, 309-10
Hawtin, Jane,
  response of to *Toronto Life* article,
    328-29
Health and Home, 192
Heard, John, 330
Himel, Susan, 43, 140

Ida (Judy's daughter), 316
Israel, Peter, 66, 67, 85, 309
Izzard, Jacqueline, 166, 186-87
  as Reiter witness, 197

Jewish Family and Child Service,
    53-54, 166, 184, 310
Joan (Wendy's sister), 272
John Fisher Public School,
    22, 310
Joint Committee on Child Custody
    and Access, 330, 332, 333, 342,
    343-44, 345
joint custody, 35
  arrangement types, 5-6
  definitions of, 34, 262
  different lifestyles and, 91
  order, 304, 311. *See also* custody;
    Gordon-Gordon custody and
    support issues
Judy (friend of Wendy), 118, 316
  introduces Ben to Wendy, 10,
    11, 12
Jules Gordon Agencies Ltd., 65, 83

Kaplovitch, Dr. Harvey, 107
Kay, Lynn, 150, 159
Kirschner, Tom, 308-309, 313, 316

Lalonde, P. Ann, 314
Larry King Live, 330
Law Times, 327
lawyers (general)
    demeanour of, 130
    expenses of, 32
    fees of, 102, 346
    female, 43
    mediation offered by, 24
    views of on clients' claims, 124
legal aid, 341
Linton, Master Ross, 172, 173, 181,
    194, 207, 223, 224, 228, 229,
    239, 242, 245, 247, 258
Lipson, Tim
    fee of, 353
    representation of Ben by, 93-99,
    101, 103
Lyons, Goodman, Iacono, Smith &
    Berkow, 39

McBride, Master Stewart, 87, 89,
    134-35, 139, 142
MacKenzie, Gavin
    on *Toronto Life* article, 327
McWhinney, Robert, 271, 276
    agrees to mediate (Wendy and
    David), 270
    fees of, 270
Mandelcorn, Dr. Berenice, 270, 271
    advises Ben, 296, 318
    recommends family mediation
    (Dennis-Wilson), 263
    as Sara's counsellor, 255, 257-58
Mann, Danny, 14
Margaret (babysitter), 290
Margaret (Ben's second cousin), 292
Marshall, Justice Lauren
    on Ben and Terry, 178
    commentary and ruling by
    (domestic assault trial), 100-102
    directs that Gordons enter into
    peace bond, 101-102, 182
    dismisses charges against Ben,
    101, 102

    presides over domestic assault trial,
    93, 99-102
Martin, Dianne
    on court prejudices, 340
media
    reaction of to *Toronto Life* article,
    327-29
    scepticism by of claims by fathers'
    groups, 343
mediation, mediators
    role of, 25, 28-29
    vs. litigation, 24, 32, 33
mediators/arbitrators. *See*
    Bartoletti, Butkowsky, Goudge,
    McWhinney
Metropolitan Toronto Police Youth
    Bureau, 302
minutes of settlement, 239
    precedence of, 277
Mobile Media Inc., 192
Mokriy, Terry, 22, 288, 289-90,
    296-97, 300, 301, 310, 312
Moody, Diane
    counsels Sara, 270, 276

nannies/housekeepers
    observations, role, treatment of,
    39, 45, 49, 51, 55, 68, 77,
    88, 95, 97, 107, 191, 206,
    210, 339
Nisan, Larry, 19, 21, 24, 48
Nusyna family, 16, 50
    debts to, 122-23
Nusyna, Morris, 52-53, 168, 207,
    217-18, 313
    debts to, 115, 116, 135, 138
    as divorce trial witness, 128
    falls out with Terry, 302
    relationship with Terry and
    grandchildren, 320
Nusyna, Ruth, 52-53, 133, 168, 191,
    207, 217-18, 245, 246, 292,
    295, 313
    debts to, 135, 138
    as divorce trial witness, 128

Nusyna, Ruth (*continued*)
  relationship with Terry and
    grandchildren, 320
Nusyna v. Gordon (divorce trial)
  adjourned, 143
  assessment (new) ordered, 139-40
  begins, 130-31
  Ben ordered to pay interim
    support, 143
  Ben testifies at, 127, 132, 134,
    135-36, 204
  cost of to taxpayers, 204
  costs requested by Terry,
    203-204
  custody issues, 122, 123, 134,
    135-36, 138, 189, 194
  divorce judgment granted, 143
  duration of, 204
  exhibits filed for, 134-35
  financial documents presented at,
    132-33, 134-35
  house sale issue, 122-23, 136-37
  mediator/arbitrator issue, 121-22
  minutes of settlement, 137, 138,
    239-40, 241, 242
  pre-trial cross-examinations (Ben),
    188-90, 191
  pre-trial cross-examinations
    (Terry), 108-10, 112-17, 191,
    192, 193
  property issues, 123, 136-37
  resumption of, 182, 183, 186
  Rule 49 offers to settle, 121, 194
  settlement negotiations during,
    135, 136-37, 138-39, 194
  Steepc evidence at, 198-99
  witness list (Reiter), 128, 197-98
  Zaldin asks for case to be thrown
    out, 131

O'Connell, Justice Hugh
  presides at fee assessment trial,
    351-52
Office of the Children's Lawyer, 43,
  313-14

Official Guardian's Office (Office of
  the Children's Lawyer), 183-84
Orbach, Carl
  representation of Terry by, 31-32,
    33, 34-39
Ostro, Michael, 285, 315, 316, 318,
  319

parental alienation syndrome, 335-41
  in Canadian context, 340
  in context of Ben Gordon's story,
    337, 340-41
  defined, 335
*Parental Alienation Syndrome:
  A Guide for Mental Health
  and Legal Professionals*
  (Gardner), 335
Paul Slavens Real Estate, 315
peace bond, 101-102, 294
Peck, Deborah, 15
Pellman, Paul, 331
Percy, Uncle (Terry's), 244, 320
Petitti, Norma, 298, 300
Pinelli, Richard, 146-47, 148-50,
  159-60, 172, 173, 221, 229
Polisuk, Rhonda, 312, 315-16
Polson, Detective Constable Michael,
  302, 303, 304, 305
Potts, Justice Joseph, 218, 219, 222,
  226, 228, 239, 266, 271
  grants divorce judgment, 143
  presides at divorce trial, 124, 131,
    132, 133, 134, 135, 136, 139-40,
    141, 142, 143, 147, 149, 153,
    154, 157, 158, 159, 160, 161,
    165, 181, 183, 184-85, 186, 188,
    189-90, 195, 196, 197, 198, 199,
    200, 201, 203, 204
property division
  selection process, 239. *See also*
    equalization payments

Reiter, Carol, 222, 228, 351
Reiter, Moishe
  Ben fires, 230-31

Ben hires, 69
Ben's concerns about, 117, 120, 228, 229-30
Ben's impressions of, 66
and Butkowsky recommendations, 74, 129-30
and child support issues, 88, 89
creditors of, 285
and custody issues, 209-11
debts of, 350
at divorce trial, 129-30, 133, 134, 135, 136, 137-39, 140, 141, 142-43, 196, 197-98, 199, 200, 202, 203-204
fee assessment of, 285, 350-52
fees and payments of, 69, 86, 117, 157, 204, 216, 228, 350, 353
financial position of, 285
and Goldstein recommendations, 206
and house and property issues, 89, 90, 147, 155, 160, 181, 220, 221, 222, 228
Izzard contacts (Steepe), 186-87
manner of, 86, 117, 125, 174, 239
meets with Steepe, 166
on petitioning for divorce, 83
and pre-trial cross-examinations, 108-16, 189-90
and Steepe allegations, 167, 197, 198, 202
on Terry-Steepe relationship, 106
and Terry's lawsuit against Steepe, 193, 195
witnesses for divorce trial, 128, 197-98
and Zaldin animosity, 183, 188
and Zaldin exchanges, 107, 151, 152-53, 154, 157-58, 160, 184, 185-86, 190, 191, 192-93
on Zaldin's reputation, 85
Reiter, Naomi, 222, 230
Revenue Canada, 350
Rock, Allan, 329-30

Roland, William, 350
Rose, Aunt (Terry's), 242-44, 245, 320, 350-52
Rule 49 (of the Rules of Civil Procedure), 121

Sadie Moranis Real Estate, 146
Schipper, Robert
    fees of, 353
    representation of Ben by (Reiter fee assessment), 350, 351
Second City, 14
separation date, official, 48
Sheehy, Gail ("The Divorced Dad's Burden"), 330
Shiffman, Gary
    representation of Slavens by, 284
Slavens, Paul, 172-73, 183, 194, 220-21, 241-42, 245, 247, 258, 283-84, 285
Smith, Bruce, 150, 159, 160
Smith, Justice Heather, 285
Southey, Justice James, 269
Spectrum Six Realty Services, 315
Spiegler, Brenda, 55, 172, 224
    as divorce trial witness, 128
spousal abuse
    broad definition of, 342. *See also* domestic violence
Stalmaster, Lynn, 16
Steepe, Randolph, 272, 305-306
    allegations made by, 166, 167, 183, 184, 186-88, 195-96, 198, 202-203
    background of, 106-107
    Ben and Wendy meet, 165
    and divorce trial, 130, 165, 197, 198-99, 200-201
    and Goldstein assessment, 173, 174, 192
    relationship with Terry, 105-107, 165-68, 228
    Terry testifies about, 183
    trial of (threatening charges), 190-91, 193

Straitman, Jack (lawyer)
  association of with Terry, 304-308
Stransman, John
  as divorce trial witness, 128
Stride Rite Canada Ltd., 83
Sunrise Films Ltd., 83, 113

Tait, Paul (Crown attorney), 93, 99
therapists
  and parental alienation syndrome,
    338
Thomas, David Clayton
  marriage to Terry, 14-15, 194
Toronto Life article ("The Divorce
    From Hell"), 324
  legal community response to, 326-27
  media response to, 325-26, 327-29
  public response to, 341

Vaccarello, Tony, 315, 316

Walsh, Justice George
  house order of, 89, 90, 107, 137,
    138, 160, 222-23
  sets cross-examination and trial
    dates, 107-108
Weiler, Justice Karen, 88-89
Westmount Collegiate Institute, 315,
    321
Wilson, David, 140, 294
  announces break-up to Sara, 8
  on Ben, 253
  child support payments by,
    7, 345-46
  disputed family issues involving,
    253-55
  enters mediation, 276
  financial settlement with Wendy, 5
  joint custody arrangement for Sara,
    3-7, 8-9, 163
  lifestyle of vs. Wendy's, 91
  marriage breakdown of, 1-2
  marriage to Jan, 10
  matrimonial home of, 3-4, 6, 9
  meets with Mandelcorn, 263

on Sara-Ben relationship, 271-72
  and Sara-related decisions, 235-37
  scheduling arrangements by, 212
  separation agreement, 5-7
  suit against Wendy by, 255,
    257-58, 269-73
  Wendy's suit against, 345-46
Wilson, Jan
  marriage to David, 10
  relationship with Sara, 237, 270
Wilson, Jeffrey, 256, 267
Wilson, Sara
  Bat Mitzvah of, 294
  budget for, 87
  child support formula for, 6-7
  counselling of, 255, 257-58, 276
  family issues of, 253-55
  Goldstein's assessment of, 173,
    174-75, 178-79
  on joint custody arrangement, 91
  joint custody, schedule for, 3-7, 19,
    135-36, 162, 163, 206, 212, 233
  mediator sought for, 270
  and parents' disputes, 235-37,
    270-73
  reaction to stepmother, 10
  relationship with Ben, 77, 80, 215,
    238, 253, 272
  relationship with Deja and Zoe,
    76-77, 78, 80, 145-46, 215, 238,
    265, 341
  response to parents' break-up, 8
  writes to Deja and Zoe, 296

Zaldin, Ronald
  on Ben-Terry relationship, 46-47
  and custody issues, 206-207, 282
  at divorce trial, 131-32, 133, 134,
    135, 136-39, 140-42, 143, 147,
    194-95, 196, 197, 198, 202, 203,
    204, 228
  and domestic assault trial, 94, 99
  early representation of Terry by, 39,
    42, 43, 48, 54, 64-67 69-71,
    72-73, 85-92

establishes own firm, 70

on Goldstein, 141

and house and property issues, 160-61, 181, 209, 222-27, 238- 42, 247, 258, 261, 268-69, 283, 293

manner and strategy of, 66, 85-86, 127, 128, 129, 130, 183, 229, 239, 293

and pre-trial cross-examinations, 107-109, 111-12, 114-15, 116, 117, 189-90, 191, 192, 193

reaction to *Toronto Life* article, 344

and Reiter animosity, 183

and Reiter exchanges, 107, 152-53, 154-55, 156, 157, 158, 184, 185-86, 188, 200, 201, 202, 203, 204, 209-11, 223, 226

and Steepe allegations concerning, 166, 195-96, 198, 202-203

suggests real estate agent, 146

The text of this book is set in Adobe Caslon, a typeface
drawn by Carol Twombly. It is closely based on the work
of William Caslon (1692-1766) and is the most
accurate modern version of the Caslon style.

The headlines are set in Franklin Gothic extra condensed.
Designed by Morris Benton in 1906, it is one of the
most enduring sans serif Gothic typefaces
spawned by the Industrial Revolution.

Designed by Wioletta Wesolowski/James Ireland Design Inc.
Typeset by Marie Jircik

A